WordPerfect®
Workbook
for IBM® Personal Computers

Version 5.1
©WordPerfect Corporation 1989
All Rights Reserved

Printed in U.S.A.
WKUSIWP51—11/89

ISBN 1-55692-476-3

WordPerfect Corporation • 1555 N. Technology Way • Orem, Utah 84057 U.S.A.
Telephone: (801) 225-5000 • Telex: 820618 • FAX: (801) 222-4477

Table of Contents

Introduction

The *WordPerfect Workbook* helps you understand how to create and format a variety of documents with WordPerfect. Along the way you are introduced to many WordPerfect features and some valuable techniques for creating and editing documents.

Because of the power and flexibility of WordPerfect, not all features or applications of the program can be covered in the workbook. However, by turning to the *WordPerfect Reference Manual*, you can find many of the answers you need when creating your own documents.

Before You Start

Before using the *WordPerfect Workbook*, you should have already installed WordPerfect and read through the *Getting Started* section of the *WordPerfect Reference Manual*.

Getting Started

Getting Started provides valuable information about starting WordPerfect, using the keyboard (or a mouse), and getting help. You are also given a quick overview of WordPerfect and the basics of word processing.

Once you feel comfortable with the information in *Getting Started*, then you are ready to begin the lessons in the workbook.

Starting WordPerfect

You need to start WordPerfect each time you use the workbook. The steps for starting WordPerfect can be found in *Getting Started* in the *WordPerfect Reference Manual*.

LEARN Files

The Learning files for the workbook should have been copied to a LEARN directory (e.g., C:\WP51\LEARN) on your hard disk during installation.

If you are running WordPerfect from two diskette drives, then turn to the Two Disk Drives *heading in the* Appendix *of the workbook for additional details.*

For WordPerfect to find these files, you need to change your default directory after starting WordPerfect and *before* starting any of the lessons.

1   After starting WordPerfect, press **List** (F5).

2   Type an equal sign (=).

3   Type **c:\wp51\learn** and press **Enter** to have WordPerfect look in the LEARN directory for the workbook files.

4 Press **Enter** to display the list of files, then press **Exit** (F7) to return to the normal editing screen.

If you copied the workbook files to a directory other than C:\WP51\LEARN, then you need to type the name of that directory before pressing Enter in step 3.

Tutorial

A tutorial program is included in your WordPerfect package that introduces you to the keyboard, some basic skills of word processing, and several WordPerfect features.

Each lesson in the tutorial displays the keys you need to press and provides comments about each step. All you need to do is match the keystroke(s) on the screen to continue a lesson.

If you are unfamiliar with computers and word processing, or find that the first few lessons in the workbook are difficult, you may want to start learning about WordPerfect from the tutorial before you move on to the workbook.

For details on starting the tutorial, turn to the On-Line Tutorial *heading under* Getting Help *in the* Getting Starting *section of the* WordPerfect Reference Manual.

Your Computer

WordPerfect is designed to take full advantage of your computer's unique capabilities. If you have a color monitor, you can change the colors of the WordPerfect editing screen. If you use a mouse, you can select WordPerfect features by using pull-down menus.

The pull-down menus can be used with or without a mouse. For details on using the pull-down menus in WordPerfect, turn to the Pull-Down Menus *heading under* The Basics *in the* Getting Starting *section of the* WordPerfect Reference Manual.

Several of the more powerful features in WordPerfect (e.g., Graphics, Equations, View Document) work much better if you have a graphics card installed in your computer.

For example, the Graphics feature lets you place graphic figures in a document. However, to actually see the figure while you are editing in WordPerfect, you need to have a graphics card installed in your computer.

Even if you aren't using graphics in a document, a graphics card is still essential for the View Document feature to accurately display what your document will look like when it is printed.

The View Document screens in the workbook illustrate what your screen should look like if you are using a high resolution graphics card in your computer. If your computer is using a lower resolution graphics card, then you may not see as much detail on your screen.

Your Printer

Once you are in WordPerfect, you can see the name of the printer you selected during installation by pressing the Print key (Shift-F7) and checking the setting for the Select Printer option.

If you selected more than one printer, then you can see all of them by choosing the Select Printer option on the Print menu (Shift-F7,s).

When selecting a printer during installation, WordPerfect creates a special file with a .PRS extension (e.g., HPLASEII.PRS for the HP LaserJet Series II). This file contains all the information WordPerfect needs to communicate with your printer.

Printer Test

Some of the features available in WordPerfect may not be available at your printer. For example, you may be able to place a graphics figure in your document, but your printer may not be able to print the figure.

To help you find out which WordPerfect features your printer can handle, try sending the PRINTER.TST file (located in your WordPerfect directory) to the printer.

Workbook Printer

All the files used in the workbook lessons were created using a special Workbook Printer definition (WORKBOOK.PRS). WordPerfect automatically selects the Workbook Printer definition for you when you retrieve any of the workbook files. You do not need to worry about selecting the printer yourself.

If WordPerfect cannot find the WORKBOOK.PRS file, then the workbook files will be converted to work with your own printer. In this case, the lesson may not work properly. Check to make sure that the WORKBOOK.PRS file is in your LEARN directory.

The Workbook Printer definition is designed to demonstrate the features of WordPerfect. It is *not* designed to be used for printing documents. Before sending a document to the printer, you need to make sure that your own printer is selected.

The workbook lessons let you know how and when you should select your own printer.

WordPerfect Settings

Each copy of WordPerfect is shipped with exactly the same settings for margins, justification, line spacing, etc. These are known as the *default* settings of WordPerfect.

The workbook lessons are designed to work with the default settings of WordPerfect. If you or someone else has used the Setup key (Shift-F1) to customize the default settings, then some of the steps in the lessons may not work properly.

For example, all measurements (e.g., position numbers, tab settings, etc.) in WordPerfect are initially set to be displayed and entered in inches. If you change the default setting to centimeters, then each measurement you enter in a lesson will be converted to centimeters and the lesson will not work properly.

If a lesson is not working properly, and someone else installed your copy of WordPerfect, check with that person to see if any of the default settings were changed.

Workbook Lessons

The workbook lessons are divided into three sections: Fundamentals I, Fundamentals II, and Special Features.

Fundamentals I introduces many of the basic word processing features you will use each time you create a document with WordPerfect. *Fundamentals II* rounds out your training by demonstrating several formatting features, some simple macros, and a simple method for merging letters.

Special Features introduces you to some of the more exciting and powerful features of WordPerfect, such as Tables and Equations, and shows you how they might be used in a document.

Lesson Order

If you are new to word processing, you should start with the lessons in Fundamentals I. If you are new to WordPerfect (but have used another word processor), you may want to start with the lessons in Fundamentals II.

If you are already familiar with WordPerfect 5.0, you may want to go straight to the Special Features lessons to try out some of the new features of WordPerfect 5.1.

The lessons listed below are designed to be completed together:

- Lessons 2-6
- Lessons 8-11
- Lessons 13-14
- Lessons 16-17
- Lessons 19-22

If you cannot complete a lesson in one sitting, save the document you are creating (use your own filename), then retrieve the file when you are ready to start the lesson again.

Lesson 1: Notes

Instead of reaching for a pen and piece of paper when you want to write a note, try using WordPerfect to quickly type and print the note.

Typing the Note

As you type in WordPerfect, press Shift to type capital (uppercase) letters. If you type an incorrect letter or word, press Backspace until the mistake is erased, then begin typing again.

1 Type the following note *without* pressing **Enter** when you reach the end of a line.

I have completed sections A through D of the medical form, but I am still confused about whether the benefits start on the last day of August or the first day of September. I would appreciate any information that you could give me. Thank you for your help. Virginia.

There are three things that you may have noticed while typing the note.

A CURSOR

B WORD WRAPPING

C STATUS LINE

```
I have completed sections A through D of the medical form, but I
am still confused about whether the benefits start on the last day  B
of August or the first day of September.  I would appreciate any
information that you could give me.  Thank you for your help.
Virginia._
           A




                              C Doc 1 Pg 1 Ln 1.67" Pos 1.9"
```

First, a cursor (usually a blinking "_") moves ahead of the text as you type, or backward if you are using Backspace to erase a mistake. The cursor indicates the place where the next character will be typed or deleted (erased).

Second, when a line fills with text, the cursor returns to the left margin in a new line. This automatic return is often referred to as *word wrapping*.

The screens shown in the workbook lessons were created with the Workbook Printer selected. Because you selected your own printer when installing WordPerfect, the words may wrap in different places than those shown in the workbook screens.

Third, the bottom line of the screen (the status line) lets you know which document (Doc) you are editing (you can edit two at once), the page you are on (Pg), how far down the page the cursor is located (Ln), and the current position of the cursor across the page (Pos).

Printing the Note

Now that you have typed the note, you are ready to print.

1 Press **Print** (Shift-F7) to display the Print menu.

⌨ *Select Print from the File menu.*

2 Select Full Document (1) from the Print menu to send the note to the printer.

If your printer does not print, check to make sure it is turned on, on-line, and that the printer cable is attached securely to your computer and printer. You may also want to read the *Printer Control* section in the *WordPerfect Reference Manual* for additional help.

Clearing the Screen

After printing the note, the screen can be cleared to begin creating or editing another document.

1 Press **Exit** (F7) to let WordPerfect know you want to remove the note from your screen.

⌨ *Select Exit from the File menu.*

A message appears on the status line asking if you want to save the document (to a disk) for future use. For some documents, like notes, there may be no real need to store the document once it is printed.

2 Type **n** (for no) to indicate that you do not want to save the note.

⌨ *Select No from the Yes/No prompt.*

A second message appears on the status line, asking if you want to exit (leave) WordPerfect.

3 Type **n** to clear the screen and stay in WordPerfect.

⌨ *Select No from the Yes/No prompt.*

Because you chose to stay in the program, WordPerfect clears the screen for you.

```
                                                        Doc 1 Pg 1 Ln 1" Pos 1"
```

By using Exit to clear the screen, you do not need to use Backspace to erase all the characters before starting a new document.

Lesson 2: Letter 1 — First Draft

One of the documents most frequently created with WordPerfect is a letter. A letter may go through several drafts before it is ready to send. You might type the document once, review and edit the document, then print a final copy.

In this lesson, you type and print the first draft of a letter for hotel reservations, and then finish making changes to the letter in lessons 4 and 6.

Typing the Inside Address

Most business letters begin with a date and an inside address. The date will be added in the final draft (lesson 6), so let's start the first draft by typing the inside address.

1 Type the first line of the inside address.

Reservations Manager

At this point, you need to start a new line at the left margin.

2 Press **Enter** to return the cursor to the left margin and start a new line.

By pressing Enter, you can start your own new line *before* the cursor reaches the right margin. Now, finish typing the inside address using Enter to end each line of the address.

3 Type the rest of the address.

Parkway Inn
1780 Delaware Ave.
Buffalo, NY 14209

Enter can also be used to add an empty line for double-spacing between blocks of text on the page.

4 Press **Enter** to add an empty line.

5 Press **Enter** again to start a new line for the subject of the letter.

Typing the Subject Line

Some people use a subject line in a letter. The subject line briefly states the purpose of the letter. Because the reservations manager needs to quickly find out the purpose of the letter, you can emphasize the subject line by typing the words in capital (uppercase) letters.

While you could hold down Shift to type the subject line, try using Caps Lock to lock all the letters on the keyboard into uppercase.

1 Press **Caps Lock** to type uppercase letters. Notice that the "Pos" on the status line switches to uppercase letters.

Number keys and punctuation keys are not affected by Caps Lock.

2 Type the subject line *without* holding down Shift.

corporate marketing conference reservations

3 Press **Enter** twice to double-space.

Now, compare your letter to the one illustrated in the screen below.

```
Reservations Manager
Parkway Inn
1780 Delaware Ave.
Buffalo, NY 14209


CORPORATE MARKETING CONFERENCE RESERVATIONS

_




                                          Doc 1 Pg 1 Ln 2.33" Pos 1"
```

From time to time during the lessons, a screen or printed document will be illustrated to help you decide if you are on the right track.

If you have made a mistake and don't know how to correct it, you can always start the lesson over by using Exit (F7,n,n) to clear your screen.

4 Press **Caps Lock** to return to typing lowercase letters. Notice that the "Pos" on the status line switches to lowercase letters again.

Typing the Message

1 Type the message of the letter.

We would like to make reservations for a marketing conference to be held on December 1, 2, and 3 of this year. A minimum of 40 people will be attending. Besides accommodations for those attending, we will also require your largest suite, a conference room, and an extra meeting room for smaller gatherings.

An early confirmation would be sincerely appreciated.

If you have not already used the arrow keys, they are usually located to the right of the typing keys on your keyboard. The arrow keys let you move the cursor up, down, left, or right through your document without disturbing the text.

Because the arrow keys are used to move the cursor through text on your screen, they are sometimes called the cursor keys.

⌨ *If you have a mouse, the cursor can be moved by placing the mouse pointer at the position on the screen where you want the cursor and clicking the left button.*

2   Place the cursor on the space *after* the word "also" in the last sentence of the first paragraph using the arrow keys.

3   Press **Backspace** until you erase the word "also" and the space before it.

The arrow keys can also be used to move to a place in your document where a word needs to be added. For example, you should probably add a word that describes the type of suite that needs to be reserved.

4   Place the cursor on the first letter of the word "suite" in the same sentence.

5   Type **executive** and press the **Space Bar**.

Notice that the text in the line moves forward to make room for the new word. You can move the cursor anywhere you want in a document and add new text just by typing.

6   Press **Down Arrow** (↓) once and watch how WordPerfect adjusts the words in each line to make room for the new text.

You may need to press Down Arrow more than once to adjust the paragraph.

This adjustment is called *rewriting* or *reformatting*, and WordPerfect does it for you as you move the cursor down through your text.

Typing the Closing

After typing the message of the letter, you are ready to type the closing.

1   Place the cursor after the period at the end of the sentence "An early confirmation. . .".

2   Press **Enter** twice for double spacing, then type **Sincerely,** to begin the closing.

3   Press **Enter** four times to leave room for a signature.

4   Type the following two lines:

Megan Sills
Marketing Director

The first draft of the letter is finished. Before printing, compare your letter to the one illustrated below.

```
Reservations Manager
Parkway Inn
1780 Delaware Ave.
Buffalo, NY 14209

CORPORATE MARKETING CONFERENCE RESERVATIONS

We would like to make reservations for a marketing conference to
be held on December 1, 2, and 3 of this year.  A minimum of 40
people will be attending.  Besides accommodations for those
attending, we will require your largest executive suite, a
conference room, and an extra meeting room for smaller gatherings.

An early confirmation would be sincerely appreciated.


Megan Sills
Marketing Director_


                                        Doc 1 Pg 1 Ln 4.17" Pos 2.8"
```

Printing the Letter

The letter can be sent to the printer using the Print menu.

1   Press **Print** (Shift-F7) and select **F**ull Document (1) from the Print menu to send the letter to the printer.

⌨ *Select **P**rint from the **F**ile menu.*

Notice that the printed page looks similar to the text on your screen. As you type, WordPerfect makes sure that each line of text contains the same words on the screen as on the printed page.

You may have also noticed that the text at the left and right margins is lined up evenly. This feature is called *full justification*, and is turned on when you first start WordPerfect.

If you prefer to have an uneven (ragged) right margin when a document is printed, you can find out how by turning to the *Special Techniques* lesson at the end of *Fundamentals I*.

Saving the Letter

With the document printed, you are ready to clear your screen with Exit. However, because the letter will be revised later on, it should be saved before clearing the screen.

1   Press **Exit** (F7) and type **y** (for yes) when you see the Save message.

⌨ *Select **E**xit from the **F**ile menu.*

A "Document to be saved:" message is displayed on the status line at the bottom of the screen. Saving a document means storing it as a file on a diskette or hard disk. Before a file can be saved, the file needs to be named.

2 Type **park** and press **Enter** to name the file in which the letter will be saved.

A light may glow on your computer to let you know that WordPerfect is saving the letter in a file on disk. After the letter has been saved, WordPerfect displays the "Exit WP? No (Yes)" message, asking if you want to exit the WordPerfect program.

3 Type **n** (for no) to stay in the program with a clear screen.

Displaying the Filename

Before finishing the lesson, let's use the List Files feature to see if the file was actually saved.

1 Press **List** (F5), then press **Enter** to display a list of files on your disk.

▢ *Select List Files from the File menu.*

```
09-14-89  02:55p              Directory C:\WP51\LEARN\*.*
Document size:      0   Free:  1,574,912 Used:    253,305    Files:      69

        Current     <Dir>              ..    Parent    <Dir>
ADDRESS .TUT         978  08-25-89 01:11p    ADDRESS .WKB        642  08-25-89 01:11p
ADVANCED.TUT           3  08-25-89 01:11p    ALTI    .WPM        132  08-25-89 01:11p
BANNER  .TUT         631  08-25-89 01:11p    BEGIN   .TUT         11  08-25-89 01:11p
BRIEF   .WKB       6,640  08-25-89 01:11p    CHART   .WKB      4,218  08-25-89 01:11p
CLIENTS .WKB       1,357  08-25-89 01:11p    COMPASS .WKB      2,924  08-25-89 01:11p
CUSTOMER.WKB       1,729  08-25-89 01:11p    FUTURE  .WKB      3,136  08-25-89 01:11p
GRAPH   .WPG       1,198  08-25-89 01:11p    INCOME  .WKB      1,823  08-25-89 01:11p
INTRO   .TUT      29,936  08-25-89 01:11p    INTRO_1 .TUT      9,408  08-25-89 01:11p
INVOICE .WKB       2,444  08-25-89 01:11p    ITINERY .WKB      2,257  08-25-89 01:11p
LABELA  .WKB         560  08-25-89 01:11p    LABELB  .WKB        929  08-25-89 01:11p
LEARN   .BAT          19  08-25-89 01:11p    LESS    .TUT         11  08-25-89 01:11p
LESS1   .TUT       4,989  08-25-89 01:11p    LESS2   .TUT      8,980  08-25-89 01:11p
LESS3   .TUT       7,631  08-25-89 01:11p    LESS4   .TUT     10,851  08-25-89 01:11p
LESS5   .TUT      13,413  08-25-89 01:11p    LESS6   .TUT      7,229  08-25-89 01:11p
LETTER  .STY         799  08-25-89 01:11p    LETTER  .TUT        653  08-25-89 01:11p
LETTER_F.TUT         679  08-25-89 01:11p    LETTER_P.TUT        652  08-25-89 01:11p
LETTER1 .TUT         778  08-25-89 01:11p    LIST    .WKB        568  08-25-89 01:11p
MASTER  .WKB         808  08-25-89 01:11p    MEMO    .TUT        569  08-25-89 01:11p

1 Retrieve; 2 Delete; 3 Move/Rename; 4 Print; 5 Short/Long Display;
6 Look: 7 Other Directory; 8 Copy; 9 Find; N Name Search: 6
```

At the top of the list is a header that includes the name of the current directory (e.g., C:\WP51\LEARN). WordPerfect saves all files to the current directory, unless you add the name of another directory to the filename when saving a file.

While all the filenames on your screen may not be displayed in the above illustration, you should be able to find the PARK filename in the alphabetized list. If the filename is not visible, then you may need to press Down Arrow (↓) until the name is displayed on the screen.

*If you are in the wrong place, press **Cancel** (F1) until you return to the document screen, then try repeating step 1 again. You should not type anything or press any other key (except Enter) after pressing List to display the correct list of files.*

After locating the file, notice that the size of the file (in bytes) and the date and time it was created (or changed) are included with the filename. This information can be important when trying to keep a large number of files organized.

2 Press **Exit** (F7) to leave the list of files and return to the WordPerfect screen.

You should now have a clear screen and be ready to continue with the next lesson.

Lesson 3: Memo Form

The heading of a memo usually includes titles for a date (Date), the name of the person receiving the memo (To), the name of the person sending the memo (From), and a brief description of the subject (Subject or RE). The area below the heading can then be used for typing a message.

One of the advantages of using a word processor is that you can create a memo form that includes only the titles, save it, then retrieve the form any time you need to type a memo.

Designing the Form

The first step in creating a memo form is to design the form. For example, a simple design for a corporate memo might include the following titles and a line to separate the heading from the message.

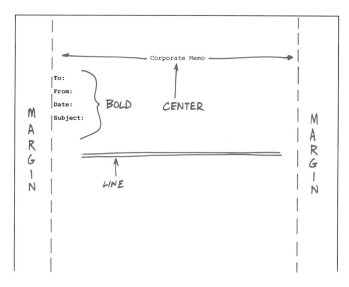

Notice that the "Corporate Memo" title is centered between the margins. The rest of the titles in the memo heading are bolded (highlighted) to help the reader quickly find information in the heading.

Centering the Memo Title

After deciding on a design, you can use the features in WordPerfect to help you create the form.

1 Press **Center** (Shift-F6) to center the cursor between the left and right margins.

The cursor moves to the center position in the first line (check the position number on the status line).

2 Type **Corporate Memo** for the memo title.

As you type, WordPerfect automatically centers the title between the margins.

3 Press **Enter** to end centering and return the cursor to the left margin.

4 Press **Enter** two more times to add extra spacing between the memo title and the memo heading.

Highlighting the Other Titles

Now that the memo title has been created, you can type the rest of the titles by using Bold to highlight the text, and Tab and Enter to add extra spacing to the right and below the title.

1 Press **Bold** (F6) to begin bolding.

🖃 *Select Appearance from the Font menu, then select Bold.*

Check the status line and notice that the "Pos" number is now as bright as the rest of the status line (monochrome screens) or a different color (color screens) to show you that Bold is on.

2 Type **To:** and press **Bold** again to end bolding.

3 Press **Tab** to add some space between the title and the text that will be filled in.

4 Press **Enter** twice to add double spacing after the To title.

Now that you have created the To title, type the From and Date titles using the same features.

5 Press **Bold**, type **From:** for the title, then press **Bold** again to end bolding.

6 Press **Tab** for extra spacing to the right of the title, then press **Enter** twice to double space after the title.

7 Press **Bold**, type **Date:** for the title, then press **Bold** again to end bolding.

8 Press **Tab** for extra spacing to the right of the title, then press **Enter** twice for double spacing after the title.

Now, try typing the Subject title on your own, following the keystrokes in steps 7 and 8.

9 Type **Subject:** for the last title using Bold, Tab, and Enter.

Your memo form should now look similar to the one illustrated below.

```
                         Corporate Memo



        To:

        From:

        Date:

        Subject:

        _




                                   Doc 1 Pg 1 Ln 2.83" Pos 1"
```

Creating a Line

Equal signs (=) can be used to draw a simple double line between the heading and the message area. However, instead of typing one character at a time, there are two ways that you can quickly create a line with equal signs.

The first way is to simply hold down the key.

1 Hold down the equal sign (=) key until the line is filled with equal sign characters, then release the key.

You may need to press Backspace to erase any equal signs that wrap to the next line.

Most of the keys on your keyboard are designed to repeat when you hold them down. This is a great feature if you want to repeat a character, or hold down an arrow key to move the cursor quickly through your text.

The function keys (F1 through F10, etc.), which are used to select WordPerfect features, also repeat when you hold them down. However, to select a feature (such as F6 for Bold), all you need to do is tap the key lightly.

2 Hold down **Backspace** to quickly erase the line of equal signs.

While repeating keys are a feature of your keyboard, WordPerfect also provides a more precise way of repeating a character by entering a repeat value, then typing the character.

3 Press **Center** (Shift-F6) to center the line of equal signs.

4 Press **Repeat** (Esc) to select the Repeat feature.

5 Type **40** for the repeat value, then type an equal sign (=).

A centered line of 40 equal signs immediately appears. By using a repeat value, you can instantly create a line that is exactly the length you need.

6 Press **Enter** twice to end centering and double space.

Your memo form should now look similar to the one illustrated below.

```
                        Corporate Memo


        To:
        From:
        Date:
        Subject:

              ========================================

          _




                                    Doc 1 Pg 1 Ln 3.17" Pos 1"
```

Inserting a Date

Before saving the memo form, an extra item can be added to the design that will save you time when filling in the memo.

1 Place the cursor on the Date title, then press **End** to move the cursor to the end of the line.

2 Press **Date/Outline** (Shift-F5) and select Date **C**ode (2).

▭ *Select Date **C**ode from the **T**ools menu.*

The current date appears! And because you selected Date Code, the displayed date will always be current whenever you fill in or print the memo.

Important: The date that appears is the date in your computer's internal clock. If the date is incorrect, check your DOS manual for details on changing the date.

Saving the Form

With the date code added, the memo form is ready to be saved.

1 Press **Exit** (F7) and type **y** (for yes) to save the memo.

2 Type **memo** for the filename, then press **Enter** to save the form.

3 Type **n** to stay in WordPerfect and clear the screen.

If you want to see if the file was actually saved on disk, go ahead and use List (F5) as you did in Lesson 2. Otherwise, you are ready to continue with the next lesson.

Lesson 4: Letter 1 — Second Draft

The first draft of the reservation letter (lesson 2) has been reviewed by the marketing director (Megan Sills) and contains a few editing remarks.

Because the first draft has already been saved in a file on disk, all you need to do is retrieve the letter, make the necessary changes, print it for final approval, then save the edited letter.

Retrieving the Letter

List Files can be used to retrieve the letter from the file on your disk.

1 Press **List** (F5), then press **Enter** to display a list of files on your disk.

⊟ *Select List Files from the File menu.*

2 Move the cursor to the PARK filename, then select **R**etrieve (1) from the menu at the bottom of the screen.

A copy of the file is retrieved to the WordPerfect screen for editing. The name of the file is displayed in the left half of the status line for your convenience.

⚠ FILENAME

```
Reservations Manager
Parkway Inn
1780 Delaware Ave.
Buffalo, NY 14209

CORPORATE MARKETING CONFERENCE RESERVATIONS

We would like to make reservations for a marketing conference to
be held on December 1, 2, and 3 of this year.  A minimum of 40
people will be attending.  Besides accommodations for those
attending, we will require your largest executive suite, a
conference room, and an extra meeting room for smaller gatherings.

An early confirmation would be sincerely appreciated.


Megan Sills
Marketing Director



C:\WP51\LEARN\PARK                          Doc 1 Pg 1 Ln 1" Pos 1"
```

Typing Over the Dates

With a copy of the first draft on the screen, you are ready to begin making changes. Checking the edited letter, it appears that the conference has been moved to December 6, 7, and 8.

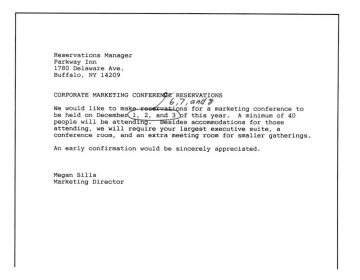

```
Reservations Manager
Parkway Inn
1780 Delaware Ave.
Buffalo, NY 14209

CORPORATE MARKETING CONFERENCE RESERVATIONS
                                    6,7, and 8
We would like to make reservations for a marketing conference to
be held on December 1, 2, and 3 of this year.  A minimum of 40
people will be attending.  Besides accommodations for those
attending, we will require your largest executive suite, a
conference room, and an extra meeting room for smaller gatherings.

An early confirmation would be sincerely appreciated.


Megan Sills
Marketing Director
```

1 Place the cursor on the number "1" in the first paragraph.

Instead of erasing each date and then typing the new date, Typeover can be used to replace the numbers as you type. Typeover is turned on and off by pressing Insert on your keyboard.

2 Press **Insert** (Ins) to turn on Typeover.

When Typeover is on, a "Typeover" message appears in the left half of the status line.

3 Type **6, 7, and 8** to replace the old with the new dates.

4 Press **Insert** again to turn off Typeover and return to inserting text.

Moving the Sentence

The sentence about the minimum number of people attending the conference needs to be moved to the beginning of the second paragraph.

One way of moving the sentence would be to erase it using Backspace, and then type it again at the beginning of the second paragraph. However, WordPerfect provides a Move feature that performs the same task with just a few keystrokes.

1 Place the cursor anywhere in the "minimum people" sentence.

2 Press **Move** (Ctrl-F4).

⌨ *Choose Select from the Edit menu.*

3 Select **S**entence (1) from the menu.

The entire sentence is immediately highlighted so you can see the text that will be moved. A menu on the status line lets you select a Move, Copy, Delete, or Append option.

4 Select **M**ove (1) to remove (cut) the sentence from the paragraph.

The sentence is removed from the screen and saved in a special file. Now all you need to do is indicate where you want the sentence placed and retrieve it with Enter (instead of Retrieve).

5 Place the cursor at the beginning of the second paragraph.

6 Press **Enter** to retrieve the sentence.

You have completed the move in just a few keystrokes. Now, check your screen to make sure that the sentence is in the correct place.

```
Reservations Manager
Parkway Inn
1780 Delaware Ave.
Buffalo, NY 14209

CORPORATE MARKETING CONFERENCE RESERVATIONS

We would like to make reservations for a marketing conference to
be held on December 6, 7, and 8 of this year.  Besides
accommodations for those attending, we will require your largest
executive suite, a conference room, and an extra meeting room for
smaller gatherings.

A minimum of 40 people will be attending.  An early confirmation
would be sincerely appreciated.


Megan Sills
Marketing Director


C:\WP51\LEARN\PARK                        Doc 1 Pg 1 Ln 3.33" Pos 1"
```

Changing the Margins

Because the letter includes only two paragraphs, the editing remarks indicate that the left and right margins should be changed to 2 inches.

```
      ┌── 2" ──┐   │              │  ┌── 2" ──┐
                   │              │
         Reservations Manager     │
         Parkway Inn              │
         1780 Delaware Ave.       │
         Buffalo, NY 14209        │

         CORPORATE MARKETING CONFERENCE RESERVATIONS    │

         We would like to make reservations for a marketing conference to
         be held on December 6, 7, and 8 of this year.  Besides
         accommodations for those attending, we will require your largest
         executive suite, a conference room, and an extra meeting room for
         smaller gatherings.

         A minimum of 40 people will be attending.  An early confirmation
         would be sincerely appreciated.


         Megan Sills               │
         Marketing Director        │
```

Margins can be changed by using the Format key. The word "format" is a standard term in word processing and indicates the style of your document or the *form* into which the text is placed.

For example, WordPerfect assumes that the paper size on which you are printing is 8.5" x 11" (unless you select another size), and that there needs to be a 1 inch margin around the edge of the page (left, right, top, and bottom).

As you type text, it is adjusted to fill in (fit) the format. When you want to change the format,

1 Press **Home** twice, then press **Up Arrow** (↑) to move the cursor to the very beginning of the text in the letter.

2 Press **Format** (Shift-F8) to display a main menu of all the formats available.

```
Format

   1 - Line
              Hyphenation                  Line Spacing
              Justification                Margins Left/Right
              Line Height                  Tab Set
              Line Numbering               Widow/Orphan Protection

   2 - Page
              Center Page (top to bottom)  Page Numbering
              Force Odd/Even Page          Paper Size/Type
              Headers and Footers          Suppress
              Margins Top/Bottom

   3 - Document
              Display Pitch                Redline Method
              Initial Codes/Font           Summary

   4 - Other
              Advance                      Overstrike
              Conditional End of Page      Printer Functions
              Decimal Characters           Underline Spaces/Tabs
              Language

   Selection: 0
```

From the main menu, you can select from one of four menus for changing the format. Because left and right margins affect the length of a line, you need to select the Line Format menu.

3 Select **L**ine Format (1).

⌨ *Select Line from the Layout menu.*

4 Select **M**argins (7) from the Line Format menu.

5 Type **2** and press **Enter** for the left margin, then type **2** and press **Enter** for the right margin.

6 Press **Exit** (F7) to return to the letter, then press **Down Arrow** (↓) to reformat the text.

You can immediately see the results of setting larger left and right margins. WordPerfect has automatically adjusted the text to fit into the new line length. Now there are more and shorter lines.

Before changing the margins, you used the Home key to move the cursor to the beginning of the letter. Each time you change a format, WordPerfect places a code in your document *at the cursor* that changes the text from that point forward through the document. In order to change the entire document, you need to have the cursor at the beginning of the text.

Format codes (and all other WordPerfect codes) can be seen by using the Reveal Codes screen.

7 Make sure the cursor is at the beginning of the letter, then press **Reveal Codes** (Alt-F3).

⌨ *Select **R**eveal Codes from the **E**dit menu.*

The screen is split in half, with the upper screen displaying the text as you normally see it when typing, and the lower screen revealing the text and all the codes WordPerfect uses to format the text exactly the way it will be printed.

A CURSOR (EDITING SCREEN)

B CURSOR (REVEAL CODES SCREEN)

```
    ▶  Reservations Manager
       Parkway Inn
       1780 Delaware Ave.
       Buffalo, NY 14209

       CORPORATE MARKETING CONFERENCE RESERVATIONS

       We would like to make reservations for a
       marketing conference to be held on December 6,
       7, and 8 of this year.  Besides accommodations
C:\WP51\LEARN\PARK                            Doc 1 Pg 1 Ln 1" Pos 2"
      ▲    {   ▲    ▲    ▲    ▲    ▲    ▲    ▲    }   ▲    ▲    ▲    ▲
[L/R Mar:2",2"]Reservations Manager[HRt]
Parkway Inn[HRt]
1780 Delaware ▲▲.[HRt]
Buffalo, NY 14209[HRt]
[HRt]
[HRt]
CORPORATE MARKETING CONFERENCE RESERVATIONS[HRt]
[HRt]
We would like to make reservations for a[SRt]
marketing conference to be held on December 6,[SRt]

Press Reveal Codes to restore screen
```

The cursor in the top screen (editing screen) is mirrored by a cursor in the bottom screen (Reveal Codes screen). The cursor in the Reveal Codes screen is normally a solid block that highlights each code or character as you move the cursor.

8 Press **Reveal Codes** to display the normal editing screen.

⌨ *Select **R**eveal Codes from the **E**dit menu.*

While in the Reveal Codes screen, you can edit and format as though you were in the normal editing screen. In fact, many people prefer to use the Reveal Codes screen when formatting a document to make sure that formatting codes are placed in the correct positions.

From time to time the Reveal Codes screen will be used in the lessons to help you understand how WordPerfect takes care of formatting your document. As you become more familiar with the screen, Reveal Codes will become much more important to you when using WordPerfect.

Centering the Letter	Although it was not mentioned in the editing remarks, a short letter usually looks better on the page if it is centered between the top and bottom margins.

You could move to the beginning of the letter and press Enter a few times to push the text down the page. However, WordPerfect provides a Center Page Top to Bottom feature that does all the work for you.

1   Press **Home** three times and then **Up Arrow** (↑) to move the cursor to the beginning of the letter.

2   Press **Format** (Shift-F8) and select **P**age (2) to display a menu of page formats.

🖳 *Select **P**age from the Layout menu.*

3   Select Center Page Top to Bottom (1) from the menu, type **y**, then press **Exit** (F7) to return to the letter.

Previewing the Letter	While the letter is not centered in the editing screen, you can see it centered in a special View Document screen. View Document lets you see how your document will appear on the printed page.

1   Press **Print** (Shift-F7).

🖳 *Select **P**rint from the **F**ile menu.*

2   Select View Document (6), then select Full Page (3) to view the entire letter.

If you have a graphics card in your computer, you should see the full page displayed on the screen.

```
1 100%   2 200%   3 Full Page   4 Facing Pages: 3              Doc 1 Pg 1
```

If you do not have a graphics card in your computer, then WordPerfect does its best to represent the printed page on your screen. You may not be able to read the text; however, you should be able to see the added space above the text that indicates the letter will be centered.

In the View Document screen, as in the editing screen, the length and number of lines in the letter will depend on which printer you selected when installing WordPerfect. The View Document screen above displays the letter with the Workbook Printer selected.

WordPerfect lets you move in for a closer look at the page by using the 100% and 200% options at the bottom of the screen.

3 Select 100% (1) from the menu line at the bottom of the preview screen.

This view represents your document at the actual size of 8.5" x 11". Because most screens are smaller than the actual size, you can only see part of the page at a time. However, you can use the arrow keys to move around on the page.

The 200% option displays your document at twice the actual size.

4 Select 200% (2) from the menu line at the bottom of the screen. Use the arrow keys to move around on the page.

You can also see two pages at a time (Facing Pages) if you are previewing a multi-page document. Since even pages are displayed on the left and odd pages on the right, page 1 is displayed by itself in Facing Pages.

Printing the Letter

After previewing the letter, you can return to the Print menu to send it to the printer.

1 Press **Exit** (F7) to return to the editing screen.

⌧ *The right-hand button on the mouse works like Cancel.*

2 Press **Print** (Shift-F7) to display the Print menu.

⌧ *Select Print from the File menu.*

3 Select **F**ull Document (1) to send the second draft of the letter to the printer.

While you cannot make any corrections to the document from the View Document screen, you can return to the editing screen, make the necessary changes, then view the document again before printing.

Looking into the File

At the beginning of the lesson you were told that the letter on your screen is only a copy of the file contents on disk. If that is true, then you have been making changes to the copy while the original has remained untouched.

1 With the printed letter in hand, press **List** (F5), then press **Enter** to display the list of files.

⌧ *Select List Files from the File menu.*

2 Move to the PARK filename and select **L**ook (6) from the menu at the bottom of the screen.

```
File: C:\WP51\LEARN\PARK                    WP5.1      Revised: 08-11-89 10:01a
Name: park                                             Created: 08-08-89 11:00a

Reservations Manager
Parkway Inn
1780 Delaware Ave.
Buffalo, NY 14209

CORPORATE MARKETING CONFERENCE RESERVATIONS

We would like to make reservations for a marketing conference to
be held on December 1, 2, and 3 of this year.  A minimum of 40
people will be attending.  Besides accommodations for those
attending, we will require your largest executive suite, a
conference room, and an extra meeting room for smaller gatherings.

An early confirmation would be sincerely appreciated.


Megan Sills
Marketing Director

Look: 1 Next Doc; 2 Prev Doc: 0
```

What you see are the actual contents of the PARK file on disk. Compare the file contents to the printed letter and you can immediately see that the document in the file has not been changed.

3 Press **Exit** (F7) once to leave the Look screen, then press **Exit** again to return to the edited letter.

Replacing the File

Although the letter on file and the edited copy on your screen are now different, they both have the same filename. Because the letter in the file on disk is no longer needed, it can be replaced with the edited version.

1 Press **Exit** (F7) and type **y** to save the edited letter.

The name PARK appears next to the "Document to be saved:" message at the bottom of the screen. When you retrieve a copy of the file, it is given the same name as the file on disk. WordPerfect always displays the name of the copy in case you want to use the same name when saving.

The name of the directory or diskette from which the document is retrieved is also included with the name of the document. When the directory or diskette name is included with the filename, it is called the "pathname" of the file. For example, C:\WP51\LEARN\PARK would be the full pathname of the PARK file if it were saved in a subdirectory called LEARN in the WP51 directory.

2 Press **Enter** to use the PARK name.

WordPerfect checks to see if there is another file on disk with the same name. Because the PARK filename already exists, WordPerfect asks if you want to replace the original letter with the edited copy on the screen.

3 Type **y** to replace the original letter with the edited version, then type **n** to stay in WordPerfect and clear the screen.

Was the original letter replaced by the edited copy? Before finishing the lesson, you can check again by using Look.

4 Press **List** (F5), then press **Enter** to display the list of files.

⌨ *Select List Files from the File menu.*

5 Move the cursor to PARK and press **Enter** to select the Look option.

You can select Look by typing a "6" or an "L", or by pressing Enter.

Compare the printed letter to the file contents. As you can see, the first draft of the letter is gone and the edited version is now in the PARK file.

6 Press **Exit** (F7) once to leave the Look screen, then press **Exit** again to return to the document screen.

The advantages of being able to work on a copy while keeping the original safely stored are important. And once you are satisfied with the changes, it only takes a few keystrokes to replace the original version with the edited copy.

Lesson 5: Memo Fill-in

A memo needs to be sent to all department managers informing them of the plans for a regional marketing conference. Because you have already created and saved a memo form (lesson 3), you can retrieve it, fill it in, and print the memo.

Retrieving the Memo Form

Beginning with a clear screen,

1 Press **List** (F5), then press **Enter** to display the list of files.

⊞ *Select List Files from the File menu.*

2 Place the cursor on the MEMO file, and then select **R**etrieve (1) to retrieve the file.

Filling In the Heading

With the memo form on the screen, you can start filling in the heading information.

1 Place the cursor on the To title and press **End** to move the cursor to the end of the line.

2 Type **All Marketing Managers** for the To information.

Editing in Reveal Codes

While filling in the memo heading, it may be useful to note some additional details about the Reveal Codes screen.

1 Place the cursor at the beginning of the From title.

2 Press **Reveal Codes** (Alt-F3) to see the WordPerfect codes in the memo.

⊞ *Select Reveal Codes from the Edit menu.*

Your screen should now look similar to the one illustrated below, with the top half of the screen displaying the memo the way it normally looks, and the bottom half of the screen displaying the memo with all the WordPerfect codes.

```
                          Corporate Memo

          To:  All Marketing Managers

          From:                                    ◄A

          Date:     September 14,1989

          Subject:

          C:\WP51\LEARN\MEMO              ▽C      Doc 1 Pg 1 Ln 1.83" Pos 1"
          ▮ ▲    ▲    ▲    ▲    ▲    ▲    ▲    ▲    )    ▲    ▲
          [HRt]
          [BOLD]To:[bold][Tab]All Marketing Managers[HRt]
          [HRt]
          [BOLD]From:[bold][Tab][HRt]
          [HRt]
          [BOLD]Date:[bold][Tab][Date:3 1,4][HRt]      ◄B
          [HRt]
          [BOLD]Subject:[bold][Tab][HRt]
          [HRt]
          [CENTER]======================================[HRt]

          Press Reveal Codes to restore screen
```

A reverse video bar divides the screen in half and indicates the position of each tab stop setting with a triangle.

Below the bar is the Reveal Codes screen, which displays the codes that WordPerfect places in a document whenever you press a key such as Tab, Enter, or Bold. Each code tells WordPerfect exactly what to do when displaying or printing the memo.

The [BOLD] and [bold] codes around the From title tell WordPerfect to begin and end printing bolded characters.

3 If it is not already there, press **Right Arrow** (→) to place the cursor between the [BOLD] and [bold] codes surrounding the From title.

When the cursor is between the Bold codes, the Position number on the status line is bolded (top half of the screen).

4 Press **Right Arrow** (→) until the cursor is on the [Tab] code.

When the cursor moves past the [bold] code, WordPerfect ends bolding and returns to displaying (and printing) normal text, and the Position number returns to a normal display.

```
                              Corporate Memo

   To:  All Marketing Managers

   From:_

   Date:       September 14,1989

   Subject:                                                    ▼Ａ
   C:\WP51\LEARN\MEMO                        Doc 1 Pg 1 Ln 1.83" Pos 1.5"
   [               ▲   ▲   ▲   ▲   ▲   ▲   ▲   ▲   ▲   )   ▲   ▲   ]
   [HRt]
   [BOLD]To:[bold][Tab]All Marketing Managers[HRt]
   [HRt]
   [BOLD]From:[bold][Tab][HRt]
   [HRt]
   [BOLD]Date:[bold][▲B][Date:3 1,4][HRt]
   [HRt]
   [BOLD]Subject:[bold][Tab][HRt]
   [HRt]
   [CENTER]=================================================[HRt]

   Press Reveal Codes to restore screen
```

The tab is shown as a [Tab] code, and moves the cursor to the next tab stop setting.

5 Press **Right Arrow** to move the cursor past [Tab].

Once you insert a tab, it can be quickly adjusted by resetting the tab stops instead of adding or erasing spaces. In addition, text will line up on a tab, but may not always line up if you have used spaces.

While you are in the Reveal Codes screen, you may want to try filling in the rest of the memo heading.

6 Make sure that the cursor is to the right of the [Tab] code in the Reveal Codes screen, and then type **Megan Sills** for the From information.

As you make changes in the bottom half of the screen (Reveal Codes), you can see the effect they are having on the memo in the upper half of the screen.

7 Place the cursor at the beginning of the Subject line, then press **End** to move the cursor to the end of the line.

When you press End, the cursor moves past all of the codes in the line to the exact place you need to enter the information for the subject. This is especially helpful when you are in the normal editing screen and cannot see the WordPerfect codes.

8 Type **Corporate Marketing Conference** for the subject information.

Before leaving the Reveal Codes screen, notice the [HRt] and [Date:3 1, 4] codes.

⚠ [HRt] CODE

⚠ [DATE:3 1, 4] CODE

```
                              Corporate Memo


      To:  All Marketing Managers

      From:    Megan Sills

      Date:    September 14,1989

      Subject:  Corporate Marketing Conference_

      C:\WP51\LEARN\MEMO                            Doc 1 Pg 1 Ln 2.5" Pos 5"
      [      ▲    ▲    ▲    ▲    ▲    ▲    ▲    ▲    ▲    ▲    }    ▲     ]
      [HRt]
      [BOLD]Date:[bold][Tab][Date:3 1,4][HRt]
      [HRt]
      [BOLD]Subject:[bold][Tab]Corporate Marketing Conference[HRt] ◁
      [HRt]
      [CENTER]========================================[HRt]
      [HRt]



      Press Reveal Codes to restore screen
```

The [HRt] codes are inserted each time you press Enter. They tell WordPerfect to end the current line and return to the left margin to start a new line. The [Date:3 1, 4] code tells WordPerfect to display and print the current date in the memo.

You are probably beginning to realize that codes are very similar to text. You insert them by pressing a key, and you can erase them with Backspace or Delete.

9 Place the cursor on the [Tab] code next to "Corporate Marketing Conference."

10 Press **Delete** (Del) to erase the code, then press **Tab** to insert another [Tab] code into the memo.

As you can see, a code is simply an instruction telling WordPerfect exactly what you want done with the text.

11 Press **Reveal Codes** to return to the document screen.

⌨ Select **Reveal Codes** from the **Edit** menu.

12 Press **Page Down** (PgDn) to move the cursor to the very end of the memo form.

Typing the Message   You can now finish filling out the memo by typing the message in the area below the line of equal signs.

1 Type the following message:

We have arranged a Corporate Marketing Conference for December 6, 7, and 8 to be held at the Parkway Inn in Buffalo, New York. All marketing managers and representatives are required to attend. If you wish to bring a spouse or friend, please let Beverly know by the end of the month so that arrangements can be made.

I will let you know when final approval has been given for the time and place.

Underlining a Word

Because the reservations at the Parkway Inn have not been confirmed, the word "tentatively" should be included before "arranged." It would also be a good idea to emphasize the word by underlining it.

1 Place the cursor on the "a" at the beginning of the word "arranged" in the first sentence of the message.

2 Press **Underline** (F8), and type **tentatively** in the memo.

⌨ *Select Appearance from the Font menu, then select Underline.*

Notice that the word is underlined as you type, and that the Position number on the status line is underlined to indicate that Underline is on.

Underlining on the screen depends on the type of monitor you are using. Color monitors may display the characters in a different color, rather than with a line beneath. Some monochrome monitors cannot display underlining at all, but in all cases the codes can be seen in Reveal Codes.

3 Press **Underline** (F8) to turn off the feature, then press the **Space Bar**.

Your filled in memo should now look similar to the one illustrated in the screen below.

```
                          Corporate Memo


         To:  All Marketing Managers

         From:     Megan Sills

         Date:     September 14,1989

         Subject:  Corporate Marketing Conference


              =========================================

         We have tentatively arranged a Corporate Marketing Conference for December 6,
         7, and 8 to be held at the Parkway Inn in Buffalo, New York.  All
         marketing managers and representatives are required to attend.  If
         you wish to bring a spouse or friend, please let Beverly know by
         the end of the month so that arrangements can be made.

         I will let you know when final approval has been given for the time
         and place.



         C:\WP51\LEARN\MEMO                    Doc 1 Pg 1 Ln 3.17" Pos 3"
```

Setting a Tab Stop

The information in the heading may not be lined up on the same tab stop, or may be too close to one or more of the titles. You could line up the information by adding one or more extra tabs on each line. However, the problem can also be corrected by setting a single tab stop for the entire memo.

1 Press **Home** twice, then **Up Arrow** (↑) to move the cursor to the beginning of the text in the memo.

2 Press **Format** (Shift-F8), select **L**ine (1) to display the menu of line formats.

⌨ *Select **Line** from the **Layout** menu.*

3 Select **T**ab Set (8).

A tab ruler appears at the bottom of the screen with a L's above ruler marking the position of each current tab stop. The memo is displayed so that you can see what happens to the document as you edit the tab stops.

⚠ MEMO
⚠ TAB STOPS

```
                        Corporate Memo

        To:  All Marketing Managers

        From:    Megan Sills

        Date:    September 14,1989

        Subject:  Corporate Marketing Conference

        ===========================================

        We have tentatively arranged a Corporate Marketing Conference for ◄
        December 6, 7, and 8 to be held at the Parkway Inn in Buffalo, New
        York.  All marketing managers and representatives are required to
        attend.  If you wish to bring a spouse or friend, please let
        Beverly know by the end of the month so that arrangements can be
        made.

        L....L....L....L....L....L....L....L....L....L....L....L....L....L...
        ¦         ¦    ⚠    ¦         ¦         ¦         ¦         ¦
        0"      +1"      +2"      +3"      +4"      +5"      +6"      +7"
        Delete EOL (clear tabs); Enter Number (set tab); Del (clear tab);
        Type; Left; Center; Right; Decimal; .= Dot Leader; Press Exit when done.
```

The numbers in the ruler represent the left margin (0") and distances from the left margin (+1",+2",+3",...). WordPerfect is set with a tab stop every half inch.

```
                          Corporate Memo

        To:  All Marketing Managers

        From:     Megan Sills

        Date:     September 14,1989

        Subject:  Corporate Marketing Conference

                  =========================================

        We have tentatively arranged a Corporate Marketing Conference for
        December 6, 7, and 8 to be held at the Parkway Inn in Buffalo, New
        York.  All marketing managers and representatives are required to
        attend.  If you wish to bring a spouse or friend, please let
        Beverly know by the end of the month so that arrangements can be
        made.    Ⓑ
      Ⓐ L....L....L....L....L....L....L....L....L....L....L....L....L....L...
        :    -    :    -    :    -    :    -    :    -    :    -    :    -
        0"       +1"       +2"       +3"       +4"       +5"       +6"       +7"
        Delete EOL (clear tabs); Enter Number (set tab); Del (clear tab);
        Type; Left; Center; Right; Decimal; .= Dot Leader; Press Exit when done.
```

Let's erase all the tab stops by using Delete to End of Line, then set a single tab stop 1.5 inches from the left margin.

4 Press **Home** and **Left Arrow** (←) to move to the beginning of the ruler.

A -1" is displayed at the beginning of the ruler. It represents the left edge of the page and the size of the left margin.

5 Press **Delete to End of Line** (Ctrl-End) to erase all the preset tab stops.

6 Type **1.5** for one and a half inches from the left margin, then press **Enter** to set the tab stop in the ruler.

An "L" is placed in the tab ruler at 1.5 inches from the left margin, and the information in the heading lines up at the new tab stop.

▲ HEADING INFORMATION
▲ NEW TAB STOP

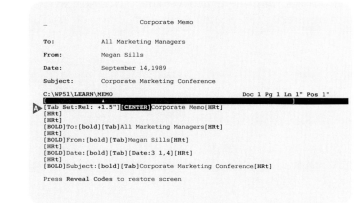

As you change the tab settings in the tab ruler, WordPerfect reformats the document so that you can see the results.

7 Press **Exit** (F7) twice to save the new tab setting and return to the memo.

Now all the information in the memo heading is lined up at 1.5 inches from the left margin (or whatever setting you selected).

8 Press **Reveal Codes** (Alt-F3) to display the Tab Setting code.

⌨ Select *Reveal Codes* from the *Edit* menu.

▲ TAB SETTING CODE

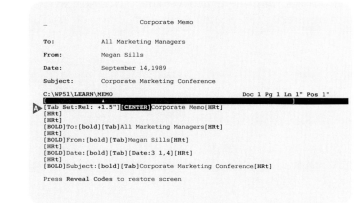

9 Press **Reveal Codes** to display to the full editing screen.

⌨ Select *Reveal Codes* from the *Edit* menu.

Printing the Memo

With the memo finished, you can send it to the printer.

1 Press **Print** (Shift-F7).

⊟ *Select Print from the File menu.*

2 Select **F**ull Document (1) to send the memo to the printer.

The printed memo should look like the version you created on your screen, with the tab setting at exactly 1.5 inches (or whatever setting you selected) from the left margin.

Saving the Memo

With the memo printed, you are ready to save it for future reference. However, because you will want to use the same memo form again, you need to create a new file for the filled-in memo.

1 Press **Exit** (F7) and type **y** to save the filled-in memo.

⊟ *Select Exit from the File menu.*

Even though the original memo form filename appears next to the "Document to be Saved:" message, you can type a new filename to have WordPerfect create a new file for the filled-in memo.

2 Type **parkmemo** and press **Enter** to create the PARKMEMO file.

3 Type **n** to clear the screen and stay in WordPerfect.

The memo is now ready to send to the marketing managers, and you have your own copy on disk in case you ever need to refer to it.

Before finishing the lesson, you may want to retrieve the MEMO file, place a tab setting of 1.5 inches at the beginning of the form, then replace the memo form on disk with the edited version. This will save you the effort of inserting a new Tab Setting code each time you use the memo form.

Lesson 6: Letter 1 — Final Draft

The second draft of the reservation letter has returned with no additional editing marks. However, the date at the top of the letter and initials below the signature block still need to be included.

Retrieving the Letter

By now you should be familiar with the filename of the letter, so try using Retrieve (instead of List Files) to retrieve a copy of the second draft to the screen.

1 Press **Retrieve** (Shift-F10) and notice that a "Document to be Retrieved:" message appears on the status line.

⌨ *Select Retrieve from the File menu.*

2 Type **park** and press **Enter** to retrieve a copy of the letter from the file.

Inserting a Date

The date of the reservation letter should be the date the letter is signed. Assuming the letter needs to go out today, you can use Date (as you did in the memo) to insert the current date. However, instead of inserting a code, you can insert the date as text.

1 Press **Reveal Codes** (Alt-F3), then place the cursor to the right of the [Center Page] and [L/R Mar] codes (if the cursor is not already there).

⌨ *Select Reveal Codes from the Edit menu.*

Important: *The Center Page code should always be at the top of the page to be centered.*

2 Press **Date/Outline** (Shift-F5) and select Date **T**ext (1).

⌨ *Select Date Text from the Tools menu.*

3 Press **Enter** four times to add extra spacing between the date and the inside address.

4 Press **Up Arrow** (↑) until the cursor is at the beginning of the date.

Instead of inserting a date code in the memo, the date is inserted as text.

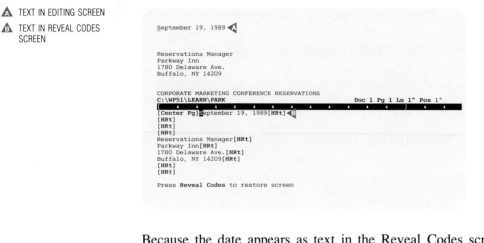

Because the date appears as text in the Reveal Codes screen, there are no instructions for WordPerfect to keep the date current if you retrieve the document later.

5   Press **Reveal Codes** to return to the normal editing screen.

▣ Select **R**eveal Codes from the **E**dit menu.

Typing the Initials

Now that the date is set, you can move to the bottom of the letter and add the initials.

1   Press **Page Down** (PgDn) to move the cursor to the end of the closing, then press **Enter** twice to double space.

2   Type **cjg** to add the typist's initials to the letter.

Spell-Checking the Letter

As a final step in the editing process, you can use the Speller to make sure there are no spelling errors, double words, or words that mistakenly contain numbers.

The Speller compares each word in the document to a dictionary list of over 120,000 words to make sure that every word is spelled correctly. Whenever

WordPerfect can't match a word against the list, the Speller stops and displays suggested spellings for the word.

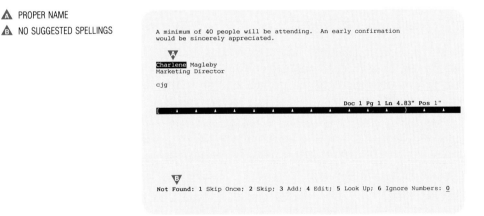

You can correct the spelling by typing the letter next to a suggested word, or by selecting Edit (4) from the menu, making the correction yourself, and pressing Exit (F7) to continue spell-checking.

Sometimes WordPerfect stops on the proper name of a person or street because the word is not found in the dictionary.

```
A minimum of 40 people will be attending.  An early confirmation
would be sincerely appreciated.

        ⚠A

Charlene Magleby
Marketing Director

cjg



                                        Doc 1 Pg 1 Ln 4.83" Pos 1"
[_____]

        ⚠B

Not Found: 1 Skip Once; 2 Skip; 3 Add; 4 Edit; 5 Look Up; 6 Ignore Numbers: 0
```

If the spelling is correct, then you can select Skip (2) from the menu to have the speller skip over that word for the rest of the document.

Important: *If you are running WordPerfect from two disk drives, insert your Speller diskette into drive B before continuing the lesson.*

With this brief introduction to the Speller, try spell-checking the reservation letter on your own. Most individuals seem to agree that the Speller is quite easy to use, and needs little or no explanation.

It is generally a good idea to save your document before spell-checking.

1 Press **Spell** (Ctrl-F2) to display the Spell menu.

⌨ *Select Spell from the Tools menu.*

2 Select **D**ocument (3) from the menu to begin spell-checking the letter.

Remember that when the Speller stops on a proper name, simply select Skip (2) to continue. If you get lost, you can always press **Cancel** (F1) one or two times to stop the spell-checking and return to the normal editing screen.

3 Spell-check the letter, skipping and editing words as described above.

After spell-checking is finished, WordPerfect displays a count of the number of words in the letter and a message telling you to press any key to continue.

4 Press any key to return to the editing screen.

Printing and Saving

Now that the final draft of the letter is finished, you can send it to the printer, then save it on disk.

Important: *If you are running WordPerfect from two disk drives, you need to replace the Speller diskette with your Workbook diskette before continuing the lesson.*

1 Press **Print** (Shift-F7) and select **F**ull Document (1).

⌨ *Select Print from the File menu.*

While the letter is printing, you can continue editing the copy of the letter on your screen, save it, send another copy to the printer, etc. In fact you can send several documents to the printer, and still continue using WordPerfect to create and edit documents.

You can display a list of documents (print job list) that you have sent to the printer by pressing Shift-F7,4. As soon as WordPerfect finishes sending the document to the printer, the document (print job) is removed from the list.

2 Press **Exit** (F7) and type **y** to save the letter.

3 Press **Enter** to use the PARK filename, type **y** to replace the original file with the edited letter on the screen, then type **n** to clear the screen and stay in WordPerfect.

The final draft is stored on disk, and you are ready to continue on to the next lesson.

You can retrieve the PARKSPEL.WKB file if you want to try using the Speller with a document that has several spelling errors. Remember to clear the screen before starting the next lesson.

Lesson 7: Getting Help

Now that you have been introduced to a few basic features of WordPerfect, let's explore the resources available for getting the help you may need to solve a problem, answer a question, or find out more about WordPerfect.

Cancel

One of the most valuable tools for helping you out of an immediate problem is the Cancel key. By pressing Cancel one or more times, you can back out of menus or messages.

When formatting a document from a menu, the Exit key is designed to save the setting and return you to the document, while the Cancel key is designed to return you to the document without saving the setting (in most cases).

Suppose you want to retrieve the PARKMEMO file to make some editing changes.

1 Press **Retrieve** (Shift-F10), type **parkmemo** for the filename, then press **Enter** to retrieve a copy of the letter.

⊟ *Select **R**etrieve from the **F**ile menu.*

After making the editing changes, you decide to save the document and clear the screen.

2 Press **Exit** (F7), type **y** to save the letter, press **Enter** to use the same filename, then type **y** to replace the letter.

You are now faced with the question "Exit WP? No (Yes)". However, you remember that you want to change the left and right margins to 2 inches.

If you type "y", you will exit WordPerfect. If you type "n", the screen will be cleared, and you will need to retrieve the letter again. However, you can press the Cancel key to keep the letter on the screen.

3 Press **Cancel** (F1) to return to the letter.

You are returned to the same place in the letter to continue editing, and can now change the margin settings.

4 Press **Format** (Shift-F8) and select **L**ine (1).

⊟ *Select **L**ine from the **L**ayout menu.*

5 Select **M**argins Left/Right (7).

As you are about to enter the new margin settings, you remember that the cursor may not be at the beginning of the memo. Pressing the Cancel key will take you out of the format menus without inserting a margin code.

6 Press **Cancel** (F1) until you return to the memo.

7 Press **Reveal Codes** (Alt-F3) and notice that a Margin Setting code was not placed in the letter.

⬚ *Select **R**eveal Codes from the **E**dit menu.*

8 Press **Page Up** (PgUp) to make sure you are at the beginning of the letter.

9 Press **Format** (Shift-F8) and select **L**ine (1).

⬚ *Select **L**ine from the **L**ayout menu.*

10 Select **M**argins Left/Right (7).

11 Type **2** and press **Enter** for the left margin, then type **2"** and press **Enter** for the right margin.

12 Press **Exit** (F7) to return to the letter.

Notice that a Margin Setting code is now inserted into the letter, and the Position number on the status line indicates the new left margin.

Besides helping you to back out of menus and messages, the Cancel key is also designed to help you restore text that you've mistakenly deleted. Because this feature of the Cancel key works differently than backing out of a menu or message, it is called "Undelete."

13 Press **Delete to End of Line** (Ctrl-End) to delete the "Corporate Memo" title.

14 Press **Cancel** (F1).

Notice that the deleted title is highlighted on your screen.

15 Select **R**estore (1) to insert the deleted title back into the memo.

Not only is the text of the title restored, but also the Center code. Let's try deleting a couple more lines, then restoring them to the memo.

16 Move the cursor to the To line, make sure the cursor in the Reveal Codes window is on the [BOLD] code, then press **Delete to End of Line** (Ctrl-End).

17 Move the cursor to the Date line, make sure the cursor is on the [BOLD] code, then press **Delete to End of Line**.

18 Press **Page Up** to move the cursor to the beginning of the memo.

19 Press **Cancel** (F1), then select **P**revious Deletion (2) several times to cycle through the deleted entries.

You can also use the Up and Down Arrow keys to cycle through previous deletions.

Notice that WordPerfect saves up to three deletions for you, and that they are displayed at the cursor position. To restore the deleted text, you need to make sure the cursor is in the same position it was before selecting Restore.

20 Press **Cancel** (F1) to back out of Undelete.

21 Restore the To and Date lines to the memo by moving the cursor to the correct position, pressing **Cancel**, then using **R**estore (1) and **P**revious Deletion (2) to insert the text back into the memo.

At this point, you may want to try experimenting with the Cancel key on your own. Remember to use Cancel as your "first line of defense" when trying to back out of a problem situation.

22 Press **Reveal Codes** to display the normal editing screen.

⊟ Select *Reveal Codes* from the *Edit* menu.

23 Press **Exit** (F7), and type **n** twice to clear the screen.

⊟ Select *Exit* from the *File* menu.

Help

Help is like having a quick reference manual at your fingertips. You can turn to Help for a list of features and keystrokes, a brief explanation of each feature, or a keyboard template.

Important: *If you are running WordPerfect from two disk drives, you need to make sure that the WordPerfect 1 diskette is in drive B before continuing the lesson. The Help files are located on the WordPerfect 1 diskette.*

For example, you may have forgotten the keystrokes for Justification.

1 Press **Help** (F3), then type **j** to display a list of all the features that start with the letter "J".

⊟ Select *Index* from the *Help* menu.

If you have forgotten what Justification does, reference information is just a keystroke away.

2 Press **Format** (Shift-F8), select **L**ine (1), then select **J**ustification (3) to display text explaining the Justification feature.

3 Press **Enter** (or the **Space Bar**) to exit Help.

Where can you find a keyboard template? Try using Help.

4 Press **Help** twice to display a keyboard template.

⊟ Select *Template* from the *Help* menu.

When you do find the keystrokes for a feature by displaying the template (or the alphabetical list), you can immediately display the reference screen from the template or list by simply pressing the keystrokes for that feature.

5 Find "Move" on the displayed keyboard template, and press the appropriate keystroke (Ctrl-F4).

While on one reference screen, you can turn to another by pressing the appropriate keystrokes for the feature, or by returning to the list, finding the keystrokes, and pressing them.

6 Press **Bold** (F6) to turn to the information on bolding.

7 Type **d** to display a list of all features that start with "D".

8 Find Date/Time and press the appropriate keystrokes to display the reference screen.

9 Press **Help** to return to the keyboard template, then press **Enter** (or the **Space Bar**) to exit Help.

WordPerfect also provides what is called *context-sensitive* help. If you are in a menu and can't remember which option to select or how a particular option works, WordPerfect senses where you are and automatically selects the help information for the menu (or feature) that you are using.

10 Press **Print** (Shift-F7), then type **s** to select a printer.

⊞ *Select Print from the File menu.*

11 Press **Help**. WordPerfect displays the information on selecting printers.

12 Press **Enter** to exit Help, then press **Exit** (F7) twice to return to the normal editing screen.

As you can see, Help is quite flexible and provides a variety of information. If you want a reminder as to how Help works, simply press the Help key.

13 Press **Help** to display instructions for using Help.

Select Help from the Help menu.

```
Help            License #  WP9991234567        WP 5.1   09/01/89


     Press any letter to get an alphabetical list of features.

          The list will include the features that start with that letter,
          along with the name of the key where the feature is found.  You
          can then press that key to get a description of how the feature
          works.


     Press any function key to get information about the use of the key.

          Some keys may let you choose from a menu to get more information
          about various options.  Press HELP again to display the template.




     Selection: 0                           (Press ENTER to exit Help)
```

Notice that your customer registration number (if you entered it), the version number, and the date of the program are listed at the top ot the screen. This information is useful to WordPerfect Customer Support when referring to problems you are having with the program.

14 Press **Enter** (or the **Space Bar**) to exit Help.

Help is a way of quickly finding the keystrokes for a particular feature, and some summary reference material. However, if you want detailed information about a feature, you should turn to your *WordPerfect Reference Manual* for an in-depth explanation.

Important: *If you are running WordPerfect from two disk drives, replace the WordPerfect 1 diskette with the Learn diskette before continuing.*

Reference Manual

The greatest amount of information available on any single WordPerfect feature can be found in the *WordPerfect Reference Manual*. The manual is divided into the following basic sections:

- Getting Started
- Reference
- Appendix
- Glossary/Index

The *Getting Started* section provides some basic information about how to begin using WordPerfect. The *Reference* section will help you find the information you need on specific features. Topics are listed alphabetically with subheadings in the text that point you to specific details.

In the *Appendix* you can find a list of the files on the diskettes in the WordPerfect package, as well as lists of codes, clip-art images, scientific and mathematical symbols, etc.

If you are having trouble locating a subject, the *Index* provides a more direct access to the information. Simply look for the topic and turn to the referenced page(s).

The primary purpose of the *WordPerfect Reference Manual* is to provide detailed, technical information on individual features. If you are looking for information on how to perform special tasks (printing envelopes) or create specialized documents (newsletters), then turn to the table of contents or index in the *WordPerfect Workbook*.

Tutorial

While the first few lessons in the workbook are designed to take you step by step through the fundamentals of WordPerfect, you may still become lost or confused by accidentally pressing the wrong key.

If you are finding it difficult to complete the initial lessons, or you want a detailed review of the lessons, try using the WordPerfect Tutorial provided on the Learning diskette in your WordPerfect package. Details on installing and using the tutorial are found in the *Getting Started* section of the *WordPerfect Reference Manual.*

Customer Support

For most people, it is comforting to know that help is as close as the nearest telephone. And WordPerfect Corporation's customer support department is among the best available in the software industry.

However, because the support is given over the telephone, you need to be able to describe the problem as clearly as possible to the person at the other end of the line. So, before picking up the receiver to call Customer Support, take a moment to collect your thoughts and any information that might be helpful.

For example, try duplicating the problem, then write down the keys you pressed that caused the error. It is also important that you know the type of computer, monitor, and printer you are using, and some basic features of the equipment (amount of memory, serial or parallel printer, DOS version, etc.).

The better the information, the quicker Customer Support can respond with a solution that will help you be successful in using WordPerfect for your personal or business needs. You will need to be at your computer before calling Customer Support.

Important: Getting Started *in the* WordPerfect Reference Manual *provides all the information you need to contact Customer Support.*

Supplemental Materials

In an effort to keep you informed of any significant changes in the program, as well as provide additional details and applications about WordPerfect features, the *WPCorp Report* is regularly sent to all registered WordPerfect users. Be sure to complete and mail your registration card to ensure that you will get all the new information.

There are many independent organizations that can give you help, advice, and new ideas for using WordPerfect. Many localities have user support groups that provide information and guidance to computer users. Bulletin Board Systems and other electronic forums are also a good place to participate in the exchange of ideas about WordPerfect.

WordPerfect Magazine is an independent publication dedicated to serving WordPerfect users. You may also want to check your local bookstore for other publications that deal with WordPerfect applications.

The views of these independent groups do not necessarily reflect the official positions of WordPerfect Corporation, its officers, or its employees.

Lesson 8: Letter 2 — First Draft

The majority of business letters are only one page in length. However, there are times when a letter may require two, three, or even more typed pages. Whatever the length, WordPerfect provides the features to make editing quick and easy.

Retrieving the Letter

For example, the first draft of a three-page letter needs some editing changes to prepare the letter for final approval.

1 Press **Retrieve** (Shift-F10) and enter **musicbox.wkb** to retrieve a copy of the rough draft.

Select ***R****etrieve from the* ***F****ile menu.*

From now on, the word "enter" will be used whenever you need to press Enter after typing the bolded text. For example, after typing MUSICBOX.WKB, you should have pressed Enter to retrieve a copy of the letter.

You may have noticed that the filename of the letter included a .WKB at the end of the name. If you want to know more about how files are named, turn to the Special Techniques *lesson at the end of* Fundamentals I.

Using the Home Key

The first correction is several lines down the page, close to the bottom of the screen.

```
Ms. Heather Wilson
Director of Sales
Swiss America, Inc.
1030 Harrington Blvd.
Newark, NJ 07112

Dear Ms. Wilson,

After recently visiting the Sundheim booth at the WURLD trade
exposition in Amsterdam, I was very impressed with both the
quality and variety of hand-crafted music boxes displayed.  While
speaking with the Sundheim marketing director, I was informed
that distribution of the music boxes in the United States is
handled directly through your company.

As you know, HALVA International has retailed an exclusive line
of jewelry from Europe for over 50 years.  Until recently, we
have handled the majority of our business through a mail order
service.

We are now planning to expand our business by opening several
retail outlets in major cities through the United States.  At the
same time, we would also like to include a complete line of
Sundheim music boxes.

We would like to order a selection of music boxes from the
following list for the conference:

Fairies
Pan's Pipes
Gondolier
Silver Harmonies
```

You could use Down Arrow to move to the correction, but a faster way is to use Home (usually on the right side of your keyboard).

1 Press **Home**, then press **Down Arrow** (↓).

Notice that the cursor moved down to the last line on your screen. Pressing Home once and then Up Arrow or Down Arrow moves you quickly backward or forward through your document a screen at a time. Home is useful for moving through large areas of text.

2 Place the cursor on the "c" in the word "complete" in the last sentence of the third paragraph.

Using the Delete Key

Instead of using Backspace to erase the word, try using Delete. Like Backspace, Delete erases both text and codes. However, it erases the character *at* the cursor instead of the character to the *left* of the cursor.

1 Press **Delete** (Del) until the word "complete" is erased.

Because the cursor stays in the same position as you press Delete, it appears as though Delete erases characters to the right of the cursor.

Restoring Deleted Text

Once you delete a word (or any text) with WordPerfect, you can bring it back by using the **Undelete** feature.

1 Press **Cancel** (F1) to bring back the deleted word.

After pressing Cancel, the deleted word is displayed at the cursor location.

▲ DELETED WORD

```
Ms. Heather Wilson
Director of Sales
Swiss America, Inc.
1030 Harrington Blvd.
Newark, NJ 07112

Dear Ms. Wilson,

After recently visiting the Sundheim booth at the WURLD trade
exposition in Amsterdam, I was very impressed with both the
quality and variety of hand-crafted music boxes displayed.  While
speaking with the Sundheim marketing director, I was informed
that distribution of the music boxes in the United States is
handled directly through your company.

As you know, HALVA International has retailed an exclusive line
of jewelry from Europe for over 50 years.  Until recently, we
have handled the majority of our business through a mail order
service.

We are now planning to expand our business by opening several
retail outlets in major cities through the United States.  At the
same time, we would also like to include a complete line of
Sundheim
Undelete: 1 Restore; 2 Previous Deletion: 0  ▲
```

WordPerfect saves up to the last three deletions. The saved deletions can be seen one at a time by selecting Previous Deletion. However, all you need to do is restore the most recent deletion.

2 Select **R**estore (1) to place the word "complete" back into the letter.

Now that you have seen how easy it is to restore deleted text, keep the Undelete feature in mind whenever you make a mistake and erase the wrong character, word, or phrase while doing the lessons.

3 Press **Backspace** until the word "complete" and the space before it are erased again.

Scrolling Through the Letter

The word "immediate" is the next word that needs to be deleted.

```
          retail outlets in major cities through the United States.  At the
          same time, we would also like to include a line of Sundheim music
          boxes.

          We would like to order a selection of music boxes from the
          following list for the conference:

          Fairies
          Pan's Pipes
          Gondolier
          Silver Harmonies
          Return to the Danube
          Patterns
          Autumn Memories
          Paris at Night
          Follow the Leader
          Secrets
          Symphony Strings
          Black Forest Summer
          Punting on the Thames
          Winter's Wonder
          Goatherd

          In addition to the above music boxes, our marketing department
          would also like to request one or more transparencies for as many
          music boxes as possible for our catalog and other advertising
          promotions.  For the immediate future, we would like to have
          transparencies sent for the following:

          Beautiful Dreamer
          Always
          Christmas Fantasy
          Little Flower Girl
```

However, the line with the correction is probably not on your screen right now. This is because most screens only let you see 24 lines at a time (the 25th line is reserved for the status line).

```
1030 Harrington Blvd.
Newark, NJ 07112

Dear Ms. Wilson,

After recently visiting the Sundheim booth at the WURLD trade
exposition in Amsterdam, I was very impressed with both the
```

```
quality and variety of hand-crafted music boxes displayed.  While
speaking with the Sundheim marketing director, I was informed
that distribution of the music boxes in the United States is
handled directly through your company.

As you know, HALVA International has retailed an exclusive line
of jewelry from Europe for over 50 years.  Until recently, we
have handled the majority of our business through a mail order
service.

We are now planning to expand our business by opening several
retail outlets in major cities through the United States.  At the
same time, we would also like to include a line of Sundheim music
boxes.

We would like to order a selection of music boxes from the
following list for the conference:

Fairies
Pan's Pipes
Gondolier
Silver Harmonies
Return to the Danube
Patterns
C:\WP51\LEARN\MUSICBOX.WKB                    Doc 1 Pg 1 Ln 6.5" Pos 5.3"
```

```
Autumn Memories
Paris at Night
Follow the Leader
Secrets
Symphony Strings
Black Forest Summer
Punting on the Thames
Winter's Wonder
```

In order to move the paragraph onto the screen, you need to use Down Arrow to scroll the top part of the letter off the screen.

1 Press **Down Arrow** (↓) several times until the paragraph following the list of music boxes is on your screen.

▲ PARAGRAPH FOLLOWING
LIST

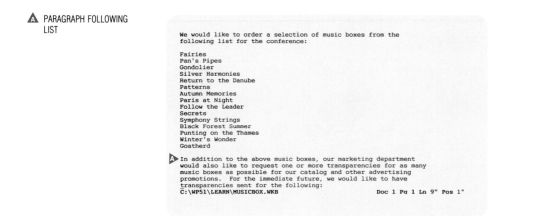

```
We would like to order a selection of music boxes from the
following list for the conference:

Fairies
Pan's Pipes
Gondolier
Silver Harmonies
Return to the Danube
Patterns
Autumn Memories
Paris at Night
Follow the Leader
Secrets
Symphony Strings
Black Forest Summer
Punting on the Thames
Winter's Wonder
Goatherd

In addition to the above music boxes, our marketing department
would also like to request one or more transparencies for as many
music boxes as possible for our catalog and other advertising
promotions.  For the immediate future, we would like to have
transparencies sent for the following:
C:\WP51\LEARN\MUSICBOX.WKB                    Doc 1 Pg 1 Ln 9" Pos 1"
```

As you press Down Arrow, the lines at the top of the screen move off to make room for the lines below. The lines that are not on the screen, which include most of the music box letter, are available at any time by simply using the Home and/or arrow keys to scroll them back onto the screen.

You may want to take a few moments right now to try scrolling through the entire letter. If you do, make sure that you return to the same paragraph before continuing the lesson.

2 Use **Backspace** or **Delete** (Del) to erase the word "immediate" from the last sentence in the paragraph below the list.

Deleting a Word

As you learn more about WordPerfect, you will discover there are several ways to move the cursor and delete text. For example, the phrase "one or more" in the same paragraph needs to be deleted.

```
retail outlets in major cities through the United States.  At the
same time, we would also like to include a line of Sundheim music
boxes.

We would like to order a selection of music boxes from the
following list for the conference:

Fairies
Pan's Pipes
Gondolier
Silver Harmonies
Return to the Danube
Patterns
Autumn Memories
Paris at Night
Follow the Leader
Secrets
Symphony Strings
Black Forest Summer
Punting on the Thames
Winter's Wonder
Goatherd

In addition to the above music boxes, our marketing department
would also like to request one or more transparencies for as many
music boxes as possible for our catalog and other advertising
promotions.  For the immediate future, we would like to have
transparencies sent for the following:

Beautiful Dreamer
Always
Christmas Fantasy
Little Flower Girl
```

You could use Backspace or Delete to delete the phrase a character at a time. However, you can also use Delete Word to delete the phrase a word at a time.

1 Place the cursor on the word "one" in the first sentence of the paragraph.

2 Press **Delete Word** (Ctrl-Backspace) to delete the word.

Once the word "one" is deleted, the text moves in from the right, and you can then use the Delete Word feature to delete the next word.

3 Press **Delete Word** (Ctrl-Backspace) to delete the word "or," then press **Delete Word** again to delete the word "more."

Deleting a Line

For the next editing change, you can use Delete to End of Line to delete "Symphony Strings" from the list of music boxes.

```
We are now planning to expand our business by opening several
retail outlets in major cities through the United States.  At the
same time, we would also like to include a line of Sundheim music
boxes.

We would like to order a selection of music boxes from the
following list for the conference:

Fairies
Pan's Pipes
Gondolier
Silver Harmonies
Return to the Danube
Patterns
Autumn Memories
Paris at Night
Follow the Leader
Secrets
(Symphony Strings)
Black Forest Summer
Punting on the Thames
Winter's Wonder
Goatherd

In addition to the above music boxes, our marketing department
would also like to request transparencies for as many music boxes
as possible for our catalog and other advertising promotions.
For the future, we would like to have transparencies sent for the
following:

Beautiful Dreamer
Always
Christmas Fantasy
Little Flower Girl
```

1 Place the cursor at the beginning of "Symphony Strings" in the list.

2 Press **Delete to End of Line** (Ctrl-End) to delete both words at the same time.

Notice that only the text in the line is deleted. The hard return [HRt] is still keeping the line open for typing more text. You can delete the hard return by simply pressing Delete.

3 Press **Delete** (Del) to delete the empty line.

Starting a New Page

When you start WordPerfect, all four margins (left, right, top, and bottom) are initially set at one inch. For example, you may have noticed that the memo you printed in lesson 5 had one-inch margins.

```
                        Corporate Memo

        To:         All Marketing Managers

        From:       Megan Sills

        Date:       September 20,1989

        Subject:    Corporate Marketing Conference

                    ========================================

        We have tentatively arranged a Corporate Marketing Conference for
        December 6, 7, and 8 to be held at the Parkway Inn in Buffalo, New
        York.  All marketing managers and representatives are required to
        attend.  If you wish to bring a spouse or friend, please let
        Beverly know by the end of the month so that arrangements can be
        made.

        I will let you know when final approval has been given for the time
        and place.
```

WordPerfect is also set (initially) to print on a standard letter-sized page (8½" x 11"). Because the size of the page and margins are already known, WordPerfect automatically wraps the cursor to the left margin when a line is full (6½").

The same is true when a page fills up. WordPerfect automatically wraps the next line to the top of a new page after reaching 9". To help you see where the old page ends and the new page begins, WordPerfect places a page break (a line of dashes) across the screen.

The Position number on the status line displays 7.5" (not 6.5") when a line is full because WordPerfect is measuring from the left edge of the page (not the left margin). The Ln number includes the top margin of the page.

For example, in the music box letter, a page break falls in the middle of the second list of music boxes.

1 Press **Down Arrow** (↓) until you see the page break on your screen.

⚠ PAGE BREAK

```
Punting on the Thames
Winter's Wonder
Goatherd

In addition to the above music boxes, our marketing department
would also like to request transparencies for as many music boxes
as possible for our catalog and other advertising promotions.
For the future, we would like to have transparencies sent for the
following:

Beautiful Dreamer
Always
Christmas Fantasy
Little Flower Girl
Just a Song
--------------------------------------------------------------------
Easter Parade                        ⚠
Somewhere, Somehow
Joplin
San Francisco Nights
Happiness
Grecian Holiday
Lazy River
Blues
C:\WP51\LEARN\MUSICBOX.WKB           Doc 1 Pg 2 Ln 2.17" Pos 1"
```

The editing remarks indicate that the beginning of the second list needs to start at the top of the second page.

```
    retail outlets in major cities through the United States.  At the
    same time, we would also like to include a line of Sundheim music
    boxes.

    We would like to order a selection of music boxes from the
    following list for the conference:

    Fairies
    Pan's Pipes
    Gondolier
    Silver Harmonies
    Return to the Danube
    Patterns
    Autumn Memories
    Paris at Night
    Follow the Leader
    Secrets
    Black Forest Summer
    Punting on the Thames
    Winter's Wonder
    Goatherd

    In addition to the above music boxes, our marketing department
    would also like to request transparencies for as many music boxes
    as possible for our catalog and other advertising promotions.
    For the future, we would like to have transparencies sent for the
    following:              ──START NEW PAGE HERE
    Beautiful Dreamer
    Always
    Christmas Fantasy
    Little Flower Girl
    Just a Song
```

One way of solving the problem is to push the beginning of the list to the top of the second page by adding some extra lines.

2 Place the cursor at the beginning of the "Beautiful Dreamer" line.

3 Press **Enter** until "Beautiful Dreamer" is at the top of the second page.

▲ TOP OF SECOND PAGE

```
Punting on the Thames
Winter's Wonder
Goatherd

In addition to the above music boxes, our marketing department
would also like to request transparencies for as many music boxes
as possible for our catalog and other advertising promotions.
For the future, we would like to have transparencies sent for the
following:



▲  ----------------------------------------------------------------------
Beautiful Dreamer
Always
Christmas Fantasy
Little Flower Girl
Just a Song
Easter Parade
Somewhere, Somehow
Joplin
C:\WP51\LEARN\MUSICBOX.WKB                        Doc 1 Pg 2 Ln 1" Pos 1"
```

Notice that the page break stayed in the same place, while the lines moved past it. This is because the page break is a *soft* page break that stays in the same place, just like the *soft* return that stays at the end of a line in a paragraph, allowing the words to wrap through it.

However, just as you can use Enter to create a shorter line, you can use Hard Page to create a shorter page. Instead of forcing the beginning of the list to the next page by adding empty lines, try using Hard Page.

4 Place the cursor at the beginning of the "Beautiful Dreamer" line (if it is not already there).

5 Press **Backspace** until the empty lines you added are deleted.

6 Press **Hard Page** (Ctrl-Enter) to insert your own page break.

```
Punting on the Thames
Winter's Wonder
Goatherd

In addition to the above music boxes, our marketing department
would also like to request transparencies for as many music boxes
as possible for our catalog and other advertising promotions.
For the future, we would like to have transparencies sent for the
following:


===========================================================================
Beautiful Dreamer
Always
Christmas Fantasy
Little Flower Girl
Just a Song
Easter Parade
Somewhere, Somehow
Joplin
San Francisco Nights
Happiness
Grecian Holiday
Lazy River
C:\WP51\LEARN\MUSICBOX.WKB                        Doc 1 Pg 2 Ln 1" Pos 1"
```

If the page break is in the wrong place, simply press Backspace to delete it, then make sure your cursor is at the very beginning of the "Beautiful Dreamer" line before pressing Hard Page.

The page break you put in with Hard Page is displayed as a line of equal signs (=====) instead of a line of dashes (-----). This is done because the hard page break stays with the text instead of remaining in the same place while the text moves past it.

7 Place the cursor at the end of the paragraph above the list.

8 Press **Enter** until a soft page break appears.

Notice that WordPerfect pushes the hard page break down and will even add a page break of its own (if necessary) to keep the list at the top of a page. WordPerfect will always keep the hard page break in exactly the same place you inserted it.

9 Press **Backspace** until you delete the empty lines you inserted with Enter and the soft page break is gone.

Saving the Letter	While editing the letter, or creating your own documents, you may have noticed a "* Please Wait *" message flash on the screen:

```
Punting on the Thames
Winter's Wonder
Goatherd

In addition to the above music boxes, our marketing department
would also like to request transparencies for as many music boxes
as possible for our catalog and other advertising promotions.
For the future, we would like to have transparencies sent for the
following:

================================================================================
Beautiful Dreamer
Always
Christmas Fantasy
Little Flower Girl
Just a Song
Easter Parade
Somewhere, Somehow
Joplin
San Francisco Nights
Happiness
Grecian Holiday
Lazy River
* Please Wait *
```

Every 30 minutes, WordPerfect automatically saves the document on your screen to a backup file on disk. If a power outage occurs, you accidentally clear your screen, or the computer fails, you can always retrieve the backup file and continue editing.

For details on retrieving the backup file, turn to the Timed Document Backup *heading in the* Special Features *lesson at the end of* Fundamentals I.

However, because the backup file is erased when you exit WordPerfect (and because you may not want to wait 30 minutes), it is also important to occasionally pause and save the changes you have made to your own file.

1 Press **Save** (F10) and enter **musicbox** to create a new file for the letter.

⊟ *Select Save from the File menu.*

Save lets you save a document as often as you like, then continue editing. By using both Save and Automatic Document Backup, you can save yourself hours of work trying to re-create or re-edit a document.

Numbering Pages

Many business letters have numbered pages when the letter is longer than one page.

1 Press **Home,Home,**↑ to move the cursor to the very beginning of the first page.

2 Press **Format** (Shift-F8) and select **P**age (2).

⊟ *Select Page from the Layout menu.*

3 Select Page **N**umbering (6) from the Page Format menu.

A menu is displayed from which you can select several options for printing page numbers. Which one should you use?

4 Press **Help** (F3) to display information about the menu.

Because you want WordPerfect to take care of positioning the page number on each page, you want to select Page Number Position.

5 Press **Enter** to exit the Help screen, then select Page Number **P**osition (4).

```
Format: Page Numbering


    Every Page                Alternating Pages
  ┌─────────────┐        ┌───────────┐ ┌───────────┐
  │ 1   2   3   │        │ 4         │ │         4 │
  │             │        │           │ │           │
  │             │        │ Even      │ │ Odd       │
  │             │        │           │ │           │
  │ 5   6   7   │        │ 8         │ │         8 │
  └─────────────┘        └───────────┘ └───────────┘

   9 - No Page Numbers




 Selection: 0
```

6 Type **2** to select the top center position for every page, then press **Exit** (F7) to return to the letter.

After selecting a numbering position, WordPerfect places a Page Numbering code in the letter.

7 Press **Reveal Codes** (Alt-F3) to see the Page Numbering code.

⌨ *Select **Reveal Codes** from the **Edit** menu.*

▲ PAGE NUMBERING CODE

```
Ms. Heather Wilson
Director of Sales
Swiss America, Inc.
1030 Harrington Blvd.
Newark, NJ 07112

Dear Ms. Wilson,

After recently visiting the Sundheim booth at the WURLD trade
exposition in Amsterdam, I was very impressed with both the
quality and variety of hand-crafted music boxes displayed.   While
C:\WP51\LEARN\MUSICBOX                        Doc 1 Pg 1 Ln 1.33" Pos 1"
[   ▲     ▲     ▲     ▲     ▲     ▲     ▲     ▲     ▲      )   ▲     ▲
▲[Pg Numbering:Top Center]Ms. Heather Wilson[HRt]
Director of Sales[HRt]
Swiss America, Inc.[HRt]
1030 Harrington Blvd.[HRt]
Newark, NJ 07112[HRt]
[HRt]
Dear Ms. Wilson,[HRt]
[HRt]
After recently visiting the Sundheim booth at the WURLD trade[SRt]
exposition in Amsterdam, I was very impressed with both the[SRt]

Press Reveal Codes to restore screen
```

Notice that the Page Numbering code is at the very beginning of the letter. All formats entered from the Page Format menu should be placed at the beginning of the page before any other text or codes; otherwise, they will not begin working until the following page.

Suppressing a Page Number

With the Page Numbering code at the beginning of the letter, every page will be numbered. However, most business letters start page numbering on the second page.

1 Press **Format** (Shift-F8), then select **Page** (2).

⌨ *Select **Page** from the **Layout** menu.*

2 Select **Suppress** (8).

A menu is displayed of all the features that you can suppress for the current page.

```
Format: Suppress (this page only)

    1 - Suppress All Page Numbering, Headers and Footers

    2 - Suppress Headers and Footers

    3 - Print Page Number at Bottom Center    No

    4 - Suppress Page Numbering               No

    5 - Suppress Header A                      No

    6 - Suppress Header B                      No

    7 - Suppress Footer A                      No

    8 - Suppress Footer B                      No



Selection: 0
```

3   Select Suppress **P**age Numbering (4), type **y** for Yes, then press **Exit** (F7) to return to the normal editing screen.

Notice that a Suppress code has been added to the top of the page.

A SUPRESS CODE

```
Ms. Heather Wilson
Director of Sales
Swiss America, Inc.
1030 Harrington Blvd.
Newark, NJ 07112

Dear Ms. Wilson,

After recently visiting the Sundheim booth at the WURLD trade
exposition in Amsterdam, I was very impressed with both the
quality and variety of hand-crafted music boxes displayed.  While
C:\WP51\LEARN\MUSICBOX                      Doc 1 Pg 1 Ln 1" Pos 1"
[Pg Numbering:Top Center][Suppress:PgNum]Ms. Heather Wilson[HRt]
Director of Sales[HRt]                     A
Swiss America, Inc.[HRt]
1030 Harrington Blvd.[HRt]
Newark, NJ 07112[HRt]
[HRt]
Dear Ms. Wilson,[HRt]
[HRt]
After recently visiting the Sundheim booth at the WURLD trade[SRt]
exposition in Amsterdam, I was very impressed with both the[SRt]

Press Reveal Codes to restore screen
```

Although the page numbering is set for every page of the letter, the page numbering will not appear on the first page of the letter because of the Suppress code.

4   Press **Reveal Codes** to display the normal editing screen.

☐ *Select **Reveal Codes** from the **Edit** menu.*

As you are beginning to see, whenever you type text *or* select a WordPerfect feature (Bold, Page Numbering, etc.), the text or code is inserted at the cursor. If you want your documents to be formatted correctly, make sure your cursor is in the right place before you begin.

Displaying a Page Number

While the page number is not displayed in the normal editing screen, it can be seen in the View Document screen and is printed when you send the letter to the printer.

1 Press **Print** (Shift-F7).

⌨ *Select **Print** from the **File** menu.*

2 Select View Document (6), then select Full Page (3).

Notice that the page number is not displayed at the top of the first page because of the Suppress code.

3 Press **Page Down** (PgDn) to view the second page.

A number for the second page appears on a separate line at the top of the page. Whenever you select page numbering, WordPerfect automatically subtracts two lines from each page—one for the number and one for spacing between the number and the text of the document.

4 Select 100% (1) for a closer view, then press **Home,↓** to move to the bottom of the page.

You can use Home to shift the page from the top to the bottom (and back again) in the View Document screen.

5 Press **Home,↑** to move to the top of the page, then press **Exit** (F7) to return to the normal editing screen.

Typing the Initials

Before printing and saving the letter, the typist's initials need to be added to the end of the letter.

1 Press **Home,Home,↓** to move to the end of the third page.

Whenever you press Home twice (before pressing an arrow key), the cursor moves to the beginning or end of the line or the document. Pressing Home once simply moves the cursor to the edges of the screen.

2   Press **Enter** twice to move the cursor two lines below "HALVA International" and type **cjg** for the initials.

```
Samuel A. Roberts
6120 Cottage Way, Suite #456
Sacramento, CA 95825
(916) 878-4550

Scott L. Ziegler
450 S. Flower St.
Los Angeles, CA 90014
(213) 937-3370

We look forward to establishing a working relationship with you,
and would be very interested in any other items you feel might
fit well with our current expansion plans.

Sincerely yours,


Bryan Metcalf
President
HALVA International
```
▲ cjg_
  C:\WP51\LEARN\MUSICBOX   Doc 1 Pg 3 Ln 5.83" Pos 1.3"

Selecting a Printer

With the editing changes completed, you may want to use Save one more time before sending the letter to the printer.

1   Press **Save** (F10), press **Enter** to use the MUSICBOX filename, then type **y** to replace the original letter with the edited version on your screen.

⌨ *Select Save from the File menu.*

It is important to save your document before printing, especially if the document is more than one page, and you have not used Save while creating or editing the document.

Now let's use Print to print the edited letter.

2   Press **Print** (Shift-F7) to display the Print menu.

⌨ *Select Print from the File menu.*

Notice that the selected printer (in the lower half of the menu) is the Workbook Printer. This is because the letter was created for the lesson with the Workbook Printer selected. When you retrieved the letter at the beginning of the lesson, WordPerfect automatically switched to the Workbook Printer for you.

However, before printing the letter, you need to select your own printer.

3 Choose **S**elect Printer (s) to display a list of printer selections.

```
Print: Select Printer

  HP LaserJet Series II
* Workbook Printer


1 Select; 2 Additional Printers; 3 Edit; 4 Copy; 5 Delete; 6 Help; 7 Update: 1
```

The list should include at least the Workbook Printer and the printer you selected when installing WordPerfect.

4 Place the cursor on the name of your printer, then press **Enter** to select the printer and return to the Print menu.

The name of the printer displayed in the Print menu should now be the one you selected from the list.

Also notice that the Text Quality is set to High. You may want to change the quality to Draft before sending the letter to the printer. With some printers, the Draft quality will print the letter faster using a lower quality font.

Printing and Saving the Letter

With your printer selected, you are ready to print the letter.

1 Select **F**ull Document (1) to send the letter to the printer.

2 Press **Exit** (F7), type **y**, then press **Enter** to use the displayed filename.

3 Type **y** to replace the file on disk with the one on the screen, then type **n** to clear the screen and stay in WordPerfect.

Now that you have saved the letter with your own printer selected, WordPerfect will automatically use that printer whenever you retrieve the letter again for editing or printing.

Most of the documents that you retrieve from the LEARN directory or Workbook diskette have been created using the Workbook Printer so that the steps in the exercises work correctly. However, you need to make sure your own printer is selected before printing a document.

Lesson 9: Editing Screens

A useful and convenient editing feature in WordPerfect is the ability to edit two documents at the same time, with each document in a separate editing screen. The first editing screen holds document 1 (Doc 1), while the second editing screen holds document 2 (Doc 2).

Opening the Second Editing Screen

Until now, you have only been using the document 1 editing screen to do word processing. In this lesson, you'll also use the document 2 editing screen. Right now, you are probably in the document 1 screen.

⚠ DOCUMENT 1

▷ Doc 1 Pg 1 Ln 1" Pos 1"

Opening the second editing screen is as easy as pressing Switch.

1 Press **Switch** (Shift-F3) to open the second editing screen.

⌨ *Select* Switch Document *from the* **E***dit menu.*

You can always check the status line to find out which editing screen is currently active (i.e., Doc 1 or Doc 2).

▲ DOCUMENT 2

▷Doc 2 Pg 1 Ln 1" Pos 1"

Switching Between Screens

When you want to return to the first editing screen, simply press Switch again.

1 Press **Switch** (Shift-F3) to return to the first editing screen.

▭ *Select Switch Document from the Edit menu.*

As you continue using the two editing screens throughout the lesson, you'll discover that all WordPerfect features are available in either screen. It's like running two copies of WordPerfect at the same time.

Filling in the Memo

Now that you have been introduced to both WordPerfect editing screens, let's retrieve a memo form in the first screen (similar to the one created in lesson 3) and fill it out.

1 Press **Retrieve** (Shift-F10), and enter **memo** for the filename.

▭ *Select Retrieve from the File menu.*

*Remember that the word "enter" means to type the bolded text and then press **Enter**.*

Because you have already filled out the memo form once (lesson 5), only the information for filling out the memo is listed below. Remember to press **Home**,→ or **End** before typing the information in the To, From, and Subject lines.

2 Fill in the memo heading with the following information:

Megan Sills (to)
Bryan Metcalf (from)
New account with Swiss America, Inc. (subject)

3 Type the following paragraph in the message area below the double line:

Following our discussion at lunch the other day, I immediately wrote a letter to Swiss America, Inc. informing them of our decision to include their music boxes in our expanded line of merchandise.

4 Press **Enter** twice at the end of the paragraph to add extra spacing.

When you finish, the memo should look similar to the one illustrated below.

```
                      Corporate Memo


      To:          Megan Sills

      From:        Bryan Metcalf

      Date:        September 20,1989

      Subject:     New Account with Swiss America, Inc.


                   ========================================

      Following our discussion at lunch the other day, I immediately
      wrote a letter to Swiss America, Inc. informing them of our
      decision to include their music boxes in our expanded line of
      merchandise.


      _


      C:\WP51\LEARN\MEMO.WKB              Doc 1 Pg 1 Ln 4" Pos 1"
```

Moving a Paragraph from the Letter

Along with the text you have already typed, some information needs to be included from the letter to Swiss America, Inc.

```
                           Corporate Memo

        To:         Megan Sills

        From:       Bryan Metcalf

        Date:       September 20,1989

        Subject:    New Account with Swiss America, Inc.

                    ==========================================

        Following our discussion at lunch the other day, I immediately
        wrote a letter to Swiss America, Inc. informing them of our
        decision to include their music boxes in our expanded line of
        merchandise.
        We would like to order a selection of music boxes from the
        following list for the conference:

        Fairies
        Pan's Pipes
        Gondolier                          — INCLUDE THIS
        Silver Harmonies                     IN MEMO
        Return to the Danube
        Patterns
        Autumn Memories
        Paris at Night
        Follow the Leader
        Secrets
        Symphony Strings
```

While you could re-type the text from a printed copy of the letter, you can save time by using the second editing screen and the Move feature to quickly copy the text from the letter into the memo.

1 Press **Switch** (Shift-F3) to display the second editing screen (check for "Doc 2" on the status line).

⌨ *Select Switch Document from the Edit menu.*

2 Press **Retrieve** (Shift-F10) and enter **musicbox.wkb** to retrieve the rough draft of the Swiss America letter.

⌨ *Select Retrieve from the File menu.*

Now you can use Move to copy and move a paragraph into the memo.

3 Press **Home** and **Down Arrow** (↓) to move to the bottom of the screen.

4 Press **Home** and **Down Arrow** (↓) again to scroll the first list of music boxes onto the screen.

5 Press **Up Arrow** (↑) until the cursor is in the "We would like to order . . ." paragraph above the list.

6 Press **Move** (Ctrl-F4).

⌨ *Choose Select from the Edit menu.*

7 Select **Paragraph** (2), then select Copy (2).

A message displayed on the status line tells you to move the cursor to the place where you want the copied text inserted, and then to press Enter to retrieve the text. This message not only applies to the document currently on your screen, but also the document in screen 1.

8 Press **Switch** (Shift-F3) to return to the memo in the first editing screen. Make sure the cursor is two lines below the text.

⌨ *Select Switch Document from the Edit menu.*

9 Press **Enter** to insert the paragraph into the memo.

While you've just completed quite a few keystrokes without much explanation, it is important to see just how quickly and smoothly you can move text between two documents in WordPerfect.

10 Press **Home** and **Down Arrow** (↓) to place the cursor at the end of the memo.

Besides moving the text of the paragraph, notice that WordPerfect also moved the two hard returns after the paragraph. Although the paragraph is only one sentence long, by selecting "Paragraph" instead of "Sentence," WordPerfect will move any extra hard returns along with the text.

Moving a List from the Letter

Now, you need to return to the letter and move the list of music boxes.

1 Press **Switch** (Shift-F3) to return to the Swiss America letter, then place the cursor on the first letter of "Fairies" at the beginning of the list.

⌨ *Select Switch Document from the Edit menu.*

The first three options on the Move menu give you the choice of moving a sentence, paragraph, or page. Once you select an option, the text to be moved is automatically blocked, or highlighted, for you.

But what about part of a sentence, paragraph, or page? Or what about text (like the list) that doesn't fit in any of the three categories?

In order to let you select exactly what you want to move, WordPerfect provides a Block feature that lets you do the highlighting yourself.

2 Press **Help** (F3) then press **Block** (Alt-F4) to display information about the Block feature.

The help information indicates that you simply place the cursor at one end of the text, turn on Block, then move the cursor to the opposite end of the text.

For example, try using Block to highlight the list. The cursor should already be at the beginning of the list.

3 Press **Enter** to exit Help.

4 Press **Block**, then move the cursor down to the beginning of the paragraph below the list.

⌨ *Block the list by holding down the left button on the mouse and dragging the pointer to the end of the list.*

Your screen should look similar to the one below, with the cursor under the "I" in the word "In," and the list completely highlighted.

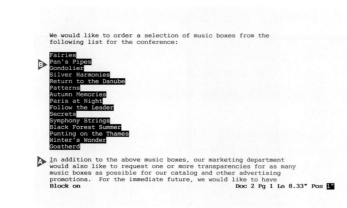

A "Block on" message at the bottom of the screen lets you know that Block is on.

5 Press **Move** (Ctrl-F4), then check the menu at the bottom of the screen.

⌨ *Select **C**opy from the **E**dit menu, then skip directly to step 8.*

Notice that three new options have replaced the original Sentence, Paragraph, Page, and Retrieve options.

6 Press **Help** for information about the new options.

After reading the Help screen, it is apparent that the list is not a tabular column or rectangle, so you simply need to select Block to copy the list.

7 Press **Enter** to exit Help, select **B**lock (1), then select **C**opy (2).

After selecting Copy, WordPerfect automatically turns off Block for you. With the list saved, you are ready to move back into the memo.

8 Press **Switch** to display the memo in the first editing screen.

⌨ *Select Switch Document from the **E**dit menu.*

9 Press **Enter** to insert the list into the memo.

Your screen should now look similar to the one below, with the cursor at the beginning of the list.

▲ CURSOR POSITION

```
                              Corporate Memo

         To:         Megan Sills

         From:       Bryan Metcalf

         Date:       September 20,1989

         Subject:    New Account with Swiss America, Inc.

                     ================================================

         Following our discussion at lunch the other day, I immediately
         wrote a letter to Swiss America, Inc. informing them of our
         decision to include their music boxes in our expanded line of
         merchandise.

         We would like to order a selection of music boxes from the
         following list for the conference:

       ▷ Fairies
         Pan's Pipes
         Gondolier
         C:\WP51\LEARN\MEMO.WKB                        Doc 1 Pg 1 Ln 4.5" Pos 1"
```

Block is a powerful editing tool that can be used with many other WordPerfect features (as indicated in the Help screen for Block).

Deleting Several Words

Before finishing the memo, the text at the beginning of the paragraph that you moved needs to be changed.

```
         same time, we would also like to include a complete line of
         Sundheim music boxes.
         I HAVE ALREADY ORDERED
         We would like to order a selection of music boxes from the
         following list for the conference:

         Fairies
         Pan's Pipes
         Gondolier
         Silver Harmonies
         Return to the Danube
         Patterns
         Autumn Memories
         Paris at Night
         Follow the Leader
         Secrets
         Symphony Strings
         Black Forest Summer
         Punting on the Thames
         Winter's Wonder
         Goatherd

         In addition to the above music boxes, our marketing department
         would also like to request one or more transparencies for as many
         music boxes as possible for our catalog and other advertising
         promotions.  For the immediate future, we would like to have
         transparencies sent for the following:

         Beautiful Dreamer
         Always
         Christmas Fantasy
         Little Flower Girl
         Just a Song
```

1 Place the cursor at the beginning of the "We would like . . ." paragraph.

2 Press **Esc**, type **5** for the repeat value, then press **Delete Word** (Ctrl-Backspace) to delete the first five words of the sentence.

When you were first introduced to the repeat value (lesson 3), you used it to automatically type a line of equal signs in the memo form. Notice that the repeat value can also be used with keys such as Delete Word to repeat the feature an exact number of times.

For a complete list of all the features that can be used with the repeat value, check your *WordPerfect Reference Manual* or use the Help feature (F3,Esc).

3 Type **I have already ordered** and press the **Space Bar**.

Finishing the Memo

Now that the first few words of the paragraph have been edited, the memo can be finished.

1 Press **Home** twice, then **Down Arrow** (↓) to move to the end of the memo.

2 Type:

An account will be set up with Swiss America within the week. Order any other samples you feel we may need for the marketing conference and charge them to the account.

With the final paragraph typed, you are ready to print and save the memo. You may want to display the memo in View Document before printing (or instead of printing).

3 Press **Print** (Shift-F7).

▭ *Select Print from the File menu.*

4 Select **F**ull Document (1) to print the memo.

Exiting the Second Editing Screen

Before saving the memo and clearing the screen, return to the letter and exit the second editing screen.

1 Press **Switch** (Shift-F3) to display the letter.

▭ *Select Switch Document from the Edit menu.*

2 Press **Exit** (F7) and type **n** to indicate that you do not want to save the letter.

When using one editing screen, WordPerfect simply asks if you want to exit the program ("Exit WP?"). Now, because there are two active editing screens, WordPerfect asks if you want to exit document 2.

```
We would like to order a selection of music boxes from the
following list for the conference:

Fairies
Pan's Pipes
Gondolier
Silver Harmonies
Return to the Danube
Patterns
Autumn Memories
Paris at Night
Follow the Leader
Secrets
Symphony Strings
Black Forest Summer
Punting on the Thames
Winter's Wonder
Goatherd

In addition to the above music boxes, our marketing department
would also like to request one or more transparencies for as many
music boxes as possible for our catalog and other advertising
promotions.  For the immediate future, we would like to have
▶ Exit doc 2? No (Yes)                          (Cancel to return to document)
```

3 Type **y** to exit the second editing screen and return to the memo.

You could have also chosen to type "n" to clear the second editing screen without exiting.

Saving the Memo

With the first editing screen displayed, you are ready to save the memo.

1 Press **Exit** (F7), type **y** to save the memo, and enter **musbmemo** to create a file for the memo.

2 Type **n** to clear the screen and stay in WordPerfect.

For details on other methods of moving a block of text, turn to the *Special Techniques* lesson at the end of *Fundamentals I*.

Lesson 10: Letter 2 — Final Draft

The second draft of the Swiss America letter has been returned with a note to alphabetize the two lists of music boxes and change the style of page numbering. The current date also needs to be added to the letter.

Inserting the Date

Let's begin by retrieving the letter and adding the date.

1 Press **List** (F5), then press **Enter** to display the list of files on your disk.

⊞ *Select List Files from the File menu.*

2 Move the cursor to the MUSICBOX filename, then select **R**etrieve (1) to retrieve the file.

3 Press **Date/Outline** (Shift-F5) and select Date **T**ext (1) to insert the current date.

⊞ *Select Date Text from the Tools menu.*

4 Press **Enter** twice to add extra spacing.

Changing the Page Numbering Style

The style of page numbering needs to be changed so that the name of the Director of Sales and the current date are printed with the page number.

```
                    ②
Beautiful Dreamer       ⌐ Change page
Always                  │ numbering style.
Christmas Fantasy       Include name and date.
Little Flower Girl
Just a Song
Easter Parade
Somewhere, Somehow
Joplin
San Francisco Nights
Happiness
Grecian Holiday
Lazy River
Blues
Copenhagen Tales

It would be greatly appreciated if you could ship an assortment of
approximately 5 music boxes to each of our regional marketing
representatives by the last week in November.  Our corporate
accountant will be in touch with you to set up an account within
the week.  If there is any charge for music boxes, transparencies,
etc., please bill them to the account.

The following is a current list of regional marketing
representatives:

Robin Pierce
544 Westminster Circle NW
Atlanta, Georgia 30327
(404) 359-2828
```

Let's check the Page Numbering menu to see what options are available.

1 Press **Format** (Shift-F8), then select **P**age (2).

⌨ *Select **P**age from the **L**ayout menu.*

2 Select Page **N**umbering (6).

3 Press **Help** for information about the options on the menu.

New Page Number lets you start page numbering over from that point, beginning with any number. A Page Number Style (format) can be set to have Insert Page Number and Page Number Position include text with the page number. However, only one line of text can be entered. What you need for this letter is several lines of the same text printed at the top of each page with a page number included.

Whenever the same text needs to be printed at the top of each page, you can create a header.

4 Press **Enter** to exit the Help screen, then press **Exit** (F7) to return to the editing screen.

Deleting a Code

Before creating the header, however, you should first delete the old Page Numbering code.

1 Press **Page Up** (PgUp) to move the cursor to the very beginning of the first page.

Because page formats need to be at the very beginning of the page (before any text) for the feature to work correctly, using Page Up and Page Down to move from page to page will always ensure that the cursor is at the top of the page.

2 Press **Reveal Codes** (Alt-F3) to display the codes at the beginning of the page.

⌨ *Select **R**eveal Codes from the **E**dit menu.*

▲ PAGE NUMBERING CODE

```
September 21, 1989

Ms. Heather Wilson
Director of Sales
Swiss America, Inc.
1030 Harrington Blvd.
Newark, NJ 07112

Dear Ms. Wilson,

After recently visiting the Sundheim booth at the WURLD trade
C:\WP51\LEARN\MUSICBOX                          Doc 1 Pg 1 Ln 1" Pos 1"
─────────────────────────────────────────────────────────────────────
▲►[Pg Numbering:Top Center][Suppress:PgNum]September 21, 1989[HRt]
[HRt]
Ms. Heather Wilson[HRt]
Director of Sales[HRt]
Swiss America, Inc.[HRt]
1030 Harrington Blvd.[HRt]
Newark, NJ 07112[HRt]
[HRt]
Dear Ms. Wilson,[HRt]
[HRt]

Press Reveal Codes to restore screen
```

Instead of deleting the Page Numbering code in the Reveal Codes screen, try erasing the code from the normal editing screen.

3   Place the cursor on the Page Numbering code (if it is not already there).

4   Press **Reveal Codes** to display the normal editing screen.

⌨ *Select **R**eveal Codes from the **E**dit menu.*

5   Press **Delete** (Del) to erase the Page Numbering code.

You should now see a message at the bottom of your screen asking if you actually want to delete the code from the letter.

⚠ DELETE MESSAGE

```
September 21, 1989

Ms. Heather Wilson
Director of Sales
Swiss America, Inc.
1030 Harrington Blvd.
Newark, NJ 07112

Dear Ms. Wilson,

After recently visiting the Sundheim booth at the WURLD trade
exposition in Amsterdam, I was very impressed with both the
quality and variety of hand-crafted music boxes displayed.  While
speaking with the Sundheim marketing director, I was informed
that distribution of the music boxes in the United States is
handled directly through your company.

As you know, HALVA International has retailed an exclusive line
of jewelry from Europe for over 50 years.  Until recently, we
have handled the majority of our business through a mail order
service.

We are now planning to expand our business by opening several
retail outlets in major cities through the United States.  At the
Delete [Pg Numbering:Top Center]? No (Yes)
```

Because you cannot see codes in the normal editing screen, WordPerfect makes sure that you know you are about to delete a formatting code whenever Backspace or Delete is being used to erase text.

6   Type **y** to have WordPerfect erase the Page Numbering code.

7   Press **Reveal Codes** (Alt-F3) to display the codes at the beginning of the page.

⌨ *Select **R**eveal Codes from the **E**dit menu.*

The Page Numbering code should no longer appear at the beginning of the page.

```
September 21, 1989

Ms. Heather Wilson
Director of Sales
Swiss America, Inc.
1030 Harrington Blvd.
Newark, NJ 07112

Dear Ms. Wilson,

After recently visiting the Sundheim booth at the WURLD trade
C:\WP51\LEARN\MUSICBOX                           Doc 1 Pg 1 Ln 1" Pos 1"
[                                      ▲    ▲    ▲   ▲   )   ▲     ▲
[Suppress:PgNum]September 21, 1989[HRt]
[HRt]
Ms. Heather Wilson[HRt]
Director of Sales[HRt]
Swiss America, Inc.[HRt]
1030 Harrington Blvd.[HRt]
Newark, NJ 07112[HRt]
[HRt]
Dear Ms. Wilson,[HRt]
[HRt]

Press Reveal Codes to restore screen
```

8 Press **Reveal Codes** to return to the normal editing screen.

⌨ Select **Reveal Codes** from the **Edit** menu.

Creating a Header

With the Page Numbering code deleted and the cursor at the very beginning of the first page, you are ready to create the header.

1 Press **Format** (Shift-F8) and select **Page** (2).

⌨ Select **Page** from the **Layout** menu.

2 Select **Headers** (3).

A menu on the status line indicates that two headers can be placed on one page.

```
Format: Page

     1 - Center Page (top to bottom)      No

     2 - Force Odd/Even Page

     3 - Headers

     4 - Footers

     5 - Margins - Top                    1"
                   Bottom                 1"

     6 - Page Numbering

     7 - Paper Size                       8.5" x 11"
                 Type                     Standard

     8 - Suppress (this page only)




▲ 1 Header A; 2 Header B: 0
```

3 Select Header **A** (1), then select Every **P**age (2) from the next menu that appears on the status line.

After selecting the type of header, WordPerfect places you in an editing screen very similar to the one you use for typing and editing documents.

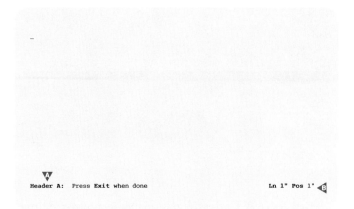

Header A: Press Exit when done   Ln 1" Pos 1"

In fact, the screens are so similar that some people have actually typed an entire document in the header/footer editing screen. If you do become confused, simply check the status line and notice the "Header A" message along with "Press Exit when done" message. Also notice that there are no document (Doc) or page (Pg) indicators on the status line, as you cannot have a header that is larger than a page.

While there is a limitation (one page) on the size of the header, there are very few limits on the features that can be used while creating a header. In other lessons we'll show you some creative ways that headers can be used.

4 Type **Ms. Wilson** and press **Enter** to return to the left margin.

5 Press **Date/Outline** (Shift-F5), select Date Code (2), then press **Enter** to return to the left margin.

▢ *Select Date Code from the Tools menu.*

6 Type **Page** and press the **Space Bar**.

For the actual page number, you need to put in a code that automatically updates the page number each time a new page is printed. However, instead of using the Page Number Position feature to place the page numbering on the page, you can use the special ^B code to print page numbers.

7 Press **Format** (Shift-F8) and select **P**age (2).

▭ *Select* ***P****age from the* ***L****ayout menu.*

8 Select Page **N**umbering (6), then select **I**nsert Page Number (3). This inserts a ^B into the text.

The current page number is substituted for the ^B when the document is displayed in View Document or printed. The header you've created should now look like the one on the header A editing screen below.

```
Ms. Wilson
September 21, 1989
Page ^B_
```

```
Header A:  Press Exit when done                    Ln 1.33" Pos 1.7"
```

You do not need to add extra spacing after the header because WordPerfect adds a blank line between a header and the text (as with Page Number Position). The lines for the header and spacing are automatically subtracted from the overall length of the page.

9 Press **Exit** (F7) to save the header, then press **Exit** again to return to the letter.

Suppressing a Header

Now that you have changed from page numbering to a header, you also need to delete the Suppress code for page numbering and replace it with a code that suppresses the header on the first page of the letter.

1 Press **Delete** (Del), then type **y** to delete the Suppress code.

2 Press **Format** (Shift-F8) and select **P**age (2).

▭ *Select* ***P****age from the* ***L****ayout menu.*

3 Select **S**uppress (8).

4 Select Suppress **H**eader A (5), type **y** for Yes, then press **Exit** (F7) to return to the editing screen.

Previewing the Header

A header (like a page number) can be seen by displaying the letter in the View Document screen.

1 Press **Print** (Shift-F7) and select **V**iew Document (6) to display the header.

⊟ *Select **P**rint from the **F**ile menu.*

2 Press **Page Up** (PgUp) or **Page Down** (PgDn) to scroll a page at a time through the letter.

Notice that the header has been suppressed on the first page of the letter.

3 Select 200% (2) to zoom in on the letter, then press **Page Up** or **Page Down** to see the text of the header at the top of page 2.

⚠ HEADER

```
        Ms. Wilson
        September 22, 1989
        Page 2

        Beautiful Dreamer
        Always
        Christmas Fantasy
    ▷   Little Flower Girl
        Just a Song
        Easter Parade
        Somewhere, Somehow
        Joplin
        San Francisco Nights
        Happiness
```

`1 100%   2 200%   3 Full Page   4 Facing Pages: 2              Doc 1 Pg 2`

While in the View Document screen, you can press **Switch** (Shift-F3) to display the text reversed out of a dark background. Pressing Switch again returns the page to a normal display. The illustrated View Document screens in the manual were created with dark text and a light background. Using the Switch feature in the View Document screen does not affect the appearance of the printed document.

4 Press **Exit** (F7) to return to the normal editing screen.

Sorting the Lists

The final editing change to the letter involves alphabetizing (sorting) the two lists of music boxes. You could retype the lists or use Move to reshuffle the music box titles.

However, there is a feature in WordPerfect that can do all the sorting for you. All you need to do is highlight the list with Block, and press two keys.

1 Place the cursor on the letter "B" in "Beautiful Dreamer" at the top of page 2 (if it is not already there).

2 Press **Block** (Alt-F4) and move the cursor to the end of the last music box title in the list (Copenhagen Tales).

With all the titles in the list completely highlighted, you are ready to begin sorting.

3 Press **Merge/Sort** (Ctrl-F9) to display the Sort menu.

⊟ *Select Sort from the Tools menu.*

The title at the top of the menu should be "Sort by Line." If another title is displayed, simply select **T**ype (7) and select **L**ine (2) before continuing.

4 Select **P**erform Action (1) from the menu that appears at the bottom of your screen.

After a moment, the menu disappears, and the letter is redisplayed with the sorted list.

▲ SORTED LIST

```
Winter's Wonder
Goatherd

In addition to the above music boxes, our marketing department
would also like to request transparencies for as many music boxes
as possible for our catalog and other advertising promotions.
For the future, we would like to have transparencies sent for the
following:


===============================================================================
Always
Beautiful Dreamer
Blues
Christmas Fantasy
Copenhagen Tales
Easter Parade        ◀
Grecian Holiday
Happiness
Joplin
Just a Song
Lazy River
Little Flower Girl
San Francisco Nights
C:\WP51\LEARN\MUSICBOX              Doc 1 Pg 2 Ln 1" Pos 1"
```

You probably noticed that the Sort menu took up half of the screen and offers several options. Although the WordPerfect sorter is a powerful feature, it is quite easy to use if all you want to do is alphabetize a list.

Now that you see how easy it is to sort a list of names, try sorting the list on the first page. However, instead of using Home and the arrow keys to move the cursor to the beginning of the list, you can use Search.

Searching for a Word

Search helps you move the cursor to an exact location in a document by letting you give WordPerfect a word to find. You already know that the first title in the list on page 1 is "Fairies," so,

1 Press ◆**Search** (Shift-F2) to search back through the letter.

⌨ *Select **B**ackward from the Search menu.*

2 Type **fairies** and press ◆**Search** (F2) to start the search.

⌨ *Select **F**orward from the Search menu.*

You can start a forward search or a backward search by pressing ◆Search.

The cursor should stop at the end of "Fairies" when the word is found.

▲ CURSOR POSITION
  AT END OF SEARCH

```
have handled the majority of our business through a mail order
service.

We are now planning to expand our business by opening several
retail outlets in major cities through the United States.  At the
same time, we would also like to include a line of Sundheim music
boxes.

We would like to order a selection of music boxes from the
following list for the conference:

Fairies▲
Pan's Pipes
Gondolier
Silver Harmonies
Return to the Danube
Patterns
Autumn Memories
Paris at Night
Follow the Leader
Secrets
Black Forest Summer
Punting on the Thames
Winter's Wonder
C:\WP51\LEARN\MUSICBOX                        Doc 1 Pg 1 Ln 6" Pos 1.7"
```

If a " Not found *" message appears, you may have typed the title incorrectly. Try repeating steps 1 and 2.*

3 Press **Home** and **Left Arrow** (←) to move to the beginning of the title.

With the cursor at the beginning of the first title in the list, you are ready to sort again.

4 Press **Block** (Alt-F4) then move the cursor to the end of the last title in the list (Goatherd).

5 Press **Merge/Sort** (Ctrl-F9).

⌨ *Select Sort from the **T**ools menu.*

6 Select **P**erform Action (1) from the Sort menu.

Finishing the Editing

Now that both lists have been sorted, you can save the letter on disk, spell-check and preview the letter, then send it to the printer. Because you have already done all three before, the steps are provided with little explanation.

Just remember that during the spell-check, WordPerfect frequently stops at proper names it does not recognize. Simply select Skip (2) to continue spell-checking.

1 Press **Save** (F10), press **Enter** to use the MUSICBOX filename, then type **y** to replace the file.

⊟ *Select Save from the File menu.*

2 Press **Spell** (Ctrl-F2) and select **D**ocument (3) to check the spelling of the letter. Press any key when the spell-checking is completed to return to the letter.

⊟ *Select Spell from the Tools menu.*

If you made changes to the document during the Spell operation, you may want to save it again by repeating step 1.

3 Press **Print** (Shift-F7), then select **F**ull Document (1) to print the letter.

⊟ *Select Print from the File menu.*

4 Press **Exit** (F7) and type **n** twice to clear the screen.

You have been introduced to headers and sorting in this lesson—both of which are powerful features of WordPerfect.

As you are introduced to other WordPerfect features, keep in mind that most features do not demand a lot of time to learn if you are using them for basic word processing. However, the flexibility is always there if you want to use the features for more advanced applications.

Lesson 11: File Management

Most of the documents you create in WordPerfect will be saved in files on disk. After several weeks, these files will begin to accumulate. Some will be worth saving; others can be erased from the disk. You may also decide that some files need to be renamed, while others can be copied to a diskette for long-term storage.

WordPerfect includes a List Files feature which lets you take care of managing your files quickly and efficiently.

Important: This lesson is designed for individuals who are running WordPerfect from a hard disk. If you are running WordPerfect from two disk drives, then turn to the Two Disk Drives *information in* Appendix *before continuing.*

Backing up Files

Let's assume that it is the end of the day, and you are about to leave the office. Is there anything you should do with your files before exiting WordPerfect and turning off your computer?

It is important to remember that your files are simply electronic information on a disk. If the disk is damaged, there is a good chance that you will not be able to recover the information. However, because the information is electronic, it can also be quickly copied to another diskette for safekeeping.

A diskette to which you copy files for safekeeping is called a *backup diskette.* Let's begin by copying the final draft of the reservation letter to a backup diskette.

For this exercise, you will need an extra formatted diskette. If you do not have a formatted diskette and do not know how to format one, turn to the *Formatting a Disk* information in *Appendix.*

1   Press **List** (F5) then press **Enter** to display a list of filenames.

▢ *Select List Files from the File menu.*

**Searching for
a Filename**

If you have completed all the lessons to this point, you should have at least the following files in the list on your screen.

```
09/22/89  10:46a              Directory C:\WP51\LFARN\*.*
Document size:       0   Free: 15,153,152 Used:      159,519     Files:        37

.    Current    <Dir>                    ..   Parent   <Dir>
ADDRESS .TUT       978  08/25/89 01:11p   ADDRESS .WKB       415  09/21/89 11:07a
ADVANCED.TUT         3  08/25/89 01:11p   BANNER  .TUT       631  08/25/89 01:11p
BEGIN   .TUT        11  08/25/89 01:11p   CUSTOMER.WKB     1,986  09/21/89 11:08a
EQUATION.WKB     6,365  09/21/89 11:03a   INTRO   .TUT    29,936  08/25/89 01:11p
INTRO_1 .TUT     9,408  08/25/89 01:11p   LESS    .TUT        11  08/25/89 01:11p
LESS1   .TUT     4,989  08/25/89 01:11p   LESS2   .TUT     8,980  08/25/89 01:11p
LESS3   .TUT     7,631  08/25/89 01:11p   LESS4   .TUT    10,851  08/25/89 01:11p
LESS5   .TUT    13,413  08/25/89 01:11p   LESS6   .TUT     7,229  08/25/89 01:11p
LETTER  .TUT       653  08/25/89 01:11p   LETTER_F.TUT       679  08/25/89 01:11p
LETTER_P.TUT       652  08/25/89 01:11p   LETTERI .TUT       778  08/25/89 01:11p
MEMO    .          768  09/20/89 04:17p   MEMO    .WKB       785  09/21/89 11:09a
MUSBMEMO.        1,509  09/20/89 04:39p   MUSICBOX.         3,320  09/20/89 11:07a
MUSICBOX.WKB     3,338  09/21/89 11:10a   NEWSLTR .WKB    14,977  09/21/89 11:05a
NEWSTABL.WKB     2,537  09/21/89 11:15a   NEWSTEXT.WKB     2,844  09/21/89 11:11a
OUTLINE .WKB     1,210  09/21/89 11:11a   PARK    .         1,002  09/19/89 02:32p
PARKMEMO.        1,253  09/14/89 05:28p   PARKSPEL.WKB       967  09/21/89 11:12a
REPORT  .WKB     9,240  09/21/89 11:12a   RETAIL  .WKB     1,435  09/21/89 11:13a
STORES  .WKB     1,476  09/21/89 11:13a ▼ TABLE   .WKB     3,808  09/21/89 11:13a

1 Retrieve; 2 Delete; 3 Move/Rename; 4 Print; 5 Short/Long Display;
6 Look; 7 Other Directory; 8 Copy; 9 Find; N Name Search: 6
```

*Other files may be listed with the ones above if you have created other files on your own. If the Learning files are not listed at all, then you are probably in the wrong directory. Select *O*ther Directory (7) and enter the name of the directory where the files are kept.*

1 Select **N**ame Search (n), type **park**, then press **Enter** to end the search.

2 Place a formatted diskette in drive A.

**Copying a Single
File**

1 Select **C**opy (8) from the menu at the bottom of the screen.

2 When you see the "Copy this file to:" message, type **a:** and press **Enter**.

The file is copied to the formatted diskette, which has now become your backup diskette for keeping an extra copy of important files. Let's check and make sure that a copy of the file is actually on the diskette in drive A.

**Checking the
Backup Diskette**

1 Move the cursor to the CURRENT directory (<Dir>) at the top of the list.

2 Press **Enter**, type **a:** and press **Enter** to display all the files on the diskette in drive A.

Unless you have other files on the diskette in drive A, your list files screen should look like the one illustrated below.

```
09/22/89  10:49a              Directory A:\*.*
Document size:        0  Free:   361,472 Used:      1,002    Files:       1
.    Current   <Dir>                  |  ..   Parent    <Dir>
PARK     .        1,002  09/19/89 02:32p




1 Retrieve; 2 Delete; 3 Move/Rename; 4 Print; 5 Short/Long Display;
6 Look; 7 Other Directory; 8 Copy; 9 Find; N Name Search: 6
```

You can return to the directory where your files are stored by using the CURRENT directory option again.

3 Make sure that the cursor is on the CURRENT directory.

4 Press **Enter**, type **c:\wp51\learn**, and press **Enter** to return to the directory where the original files are stored.

If you are keeping your WordPerfect Learning files in a directory other than "C:\WP51\LEARN," you need to type the name of that directory for step 4.

Copying Several Files

While you're copying files to a backup diskette, you may as well copy any other important files. For example, you should make sure that the two memos, the memo form, and the music box letter are also copied to the backup diskette.

However, instead of copying them one at a time, you can use the WordPerfect file marking feature to mark each file, and copy them all at once.

1 Move the cursor to PARKMEMO by using the arrow keys or **Name** Search (n).

*If you use Name Search, remember to press **Enter** to end the search.*

2 Type an asterisk (*) to mark the file. Notice that the cursor moves to the next file.

An asterisk should appear next to the filename, indicating that the file has been marked. Now that you know how to mark one file, go ahead and mark the rest of the files you need to copy.

3 Mark the following files:

MEMO
MUSBMEMO
MUSICBOX

Once you have marked the files, the rest is as easy as copying a single file to the backup diskette.

4 Select Copy (8) and type **y** (for yes) when you see the "Copy marked files?" question at the bottom of the screen.

5 When the "Copy all marked files to:" message is displayed, enter **a:** to copy the files to the diskette in drive A.

The files are copied one at a time while a "* Please Wait *" message is displayed at the bottom of the screen.

When the copying is completed, the files are still marked. Often when you copy files to a backup diskette, you may no longer want them on your hard disk. This is especially true if the files have been stored for several weeks and are no longer useful.

Deleting Several Files

Let's assume that the memos and letters do not need to be kept on the hard disk. However, you will probably still want to keep the MEMO file for creating other memos.

1 Place the cursor on the MEMO file, then type an asterisk (*) to unmark the file.

With the memo form unmarked, Delete can be used to erase the rest of the files from the list. Before using Delete, check your screen to make sure that only the following files are marked.

A MARKED FILES

```
09/22/89  10:55a           Directory C:\WP51\LEARN\*.*
Document size:       0  Free: 15,153,152 Used:      6,082    Marked:       3

       .  Current   <Dir>                    ..  Parent   <Dir>
    ADDRESS .TUT        978  08/25/89 01:11p  ADDRESS .WKB        415  09/21/89 11:07a
    ADVANCED.TUT          3  08/25/89 01:11p  BANNER  .TUT        631  08/25/89 01:11p
    BEGIN   .TUT         11  08/25/89 01:11p  CUSTOMER.WKB      1,986  09/21/89 11:08a
    EQUATION.WKB      6,365  09/21/89 11:03a  INTRO   .TUT     29,936  08/25/89 01:11p
    INTRO_1 .TUT      9,408  08/25/89 01:11p  LESS    .TUT         11  08/25/89 01:11p
    LESS1   .TUT      4,989  08/25/89 01:11p  LESS2   .TUT      8,980  08/25/89 01:11p
    LESS3   .TUT      7,631  08/25/89 01:11p  LESS4   .TUT     10,851  08/25/89 01:11p
    LESS5   .TUT     13,413  08/25/89 01:11p  LESS6   .TUT      7,229  08/25/89 01:11p
    LETTER  .TUT        653  08/25/89 01:11p  LETTER_F.TUT        679  08/25/89 01:11p
    LETTER_P.TUT        652  08/25/89 01:11p  LETTER1 .TUT        778  08/25/89 01:11p
    MEMO    .            768  09/20/89 04:17p MEMO    .WKB        785  09/21/89 11:09a
  A*MUSBMEMO.        1,509  09/20/89 04:39p *MUSICBOX.        3,320  09/20/89 11:07a
    MUSICBOX.WKB      3,338  09/21/89 11:10a  NEWSLTR .WKB     14,977  09/21/89 11:05a
    NEWSTABL.WKB      2,537  09/21/89 11:15a  NEWSTEXT.WKB      2,844  09/21/89 11:11a
    OUTLINE .WKB      1,210  09/21/89 11:11a  PARK    .        1,002  09/19/89 02:32p
  A*PARKMEMO.        1,253  09/14/89 05:28p  PARKSPEL.WKB        967  09/21/89 11:12a
    REPORT  .WKB      9,240  09/21/89 11:12a  RETAIL  .WKB      1,435  09/21/89 11:13a
    STORES  .WKB      1,476  09/21/89 11:13a  TABLE   .WKB      3,808  09/21/89 11:13a

    1 Retrieve; 2 Delete; 3 Move/Rename; 4 Print; 5 Short/Long Display;
    6 Look; 7 Other Directory; 8 Copy; 9 Find; N Name Search: 6
```

It is important to understand that once a file is erased, you cannot get it back without using special recovery programs. (These recovery programs are not WordPerfect products. See your dealer.) Even then, the file may never be put back together exactly the way it was first created. So, always check twice to make sure that you are deleting the file(s) you no longer want on your disk.

2 Select **D**elete (2) and type **y** when you see the "Delete marked files?" message.

A second message appears, letting you know that the marked files will be deleted if you continue. Because the marked files have already been copied to a backup diskette, it is safe to go ahead and delete them from the hard disk. They can always be copied back onto the hard disk when they are needed.

3 Type **y** to delete the marked files.

WordPerfect erases the files from the directory, then redisplays the list with the remaining files in alphabetical order.

While keeping the files in your directory well-organized is easier if you backup and delete every day, some people wait until their hard disk "crashes" (i.e., is damaged with resulting loss of data). They then realize that there are no backup copies of their files and no way of getting them from the hard disk.

If you do nothing else, always take a moment to make a copy of the files you create or edit before exiting WordPerfect or turning off your computer. It's the best protection available for your files, and can be done quickly and easily from the List Files screen.

Deleting a Single File

The first ten lessons in *Fundamentals I* provide an overview of some basic word processing skills. If you want to set up your directory for repeating these lessons, you should also delete the MEMO file.

1 Move the cursor to MEMO, select **D**elete (2), then type **y** to delete the file.

Moving a File

You have already been shown how to copy files to a diskette with Copy, then erase them from your hard disk with Delete. If you want to have WordPerfect perform both jobs at the same time, then you can use the Move/Rename option.

For example, the PARK letter still needs to be removed from the hard disk.

1 Move the cursor to PARK and select **M**ove/Rename (3).

A "New name:" message appears with the filename C:\WP51\LEARN\PARK displayed. By simply deleting the "C:\WP51\LEARN" and typing an "A:," you can have WordPerfect move the file from the hard disk to the A drive.

2 Press **Delete** (Del) to erase "C:\WP51\LEARN," type **a:** for the new drive, then press **Enter**.

A second message appears asking if you want to replace the PARK file already on the diskette. This message is displayed when you copy or move a file to a new location and the same filename already exists on the disk.

3 Type **y** to replace the PARK file.

Notice that not only does WordPerfect copy the file to drive A, but the file is automatically removed from the file list on the screen. Like the Copy option, you can mark several files to move to the same location.

Printing a List of Files

To help you keep a record of your files, you can use Print to send a copy of the file list on your screen to the printer. All files in the directory or on the diskette are included— even those not currently on the screen.

1 Press **Print** (Shift-F7) to send the list of files on your screen to the printer.

The printed list includes the heading information you see on your screen with the current date, time, and directory. Other items include the size of the document currently on your screen, the amount of free space on the disk, the amount used by the directory, and the number of files in the directory.

All this information can be valuable in helping you to keep your diskettes or hard disk organized. You may want to keep a printed list of each directory and backup diskette for quick and easy reference.

Exiting WordPerfect

WordPerfect creates several files of its own each time you start the program. By using Exit to leave the program, WordPerfect has a chance to erase these program files.

If you simply turn off the computer without exiting properly, WordPerfect is not able to erase the files, and the next time you start WordPerfect you will probably see a message asking if there is another copy of WordPerfect running. Type **n** (for no), and WordPerfect will delete the old temporary files and replace them with new ones.

You may also see a message asking if you want to rename or delete your timed backup files. Select Rename if you want to restore the document that was on your screen; otherwise, select Delete. Turn to Timed Document Backup *in* lesson 12 *for details.*

Assuming that you have finished your file management for the day, it's time to exit WordPerfect and turn off the computer before leaving the office.

1 Press **Exit** (F7) to return to the normal editing screen.

2 Press **Exit** again, type **n** to indicate that you do not want to save anything from your screen, then type **y** to exit WordPerfect.

Once you leave WordPerfect, you are returned to the place where you started the program. If you started from DOS, then you should see the DOS prompt at the top of the screen.

▲ DOS PROMPT

```
▲ C>_
```

If you started WordPerfect from a menu, such as the one in the WordPerfect Library program, then you are returned to that menu.

```
┌─────────────────────────────────────────────────────────────────────┐
│ WordPerfect Library              Friday, September 22, 1989, 1:03pm   │
├─────────────────────────────────────────────────────────────────────┤
│  A - Appointment Calendar          P - PlanPerfect                    │
│                                                                       │
│  C - Calculator                    W - WordPerfect                    │
│                                                                       │
│  E - Edit Macros                                                      │
│                                                                       │
│  F - File Manager                                                     │
│                                                                       │
│  G - Go to DOS for One Command                                        │
│                                                                       │
│  N - NoteBook                                                         │
│                                                                       │
│  T - Program Editor                                                   │
│                                                                       │
│  D - DataPerfect                                                      │
│                                                                       │
│                                                                       │
└─────────────────────────────────────────────────────────────────────┘
C:\LIBRARY
1 Go to DOS; 2 Clipboard; 3 Other Dir; 4 Setup; 5 Mem Map; 6 Log: _   (F7 = Exit)
```

The topic of file management includes a lot of information about the way your computer stores and organizes files. In this lesson you have been introduced to copying and deleting files as an important part of word processing. You have also been introduced to some terms, such as "directory," that may be unfamiliar to you.

If you feel you need more information about maintaining files, turn to the *List Files* heading in the *WordPerfect Reference Manual* for detailed instructions.

An exercise on document summaries in the Document Management *lesson (lesson 27) in* Special Features *gives you additional information on how to find files from the List Files screen.*

Lesson 12: Special Techniques

Now that you have completed *Fundamentals I*, there are some additional features and insights in this lesson that you might find helpful when first learning WordPerfect.

Each feature (e.g., Date Format, Initial Settings) is written as a separate exercise. Simply select a feature you want to learn about, then read through the material and complete the steps. You do not need to finish the entire lesson from beginning to end.

Date Format

When you select Date Code (2) from the Date/Outline menu (Shift-F5), the current date is displayed as month, day, and year (e.g., July 14, 1991). The same menu also lets you change the way the date is displayed (the format), as well as add the time to the date.

1 Press **Date/Outline** (Shift-F5), then select Date **F**ormat (3).

⌨ *Select Date **F**ormat from the **T**ools menu.*

The top half of the screen displays a table of characters you can use to create a format, while examples of formats are provided below the table.

A FORMAT CHARACTERS

B FORMAT EXAMPLES

```
Date Format

A▶ Character    Meaning
      1         Day of the Month
      2         Month (number)
      3         Month (word)
      4         Year (all four digits)
      5         Year (last two digits)
      6         Day of the Week (word)
      7         Hour (24-hour clock)
      8         Hour (12-hour clock)
      9         Minute
      0         am / pm
      %,$       Used before a number, will:
                   Pad numbers less than 10 with a leading zero or space
                   Abbreviate the month or day of the week

B▶ Examples:   3 1, 4        = December 25, 1984
               %6 %3 1, 4    = Tue Dec 25, 1984
               %2/%1/5 (6)   = 01/01/85 (Tuesday)
               $2/$1/5 ($6)  =  1/ 1/85 (Tue)
               8:90          = 10:55am


Date format: 3 1, 4
```

2 Type the following date format:

%6 %3 1, 4 (8:90)

3 Press **Enter**, then press **Exit** (F7) to return to the editing screen.

4 Press **Reveal Codes** (Alt-F3).

⌨ *Select **R**eveal Codes from the **E**dit menu.*

Notice that a Date Format code is *not* placed in the editing screen.

5 Press **Date/Outline** (Shift-F5), then select Date Code (2).

⊟ *Select Date Code from the Tools menu.*

The inserted Date code not only displays the current date and time in the editing screen, but includes the format that you set for the Date feature.

▲ DATE FORMAT

```
▶Fri Sept 22, 1989 (1:50pm)_




                                            Doc 1 Pg 1 Ln 1" Pos 3.6"
[                                                          ]
[Date:%6 %3 1, 4 (8:90)]



Press Reveal Codes to restore screen
```

Because the format is included with the Date code, you can change the format as often as you like in a document, and the date codes that already exist will remain the same.

6 Press **Reveal Codes** to display the normal editing screen.

⊟ *Select Reveal Codes from the Edit menu.*

7 Press **Exit**, then type **n** twice to clear the screen.

Once you set the date format it remains the same until you change it or exit WordPerfect.

You can change the initial setting of the date format by using the Setup key. Turn to Initial Settings *in this lesson for an example.*

Filenames

The DOS operating system limits the number of characters in a filename to a maximum of 8 with an additional extension of 3 characters if you type a period. As soon as you type a period, you can only type three more characters, even if there are fewer than 8 characters in the filename.

Only the following characters can be used to create a filename. *A space should never be used in a filename.*

  A-Z   all letters
  0-9   all numbers

!	exclamation point
@	at sign
#	numbers/pound sign
$	dollar sign
%	percent sign
&	ampersand
(	left parenthesis
)	right parenthesis
-	hyphen
`	grave
'	single quote
_	underscore

If you want to add an extension to a filename, do not use .COM, .EXE, or .BAT as these extensions are used for program files.

Fixed Pitch and Proportional Spacing

Depending on the type of font selected for your document, WordPerfect may be printing characters with *fixed pitch* or *proportional* spacing. Fixed pitch spacing means that each character you type in a line takes up an equal amount of space. Proportional spacing means that each character you type is given space in proportion to its width (e.g., a "w" takes more space than an "i").

Fixed Pitch Fonts

Let's retrieve a document that automatically selects the Workbook printer, delete the text on the screen, then type three lines of characters.

1 Press **Retrieve** (Shift-F10), then enter **address.wkb** to retrieve an inside address and salutation.

⊟ *Select Retrieve from the File menu.*

2 Press **Delete to End of Page** (Ctrl-PgDn), then type **y** to delete the text on the screen.

3 Press **Repeat** (Esc), type **30**, then type **W** to create a line of characters.

4 Press **Enter** to start a new line, press **Repeat**, type **30**, then type **i** to create a second line of characters.

5 Press **Enter** to start a new line, press **Repeat**, type **30**, then type **?** to create a third line of characters.

The three lines of characters appear to be the same length in the editing screen. Let's check them in the View Document screen.

6 Press **Print** (Shift-F7), select **V**iew Document (6), then select 100% (1).

⊟ *Select Print from the File menu.*

Each line is exactly the same length, even though the "i" is narrower than the "?" or "W."

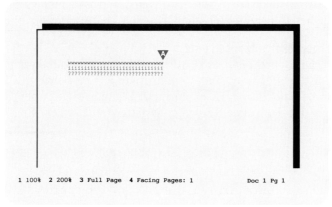

If each line is the same length, then each character is assigned an equal amount of space. The font selected for the text is a fixed pitch font.

7 Press **Exit** (F7) to return to the editing screen.

8 Press **Home,Home,↑** to move the cursor to the beginning of the lines.

9 Press **Font** (Ctrl-F8), then select Base **F**ont (4).

⌨ *Select Base Font from the Font menu.*

WordPerfect displays a list of fonts available for the Workbook printer.

The font currently selected is marked with an asterisk (*) and is the Courier 10cpi font. The "cpi" stands for **c**haracters **p**er **i**nch and lets you know how many characters will print in one inch of space. Fonts with cpi measurements are fixed pitch fonts, and will always print the same number of characters per inch no matter which characters you type.

Proportionally-Spaced Fonts

Because each character can be a different width in a proportionally-spaced font, the Helvetica and Roman fonts are measured by height. The Helvetica 10pt (1 **point** = 1/72 of an inch) is taller (and larger) than the Helvetica 8pt font; the Helvetica 12pt font is taller (and larger) than the Helvetica 10pt font.

Let's select the Helvetica 12pt font, then check the lines of text in the View Document screen.

1 Press **Down Arrow** (↓) until the cursor highlights the Helvetica 12pt font.

2 Press **Enter** to select the font.

3 Press **Print**, then select **V**iew Document.

⌨ *Select **P**rint from the **F**ile menu.*

Because each character in the Helvetica 10pt font is given a customized width, the line of W's is much longer than the line of question marks, and the line of question marks is longer than the line of i's.

△ UNEQUAL LENGTHS

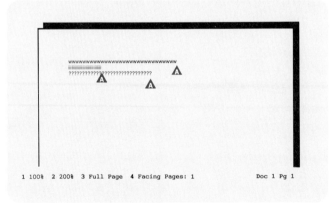

Let's check the line length in the editing screen.

4 Press **Exit** to return to the editing screen.

Each line is displayed as equal in length because the editing screen is *not* in a graphics mode, and assigns the same width to each character on the screen.

You can check the length of each line in the editing screen by using the Position number (Pos) on the status line.

5   Press **Home,**→ to move the cursor to the end of the W's line.

The Position number should be 7", which means that the end of the line of W's is 7" from the left edge of the page.

6   Press **Down Arrow** (↓), then check the Position number for the line of i's.

The Position number is 2.65", which is much shorter than the line length of the W's. Even though WordPerfect can't display proportional spacing in the editing screen, you can still check the actual line length by using the status line.

7   Press **Exit**, then type **n** twice to clear the screen.

Editing and Proportional Spacing

Now that you have been introduced to fixed pitch and proportionally-spaced fonts, let's see what font spacing means when editing a document.

1   Press **Retrieve**, then enter **musicbox.wkb** to retrieve a letter.

⌨ *Select **R**etrieve from the **F**ile menu.*

The full length of each line is displayed on the screen with space displayed to the right of each line.

2   Press **Font** (Ctrl-F8), then select Base **F**ont (4).

⌨ *Select Base **F**ont from the **F**ont menu.*

The font currently selected is the Courier 10cpi fixed pitch font. Let's select the Helvetica 10pt proportionally-spaced font and see what happens.

3   Press **Down Arrow** until the Helvetica 10pt font is highlighted, then press **Enter** to select the font.

4   Press **Home,**↓ to reformat the text of the letter.

Because the Helvetica 10pt is proportionally-spaced (and because the font is smaller), more characters can be printed in a line than with the Courier 10cpi font.

However, the editing screen still only displays 80 characters per line. Lines with more than 80 characters are longer than the width of the screen, and can only be displayed a section at a time.

5 Move the cursor to the second line of the first paragraph, then press **Home,Home,→** to display the lines at the right margin.

```
ng the Sundheim booth at the WURLD trade exposition in
 impressed with both the quality and variety of hand-crafted_
 . While speaking with the Sundheim marketing director, I was
ution of the music boxes in the United States is handled directly
                                                               ▲
ternational has retailed an exclusive line of jewelry from
ars.  Until recently, we have handled the majority of our
il order service.

o expand our business by opening several retail outlets in
the United States.  At the same time, we would also like to
ne of Sundheim music boxes.

r a selection of music boxes from the following list for the

C:\WP51\LEARN\MUSICBOX.WKB                    Doc 1 Pg 1 Ln 2.5" Pos 7.32"
```

You can use the Home and arrow keys to shift the lines back and forth on the screen for editing, or display the entire length of the lines in the View Document screen using the 100% (on most monitors) or Full Page option.

6 Press **Home,Home,←** to display the lines at the left margin.

Now that you have learned a little about fixed pitch and proportional spacing, you may want to try lessons 16 and 17 in the workbook to see what it is like to edit with a proportionally-spaced font selected.

7 Press **Exit**, then type **n** twice to clear the screen.

Initial Settings

As you may have noticed, many of the formatting features (justification, tabs, margins, etc.) are already set for you when you start creating a document. For example, the left/right margins are set for one inch every time you clear the screen and start typing.

These settings are called the *default settings* of WordPerfect, and are included so that you can begin typing immediately when you first start the program.

If you want to change a setting for a document you are typing, use Format (as you did in lesson 5) to insert a formatting code. The new setting will change the text from the code *forward* through the document.

However, if you want to change a format setting so that WordPerfect uses it each time you start the program or clear the screen, use the Initial Codes option on the Setup key.

1 Press **Setup** (Shift-F1).

⊟ *Select Setup from the File menu.*

2 Select Initial Settings (4), then select Initial Codes (5).

A Reveal Codes screen is displayed that lets you enter a new setting by simply pressing the appropriate keys to insert a WordPerfect code.

3 Press **Format** (Shift-F8), select **L**ine (1), then select **M**argins Left/ Right (7).

⊟ *Select Line from the Layout menu, then select Margins Left/Right (7).*

4 Enter **2** for the left margin, enter **2** for the right margin, then press **Exit** (F7) to return to the Initial Codes editing screen.

A Left/Right Margin code is displayed in the Initial Codes editing screen.

▲ LEFT/RIGHT MARGIN CODE

```
Initial Codes:  Press Exit when done                    Ln 1" Pos 2"
       ▲      (      ▲      ▲      ▲      ▲      ▲      ▲      )      ▲      ▲      ▲
▶[L/R Mar:2",2"]
```

If you returned to the normal editing screen at this point, each new document you created would have 2" left and right margins.

5 Press **Backspace** to delete the Left/Right Margin code, then press **Exit** to return to the Initial Settings menu.

Besides setting formats for each document, you can also use the Initial Settings menu to change settings for Date Format, Repeat Value, and several of the Print options.

```
Setup: Initial Settings

    1 - Merge

    2 - Date Format                          3 1, 4
                                             September 22, 1989
    3 - Equations

    4 - Format Retrieved Documents           No
        for Default Printer

    5 - Initial Codes

    6 - Repeat Value                         8

    7 - Table of Authorities

    8 - Print Options




Selection: 0
```

6 Press **Exit** (F7) to return to the normal editing screen.

If you find that you are changing an initial setting frequently with the Setup key, then it would be wise to leave the initial settings alone and use keys such as Format, Date/Outline, Repeat, and Print to make any changes to the document or WordPerfect.

Check the index at the end of the workbook for other lessons that discuss Setup or Initial Settings. You may also want to turn to the Setup *heading in the* WordPerfect Reference Manual *for details on using Setup to customize your copy of WordPerfect.*

Justification

WordPerfect is set to keep all lines ending with a soft return [SRt] exactly the same length when a document is printed. This is called full justification because text at both the left and right margins is lined up evenly.

Because many business offices no longer use full justification for their correspondence, most of the illustrations of printed pages in the workbook show an unjustified (uneven or ragged) right margin.

If you want your printed documents to have an uneven right margin, but keep the left margin even, use Setup to turn on Left Justification.

1 Press **Setup** (Shift-F1).

⌨ *Select Setup from the File menu.*

2 Select **I**nitial Settings (4), then select Initial Codes (5).

3 Press **Format** (Shift-F8), then select **L**ine (1).

⌨ *Select Line from the Layout menu.*

4 Select **J**ustification (3), select **L**eft (1), then press **Exit** (F7) to return to the Initial Codes screen.

A [Just:Left] code should be displayed in the Reveal Codes screen.

5 Press **Exit** twice to return to the normal editing screen.

Now each document you create will have left justification only. If you want to turn full justification back on for a single document, then place your cursor at the beginning of the document, and follow steps 3 and 4 above before printing (select **F**ull (4) to turn on full justification).

Moving Text

Although the Move feature is specifically designed for moving text from one location to another, there are two other methods of copying or moving text that some people prefer to use while editing in WordPerfect. These methods are particularly useful if you are blocking text that needs to be moved.

For details on some shortcuts, see Move, Block *in the* WordPerfect Reference Manual.

Copying a Block of Text
To copy a block of text *without* using Move,

1 Highlight the text with **Block** (Alt-F4).

2 Press **Save** (F10), then press **Enter** to save the highlighted text. You do not need to type a name to save blocked text.

⌨ *Select Save from the File menu.*

The text is saved in memory until you exit WordPerfect. Replace it by using Enter to save another block of text, or use Block Move or Copy with the Move key.

3 Place the cursor at the location where you want the text inserted.

4 Press **Retrieve** (Shift-F10), then press **Enter** to insert the text into your document. You do not need to type a name to retrieve the blocked text.

⌨ *Select Retrieve from the File menu.*

Moving a Block of Text
To delete and move a block of text *without* using Move,

1 Highlight the text with **Block** (Alt-F4).

2 Press **Backspace** or **Delete**, then type **y** to erase the text from your document.

3 Place the cursor at the location where you want the text inserted.

4 Press **Cancel** (F1) then select **R**estore (1) to insert the text into your document.

You can delete up to three blocks of text before moving them by repeating steps 1 and 2 for each block of text.

When you want to insert the text at the new location, simply press **Cancel** (F1), select **P**revious Deletion (2) until the text you want to insert is displayed, then select **R**estore (1) to insert the text. You can also press **Up Arrow** or **Down Arrow** to display the deletions.

For details on what WordPerfect considers a deletion, turn to *Undelete* in the *WordPerfect Reference Manual*.

Printer Help

There are thousands of printers available, each one with its own unique printer language, capabilities, and requirements. What you can do with WordPerfect often depends on the features that may or may not be available at your printer.

To help you become aware of the limitations or possibilities your printer may have when used with WordPerfect, a Printer Help screen is provided with each printer that WordPerfect supports.

1 Press **Retrieve** (Shift-F10), then enter **memo.wkb** to retrieve the memo form.

⊟ *Select Retrieve from the File menu.*

When you retrieve the memo form, WordPerfect selects the Workbook Printer. Let's check the Printer Help screen for the Workbook Printer.

2 Press **Print** (Shift-F7).

⊟ *Select Print from the File menu.*

3 Choose **S**elect Printer (s), then select **H**elp (6) to display information about the Workbook Printer.

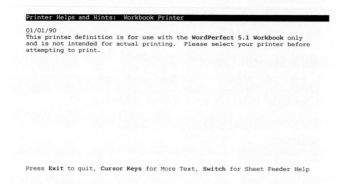

A screen is displayed telling you that the Workbook Printer is only designed to be used with the exercises in the Workbook. If you want to print a document, you need to select your own printer.

4 Press **Exit** (F7) to return to the list of printers.

5 Move the cursor with **Up Arrow** (↑) or **Down Arrow** (↓) until your printer is highlighted, then select **H**elp (6).

If you did not select a printer during installation, then the only printer displayed may be the Workbook Printer.

Take a moment to read the information provided about your printer and WordPerfect. There may be some details listed that can help you when trying to use a WordPerfect feature.

For example, the Printer Help screen for the HP LaserJet Series II printer lets you know that the Line Draw feature does not work correctly with a proportionally-spaced font selected.

A LINE DRAW NOTE

```
 Printer Helps and Hints:  HP LaserJet Series II

 01/01/90
▲► Line draw is not supported with proportionally spaced fonts.












      Press Exit to quit, Cursor Keys for More Text, Switch for Sheet Feeder Help
```

6 When you finish reading the Printer Help screen, press **Exit** three times to return to the editing screen.

7 Press **Exit** again, then type **n** twice to clear the screen.

If you are having problems printing, try checking the Printer Help screen first for information to help you solve the problem.

You can also send the PRINTER.TST file in your WordPerfect directory to your printer to examine your printer's capabilities.

Split Screen

You have already been introduced to using two document editing screens to edit more than one document at a time (lesson 9). By pressing Switch, you can quickly move back and forth between the documents, but you cannot see them both on the same screen.

If you want to display two documents at once, you can use Window to open a window for the document 2 editing screen.

1 Press **Retrieve** (Shift-F10), then enter **musicbox.wkb** to retrieve a letter.

⌨ *Select **R**etrieve from the **F**ile menu.*

2 Press **Screen** (Ctrl-F3), select **W**indow (1), then enter **12** (for twelve lines) to split the screen in half.

⌨ *Select **W**indow from the **E**dit menu.*

The screen is now shared by both the document 1 and document 2 editing screens.

▲ DOCUMENT 1 EDITING
SCREEN
🄰 DOCUMENT 2 EDITING
SCREEN

```
Ms. Heather Wilson
Director of Sales
Swiss America, Inc.
1030 Harrington Blvd.
Newark, NJ 07112

Dear Ms. Wilson,

After recently visiting the Sundheim booth at the WURLD trade
exposition in Amsterdam, I was very impressed with both the
quality and variety of hand-crafted music boxes displayed.  While
speaking with the Sundheim marketing director, I was informed
C:\WP51\LEARN\MUSICBOX.WKB                          Doc 1 Pg 1 Ln 1" Pos 1"




                                        ▼B
                                 Doc 2 Pg 1 Ln 1" Pos 1"
```

You can move back and forth between the two screens by using Switch.

3 Press **Switch** (Shift-F3) to move the cursor to the document 2 editing screen.

⌨ *Select **S**witch Document from the **E**dit menu.*

4 Press **Retrieve**, then enter **memo.wkb** to retrieve the memo form.

⌨ *Select **R**etrieve from the **F**ile menu.*

You should now have the letter in the document 1 editing screen, and the memo form in the document 2 editing screen.

A LETTER
B MEMO FORM

```
Ms. Heather Wilson
Director of Sales
Swiss America, Inc.
1030 Harrington Blvd.
Newark, NJ 07112

Dear Ms. Wilson,

After recently visiting the Sundheim booth at the WURLD trade
exposition in Amsterdam, I was very impressed with both the
quality and variety of hand-crafted music boxes displayed.  While
speaking with the Sundheim marketing director, I was informed
C:\WP51\LEARN\MUSICBOX.WKB                        Doc 1 Pg 1 Ln 1" Pos 1"

                           Corporate Memo

To:

From:

Date:          September 22, 1989

Subject:       B

C:\WP51\LEARN\MEMO.WKB                            Doc 2 Pg 1 Ln 1" Pos 1"
```

You can use all the features of WordPerfect in both screens, just as you can when switching back and forth between the full-size editing screens.

When you want to change the size of one of the editing screens, use Window again.

5 Press **Screen** (Ctrl-F3), then select **W**indow (1).

⊟ *Select Window from the Edit menu.*

6 Enter **6** to reduce the size of the document 2 editing screen.

7 Press **Switch**, select **Screen**, then select **W**indow.

⊟ *Select Switch Document from the Edit menu.*

8 Press **Up Arrow** (↑) six times, then press **Enter** to reduce the size of the document 1 editing screen.

You can either enter a number or use the Up/Down Arrows to size the editing screen where the cursor is located.

9 Press **Switch** to move the cursor to the document 2 editing screen.

⊟ *Select Switch Document from the Edit menu.*

10 Press **Exit** (F7), type **n** to clear the screen, then type **y** to exit the document 2 editing screen.

Even though the document 2 editing screen is cleared, the two editing screens are still displayed.

11 Press **Screen**, select **W**indow, then enter **0** to close the window for the document 2 editing screen.

⌨ *Select* **W***indow from the* **E***dit menu.*

12 Press **Exit**, then type **n** twice to clear the screen.

For additional details about the Window feature of WordPerfect, turn to the *Screen* heading in the *WordPerfect Reference Manual*.

**Timed Document
Backup**

WordPerfect helps you save work by backing up the document on your screen every 30 minutes. When you see a "* Please Wait *" message while editing, you know that WordPerfect is saving the document on your screen to a special backup file.

There is one backup file for each editing screen. The document 1 backup file is named WP{WP}.BK1 and the document 2 backup file is named WP{WP}.BK2.

In case of a power outage or computer failure, these files stay on disk. When you start WordPerfect again, you can use the List Files feature to rename the backup files, then retrieve them into WordPerfect and start editing again.

If you don't want the files, simply delete them after you start WordPerfect.

WordPerfect checks for the files when you first start the program. If they already exist on your disk, a menu is displayed that lets you rename them or delete them from disk.

The timed backup files are saved in the directory where WordPerfect is located (unless you have indicated another directory). You can change both the directory where the backup files are saved and the interval between backups by using the Setup key.

1 Press **Setup** (Shift-F1), then select **E**nvironment (3).

⌨ *Select* **S***etup from the* **F***ile menu, then select* **E***nvironment.*

2 Select **B**ackup Options (1).

A menu is displayed that includes information about Timed Document Backup in the top half of the screen.

△ TIMED DOCUMENT BACKUP

⒝ BACKUP DIRECTORY

```
Setup: Backup

 ▶ Timed backup files are deleted when you exit WP normally.  If you
   have a power or machine failure, you will find the backup file in the
   backup directory indicated in Setup: Location of Files.

   ⒝▶ Backup Directory

   1 - Timed Document Backup               Yes
       Minutes Between Backups             30

   Original backup will save the original document with a .BK! extension
   whenever you replace it during a Save or Exit.

   2 - Original Document Backup            No




Selection: 0
```

If there is a backup directory displayed, then the timed backup files are saved in that directory. Otherwise, they are saved in the WordPerfect directory (e.g., C:\WP51).

By selecting Timed Document Backup (1), you can turn off the Backup feature and/or change the number of minutes between backups.

3 Press **Cancel** (F1) twice to display the Setup menu, then select Location of Files (6).

The first option on the Location of Files menu lets you enter a directory in which you want WordPerfect to save the timed backup files. The directory you enter here is displayed on the Backup menu.

4 Press **Exit** (F7) to return to the normal editing screen.

Because the timed backup files are designed for emergencies only, WordPerfect deletes them from your disk as soon as you exit the program. You should not substitute the Timed Document Backup feature for saving (and replacing) your documents in files that you have created.

Units of Measure

WordPerfect is initially set to display all measurements on the status line and menus in inches. However, you can change the measurements displayed to centimeters, points, or WordPerfect units (1200ths of an inch) by using the Setup key.

1 Press **Setup** (Shift-F1), then select Environment (3).

⌨ *Select Setup from the File menu, then select Environment.*

2 Select Units of Measure (8).

A screen is displayed that lists the choices you have for displaying and entering measurements, and displaying measurements on the status line.

```
Setup: Units of Measure                              ▼
                                                     ▲
       1 - Display and Entry of Numbers              "
               for Margins, Tabs, etc.

       2 - Status Line Display                       "


  Legend:

       " = inches
       i = inches
       c = centimeters
       p = points
       w = 1200ths of an inch
       u = WordPerfect 4.2 Units (Lines/Columns)




  Selection: 0
```

3 Select **D**isplay and Entry of Numbers (1), then type **p** for points.

4 Select **S**tatus Line Display (2), then type **p** for points.

5 Press **Exit** (F7) to return to the normal editing screen.

Points are a measurement used in publishing. There are 72 points in one inch. If you are using one-inch margins, then the Line and Position numbers on the status line should read 72p (one inch).

6 Press **Format** (Shift-F8), then select **L**ine (1).

⊟ *Select **L**ine from the Layout menu.*

Because the default setting for the menu is now points, any number you enter to change a setting will also be in points.

7 Select **M**argins Left/Right (7), then enter **144** (two inches) for the left margin and **144** for the right margin.

However, what if you need to enter a number using another measurement?

8 Select **M**argins Left/Right again, then enter **1.5"** for the left margin and **1.5"** for the right margin.

By typing a quotation mark (") with the measurement, WordPerfect recognizes that the measurement is in inches, and converts the number to points.

⚠ 108 POINTS

```
Format: Line

        1 - Hyphenation                    No

        2 - Hyphenation Zone - Left        10%
                            Right          4%

        3 - Justification                  Left

        4 - Line Height                    Auto

        5 - Line Numbering                 No

        6 - Line Spacing                   1 ▼▼

        7 - Margins - Left                 108p
                    Right                  108p

        8 - Tab Set                        Rel: -72p, every 36p

        9 - Widow/Orphan Protection        No


    Selection: 0
```

The same is true of any measurement displayed on the Units of Measure menu. If you simply enter the number, then WordPerfect assumes you are using the default measurement. If you enter a measurement symbol (",i,c,p,u) with the number, then WordPerfect converts the number to the default units of measure.

9 Press **Exit** to return to the normal editing screen.

10 Press **Setup** (Shift-F1), then select **Environment** (3).

⌨ *Select Setup from the File menu, then select Environment.*

11 Select **Units of Measure** (8).

12 Select **Display and Entry of Numbers** (1), then type **"** for inches.

13 Select **Status Line Display** (2), then type **"** for inches.

14 Press **Exit** to return to the normal editing screen.

The lessons in the workbook assume that you have the default units of measure set for inches (the setting that came with your original copy of WordPerfect). If you decide to switch to another unit of measure, then make sure you include **"** or i at the end of any number you enter when formatting a document for these lessons.

Lesson 13: Formatting a Letter   Part I

Formatting a document can be as simple as double spacing with the Enter key, or as sophisticated as creating footers for odd/even page numbering.

In this lesson you begin formatting the MUSICBOX.WKB letter (lessons 8 and 10) by adding spacing for a letterhead, changing the line spacing, and creating tabbed and newspaper columns. Along the way you are introduced to other formatting features that can be very helpful when creating a document with WordPerfect.

Adding Space for a Letterhead

Let's begin by retrieving the letter and adding some space at the top of the first page for a letterhead.

1 Press **Retrieve** (Shift-F10), then enter **musicbox.wkb** to retrieve the letter.

Select **Retrieve** *from the* **File** *menu.*

Many companies print the first page of a letter on a sheet of paper that includes the letterhead of the company. In order to avoid printing on the letterhead, extra space is normally placed at the top of the first page for the letterhead.

For example, the letterhead for HALVA International needs approximately two inches of space at the top of the page. If you check the Line number on the status line, you can see that there is already a one-inch margin.

⚠ ONE-INCH TOP MARGIN

```
Ms. Heather Wilson
Director of Sales
Swiss America, Inc.
1030 Harrington Blvd.
Newark, NJ 07112

Dear Ms. Wilson,

After recently visiting the Sundheim booth at the WORLD trade
exposition in Amsterdam, I was very impressed with both the
quality and variety of hand-crafted music boxes displayed.  While
speaking with the Sundheim marketing director, I was informed
that distribution of the music boxes in the United States is
handled directly through your company.

As you know, HALVA International has retailed an exclusive line
of jewelry from Europe for over 50 years.  Until recently, we
have handled the majority of our business through a mail order
service.

We are now planning to expand our business by opening several
retail outlets in major cities through the United States.  At the
same time, we would also like to include a complete line of    ▼
Sundheim music boxes.
C:\WP51\LEARN\MUSICBOX.WKB                    Doc 1 Pg 1 Ln 1" Pos 1"
```

All you need to do is add about one more inch of space for the letterhead.

2 Press **Enter** until the Line number on the status line displays 2".

If you add too many lines, press **Backspace** until 2" is displayed. As you use WordPerfect, remember to check the status line when adding space in your document.

Changing the Line Spacing

The letter is currently set for single line spacing. In order to make the letter easier to read, you can increase the space for each line in the body of the letter.

1 Press **Down Arrow** (↓) until the cursor is at the beginning of the "Dear Ms. Wilson," line.

2 Press **Format** (Shift-F8), then select **Line** (1).

⌨ *Select Line from the Layout menu.*

Notice that there are two options in the Line Format menu that you can use to increase the line spacing.

A LINE HEIGHT

B LINE SPACING

```
Format: Line

      1 - Hyphenation                      No

      2 - Hyphenation Zone - Left          10%
                            Right          4%

      3 - Justification                    Left

A ▶   4 - Line Height                      Auto

      5 - Line Numbering                   No

B ▶   6 - Line Spacing                     1

      7 - Margins - Left                   1"
                    Right                  1"

      8 - Tab Set                          Rel: -1", every 0.5"

      9 - Widow/Orphan Protection          No


  Selection: 0
```

Line Height lets you enter an exact amount of space to be used for each line (or automatically use the height of the largest font in the line), and is important when creating documents that need to meet exact publishing specifications.

Line Spacing lets you increase the line spacing by multiplying. For example, entering "2" for the line spacing doubles the current setting and creates double spacing. You can also enter numbers such as 1.5", 1.7", 2.3", and 3.1" to more accurately adjust the line spacing.

3 Select Line **S**pacing (6), then enter **1.5** to increase the line spacing one and a half times.

4 Press **Exit** (F7) to return to the editing screen.

5 Press **Reveal Codes** (Alt-F3) to display the Line Spacing code.

▣ *Select **R**eveal Codes from the **E**dit menu.*

▲ LINE SPACING CODE

```
Ms. Heather Wilson
Director of Sales
Swiss America, Inc.
1030 Harrington Blvd.
Newark, NJ 07112

Dear Ms. Wilson,
C:\WP51\LEARN\MUSICBOX.WKB                      Doc 1 Pg 1 Ln 3" Pos 1"
[    ▲    ▲     ▲     ▲     ▲     ▲      ▲     ▲     ▲   }  ▲    ▲    ▲
1030 Harrington Blvd.[HRt]
Newark, NJ 07112[HRt]
[HRt]
[Ln Spacing:1.5]Dear Ms. Wilson,[HRt]
[HRt]
After recently visiting the Sundheim booth at the WURLD trade[SRt]
exposition in Amsterdam, I was very impressed with both the[SRt]
quality and variety of hand[-]crafted music boxes displayed.  While[SRt]
speaking with the Sundheim marketing director, I was informed[SRt]
that distribution of the music boxes in the United States is[SRt]

Press Reveal Codes to restore screen
```

6 Press **Reveal Codes** to display the normal editing screen.

▣ *Select **R**eveal Codes from the **E**dit menu*

The inside address is still single-spaced, while the rest of the letter is using the new setting.

▲ SINGLE LINE SPACING
🅱 1.5 LINE SPACING

```
Ms. Heather Wilson
Director of Sales
Swiss America, Inc.
1030 Harrington Blvd.
Newark, NJ 07112

Dear Ms. Wilson,


After recently visiting the Sundheim booth at the WURLD trade

exposition in Amsterdam, I was very impressed with both the

quality and variety of hand-crafted music boxes displayed.  While

speaking with the Sundheim marketing director, I was informed

that distribution of the music boxes in the United States is
C:\WP51\LEARN\MUSICBOX.WKB                      Doc 1 Pg 1 Ln 3" Pos 1"
```

As you can see, WordPerfect only starts increasing the line spacing *after* the [Ln Spacing:1.5] code. Any text before the code uses the previous setting. This feature of WordPerfect makes it easy to change the format at any point in the document.

Viewing the Line Spacing

Now that the letter is set for 1.5 line spacing, let's use the View Document screen to see the new format.

1 Press **Print** (Shift-F7).

▣ *Select **P**rint from the **F**ile menu.*

2 Select **V**iew Document (6), then select Facing Pages (4).

3 Press **Page Down** (PgDn) to display pages 2 and 3 of the letter.

Not only is the text of the letter in 1.5 line spacing, but the lists of music boxes and the list of regional marketing representatives are as well.

A MUSIC BOX LISTS
B LIST OF REPRESENTATIVES

1 100% 2 200% 3 Full Page **4** Facing Pages: **4**   Doc 1 Pg 2-3

In order to format the lists for single spacing, another Line Spacing code needs to be placed at the beginning of each list.

4 Press **Exit** (F7) to return to the editing screen, then press **Home,Home,↑** to move the cursor to the beginning of the letter.

Formatting Part of a Document

Let's begin by formatting the first music box list for single line spacing.

1 Press **Go To** (Ctrl-Home), then **Down Arrow** (↓) to move to the bottom of the first page.

2 Press **Up Arrow** (↑) until the cursor is at the beginning of the word "Fairies."

3 Press **Format** (Shift-F8) and select **L**ine (1).

▣ *Select **L**ine from the **L**ayout menu.*

4 Select Line **S**pacing (6), then enter **1** for single line spacing.

5 Press **Exit** (F7) to return to the editing screen.

The list is now single-spaced, but what about the rest of the letter?

6 Press **Down Arrow** (↓) until the paragraph below the list is displayed on the screen.

Not only is the list single-spaced, but also the rest of the letter. To start 1.5 line spacing again, you need to insert another code.

7 Place the cursor in the last line of the music box list (Goatherd), then press **End** to move the cursor to the end of the line.

The Line Spacing code is placed at the end of the line to make sure it stays with the list when editing the document.

8 Press **Format** (Shift-F8) and select **L**ine (1).

▣ *Select* **L**ine *from the Layout menu.*

9 Select Line **S**pacing (6), then enter **1.5** for the line spacing number.

10 Press **Exit** (F7) to return to the editing screen.

11 Press **Down Arrow** (↓) until the second list of music boxes is displayed.

Now that you have changed the line spacing back to 1.5, both the second music box list and the list of representatives need to be formatted for single line spacing.

12 Set single line spacing at the beginning of the music box list, then move the cursor to the end of the last line (Copenhagen Tales), then set the line spacing back to 1.5.

If you can't remember the exact keystrokes for setting the line spacing, they are provided in steps 8, 9, and 10.

13 Move the cursor to the beginning of the list of representatives, set single line spacing, then set the line spacing back to 1.5 at the end of the last line in the list ((213)937-3370).

14 When you finish formatting the lists, move the cursor to the beginning of the "Sincerely yours," line and set the closing for single line spacing.

From time to time in the *Fundamentals II* lessons, you will be given the chance to complete an exercise on your own *without* being given specific keystrokes. However, you will always be guided through the steps before the exercise begins.

Indenting the First Line of a Paragraph

Another way of making a letter easier to read is to indent the first line of each paragraph with a tab.

1 Press **Home,Home,**↑ to move the cursor to the beginning of the letter.

2 Place the cursor at the beginning of each paragraph in the letter, then press **Tab** to indent the first line of the paragraph.

Do not indent the inside address, lists, or closing.

Creating Tabbed Columns

Now that the text has been changed to 1.5 line spacing, the letter is longer than at the beginning of the lesson. Is there a way to make the letter shorter without losing the advantages of 1.5 line spacing?

1 Press **Home,Home,**↑ to move the cursor to the beginning of the letter.

2 Press **Go To** (Ctrl-Home), **Down Arrow** (↓) to display the first list of music boxes.

Because the music box titles are short, there is enough room on the right side of the page to create a second column of titles.

3 Move the cursor to the beginning of the "Pan's Pipes" title (second in the list).

4 Press **Backspace** to delete the hard return, then press **Tab** six times to move the title to a new, second column.

5 Move the cursor to the beginning of "Silver Harmonies," press **Backspace**, then press **Tab** six times to move the title to the new column.

6 Move the cursor to the beginning of "Patterns," press **Backspace**, then press **Tab** three times to move the title to the new column.

```
several retail outlets in major cities through the United States.
At the same time, we would also like to include a complete line
of Sundheim music boxes.

     We would like to order a selection of music boxes from the
following list for the conference:


Fairies                     Pan's Pipes
Gondolier                   Silver Harmonies
Return to the Danube        Patterns
Autumn Memories
Paris at Night
Follow the Leader
Secrets
Symphony Strings
Black Forest Summer
--------------------------------------------------------------
C:\WP51\LEARN\MUSICBOX.WKB              Doc 1 Pg 1 Ln 8.83" Pos 4.5"
```

Setting a Tab for the Columns

You could continue lining up titles in a second column by adding several tabs between the music box titles. However, if you ever selected another font, you might need to add or delete tabs to line up the second column again.

An easier way of lining up the second column of titles is to insert a single tab between the columns, then set a tab stop near the middle of the page.

1   Press **Reveal Codes** (Alt-F3) to see the tabs between the columns, then delete all but one tab from between the three pairs of music box titles.

Select Reveal Codes from the Edit menu.

You should now have only one tab between the columns.

▲ ONE TAB

```
    We would like to order a selection of music boxes from the
following list for the conference:


Fairies    Pan's Pipes
Gondolier  Silver Harmonies
Return to the Danube      Patterns
C:\WP51\LEARN\MUSICBOX.WKB               Doc 1 Pg 1 Ln 8.5" Pos 2"
[Tab]We would like to order a selection of music boxes from the[SRt]
following list for the conference:[HRt]
[HRt]
[Ln Spacing:1]Fairies[Tab]Pan's Pipes[HRt]
Gondolier[Tab]Silver Harmonies[HRt]
Return to the Danube[Tab]Patterns[HRt]
Autumn Memories[HRt]
Paris at Night[HRt]
Follow the Leader[HRt]
Secrets[HRt]

Press Reveal Codes to restore screen
```

2   Move the cursor to "F" in "Fairies" (next to the [Ln Spacing:1] code).

3   Press **Reveal Codes** to display the normal editing screen.

⌨ *Select Reveal Codes from the Edit menu.*

4   Press **Format** (Shift-F8) and select **Line** (1).

⌨ *Select Line from the Layout menu.*

5   Select **Tab Set** (8).

6   Press **Delete to End of Line** (Ctrl-End) to clear the tabs from the tab ruler, then enter **3.5** for the tab setting.

7   Press **Exit** (F7) twice to return to the normal editing screen.

The music box titles in the second column have lined up at the 3.5" tab stop (4.5 inches from the left edge of the page). You are ready to continue creating the tabbed columns.

8   Move the cursor to the beginning of "Paris at Night," press **Backspace**, then press **Tab** to move the title to the second column.

9   Place the cursor at the beginning of the following titles, then repeat step 8 to move the titles to the second column.

Secrets
Black Forest Summer
Winter's Wonder

When you finish creating the second column, notice the first line of the paragraph that follows the list.

△ PARAGRAPH TAB

```
     We would like to order a selection of music boxes from the

following list for the conference:

                                        ▼▼
Fairies                            Pan's Pipes
Gondolier                          Silver Harmonies
Return to the Danube               Patterns
Autumn Memories                    Paris at Night
Follow the Leader                  Secrets
Symphony Strings                   Black Forest Summer
Punting on the Thames              Winter's Wonder
Goatherd

-----------------------------------------------------------------
                                   In addition to the above music

boxes, our marketing department would also like to request one or

more transparencies for as many music boxes as possible for our

C:\WP51\LEARN\MUSICBOX.WKB                  Doc 1 Pg 1 Ln 9.5" Pos 4.5"
```

Because there is only one tab set at the beginning of the list, there is only one tab set for the rest of the document. The first line of each paragraph below the list is now indented 4.5" from the left edge of the page.

To set the tabs back to one tab for every half inch (default setting), you could insert a new tab code at the end of the list. However, since there are only two tab settings being used in the letter (one for the lists and one for the first line of the paragraphs), you could also set two tabs for the entire document.

1   Move the cursor to the "Fairies" music box title, then press **Home,←** to place the cursor at the beginning of the title.

2   Press **Backspace**, then type **y** to delete the Tab Setting code.

3   Press **Home,Home,↑** to move the cursor to the beginning of the letter.

4   Press **Format** (Shift-F8), then select **Line** (1).

⌨ *Select Line from the Layout menu.*

5   Select **Tab Set** (8), then press **Delete to End of Line** (Ctrl-End) to erase all the tab settings.

6   Enter **0.5** for the tab at the beginning of each paragraph, then enter **3.5** for the second column in the music box list.

7   Press **Exit** twice to return to the editing screen.

8 Press **Go To** (Ctrl-Home), then press **Down Arrow** (↓) to display the music box list on the screen.

9 Press **Down Arrow** until the paragraph below the list is displayed.

The tab at the beginning of the paragraph has returned to its original position, as well as all other paragraph tabs below the list.

Formatting the Second List

Now that you have formatted the first music box list using tabbed columns, try placing the second music box list in tabbed columns.

1 Place the cursor at the beginning of the following titles in the second list, press **Backspace**, then press **Tab** to move them to the second column.

Always
Little Flower Girl
Easter Parade
Joplin
Happiness
Lazy River
Copenhagen Tales

When you finish, the second list of music boxes should look similar to the following illustration.

```
Punting on the Thames          Winter's Wonder
Goatherd

--------------------------------------------------------------------------------
        In addition to the above music boxes, our marketing
department would also like to request one or more transparencies
for as many music boxes as possible for our catalog and other
advertising promotions.  For the immediate future, we would like
to have transparencies sent for the following:


Beautiful Dreamer              Always
Christmas Fantasy              Little Flower Girl
Just a Song                   Easter Parade
Somewhere, Somehow            Joplin
San Francisco Nights          Happiness
Grecian Holiday               Lazy River
Blues                         Copenhagen Tales

C:\WP51\LEARN\MUSICBOX.WKB              Doc 1 Pg 2 Ln 3.5" Pos 4.5"
```

Because you are using a single tab for the second column of each music box list, the second column will stay lined up at 4.5", even if you select a different font or printer for the letter.

Creating Newspaper Columns

While placing the music box lists in tabbed columns has saved a lot of space in the letter, you could save even more space by also placing the list of marketing representatives in columns.

1 Press **Go To** (Ctrl-Home), then press **Down Arrow** (↓) to display the list of representatives.

2 Place the cursor at the beginning of "Jayna Wilder-Smith."

3 Press **Backspace** twice, then press **Tab** to move Jayna Wilder-Smith to the second column.

As you can see, only the name moved to the second column. The address and phone number stayed at the left margin.

Ⓐ NAME

Ⓑ ADDRESS AND PHONE

```
        Robin Pierce
        544 Westminster Circle NW
        Atlanta, Georgia 30327
      Ⓑ (404) 359-2828           Ⓐ Jayna Wilder-Smith
      ▶ 8611 Market St.
        San Francisco, CA 94102
        (415) 987-4598

        Anna Lee Pierce
        P.O. Box 1392
        Central Park Station
        Buffalo, NY 14215
        (716) 453-5678

        Kathleen O'Hara
        678 Forestvale Road
        Boston, MA 02136
        (617) 789-2027

        Mary Anna Pickford
        Route 1, Box 196
        ----------------------------------------------------------------
        C:\WP51\LEARN\MUSICBOX.WKB              Doc 1 Pg 2 Ln 7" Pos 4.5"
```

Although single lines of text (such as titles) work well in tabbed columns, it is very difficult to place an item in tabbed columns if it includes more than one line of text.

If you want to place multiple-line items in columns, try using the Text Columns feature.

4 Press **Backspace** to delete the tab, then press **Enter** twice to restore the double spacing between the first and second representatives.

5 Move the cursor to the beginning of the first representative's name (Robin Pierce).

6 Press **Columns/Table** (Alt-F7), select Columns (1), then select **Define** (3).

⌨ *Select Columns from the Layout menu, then select Define.*

A menu fills the screen that includes settings for Newspaper columns and two columns across the page. Because these settings are exactly what you need for the list of representatives, you can simply press Exit to use the settings.

7 Press **Exit** (F7) to use the settings, then select **On** (1) to turn on the Newspaper columns.

8 Press **Home,↓** to format the list.

The marketing representatives are placed in two Newspaper columns.

9 Press **Down Arrow** (↓) four times to display the paragraph below the list.

Not only is the list in Newspaper columns, but the rest of the letter is placed into columns.

A MARKETING REPRESENTATIVES LIST

B REST OF LETTER

```
                            (415) 987-4598                 Chicago, IL 60617
                                                           (312) 377-3980
A ▷ Anna Lee Pierce
      P.O. Box 1392                                        Samuel A. Roberts
      Central Park Station                                 6120 Cottage Way, Suite #456
      Buffalo, NY 14215                                    Sacramento, CA 95825
      (716) 453-5678                                       (916) 878-4550

      Kathleen O'Hara                                      Scott L. Ziegler
      678 Forestvale Road                                  450 S. Flower St.
      Boston, MA 02136                                     Los Angeles, CA 90014
      (617) 789-2027                                       (213) 937-3370

B ▷ -----------------------------------------------------------------------------
          We look forward to

      establishing a working

      relationship with you, and

      would be very interested in

      any other items you feel might
      C:\WP51\LEARN\MUSICBOX.WKB           Col 1 Doc 1 Pg 3 Ln 2" Pos 1"
```

The columns need to be turned off at the end of the list for the rest of the letter to return to the original margin settings.

10 Press **Go To** (Ctrl-Home), then press **Up Arrow** (↑) to move the cursor to the top of the page.

11 Press **Left Arrow** (←) twice to place the cursor at the end of the second column in the list of representatives (before the Line Spacing code).

12 Press **Columns/Table**, select Columns, then select Off.

⌨ *Select Columns from the Layout menu, then select Off.*

13 Press **Home,↓** to reformat the text below the Newspaper columns.

◢ ORIGINAL MARGINS

```
Kathleen O'Hara                        Scott L. Ziegler
678 Forestvale Road                    450 S. Flower St.
Boston, MA 02136                       Los Angeles, CA 90014
(617) 789-2027                         (213) 937-3370          ▼▼
------------------------------------------------------------------------
▼▼    We look forward to establishing a working relationship with

you, and would be very interested in any other items you feel

might fit well with our current expansion plans.


Sincerely yours,


Bryan Metcalf
President
HALVA International


C:\WP51\LEARN\MUSICBOX.WKB                  Doc 1 Pg 3 Ln 3" Pos 1"
```

Placing a list of items in Newspaper columns can make it easier to format the list and use a feature such as Sort to alphabetize the list. Even single-line items such as the titles in the music box list can be placed in columns instead of using tabs.

Whether you choose tabbed columns or Newspaper columns to format a list, you should always be aware that the formatting for the columns usually affects the rest of the document until you change the format again.

Viewing and Saving the Letter

With the formatting changes completed, you may want to use the View Document screen to see the results of your work.

1 Press **Print** (Shift-F7), select **V**iew Document (6), then select 100% (1).

2 Use **Page Up** (PgUp), **Page Down** (PgDn), and the arrow keys to scroll through the letter.

▭ *Select Print from the File menu.*

Try using all the View Document options (200%, Full Page, Facing Pages) for a closer or overall view of the pages. The higher the resolution of your monitor, the better you will be able to read characters in Full Page and Facing Pages.

3 When you finish, press **Exit** (F7) to return to the editing screen.

4 Press **Exit** again, type **y** to save the letter, then enter **musicbox.ltr** for the filename.

5 Type **n** to clear the screen and stay in WordPerfect.

In this lesson you have been introduced to several ways of formatting the text in your document. Remember that when you change a format such as line spacing, you are telling WordPerfect to use the new format for the *rest of the document*. It is up to you to let WordPerfect know when to start using the original format again (by inserting another formatting code).

Important: *Some of the lessons in the rest of the workbook are long enough that you may not have time to complete them in a single session. If you run out of time, you can always use the Exit key to save the document (use a filename like LESSON13), then retrieve it at a more convenient time to complete the lesson.*

Lesson 14: Formatting a Letter — Part II

In this lesson you finish editing and formatting the letter from lesson 13, then spell-check, save, and print the final draft.

Replacing a Word

Whenever you want to find a word in a document, you can always use the ♦Search key. This can be especially useful when you need to replace a word. For example, the name of the Sundheim music box company has been changed to SoundMaster.

1 Press **Retrieve** (Shift-F10), then enter **musicbox.ltr** to retrieve the letter.

⌨ *Select Retrieve from the File menu.*

You need to find every occurrence of "Sundheim" in the letter, delete it, then type in the new company name.

2 Press ♦**Search** (F2), type **sundheim** and press ♦**Search** again to begin looking for the company name.

⌨ *Select Forward from the Search menu.*

3 Press **Delete Word** (Ctrl-Backspace) to erase "Sundheim," then type **SoundMaster** and press the **Space Bar** for the new company name.

4 Continue repeating steps 2 and 3 until you find and replace all occurrences of "Sundheim" in the letter.

You do not need to type "Sundheim" again to search for the word because WordPerfect saves the last text you type in case you want to look for it again.

5 When the "*Not found*" message is displayed, press **Home,Home,↑** to return to the beginning of the letter.

You should have found and replaced the "Sundheim" company name three times.

Replacing Several Words

Even though ♦Search is convenient for finding and editing text in a document, you can still spend a lot of time making changes if the same word needs to be replaced several times.

Now that the Sundheim company has changed their name, they have also changed their line of merchandise from music boxes to harmonicas.

1 Press ♦**Search** (F2), type **music boxes** and press ♦**Search** again to begin looking.

⌨ *Select Forward from the Search menu.*

The cursor stops next to the "hand-crafted music boxes" phrase. You could erase "music boxes," type "harmonicas," then continue searching, but how many times would you need to find and replace "music boxes" in the letter?

2 Continue using ◆**Search** to count the number of "music boxes" in the letter.

3 When you finish counting, press **Home,Home,↑** to return to the beginning of the letter.

You should have counted a total of 8 "music boxes" in the letter. When there are several occurrences of a word or phrase that need to be changed, it is much easier to let WordPerfect do the editing for you by using the Replace feature.

4 Press **Replace** (Alt-F2), then type **n** when you see "w/Confirm?".

⌨ *Select **R**eplace from the Search menu.*

If you type "y" for Yes, then WordPerfect stops each time it finds the word to let you decide whether or not to replace it.

5 Type **music boxes** and press ◆**Search** to have WordPerfect look for the words "music boxes."

6 Type **harmonicas** and press ◆**Search** to have WordPerfect replace "music boxes" with "harmonicas."

When the replacing is completed, the cursor stops at the last "music boxes" in the letter. The word "harmonicas" is now in its place.

▲ REPLACED WORD

```
                              ▼
account within the week.  If there is any charge for harmonicas,

transparencies, etc., please bill them to the account.


    The following is a current list of regional marketing

representatives:


Robin Pierce                  Mary Anna Pickford
544 Westminster Circle NW     Route 1, Box 196
Atlanta, Georgia 30327        Louisville, KY 40222
(404) 359-2828                Mary
                              (502) 224-7273
Jayna Wilder-Smith
8611 Market St.               Paul Magleby
San Francisco, CA 94102       1820 Harbor Ave S.
(415) 987-4598                Chicago, IL 60617
                              (312) 377-3980
Anna Lee Pierce
P.O. Box 1392                 Samuel A. Roberts
C:\WP51\LEARN\MUSICBOX.LTR                      Doc 1 Pg 2 Ln 5" Pos 6.4"
```

7 Press ◆**Search** twice to check for any "music boxes" from the cursor to the end of the letter.

8 Press **◆Search** (Shift-F2), then press **◆Search** to check for any "music boxes" from the cursor back to the beginning of the letter.

⊞ Select *Backward from the Search menu.*

You should see a "*Not found*" message briefly displayed at the end of each search. After replacing "music boxes," you should also check for any occurrences of "music box."

9 Press **Home,Home,↑** to return to the beginning of the letter, then use **◆Search** to find the words "music box."

The words are not found, so you do not need to use Replace to change them to "harmonica." You are ready to finish formatting the letter.

Numbering Pages with a Footer

Just as a header can be used for printing the same text at the top of each page (lesson 10), a footer can be used to print the same text at the *bottom* of every page in a document.

For example, you may decide that you want page numbering at the bottom of each page in the letter.

1 Press **Format** (Shift-F8) and select **P**age (2).

⊞ Select *Page from the Layout menu.*

2 Select **F**ooters (4).

While you can create up to two footers (A and B) per page, you only need one footer for page numbering in the MUSICBOX.LTR letter.

3 Select Footer **A** (1), then select Every **P**age (2) to have a footer printed on every page of the letter.

The footer editing screen is exactly like the header editing screen, except that the message in the lower left corner indicates that you are now editing footer A.

▲ FOOTER A EDITING SCREEN

```
          ▼
          A


Footer A:  Press Exit when done                    Ln 1" Pos 1"
```

While a standard way of numbering pages is to place the page number at the bottom center of each page, you can also separate the page number from the rest of the letter with a line.

4 Press **Graphics** (Alt-F9), select **L**ine (5), then select **H**orizontal (1).

⌨ *Select **L**ine from the **G**raphics menu, then select Create **H**orizontal.*

A menu fills the screen that includes settings for a thin (.013"), black (100%) line that extends from the left margin to the right margin (Full).

```
Graphics: Horizontal Line

    1 - Horizontal Position        Full

    2 - Vertical Position          Baseline

    3 - Length of Line

    4 - Width of Line              0.013"

    5 - Gray Shading (% of black) 100%




Selection: 0
```

Because these settings are exactly what you need for the line in the footer, you can simply press Exit to use the settings.

5 Press **Exit** (F7) to use the settings in the Horizontal Line menu.

6 Press **Reveal Codes** (Alt-F3) to see the code for the horizontal line.

⌨ *Select **R**eveal Codes from the **E**dit menu.*

Like a Date code that inserts the current date in your document, a Graphics Line code prints a line using the settings in the code.

Footer A: Press **Exit** when done   Ln 1" Pos 1"
▲▶[HLine:Full,Baseline,6.5",0.013",100%]

Press **Reveal Codes** to restore screen

While you cannot see the line in an editing screen (such as the one for footer A), the line can be displayed in the View Document screen.

7 Press **Reveal Codes** to display the normal editing screen.

⌨ Select *Reveal Codes* from the *Edit* menu.

8 Press **Enter** twice to double space.

9 Press **Center** (Shift-F6) to center the page number in the line.

10 Press **Format** (Shift-F8) and select **P**age (2).

⌨ Select *Page* from the *Layout* menu.

11 Select Page **N**umbering (6), then select **I**nsert Page Number (3) to insert a ^B into the footer.

The ^B can be used anywhere in a document to have WordPerfect print the current page number. This feature is especially useful when creating a header or footer because it lets you put a page number anywhere in a line with any text you choose.

12 Press **Exit** twice to exit the footer editing screen and return to the normal editing screen.

Because the footer editing screen is so similar to the normal editing screen, you can easily forget that you are creating a footer, and may begin to type your document text in the footer editing screen. If you do so, simply use Block and Move to move the text out of the screen and into the normal editing screen.

Viewing the Formatted Letter

While you can see the effects of many features in the normal editing screen, footers, graphic lines, and the page number for ^B are only displayed in the View Document screen.

1 Press **Print** (Shift-F7), select **V**iew Document (6), then select 100% (1) to view the page at the actual size it will be printed.

⊟ *Select **Print** from the **File** menu.*

2 Press **Go To** (Ctrl-Home), then press **Down Arrow** (↓) to display the footer on the first page.

▲ PAGE NUMBERING FOOTER

```
        We are now planning to expand our business by opening
    several retail outlets in major cities through the United States.
    At the same time, we would also like to include a complete line
    of SoundMaster harmonicas.

        We would like to order a selection of harmonicas from the
    following list for the conference:

    Fairies                     Pan's Pipes
    Gondolier                   Silver Harmonies
    Return to the Danube        Patterns
    Autumn Memories             Paris at Night
    Follow the Leader           Secrets


                            1
                            ▲
```
```
1 100%  2 200%  3 Full Page  4 Facing Pages: 1                 Doc 1 Pg 1
```

The ^B is replaced by a page number, and the Graphics Line code displays the line as it will be printed.

3 Select **F**acing Pages (4), then press **Page Down** (PgDn) to display pages 2 and 3 of the letter.

Notice that both the first harmonica list and the list of representatives are split by page breaks.

▲ FIRST HARMONICA LIST
▲ LIST OF REPRESENTATIVES

1 100%   2 200%   3 Full Page   4 Facing Pages: 4   Doc 1 Pg 2-3

Setting the Top and Bottom Margins

You could move the entire harmonica list to the top of page 2 by using a hard page break, but the list of representatives would still be divided between pages 2 and 3.

1 Press **Exit** (F7) to return to the editing screen.

Although it may be important to keep a 1 inch margin on the left and right sides of the page, you could increase the space for text on each page by decreasing the size of the top and bottom margins.

2 Press **Home,Home,Home,**↑ to move the cursor to the very beginning of the letter.

3 Press **Format** (Shift-F8) and select **P**age (2).

📋 *Select Page from the Layout menu.*

4 Select **M**argins (5).

5 Enter ½" for the top margin, then enter ½" for the bottom margin.

Notice that WordPerfect changes the fractional amount (½) to a decimal number (.5) for the setting. Any time you have a fractional number such as 3/8, 7/32, or 13/64, you can enter the fraction and WordPerfect will change it to a decimal amount for you.

6 Press **Exit** to return to the editing screen.

Let's check the results of the smaller top and bottom margins in the View Document screen.

7 Press **Print** (Shift-F7), select **V**iew Document (6), then select Full Page (3).

The harmonica list has moved back to the first page of the letter. However, the first line of the paragraph below the list is separated by a soft page break from the rest of the paragraph.

1 100%   2 200%   3 Full Page   4 Facing Pages: 3   Doc 1 Pg 1

Setting Widow/ Orphan Protection

This type of break in a paragraph is called an "orphan." If the last line of a paragraph is by itself at the top of a page, the line is called a "widow."

Some dictionaries and style books call both types of lines a widow.

In order to help you prevent widows and orphans, WordPerfect provides a Widow/Orphan Protection feature.

1   Press **Exit** (F7) to return to the editing screen.

2   Press **Home,Home,↑** to move the cursor to the beginning of the letter.

3   Press **Format** (Shift-F8) and select **Line** (1).

⌨ *Select Line from the Layout menu.*

4   Select **Widow/Orphan** Protection (9).

5   Type **y** (for Yes) to turn on the protection, then press **Exit** to return to the editing screen.

6   Press **Down Arrow** (↓) to scroll through the letter to the top of the second page.

As you move past the harmonica list on page 1, WordPerfect moves the orphaned line to the top of page 2.

Any time the first or last line of a paragraph is separated from the paragraph by a soft page break, WordPerfect will use Widow/Orphan Protection to make sure that the paragraph stays together.

Adjusting the Letterhead Spacing

Now that the top margin is smaller by one-half inch, what has happened to the two inches of spacing for the letterhead?

1 Press **Home,Home,↑** to move the cursor to the beginning of the letter.

2 Press **Down Arrow** (↓) until the cursor is at the beginning of the "Ms. Heather Wilson" line.

The Line number on the status line lets you know that instead of 2" for the letterhead, there is only 1.5" from the top of the page to the first line of the inside address.

You could add more lines to leave enough room for the letterhead. However, if you change the top margin, create a header, select another printer or font, etc., you will probably have to adjust the letterhead spacing again.

3 Press **Backspace** six times to delete the six empty lines at the top of the letter.

To make sure that the first line of the letter will always be printed 2 inches down from the top edge of the page, you can use the Advance Line feature.

4 Press **Format** (Shift-F8), select **O**ther (4), then select **A**dvance (1).

⌨ *Select **O**ther From the Layout menu, then select **A**dvance.*

5 Select **L**ine (3), then enter **2** to have the first line of the letter printed 2 inches down from the top edge of the page.

6 Press **Exit** (F7) to return to the editing screen.

The Line number on the status line displays 2" for the position of the first line of the letter, but no extra space is displayed above the first line on the screen. Whenever you use any of the Advance features, the cursor position is updated on the status line, but the actual spacing can only be seen in View Document or when you print.

7 Press **Print** (Shift-F7), then select **View Document** (6).

⌨ *Select **Print** from the **File** menu.*

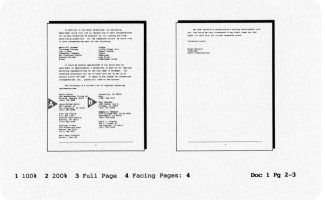

1 100%   2 200%   3 Full Page   **4** Facing Pages: 3   Doc 1 Pg 1

**Adjusting the
Newspaper Columns**

While you are in the View Document screen, let's check pages 2 and 3 to see what happened to the list of representatives.

1 Select Facing Pages (4), then press **Page Down** (PgDn) to display pages 2 and 3 on the screen.

The entire list has moved back to the bottom of page 2, but the columns are uneven.

1 100%   2 200%   3 Full Page   **4** Facing Pages: **4**   Doc 1 Pg 2-3

2 Press **Exit** (F7) to return to the editing screen.

3 Press **Go To** (Ctrl-Home), then press **Down Arrow** (↓) to move the cursor to the bottom of page 2.

When there is more text in one column than another, you can use Hard Page to rearrange the text in the columns.

4   Press **Go To**, then press **Left Arrow** (←) to move the cursor to the first column.

5   Press **Down Arrow** until the cursor is at the beginning of the "Mary Anna Pickford" line.

6   Press **Hard Page** (Ctrl-Enter) to move Mary Anna Pickford to the top of the second column.

Both columns are now even, with four representatives in each column.

7   Press **Print** (Shift-F7), then select **V**iew Document (6).

8   Press **Page Up** (PgUp) and **Page Down** (PgDn) to display the formatted letter.

The harmonica lists are on pages 1 and 2, with the evenly-divided list of representatives at the bottom of page 2. The final paragraph and closing are on page 3, there are no widows or orphans, and each page is numbered with a footer.

9   Press **Exit** to return to the editing screen.

You have completed editing and formatting the letter, and are ready to spell-check and print the final draft.

Spell-checking the Letter

Before checking the spelling or printing the letter, it would be a good idea to save the changes you have made.

1   Press **Save** (F10), then press **Enter** and type **y** to replace the letter on disk with the edited version.

⌨ *Select Save from the **F**ile menu.*

If you have been careful when formatting, there should be very few (or no) spelling errors in the letter.

2   Press **Spell** (Ctrl-F2).

⌨ *Select Spell from the **T**ools menu.*

3   Select **D**ocument (3) to begin spell-checking.

If WordPerfect stops on a proper name such as "Harrington" or "SoundMaster" that is spelled correctly, simply select Skip (2) to have WordPerfect skip over the word for the rest of the letter.

4   When the spell-checking is completed, press **Exit** (F7) or any other key to exit the Word Count message.

Printing the Letter

With the spell-checking completed, you can send the letter to the printer. However, because the letter was formatted using the Workbook printer, you need to select your own printer before printing.

1 Press **Print** (Shift-F7).

⌨ *Select Print from the File menu.*

2 Type **s** for Select Printer.

3 Using the arrow keys, highlight the name of your printer, then press **Enter** to select the printer.

⌨ *Highlight your printer by placing the mouse pointer on it and clicking the left button.*

You are returned to the Print menu. At this point, you may want to check the letter in the View Document screen to see what formatting adjustments have been made for your printer.

4 Select View Document (6), then use **Page Up** (PgUp) and **Page Down** (PgDn) to scroll through the letter.

5 When you finish, press **Cancel** (F1), then select Full Document (1) to print the letter.

6 Press **Exit**, press **Enter** twice, then type **y** to replace the letter on disk.

7 Type **n** to clear the screen.

While formatting the letter in lessons 13 and 14, you have discovered that WordPerfect lets you decide where a format begins and where it should end.

As you learn more about WordPerfect, you will also learn more about how one feature affects another, and what you can do to make sure that your document is formatted exactly the way you want it to look.

Lesson 15: Office Automation

Typing a company name, setting margins, printing a page, and filling in a memo are just a few of the word processing tasks you may find yourself repeating over and over again as you create documents.

In this lesson you are introduced to a feature that can save you time and effort by performing these tasks for you. All you need to do is show exactly what you want done, then let WordPerfect do the rest.

Automating with Macros

When you think of the word "computer," you may also think of words like "labor-saving," "self-running," or "automatic." While there are many features in WordPerfect (such as Headers or Date Code) that can make it easier to create or format a document, there are still many tasks you do that are *not* included as a feature.

However, you can have WordPerfect do the work for you by using a feature called Macros. Simply give the task a name, record the keystrokes, then have WordPerfect repeat the keystrokes by typing in the name of the task.

Typing a Company Name

For example, you may type a company name such as "HALVA International" hundreds of times during a week. It would be wonderful if WordPerfect could do the typing for you.

1 Press **Macro Define** (Ctrl-F10).

⌨ *Select Macro from the Tools menu, then select Define.*

2 Enter **hi** (for **HA**LVA **I**nternational) to name the task when you see the "Define Macro:" message.

3 Press **Enter** when you see the "Description:" message (you do not need a description right now).

A "Macro Def" message is displayed at the bottom of the screen to let you know that each time you press a key, the keystroke will be recorded in a file named HI.WPM (WPM = **W**ord**P**erfect **M**acro).

The .WPM extension is added to every macro that you create in WordPerfect.

4 Type **HALVA International** to record the keystrokes for typing the company name in the HI.WPM file.

The words are displayed on the screen, which gives you the chance to make any corrections before ending the recording.

5 Press **Macro Define** (Ctrl-F10) when you finish typing to stop recording keystrokes.

⌨ *Select Macro from the Tools menu, then select* **Define***.*

The keystrokes are now ready to play back any time you need them.

6 Press **Enter** to start a new line.

7 Press **Macro** (Alt-F10).

⌨ *Select Macro from the Tools menu, then select* **Execute***.*

8 Enter **hi** to play back the keystrokes you recorded.

Because a computer processes information so rapidly, it probably looked as though "HALVA International" was retrieved to the screen. However, WordPerfect actually "typed" the keystrokes for you, even those you may have used when correcting the text with Backspace or Delete.

Important: *If you want to stop defining a macro and start over again, simply press Macro Define (Ctrl-F10) to stop recording keystrokes, then press Macro Define and enter the same macro name. Select* **Replace** *(1) from the menu that appears, then type "y" to answer Yes when you are asked if you want to replace the macro. You can then enter a description and begin recording keystrokes in a new file.*

Typing a Closing

Now that you have been introduced to the Macro feature, let's try using it to create a closing for a letter.

1 Press **Enter** to start a new line.

2 Press **Macro Define** (Ctrl-F10).

⌨ *Select Macro from the Tools menu, then select* **Define***.*

3 Enter **close** for the macro name, then press **Enter** for no description.

The "Macro Def" message begins blinking to let you know that WordPerfect is ready to record keystrokes.

4 Type **Sincere regards**, and press **Enter** four times.

5 Type your name, press **Enter** then type the following two lines:

President
HALVA International

6 When you finish, press **Macro Define** (Ctrl-F10) to end recording keystrokes.

⌨ *Select Macro from the Tools menu, then select* **Define***.*

Now, let's test the macro to see if it actually types the letter closing.

7 Press **Enter** to start a new line.

8 Press **Macro** (Alt-F10).

☐ *Select Macro from the Tools menu, then select Execute.*

9 Enter **close** for the macro name.

Notice that only the keystrokes you recorded are played back on the screen.

```
△ HALVA International
  HALVA International
  Sincere regards,


  President
  HALVA International
△ Sincere regards,


  President
  HALVA International_
```

Doc 1 Pg 1 Ln 3.17" Pos 2.9"

The two "HALVA International's" and the first closing are *not* part of the CLOSE.WPM macro. Only the keystrokes you type while "Macro Def" is blinking are recorded in the macro file.

10 Press **Exit** (F7), then type **n** twice to clear the screen.

Let's replace the closing to the MUSICBOX.WKB letter with the one you've created using the Macro feature.

11 Press **Retrieve** (Shift-F10), then enter **musicbox.wkb** to retrieve the letter.

☐ *Select Retrieve from the File menu.*

12 Press **Home,Home,↓** then move the cursor to the beginning of the "Sincerely yours," line.

13 Press **Delete to End of Page** (Ctrl-PgDn) and type **y** to delete the current closing.

14 Press **Macro** (Alt-F10).

☐ *Select Macro from the Tools menu, then select Execute.*

15 Enter **close** for the macro name.

Your closing is typed at the end of the letter, saving you time and keystrokes.

Inserting Format Codes

Characters are not the only keystrokes that can be recorded in a macro file. The same is true for *any* keystrokes you press—including the Format key. For example, you may always set the left and right margins to two inches and set full justification when creating letters.

By recording the keystrokes for the formats as a macro, you can save additional time when creating a letter.

1 Press **Home,Home,**↑ to move the cursor to the beginning of the letter.

2 Press **Macro Define** (Ctrl-F10).

   ⊟ *Select Macro from the Tools menu, then select Define.*

3 Enter **format** for the macro name, then press **Enter** for no description.

You are now ready to begin recording the keystrokes to set the margins and justification.

4 Press **Format** (Shift-F8).

   ⊟ *Select Line from the Layout menu.*

5 Select **L**ine (1), then select **M**argins Left/Right (7).

6 Enter **2** for the left margin, then enter **2** for the right margin.

7 Select **J**ustification (3), then select **F**ull (4).

8 Press **Exit** (F7) to return to the editing screen.

9 Press **Home,**↓ to display the text in the new margins, then press **Home,Home,**↑ to return the cursor to the beginning of the letter.

10 Press **Macro Define** to end recording keystrokes in the FORMAT.WPM file.

   ⊟ *Select Macro from the Tools menu, then select Define.*

11 Press **Reveal Codes** (Alt-F3) to display the codes at the beginning of the letter.

⌨ *Select* **R***eveal Codes from the* **E***dit menu.*

▲ LEFT/RIGHT MARGIN CODE

Ⓑ JUSTIFICATION CODE

```
            Ms. Heather Wilson
            Director of Sales
            Swiss America, Inc.
            1030 Harrington Blvd.
            Newark, NJ 07112

            Dear Ms. Wilson,

            After recently visiting the Sundheim booth at
            the WURLD trade exposition in Amsterdam, I was
            very impressed with both the quality and
C:\WP51\LEARN\MUSICBOX.WKB                    Doc 1 Pg 1 Ln 1" Pos 2"

[L/R Mar:2",2"][Just:Full]Ms. Heather Wilson[HRt]
Director of Sales[HRt]
Swiss America, Inc.[HRt]
1030 Harrington Blvd.[HRt]
Newark, NJ 07112[HRt]
[HRt]
Dear Ms. Wilson,[HRt]
[HRt]
After recently visiting the Sundheim booth at[SRt]
the WURLD trade exposition in Amsterdam, I was[SRt]

Press Reveal Codes to restore screen
```

Just like typing text when defining a macro, WordPerfect also inserts the formatting codes you select so that you can see exactly how the text will be formatted when you use the macro.

12 Press **Backspace** twice to delete the justification and margin codes.

13 Press **Reveal Codes** to display the normal editing screen.

⌨ *Select* **R***eveal Codes from the* **E***dit menu.*

14 Press **Macro** (Alt-F10).

⌨ *Select* **M***acro from the* **T***ools menu, then select* **E***xecute.*

15 Enter **format** to start the macro.

WordPerfect repeats the same keystrokes to change the margins, the justification, then reformats the text in the new margins.

16 Press **Exit**, then type **n** twice to clear the screen.

You could save the formatting codes as a WordPerfect document with Exit or Save, then retrieve the codes into a letter using List Files or Retrieve. However, you could *not* save the Home and arrow keys that reformat the text on the screen.

Retrieving a Memo Form

The memo you created in lesson 3 of the workbook is designed to save you time by providing a form that can be filled in whenever you want to create a memo. However, a macro could increase the convenience of the memo form by retrieving the form for you.

1 Press **Macro Define** (Ctrl-F10).

⊟ *Select* ***Macro*** *from the* ***Tools*** *menu, then select* ***Define***.

2 Enter **memo** for the name of the macro.

3 Enter **Retrieves memo form.** for the description.

4 Press **Retrieve** (Shift-F10), then enter **memo.wkb** to retrieve the memo form.

⊟ *Select* ***Retrieve*** *from the* ***File*** *menu.*

5 Press **Down Arrow** (↓) twice, then press **End** to move the cursor to the first place that you enter text.

6 Press **Macro Define** to end defining the macro.

⊟ *Select* ***Macro*** *from the* ***Tools*** *menu, then select* ***Define***.

7 Press **Exit** (F7), then type **n** twice to clear the screen.

Now that you have entered a description for the MEMO.WPM macro, you can see the description each time you use Look to view the macro from the List Files screen.

8 Press **List** (F5), type ***.wpm** to list only WordPerfect macros, then press **Enter** to display the macros on the screen.

The asterisk (*) can be used to represent several characters in a filename. By typing an asterisk and then an extension, only filenames with that extension are displayed.

```
09/23/89  11:35a              Directory C:\WP51\*.WPM
Document size:          0   Free: 15,151,104 Used:        541    Files:

.      Current   <Dir>              ..    Parent    <Dir>
CLOSE    .WPM       167  09/23/89 11:21a  FORMAT   .WPM      93  09/23/89 11:26a
HI       .WPM        99  09/23/89 11:07a  MEMO     .WPM     121  09/23/89 11:31a
WP{WP}   .WPM        61  02/01/89 10:04a




1 Retrieve; 2 Delete; 3 Move/Rename; 4 Print; 5 Short/Long Display;
6 Look; 7 Other Directory; 8 Copy; 9 Find; N Name Search: 6
```

9 Move the cursor to the MEMO.WPM filename, then press **Enter** to display the contents of the file.

The macro description is displayed at the top of the screen, with the macro keystrokes (displayed as special characters) below the hard page break.

A MACRO DESCRIPTION

B MACRO KEYSTROKES

```
File: C: WP51 MEMO.WPM                        Revised: 09/23/89 11:31a

A  Retrieves memo form.
   ==================================================================
B  n5Çl
   Ç


   _





   Look: 1 Next Doc; 2 Prev Doc: 0
```

Any time you are trying to find a particular macro, or have forgotten what a macro does, you can always check the Look screen for brief description of the macro (if you entered a description when creating the macro).

10 Press **Exit** twice to return to the editing screen.

The description can also be seen when editing a macro. For details on macro editing, turn to the Macros *heading in the* WordPerfect Reference Manual.

You are now ready to try using the macro to retrieve the memo form.

11 Press **Macro** (Alt-F10).

⌨ *Select* **Ma***cro from the* **T***ools menu, then select Execute.*

12 Enter **memo** to start the macro.

Not only is the memo form retrieved, but the cursor is moved to the exact location you need to start filling in the memo.

13 Press **Exit**, then type **n** twice to clear the screen.

Filling In a Memo Form

Before finishing the lesson, you may want to become more familiar with another Macro feature that can help you to automate filling in a document such as a memo form.

Let's create the same MEMO macro again, but this time add a feature that pauses at each place where information is filled in.

1 Press **Macro Define** (Ctrl-F10).

⌨ *Select* **Ma***cro from the* **T***ools menu, then select* **De***fine.*

2 Enter **memo** for the macro name.

Because the MEMO.WPM macro already exists, WordPerfect displays a menu with a choice of replacing the old macro with the new one, editing the macro in a special editing screen, or editing the description.

3 Select **R**eplace (1), then type **y** to replace the MEMO.WPM macro.

4 Enter **Retrieves memo form and pauses.** for the description.

You can now begin recording new keystrokes for the same macro.

5 Press **Retrieve** (Shift-F10), then enter **memo.wkb** to retrieve the memo form.

⬚ *Select **R**etrieve from the File menu.*

6 Press **Down Arrow** (↓) twice, then press **End** to move the cursor to the end of the To: line.

7 Press **Macro Commands** (Ctrl-PgUp) to display a menu of macro commands.

```
                        Corporate Memo
        To:
        From:
        Date:      September 23, 1989
        Subject:

                   ----------------------------------------
```

▶1 Pause; 2 Display; 3 Assign; 4 Comment: 0

The macro commands provide extra power and flexibility when creating macros. For example, the Pause option pauses a macro while it is running to let you type text from the keyboard.

8 Select **P**ause (1), then press **Enter** to let WordPerfect know you want to continue defining the macro.

9 Press **Down Arrow** twice to move the cursor to the end of the From: line.

10 Press **Macro Commands** (Ctrl-PgUp), select **P**ause, then press **Enter** to let WordPerfect know you want to continue defining the macro.

11 Press **Down Arrow** four times to move the cursor to the end of the Subject: line.

12 Press **Macro Commands**, select **P**ause, then press **Enter** to let WordPerfect know you want to continue defining the macro.

13 Press **Home,Home,↓** to move the cursor to the end of the memo, then press **Macro Define** to end defining the macro.

⊟ *Select Macro from the Tools menu, then select Define.*

14 Press **Exit** (F7), then type **n** twice to clear the screen.

Try using the MEMO.WPM macro (Alt-F10) to fill in the memo form. As soon as you press Enter, the cursor will move to the next title. When the cursor moves to the end of the memo, the macro ends and you can fill in the text of the memo. You can either save the memo (do *not* use the MEMO filename) or simply clear the screen with Exit.

This lesson has introduced you to a few ways that macros can help you automate WordPerfect for office or home use. While there are many other options and commands you can use to build very elaborate macros, creating a simple macro may be all you ever need to make your time at the computer with WordPerfect more pleasant and productive.

Lesson 16: Formatting a Newsletter — Part I

Newsletters are a popular way of providing information to a group of people. In this lesson you begin creating a newsletter by formatting three articles with features such as Graphics and Newspaper Columns. You are also introduced to some ideas that can help you create a more professional-looking newsletter.

Important: *For lessons 16 and 17 to work properly, the WORKBOOK.PRS file needs to be in your WordPerfect directory (i.e., C:\WP51). If you copied the LEARN files during installation, then the WORKBOOK.PRS file should already be in the correct directory.*

Displaying Longer Lines

Let's begin by retrieving the three articles for the newsletter.

1 Press **Retrieve** (Shift-F10), then enter **newstext.wkb** to retrieve the three newsletter articles.

⌨ *Select **R**etrieve from the **F**ile menu.*

Notice that the lines in the newsletter paragraphs are longer than the screen.

▲ LINES LONGER THAN SCREEN

```
  Sales Up by Two Million

▷ Record sales of the new line of music boxes has boosted first quarter revenues t
  the tune of 2 million dollars.  It is expected that by the year 1995, one out of
  3 people in the United States and Canada will own a music box.

  On the drawing boards are music box watches, dash-board models for cars,
  waterproof boxes for showers, ultra-light boxes for backpackers, and even an
  amplified music box that plays a disco version of "Que Sera Sera."

  Music boxes with figurines depicting the following occupational motifs will be
  available in June:

  Airline Navigators
  Dog Trainers
  Lottery Winners
  Mercenaries
  Quilters

  Research indicates that the upsurge in purchasing music boxes stems from a trend
  towards the traditional.  In addition, the actual music has been found to be
  beneficial to the physical well-being.

▷ After extensive testing, Dr. Hugo Nebula, famous tonal physicist, claims that th
  C:\WP51\LEARN\NEWSTEXT.WKB                        Doc 1 Pg 1 Ln 1" Pos 1"
```

Whenever you retrieve a document into the editing screen, WordPerfect displays each line with the words that will be printed in that line. The number of words (or characters) in a line depends on which font is selected for your printer.

Most computer screens display 80 characters in a line—enough room to display all the words in a line for a standard font such as Courier 12 cpi (characters per inch). However, if you are using a font that prints *more than* 80 characters in a line, WordPerfect may only be able to display part of the line at a time.

For an explanation of how character spacing in a font can affect the number of characters printed in a line, turn to the Fixed Pitch and Proportional Spacing *exercise in* lesson 12 *of the workbook.*

The newsletter articles were created using a Helvetica 10pt font, which means that there are more characters in the paragraph lines than can be displayed on your screen at one time.

2 Press **Down Arrow** (↓) twice, then press **Home,**→ to move the cursor to the right edge of the screen.

The cursor moves to edge of the screen, but *not* to the end of the line.

3 Press **Home,**→ again.

This time the entire page shifts to the left, so that you can see the end of every line on the screen.

⚠ ENDS OF LINES

```
on

ew line of music boxes has boosted first quarter revenues to_
  dollars.  It is expected that by the year 1995, one out of every
d States and Canada will own a music box.                    ⚠

  are music box watches, dash-board models for cars,
showers, ultra-light boxes for backpackers, and even an
hat plays a disco version of "Que Sera Sera."

rines depicting the following occupational motifs will be




at the upsurge in purchasing music boxes stems from a trend
al.  In addition, the actual music has been found to be
sical well-being.

ng, Dr. Hugo Nebula, famous tonal physicist, claims that the ◁
C:\WP51\LEARN\NEWSTEXT.WKB                    Doc 1 Pg 1 Ln 1.33" Pos 7.25"
```

4 Press **Home,**← three times to return to the left margin of the page.

Pressing Home once then Left or Right Arrow shifts the page to the left or the right a section at a time. However, pressing Home twice with the Left or Right Arrow can shift the entire page in one movement.

5 Press **Home,Home,**→ then press **Home,Home,**← to shift the page between the right and left margins.

6 Press **Up Arrow** (↑) twice to move to the "Sales Up by Two Million" headline.

7 Press **Home,Home,**→ to move the cursor to the end of the line.

WordPerfect only moves the cursor to the end of the line, even when using the Home key twice. If you want to shift the entire page to the left or right when displaying longer lines, you should always make sure that the cursor is in a line that extends beyond the screen.

8 Press **Home,←** to move the cursor to the beginning of the headline.

Now that you know how to move through longer lines on your screen, let's begin formatting the newsletter.

Creating a Full Page Border

You have already used the Graphics feature to create a horizontal line for a footer (lesson 14). Another way of using Graphics is to create a box with a border.

1 Select **Graphics** (Alt-F9), select **F**igure (1), then select **C**reate (1).

⊞ *Select **Figure** from the Graphics menu, then select **Create**.*

Whenever you select Figure, you are creating a box that you can fill with text, a graphics figure, an equation, etc. The menu that appears when you select Create lets you change the contents, size, and position of the box on the page.

```
Definition: Figure
      1 - Filename
      2 - Contents          Empty
      3 - Caption
      4 - Anchor Type        Paragraph
      5 - Vertical Position  0"
      6 - Horizontal Position Right
      7 - Size               3.25" wide x 3.25" (high)
      8 - Wrap Text Around Box Yes
      9 - Edit


Selection: 0
```

For the newsletter, you simply want an empty, full page box that prints a border around the text on the page.

2 Select Anchor **T**ype (4), select **P**age (2), then press **Enter** to have the box stay on the current page.

3 Select **V**ertical Position (5), then select **F**ull Page (1) to create a box the size of the margins.

4 Select **W**rap Text Around Box (8), then type **n** for No, to have the box and the newsletter articles printed together on the same page.

5 Press **Exit** (F7) to return to the editing screen.

6 Press **Reveal Codes** (Alt-F3) to display the codes in the newsletter.

⌨ *Select* **R***eveal Codes from the* **E***dit menu.*

A Figure code is placed at the cursor position (top of the page) that creates a border around the text that can be seen in the View Document screen.

▲ FIGURE CODE

```
Sales Up by Two Million

Record sales of the new line of music boxes has boosted first quarter revenues t
the tune of 2 million dollars.  It is expected that by the year 1995, one out of
3 people in the United States and Canada will own a music box.

On the drawing boards are music box watches, dash-board models for cars,
waterproof boxes for showers, ultra-light boxes for backpackers, and even an
amplified music box that plays a disco version of "Que Sera Sera."

Music boxes with figurines depicting the following occupational motifs will be
C:\WP51\LEARN\NEWSTEXT.WKB                          Doc 1 Pg 1 Ln 1" Pos 1"
[▲    ▲    ▲    ▲    ▲    ▲    ▲    ▲    ▲    ▲    ▲    )    ▲    ▲ ]
[Figure:1;;]Sales Up by Two Million[HRt]
[HRt]      ▲
Record sales of the new line of music boxes has boosted first quarter revenues t
o[SRt]
the tune of 2 million dollars.  It is expected that by the year 1995, one out of
 every[SRt]
3 people in the United States and Canada will own a music box.[HRt]
[HRt]
On the drawing boards are music box watches, dash[-]board models for cars,[SRt]
waterproof boxes for showers, ultra[-]light boxes for backpackers, and even an[S

Press Reveal Codes to restore screen
```

7 Press **Print** (Shift-F7), select **V**iew Document (6), then select Full Page (3).

⌨ *Select* **P***rint from the* **F***ile menu.*

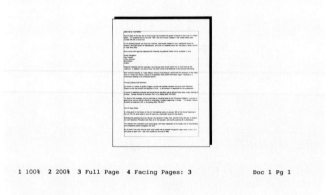

1 100% 2 200% **3** Full Page **4** Facing Pages: 3   Doc 1 Pg 1

Important: *If you do not have a graphics card in your computer, then you will not be able to see the Graphics features (or the Font attributes in lesson 17) displayed. However, you can print the document to see the results of these features.*

Although the newsletter articles and the border of the Figure box are displayed (and printed) together on the same page, the articles are *not* inside or part of the box. If you had selected Yes in step 4 to have the text wrap around the box, then the box border would be printed on page 1 by itself, with the newsletter articles moved to page 2.

By selecting No for text wrapping, you are telling WordPerfect to overlay (print) the box border on *top* of the newsletter articles.

8 Select 200% (2) for a closer look at the border and text.

Setting the Margins

Notice that the edges of the text are touching the border of the full page box.

A NEWSLETTER TEXT

B BOX BORDER

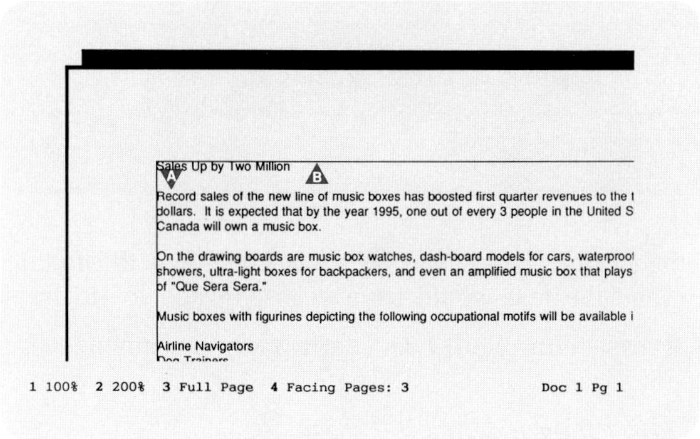

Because the box border and the text are using the same margin settings, the text completely fills the inside of the box. You can add space between the border and the text by increasing the size of the margins surrounding the text.

1 Press **Exit** (F7) to return to the editing screen.

2 Make sure that the cursor is on the letter "S" in "Sales" (to the right of the Figure code), then press **Format** (Shift-F8) and select **Line** (1).

*Select **L**ine from the **L**ayout menu.*

3 Select **M**argins Left/Right (7), enter **1.25** for the left margin, then enter **1.25** for the right margin.

4 Press **Enter** to return to the main Format menu.

5 Select **P**age (2), select **M**argins Top/Bottom (5), then enter **1.25** for the top margin and **1.25** for the bottom margin.

6 Press **Exit** (F7) to return to the editing screen.

Notice that the Margin codes are placed between the Figure code and the text.

```
Sales Up by Two Million

Record sales of the new line of music boxes has boosted first quarter revenues
the tune of 2 million dollars.  It is expected that by the year 1995, one out
3 people in the United States and Canada will own a music box.

On the drawing boards are music box watches, dash-board models for cars,
waterproof boxes for showers, ultra-light boxes for backpackers, and even an
amplified music box that plays a disco version of "Que Sera Sera."

Music boxes with figurines depicting the following occupational motifs will be
C:\WP51\LEARN\NEWSTEXT.WKB                    Doc 1 Pg 1 Ln 1.25" Pos 1.25"
▬▬▬▬▬▬▬▬▬▬▬▬▬▬▬▬▬▬▬▬▬▬▬▬▬▬▬▬▬▬▬▬▬▬▬▬▬▬▬▬▬▬▬▬▬▬▬▬▬▬▬
{         ▲      ▲      ▲    ▲      ▲     ▲    ▲    ▲   }     ▲
[Figure:1;;][L/R Mar:1.25",1.25"][T/B Mar:1.25",1.25"]Sales Up by Two Million[HR
t]
[HRt]       ▲                  ▲
Record sales of the new line of music boxes has boosted first quarter revenues t
o[SRt]
the tune of 2 million dollars.  It is expected that by the year 1995, one out of
 every[SRt]
3 people in the United States and Canada will own a music box.[HRt]
[HRt]
On the drawing boards are music box watches, dash[-]board models for cars,[SRt]

Press Reveal Codes to restore screen
```

If the Margin codes had been placed *before* the Figure code, then both the box and the text would have been adjusted to fit the new margins.

7 Press **Print** (Shift-F7), select **V**iew Document (6), then select Full Page (3).

⌨ Select **Print** from the **File** menu.

A quarter inch of space surrounds the articles between the border and the text. This type of space is called "white space," and always helps to make the page look more inviting to read.

8 Press **Exit** (F7) to return to the editing screen.

Setting the Newspaper Columns

Most newsletters place the articles in at least two columns across the page. The columns not only make the page look more interesting, but the shorter lines in the columns are easier to read.

1 Press **Columns/Table** (Alt-F7), select **C**olumns (1), then select **D**efine (3).

⌨ Select **Columns** from the **Layout** menu, then select **Define**.

There are two newspaper columns set up in the Text Column Definition menu. The margins for both columns are set from the left margin (1.25" to

4" and 4.5" to 7.25"). The two columns are equal in width (3.25") with a half inch of space between the columns (4" to 4.5").

```
Text Column Definition

    1 - Type                        Newspaper

    2 - Number of Columns          ▶2

    3 - Distance Between Columns

    4 - Margins

    Column    Left      Right      Column    Left      Right
      1:      1.25"     4"           13:
      2:      4.5"      7.25"        14:
      3:      A         A            15:
      4:                             16:
      5:                             17:
      6:                             18:
      7:                             19:
      8:                             20:
      9:                             21:
     10:                             22:
     11:                             23:
     12:                             24:

    Selection: 0
```

The 1.25" margins that you set for the text are reflected in the margins for the columns. Text columns are always calculated using the current margin settings.

2 Press **Exit** (F7) to leave the Text Column definition menu.

3 Select **On** (1) to turn on the Newspaper columns.

A Column Define and Column On code have been added to the other formatting codes at the beginning of the newsletter. Notice that a "Col 1" message is displayed on the status line with the rest of the cursor position indicators.

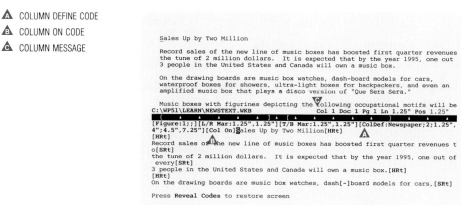

The Col message appears whenever the cursor is in text columns between the Column On and Column Off codes. The message lets you know in which column on the page the cursor is located.

4 Press **Print** (Shift-F7), then select **View** Document (6) to display the newsletter in columns.

⌨ *Select* **Print** *from the* **File** *menu.*

You may want to select 100% or 200% to move in for a closer look at the page.

5 When you finish, press **Exit** to return to the normal editing screen.

Creating a Masthead
Now that the basic format of the page has been set, let's try adding a masthead for the newsletter that is centered above the columns.

1 Place the cursor on the [Col On] code, press **Enter** twice, then press **Up Arrow** (↑).

Notice that both columns moved down the page when you pressed Enter. The Column On code marks the beginning of the columns—not the Column Define code. Once you define text columns, you can place the Column On code anywhere in the document to start formatting text in columns.

2 Press **Center** (Shift-F6), type **HALVA Herald** for the masthead, then press **Enter** twice for double spacing.

A horizontal line would help to separate the masthead from the newsletter articles. And the quickest way to create a horizontal line is with Graphics.

3 Press **Graphics** (Alt-F9), select **Line** (5), then select **Horizontal** (1).

⌨ *Select* **Line** *from the* **Graphics** *menu, then select* **Create Horizontal**.

4 Press **Exit** (F7) to use the settings in the Horizontal Line menu.

5 Press **Enter** to add extra spacing.

6 Press **Print** (Shift-F7), select **View** Document (6), then select **Full Page** (3).

⌨ *Select* **Print** *from the* **File** *menu.*

Moving in Columns

Notice that the headline for the second article is at the bottom of the first column.

⚠ SECOND ARTICLE HEADLINE

```
1 100%  2 200%  3 Full Page  4 Facing Pages: 3            Doc 1 Pg 1
```

It should be placed at the top of the second column with the rest of the article.

1 Press **Exit** (F7) to return to the editing screen.

2 Press **Reveal Codes** (Alt-F3) to display the normal editing screen.

⊞ *Select Reveal Codes from the Edit menu.*

3 Press **Repeat** (Esc) then **Down Arrow** (↓) to move the cursor past the Column On code and into the first article.

Once you are in columns (and the Col message is displayed on the status line), each column is seen by WordPerfect as a separate page.

4 Press **Go To** (Ctrl-Home) then **Down Arrow** (↓) to move the cursor to the bottom of the first column.

⊞ *Select Goto from the Search menu.*

The cursor moves to the bottom of the first column instead of the bottom of the page (the end of the second column).

5 Press **Hard Page** (Ctrl-Enter) to move the headline of the second article to the top of the second column.

Pressing Hard Page starts a second column instead of a new page. And because each column has its own left and right margins, using the Left and Right Arrows with Home only moves the cursor between the margins in a column.

6 Press **Down Arrow** (↓) twice, then press **Home,Home,**→ to move the cursor to the end of the line.

7 Press **Home,Home,**← to move the cursor to the beginning of the line.

The cursor only moves as far as the left margin of the second column, then stops. To move back into the first column you need to use Go To.

8 Press **Go To** (Ctrl-Home) then press **Left Arrow** (←) to move the cursor to the first column.

⌨ *Select Goto from the Search menu.*

Although using Home with the Left and Right Arrows is limited to the margins of a column, using Home with the Up and Down Arrows still moves the cursor up and down the entire page.

9 Press **Home,Home,**↑ to move the cursor to the beginning of the newsletter.

Saving the Newsletter

With the articles in columns, a border around the articles, and a masthead at the top of the page, you are ready to end the lesson by saving the formatted newsletter.

1 Press **Exit** (F7), type **y** to save the newsletter, then enter **newsltr** for the filename.

⌨ *Select Exit from the File menu.*

2 Type **n** to clear the screen and stay in WordPerfect.

Like formatting a letter (lessons 13 and 14), formatting a newsletter gives you a chance to see how WordPerfect features work together to give you a more professional-looking document. At the same time, you also learn that setting one format (e.g., a full page border) may require you to change another format (e.g., margins) in a document.

Lesson 17: Formatting a Newsletter — Part II

In this lesson you finish formatting the newsletter by using the Font key to change both the size and appearance of text. You are also introduced to base fonts, page numbering formats, and how to print a border on each page of a newsletter.

Attributes and Fonts

Let's begin by retrieving the newsletter you formatted in lesson 16, then take a look at the features available on the Font key.

1 Press **Retrieve** (Shift-F10), then enter **newsltr** to retrieve the formatted newsletter.

Bold and Underline are attributes that let you change the appearance of printed text. How the text is actually bolded or underlined depends on what resources are available at your printer.

For example, some printers have a darker font that WordPerfect can use for bolding text. When a printer does not have a bold font, WordPerfect may bold the text by causing the printer to strike each character three or four times.

Besides Bold and Underline, you can also use several other attributes that let you change both the size and appearance of printed text.

2 Press **Font** (Ctrl-F8), then select **Size** (1) to display a menu of the size attributes.

⌨ *The size attributes are listed on the Font menu.*

The size attributes are Superscript, Subscript, Fine, Small, Large, Very Large, and Extra Large.

You can format text with any of the size attributes. However, what your printer can actually do depends on what fonts are available.

For example, if you select Large for a headline, then select Very Large for the masthead, your printer may only be able to print one size for both selections because there is only one larger font at the printer.

3 Press **Exit** (F7) to exit the Size attributes menu.

4 Press **Font** and select Appearance (2) to display a menu of the appearance attributes.

⌨ *Select Appearance from the Font menu.*

The appearance attributes are Bold, Underline, Double Underline, Italic, Outline, Shadow, Small Caps, Redline, and Strikeout.

You can format text with any of the appearance attributes, but (just like the size attributes) what actually happens on the printed page depends on the capabilities of your printer.

5 Press **Exit** to exit the Appearance attributes menu.

6 Press **Font**, then select Base **F**ont (4) to display a list of fonts available for the Workbook printer.

⌨ *Select Base Font from the Font menu.*

The current font selected for the newspaper articles is Helvetica 10pt (marked with an asterisk).

▲ CURRENT FONT

```
Base Font

    Courier 10cpi
    Courier 10cpi Italic
    Helvetica  6pt
    Helvetica  6pt Italic
    Helvetica  8pt
    Helvetica  8pt Italic
  ▶ *Helvetica 10pt
    Helvetica 10pt Italic
    Helvetica 12pt
    Helvetica 12pt Italic
    Helvetica 15pt
    Helvetica 15pt Italic
    Helvetica 18pt
    Helvetica 18pt Italic
    Roman   6pt
    Roman   6pt Italic
    Roman   8pt
    Roman   8pt Italic
    Roman  10pt
    Roman  10pt Italic
    Roman  12pt

  1 Select; N Name search: 1
```

There are several fonts smaller and larger than 10 points (1 point = 1/72 of an inch), so WordPerfect is able to provide a font for each size attribute when using Helvetica.

However, if you were printing the newspaper articles with Helvetica 18pt, WordPerfect could not print larger text for Large, Very Large, and Extra Large because 18 points is already the largest font available.

The list also includes italic Helvetica fonts, which means WordPerfect can print italicized text for the same sizes of fonts.

7 Press **Exit** to return to the editing screen.

Formatting the Masthead and Headlines

Now that you have been introduced to fonts and attributes, let's try using some of the attributes to format the masthead and headlines.

1 Move the cursor to the beginning of the "HALVA Herald" masthead.

2 Press **Block** (Alt-F4), then press **Home,**→ to block the masthead.

> ▢ *Block the masthead by holding down the left mouse button and dragging the mouse pointer to the end of the line.*

3 Press **Font** (Ctrl-F8), select **S**ize (1), then select **E**xtra Large (7).

> ▢ *Select **E**xtra Large from the **F**ont menu.*

4 Press **Reveal Codes** (Alt-F3) to display the codes for the formatted masthead.

> ▢ *Select **R**eveal Codes from the **E**dit menu.*

An [EXT LARGE] code appears at the beginning of the masthead, with an [ext large] code at the end of the masthead.

HALVA Herald_

Sales Up by Two Million   Training Classes and Seminars

Record sales of the new line of   Our fourth in a series of guided
music boxes has boosted first   imagery revivals will mentally
quarter revenues to the tune of 2   transport everyone from Pokorney
million dollars. It is expected that   Stadium to the rain forests and
C:\WP51\LEARN\NEWSLTR   Doc 1 Pg 1 Ln 1.42" Pos 5.29"

[Figure:1;;][L/R Mar:1.25",1.25"][T/B Mar:1.25",1.25"][Col Def:Newspaper ;2;1.25
",4";4.5",7.25"][HRt]
[Center][EXT LARGE]HALVA Herald[ext large][HRt]
[HRt]
[HLine:Full,Baseline,6",0.013",100%][HRt]
[HRt]
[Col On]Sales Up by Two Million[HRt]
[HRt]
Record sales of the new line of[SRt]
music boxes has boosted first[SRt]

Press **Reveal Codes** to restore screen

Just like Bold and Underline, each attribute surrounds the text with an on and off code that lets WordPerfect know when to begin and end formatting the text.

This type of code is called a "paired" code in WordPerfect. Other formatting codes that are inserted one at a time (e.g., Margins, Line Spacing) are called "open" codes because you need to insert another formatting code for the same feature before WordPerfect ends the current setting and begins using another setting.

5 Press **Block**, then press **Go To** (Ctrl-Home) twice to highlight the masthead.

By using Go To with Block, you can highlight the same text again to make it easier to format the text with more than one feature.

6 Press **Font** (Ctrl-F8), select **A**ppearance (2), then select Shadow (6).

> ▢ *Select **A**ppearance from the **F**ont menu, then select Sha**d**ow.*

A pair of Shadow codes has been included with the Extra Large codes to format the text.

7 Press **Reveal Codes** to display the normal editing screen.

⌨ *Select **R**eveal Codes from the **E**dit menu.*

With the masthead formatted, let's try formatting the headlines with the Bold and Large attributes.

8 Place the cursor at the beginning of the "Sales Up by Two Million" headline.

9 Press **Block**, press **End** to highlight the entire headline, then press **Bold** (F6).

⌨ *Block the headline by holding down the left mouse button and dragging the mouse pointer to the end. Select **A**ppearance from the **F**ont menu, then select **B**old.*

The Bold attribute can be selected by using the Bold key or the appearance attributes on the Font key or Font pull-down menu. The same is true of the Underline attribute.

10 Press **Block** then press **Go To** (Ctrl-Home) twice to highlight the same headline.

11 Press **Font**, select **S**ize, then select **L**arge (5).

⌨ *Select **L**arge from the **F**ont menu.*

There are two more headlines that need to be formatted with the Bold and Large attributes. If you need help formatting the headlines, use steps 8 through 11 as a guide. Remember that to move to the second column, you need to press Go To then the Right Arrow.

12 Format the "Training Classes and Seminars" and "HALVA Goes Retail" headlines with the Bold and Large attributes.

13 When you finish formatting the headlines, press **Home,Home,↑** to return to the beginning of the report.

14 Press **Print** (Shift-F7), select **V**iew Document (6), then select 100% (1) to display the results.

15 Select 200% (2) for a closer look at the masthead.

WordPerfect is creating a shadow effect by printing the same text twice with a slight offset.

16 Press **Exit** (F7) to return to the editing screen.

Whenever a font is not available for an appearance attribute, WordPerfect tries to use the capabilities of your printer to produce the same effect.

Changing the Base Font

The newsletter is formatted with a Helvetica 10pt font, which means that WordPerfect will try to use only Helvetica fonts for the size and appearance attributes.

What happens if you decide to change the font for the newsletter to a different style (typeface)?

1 Press **Home,Home,↑** to make sure the cursor is at the beginning of the newsletter.

2 Press **Font** (Ctrl-F8), then select Base **F**ont (4).

⊟ *Select Base Font from the Font menu.*

3 Press **Down Arrow** (↓) until the cursor highlights the Roman 10pt font.

4 Press **Enter** to select the font, then press **Reveal Codes** (Alt-F3) to display the Font code.

⊟ *Select **R**eveal Codes from the **E**dit menu.*

▲ BASE FONT CODE

```
                              HALVA Herald

    Sales Up by Two Million              Training Classes and
                                         Seminars
    Record sales of the new line of
    music boxes has boosted first        Our fourth in a series of guided
    quarter revenues to the tune of 2    imagery revivals will mentally
    million dollars.  It is expected that transport everyone from Pokorney
C:\WP51\LEARN\NEWSLTR                              Doc 1 Pg 1 Ln 1.25" Pos 1.25"
    {        ▲        ▲        ▲        ▲        ▲        ▲        ▲        }
[Figure:1;;][L/R Mar:1.25",1.25"][T/B Mar:1.25",1.25"][ColDef:Newspaper;2;1.25",
4";4.5",7.25"][Font:Roman 10pt][HRt]
[Center][EXT LARGE][SHADW]HALVA Herald[ext large][shadw][HRt]
[HRt]
[HLine:Full,Baseline,6",0.013",100%][HRt]
[HRt]
[Col On][LARGE][BOLD]Sales Up by Two Million[bold][large][HRt]
[HRt]
Record sales of the new line of[SRt]
music boxes has boosted first[SRt]

Press Reveal Codes to restore screen
```

The Font code not only changes the text of the newsletter to Roman 10pt, but changes the fonts WordPerfect uses for the attributes to the Roman typeface.

5 Press **Print** (Shift-F7), select **V**iew Document (6), then select 200% (2).

⊟ *Select **P**rint from the **F**ile menu.*

Notice that characters such as "H," "T," and "M" have short, horizontal lines (serifs) at the top and/or bottom of the letters in the Roman typeface.

▷ **HALVA Herald**

Sales Up by Two Million

Record sales of the new line of
music boxes has boosted first
quarter revenues to the tune of 2
million dollars. It is expected that

Training Classes and Seminars

Our fourth in a series of gu
imagery revivals will menta
transport everyone from Po

1 100%   2 200%   3 Full Page   4 Facing Pages: 2   Doc 1 Pg 1

6 Press **Exit** (F7) to return to the editing screen, then press **Backspace** to delete the Font code.

7 Press **Print**, then select **V**iew Document to see the same text in the original Helvetica typeface.

⌨ *Select Print from the File menu.*

Notice that the short lines (serifs) at the top and the bottom of the characters are gone, and that the typeface is simpler.

▷ **HALVA Herald**

Sales Up by Two Million

Record sales of the new line of
music boxes has boosted first
quarter revenues to the tune of 2
million dollars. It is expected that

Training Classes and Seminars

Our fourth in a series of g
imagery revivals will ment
transport everyone from P
Stadium to the rain forest

1 100%   2 200%   3 Full Page   4 Facing Pages: 2   Doc 1 Pg 1

8 Press **Exit** to return to the editing screen.

9 Make sure the cursor is in the same place, press **Cancel** (F1), then select **R**estore (1) to insert the Font code for Roman 10pt.

Select Undelete from the Edit menu, then select Restore.

10 Press **Reveal Codes** to display the normal editing screen.

Select Reveal Codes from the Edit menu.

The list of fonts are called "Base Fonts" because each time you use the list to change a font, both the text of the document *and* the attributes are adjusted for the new font.

If you select a larger base font, then WordPerfect tries to use larger fonts for the size attributes. If you select a base font with a different typeface, then WordPerfect tries to use fonts for the attributes that match the new typeface.

If the same typeface is not available for an attribute, then whatever fonts are available are used for the attribute (no matter what the typeface).

Placing a Line Chart in the First Article

Drawings, charts, and graphs are often used in a newsletter to help emphasize the information in an article. Let's add some interest to the first article by including a line chart showing the predicted growth of music box customers.

1 Move the cursor to the beginning of the first paragraph in the "Sales Up by Two Million" article.

2 Press **Graphics** (Alt-F9), select **F**igure (1), then select **C**reate (1).

Select Figure from the Graphics menu, then select Create.

You have already created an empty graphics box to use as a border around the newsletter. This time you will fill a box with a graphics image.

3 Select **F**ilename (1), then enter **graph.wpg** for the name of the graph to place in the box.

The Contents setting has changed from "Empty" to "Graphic" to let you know that there is a graphic image in the box.

The anchor type is "Paragraph" which keeps the graph with the first paragraph of the article during editing. The rest of the settings place the graph at the right side of the column with text wrapping around the left side of the box.

4 Press **Exit** (F7) to return to the editing screen, then press **Down Arrow** (↓) to reformat the text on the screen.

Notice that a "Figure 2" box is displayed in the place where the graph will be printed in the paragraph (Figure 1 is the border of the newsletter).

▲ FIGURE 2 BOX

```
                                    HALVA Herald

        Sales Up by Two Million                    the lumbar region, resulti
                                                    harmonious healing of the
        Record sales of    ┌FIG 2──────────        emotional psyche.
        the new line of  ▲ │
        music boxes        │
        has boosted        │
        first quarter      │
        revenues to the    │
        tune of 2          │
        million dollars.   │
        It is expected     │
        that by the        └───────────────
        year 1995, one out of every 3
        people in the United States and
        Canada will own a music box.

        On the drawing boards are music
        box watches, dash-board models for
        cars, waterproof boxes for showers,
C:\WP51\LEARN\NEWSLTR                   Col 1 Doc 1 Pg 1 Ln 4.76" Pos 1.25"
```

You can also see that the second (and third) articles are missing from the second column. Where are they?

5 Press **Page Down** (PgDn) to display the missing articles.

When you added the graphics box, text from the first article spilled over into the second column. Because there was a Hard Page break at the top of the second column, the rest of the newsletter moved to the beginning of the second page.

6 Press **Backspace** to erase the Hard Page break at the beginning of the second article.

The rest of the newsletter returns to the second column, and fills in the first page.

7 Press **Print** (Shift-F7), select **V**iew Document (6), then select Full Page (3).

⌨ Select **Print** from the **F**ile menu.

Moving the Line Chart

The line chart makes the newsletter look more interesting. However, the chart could be moved down into the paragraph to have the text wrap around the top and sides of the chart.

1 Press **Exit** (F7) to return to the editing screen.

2 Press **Graphics** (Alt-F9), select **F**igure (1), select **E**dit (2), then enter **2** to edit the graphics box for figure 2 (the line chart).

⌨ Select **Figure** from the **Graphics** menu, then select **Edit**.

3 Select **Vertical Position** (5), then enter **.5** to place the figure box one-half inch down into the paragraph.

A caption could also be added to the figure box to label the chart.

4 Select **Caption** (3), then press **Backspace** to erase the figure number provided by WordPerfect.

The Box Caption editing screen gives you the same flexibility as editing screens for headers and footers. You can even use the attributes on the Font key.

5 Press **Bold** (F6) to bold the caption.

⌨ *Select Appearance from the Font menu, then select **B**old.*

6 Press **Font** (Ctrl-F8), select **Size** (1), then select **Small** (4).

⌨ *Select Small from the Font menu.*

7 Type **Music Box Sales Soar** for the caption, then press **Exit** (F7) twice to return to the normal editing screen.

8 Press **Print** (Shift-F7), then select **View Document** (6).

⌨ *Select Print from the File menu.*

9 Select **200%** (2), then press **Down Arrow** (↓) four times for a closer view of the graph and caption.

The figure box has been moved one-half inch into the paragraph, and is surrounded on the top, left, and bottom by text from the first and second paragraphs.

Ⓐ ONE-HALF INCH
Ⓑ GRAPHICS BOX

Sales Up by Two Million

Record sales of the new line of music boxes has boosted first quarter revenues ▼▲the tune of 2 million dollars.
It is expected that by the year 1995, one out of every 3 people in the United States and Canada will own a music box.

Ⓑ

Music Box Sales Soar

On the drawing boards are music box watches, dash-board models for cars, waterproof

the lumbar region, resulting i harmonious healing of the emotional psyche.

Training Classes and Seminars

Our fourth in a series of guid imagery revivals will mentall transport everyone from Poko Stadium to the rain forests an beaches of Kuai. (A $5 dona requested for the experience.,

A course in telephone etiquet actual phone operation will b offered three times a day star on Monday. Contact Wendy extension 345, or by dialing (

1 100%   2 200%   3 Full Page   4 Facing Pages: 2   Doc 1 Pg 1

Placing the Full Page Border in a Header

Now that a graph has been added, part of the last article has moved to a second page.

1 Select Full Page (3), then press **Page Down** (PgDn).

▲ LAST ARTICLE

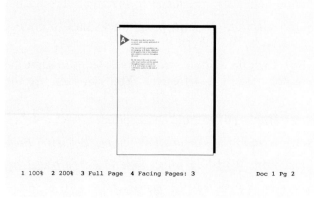

```
1 100%   2 200%   3 Full Page   4 Facing Pages: 3                    Doc 1 Pg 2
```

Let's return to the editing screen and add a border to the second page.

2 Press **Exit** (F7), then press **Page Up** (PgUp) to move to the top of the first page.

3 Press **Reveal Codes** (Alt-F3).

⌨ *Select **R**eveal Codes from the **E**dit menu.*

4 Press **Block** (Alt-F4), then press **Right Arrow** (→) to block the Figure 1 code.

5 Press **Move** (Ctrl-F4), select **B**lock (1), then select **C**opy (2).

6 Press **Page Down** (PgDn) to move the cursor to the beginning of the second page, then press **Enter** to retrieve the Figure code.

You have now copied the same box used for the border on the first page to the top of the second page. The figure number has been updated to "3" to let you know that the box is the third figure in the newsletter.

7 Press **Print** (Shift-F7), then select **V**iew Document (6).

⌨ *Select **P**rint from the **F**ile menu.*

You may have expected the box to frame the entire page (as it did on the first page). However, because each column is a "page," the "Full Page" box only frames a single column.

▲ FULL PAGE BOX
ⒶＡ FIRST COLUMN

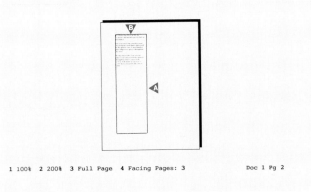

1 100% 2 200% 3 Full Page 4 Facing Pages: 3   Doc 1 Pg 2

The graphics box on the first page frames the entire page because the Figure 1 code comes *before* the Column On code.

A simple way of solving the problem is to include the graphics box in a header. Then each page will have a border printed the size of the full page.

8 Press **Exit** to return to the editing screen.

9 Press **Delete** (Del) to delete the Figure 3 code.

10 Press **Page Up** and **Delete** (Del) to delete the Figure 1 code.

11 Press **Format** (Shift-F8) and select **P**age (2).

⌨ *Select **P**age from the Layout menu.*

12 Select **H**eaders (3), select Header **A** (1), then select Every **P**age (2).

Now that you are in the Header A editing screen, you could create a new Full Page figure box using the Graphics key. However, you could also use Undelete to restore one of the boxes you just deleted.

13 Press **Cancel** (F1), then select **R**estore (1) to insert the Figure 1 code you deleted.

⌨ *Select Undelete from the Edit menu, then select **R**estore.*

14 Press **Exit** twice to return to the newsletter.

15 Press **Print**, then select View Document.

⌨ *Select Print from the File menu.*

The first page of the newsletter has a full page border, but what about the second page?

16 Press **Page Down** to display the second page.

Because the figure box is in a header, the box is not affected by the Newspaper column. A full page border is also printed on the second page.

▲ FULL PAGE BORDER

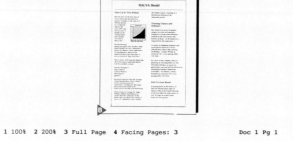

1 100% 2 200% 3 Full Page 4 Facing Pages: 3   Doc 1 Pg 2

17 Press **Page Up** to return to the first page of the newsletter.

Changing the Top Margin

You may have noticed in the View Document screen that the border has shifted down the page. There is more space above the border than below the border on the page.

▲ MORE SPACE
Ⓑ LESS SPACE

1 100% 2 200% 3 Full Page 4 Facing Pages: 3   Doc 1 Pg 1

Because the graphics box is in a header, WordPerfect moves the newsletter articles down the page to add extra spacing between the header and the text.

However, the graphics box moves down the page because it is now using the 1.25" top margin setting that comes *after* the Header code.

1 Press **Exit** (F7) to return to the editing screen.

2 Press **Right Arrow** (→) three times to move the cursor to the right of the Top/Bottom Margin code.

3 Press **Format** (Shift-F8) and select **P**age (2).

⌨ Select **P**age from the **L**ayout menu.

4 Select **M**argins Top/Bottom (5).

5 Enter **1** (one) for the top margin, press **Enter** to keep the 1.25" setting for the bottom margin.

6 Press **Exit** to return to the editing screen.

Once you create a new Top/Bottom Margin code, you should delete the old code before continuing to edit.

7 Press **Left Arrow** (←), then press **Backspace** to delete the [T/B Mar:1.25",1.25"] code.

8 Press **Print** (Shift-F7), then select **V**iew Document (6).

⌨ Select **P**rint from the **F**ile menu.

By setting the top margin to 1", both the text and the figure box have shifted back up the page so that there is an equal amount of space above and below the border.

▲ EQUAL SPACE

1 100% 2 200% 3 Full Page 4 Facing Pages: 3   Doc 1 Pg 1

9 Press **Exit** to return to the editing screen.

Changing the Style for Page Numbering

To finish formatting the newsletter, let's add page numbering at the bottom center of each page.

1 Press **Right Arrow** (→) to place the cursor to the right of the Top/Bottom Margin code.

2 Select **Format** (Shift-F8) and select **P**age (2).

⊟ *Select **P**age from the Layout menu.*

3 Select Page **N**umbering (6).

A menu of page numbering options is displayed.

```
Format: Page Numbering

    1 - New Page Number         1

    2 - Page Number Style       ^B

    3 - Insert Page Number

    4 - Page Number Position    No page numbering




Selection: 0
```

You are already familiar with using Page Number Position (lesson 10) to print a page number on every page, but this time it would be nice to include the word "Page" with the page number.

Whenever you want to add text to the page number, you can use Page Number Style. The ^B currently set for the style represents the page number. At this moment, only a page number is printed when you select Page Number Position (or Insert Page Number).

4 Select Page Number **S**tyle (2), then type **Page** and press the **Space Bar**.

5 Hold down **Ctrl** then type **b** to insert a ^B character into the style.

The "^B" is a single code that can only be inserted by using the Ctrl key.

6 Press **Backspace** and notice that both "^" and the "B" are deleted as if they were one character.

7 Hold down **Ctrl** and type **b** to insert another ^B character into the style.

You could type a "^" (Shift-6) then a "B" from the keyboard, but they would be seen as two characters by WordPerfect and print a "^B" on each page instead of a page number.

8 Press **Enter** to finish creating the page numbering style.

9 Select Page Number **P**osition (4), then type **6** to have the page number printed at the bottom center of every page.

10 Press **Exit** (F7) to return to the editing screen.

Notice that two formatting codes have been inserted—one for the Page Number Style and one for the Page Number Position. You can change the style as often as you like without changing the position on the page where the page number is printed.

11 Press **Print** (Shift-F7), select **V**iew Document (6), then select 100% (1).

☐ *Select **P**rint from the **F**ile menu.*

12 Press **Go To** (Ctrl-Home), then **Down Arrow** (↓) to display the page number at the bottom of the newsletter.

The word "Page" has been included with the page number as you indicated in the page number style.

13 Press **Page Down** (PgDn), then press **Go To** (Ctrl-Home) and **Down Arrow** to display the page number at the bottom of the second page.

14 Press **Exit** to return to the normal editing screen.

15 Press **Reveal Codes** (Alt-F3) to display the normal editing screen.

☐ *Select **R**eveal Codes from the **E**dit menu.*

Saving the Newsletter

With the page numbering added, and the formatting completed, you are ready to save the newsletter.

1 Press **Save** (F10), press **Enter**, then type **y** to replace the original newsletter with the final copy.

☐ *Select **S**ave from the **F**ile menu.*

Try selecting your own printer, then display the newsletter in the View Document screen or send it to the printer. If your printer cannot print graphics, or has no large fonts, then you may not be able to print the graphics images or larger text for the Large and Extra Large attributes.

2 When you finish, press **Exit** (F7) and type **n** twice to clear the screen.

When you want to change the size or appearance of text in your document, try using attributes instead of changing base fonts. Then, if you decide to select a new base font, the attributes will be adjusted to match the new typeface and/or size.

If there is a printer with better font capability (e.g., a laser printer) available to you that can be run from WordPerfect (version 5.1), you can create a document with your printer selected, save the document on disk, then retrieve and print the document using the other printer. This "document portability" feature lets you move a document from printer to printer to take advantage of each printer's unique capabilities.

Lesson 18: Corporate Report — Outline

An outline is an important way of organizing the ideas and information that you want to present in a longer document such as a research paper or a report. In this lesson, you use the Outline features of WordPerfect to create and format an outline for a corporate report on the past, present, and future of HALVA International.

Organizing the Outline

The outline that needs to be created for the report includes several levels of headings.

△ LEVEL 1 HEADING

△ LEVEL 2 HEADING

△ LEVEL 3 HEADING

△ LEVEL 4 HEADING

Each level has its own style of numbering. For example, "The First Fifty Years" and "A Time for Reflection" are both level 1 headings and use Roman numerals. "The European Connection" and "Maximizing the Organization" are both level 2 headings and use capital letters for numbering.

WordPerfect lets you use up to eight different levels of numbering with the Outline feature.

Turning On Outline

Now that you have seen the outline that needs to be typed, and know about numbering levels, let's retrieve the outline title and start creating the outline.

1 Press **Retrieve** (Shift-F10), then enter **outline.wkb** to retrieve the title for the outline.

⌨ *Select **R**etrieve from the **F**ile menu.*

2 Press **Home,↓** then press **Reveal Codes** (Alt-F3) to display the codes in the outline.

⊟ *Select Reveal Codes from the Edit menu.*

3 Press **Date/Outline** (Shift-F5), select **Outline** (4), then select **On** (1).

⊟ *Select Outline from the Tools menu, then select On.*

Just like a Column On code for Newspaper columns (lessons 13 and 16), an Outline On code is placed in your document when you turn on the Outline feature.

△ OUTLINE ON CODE
△ OUTLINE MESSAGE

```
                         HALVA International
                       Annual Corporate Report




Outline                                          Doc 1 Pg 1 Ln 1.56" Pos 1"
[      ▲    ▲   ▲  ▲   ▲   ▲    ▲  .▲   ▲   ▲   ▲   ▲  )  ▲    ▲    ▲
[Par Num Def:][Center][VRY LARGE][BOLD]HALVA International[bold][vry large][HRt]

[Center][ITALC]Annual Corporate Report[italc][HRt]
[HRt]
B▶[Outline On]█




A▶Press Reveal Codes to restore screen
```

An "Outline" message is displayed on the status line to let you know that outline is on, even when the Reveal Codes screen is off.

Typing the Outline

Now that Outline is on, WordPerfect is ready to help you create an outline by automatically inserting the numbers and letting you type the headings. Watch the Reveal Codes screen carefully as you press Enter to start the first heading.

1 Press **Enter** to start a new line.

A Paragraph Number code has been added to the outline, and is displayed as a Roman numeral "I." in the editing screen. Because the numbering in an outline is done with Automatic Paragraph Number codes, WordPerfect can update the numbers for you as you create and edit the outline.

2 Press **◆Indent** (F4), then type **The First Fifty Years** for the heading.

3 Press **Enter** to insert another Paragraph Number code, then press **Tab** to move the code to the next level of numbering.

Pressing Tab moves the number to the next tab stop and updates the number to the next level. If you want to move the number back a level, then use Shift-Tab.

4 Press **Shift-Tab** to move the number back to level 1, then press **Tab** to move the number forward again to level 2.

5 Press ◆**Indent** and type **The European Connection** for the heading.

You now have two levels in the outline, with a paragraph number for each level.

LEVEL 1
LEVEL 2

```
                        HALVA International
                        Annual Corporate Report

I.   The First Fifty Years
     A.    The European Connection_



Outline                                    Doc 1 Pg 1 Ln 1.9" Pos 4.3"

[HRt]
[Outline On][HRt]
[Par Num:Auto][→Indent]The First Fifty Years[HRt]
[TAB][Par Num:Auto][→Indent]The European Connection



Press Reveal Codes to restore screen
```

6 Press **Enter** to insert another Paragraph Number code.

This time the cursor returned to level 2 and inserted a "B." in the outline.

7 Press ◆**Indent**, type **The Roots of Mail Order** for the heading, then press **Enter**.

Once you are finished with a section of the outline, you can use Shift-Tab to return the paragraph number to level 1, then press Enter to double space for the next section.

8 Press **Shift-Tab** to move the paragraph number back to level 1.

9 Press **Enter** to move the paragraph number down a line.

10 Press **Reveal Codes** to display the normal editing screen.

⌨ *Select **Reveal Codes** from the **Edit** menu.*

Copying a Family

Each time you start over with a level 1 number, you start a new section of the outline. All or part of a section can be quickly moved, copied, or deleted by identifying a *family* in the section.

For example, all three headings in the section you have created can be copied by placing the cursor on the level 1 heading.

1 Press **Backspace** to delete the "II." paragraph number.

2 Move the cursor to the level 1 heading (The First Fifty Years).

3 Press **Date/Outline** (Shift-F5), select **O**utline (4), then select **C**opy Family (4).

⬛ Select **O**utline from the **T**ools menu, then select **C**opy Family.

A copy of the section is highlighted and displayed above the original section. Because the cursor is at level 1 in the section, the entire section becomes a family.

```
                          HALVA International
                        Annual Corporate Report

     I.   The First Fifty Years
  ▷    A.    The European Connection
         B.    The Roots of Mail Order

    II.   The First Fifty Years
            A.    The European Connection
            B.    The Roots of Mail Order




    Press Arrows to Move Family; Enter when done.
```

You can use the arrow keys to move the family all at the same time.

4 Press **Down Arrow** (↓) to place the copy below the original section, then press **Enter** to insert the copy into the outline.

With the first section copied, you can use Typeover to replace the text in the copied section with new headings.

5 Press **Word Right** (Ctrl-→) to place the cursor at the beginning of "The First Fifty Years" in the copied section.

6 Press **Typeover** (Ins), then type **A Time for Reflection** for the level 1 heading.

7 Press **Down Arrow**, then press **Word Left** (Ctrl-←) three times to place the cursor at the beginning of "The European Connection."

8 Type **Maximizing the Organization** for heading "A."

9 Press **Down Arrow**, then press **Word Left** five times to place the cursor at the beginning of "The Roots of Mail Order."

172 LESSON 18: CORPORATE REPORT — OUTLINE

10 Type **Mail Order Marketing** for heading "B.", then press **Delete to End of Line** (Ctrl-End) to erase the characters left from the original heading.

11 Press **Typeover** (Ins) to return to inserting text.

When you finish, your outline should have two sections with two numbering levels in each section.

```
I.   The First Fifty Years
     A.   The European Connection
     B.   The Roots of Mail Order

II.  A Time for Reflection
     A.   Maximizing the Organization
     B.   Mail Order Marketing_
```

Outline   Doc 1 Pg 1 Ln 2.73" Pos 4"

Editing the Outline

As you move a paragraph number in a line with Tab and Shift-Tab, the number updates as soon as it reaches a new level. Paragraph numbers also update as you add new headings to the outline.

1 Place the cursor at the end of the "A Time for Reflection" heading.

2 Press **Enter** to insert a new paragraph number, then press **Tab** to move the number to level 2.

As soon as you pressed Tab, the "III." updated to "A."

3 Press **Down Arrow** (↓) twice to update the numbering in the outline.

The original "A." and "B." paragraph numbers updated to "B." and "C.".

4 Press **Up Arrow** (↑) twice to return to the new paragraph number.

5 Press ◆**Indent** (F4), then type **Direction vs. Management** for the new heading.

Let's try adding two more headings to the outline.

6 Press **Enter**, press **Tab** to move to level 3, then press ◆**Indent** and type **The Founder** for the heading.

7 Press **Enter**, press ◆**Indent**, then type **The Employees** for the heading.

Just as you can copy a family of headings, you can also select and delete a family of headings.

8 Place the cursor on the "Direction vs. Management" heading.

9 Press **Date/Outline** (Shift-F5), select **O**utline (4), then select **D**elete Family (5).

⌨ Select **O**utline from the **T**ools menu, then select **D**elete Family.

This time only the "Direction vs. Management" heading and the two headings at level 3 are highlighted.

▲ FAMILY

```
I.    The First Fifty Years
      A.    The European Connection
      B.    The Roots of Mail Order

II.   A Time for Reflection
      A.    Direction vs. Management
            1.    The Founder
            2.    The Employees
      B.    Maximizing the Organization
      C.    Mail Order Marketing




Delete Outline Family? No (Yes)
```

10 Type **y** for Yes to delete the family of headings.

The level of a heading determines if all or part of a section is a family. If the cursor is resting on a level 1 heading, then all the headings to the next level 1 paragraph number are a family. If you move the cursor to a level 2 heading, then all the headings to the next level 2 paragraph number (in the same section) are family.

The same is true of all other paragraph numbering levels. The family always stays within the same level.

Turning Off Outline

If the outline is part of a larger document, then you should insert an Outline Off code to end the outline.

1 Press **Home,Home,↓** to move the cursor to the end of the outline.

2 Press **Date/Outline** (Shift-F5), select **O**utline (4), then select Off (2).

⌨ Select **O**utline from the **T**ools menu, then select **O**ff.

3 Press **Reveal Codes** (Alt-F3) to see the Outline Off code.

▭ *Select **R**eveal Codes from the **E**dit menu.*

```
     I.    The First Fifty Years
           A.    The European Connection
           B.    The Roots of Mail Order

     II.   A Time for Reflection
           A.    Maximizing the Organization
           B.    Mail Order Marketing


C:\WP51\LEARN\OUTLINE.WKB                        Doc 1 Pg 1 Ln 3.23" Pos 1"
[TAB][Par Num:Auto][→Indent]Mail Order Marketing[HRt]
[TAB][HRt]
[HRt]
[Outline Off]█




Press Reveal Codes to restore screen
```

With the cursor to the right of Outline Off code, the Outline message is no longer displayed on the status line.

4 Press **Left Arrow** (←), then press **Up Arrow** (↑) twice.

As soon as you place the cursor on the Outline Off code, or somewhere in the outline, the "Outline" message reappears on the status line.

The Outline On and Off codes help you when editing to make sure that you do not type any text in the outline that belongs in the main part of the document. You can also tell when keys like Enter and Tab will start inserting and updating paragraph numbers by watching for the "Outline" message on the status line.

5 Press **Reveal Codes** to display the normal editing screen.

▭ *Select **R**eveal Codes from the **E**dit menu.*

Selecting a Numbering Style

While Roman numerals, uppercase letters, and numbers are frequently used when creating an outline, other styles of numbering are also important for paragraphs, legal documents, presentations, etc.

1 Press **Home,Home,**↑ to move the cursor to the beginning of the outline.

2 Press **Down Arrow** (↓) twice to move the cursor to the line below the "Annual Corporate Report" title.

3 Press **Date/Outline** (Shift-F5), then select **D**efine (6).

▭ *Select **D**efine from the **T**ools menu.*

Several numbering styles (Paragraph, Outline, Legal, and Bullets) are displayed in the top half of the screen. The current definition is displayed in the middle of the screen.

▲ CURRENT DEFINITION

```
Paragraph Number Definition

1 - Starting Paragraph Number                 1
    (in legal style)
                                   Levels
                        1     2     3     4     5     6     7     8
2 - Paragraph          1.    a.    i.   (1)   (a)   (i)   1)    a)
3 - Outline            I.    A.    1.    a.   (1)   (a)   i)    a)
4 - Legal (1.1.1)      1     .1    .1    .1    .1    .1    .1    .1
5 - Bullets            •     o     -     ■     *     +     ·     x
6 - User-defined

▷ Current Definition   I.    A.    1.    a.   (1)   (a)   i)    a)
  Attach Previous Level      No    No    No    No    No    No    No

7 - Enter Inserts Paragraph Number            Yes

8 - Automatically Adjust to Current Level      Yes

9 - Outline Style Name


Selection: 0
```

4 Select **P**aragraph (2), then press **Exit** (F7) twice to return to the editing screen.

5 Press **Screen** (Ctrl-F3), then press **Enter** to reformat the outline.

The paragraph numbers in the outline are reformatted for the Paragraph style.

6 Press **Date/Outline**, then select **D**efine.

⌨ *Select Define from the Tools menu.*

7 Select **L**egal (4), then press **Exit** twice to return to the editing screen.

8 Press **Screen** (Ctrl-F3), then press **Enter** to format the outline.

Notice that the numbering from level 1 is attached to the numbering in level 2 for the legal style.

```
                              HALVA International
                            Annual Corporate Report

            1       The First Fifty Years
              ▲▶ 1.1   The European Connection
                 1.2   The Roots of Mail Order

            2  ▲▶  A Time for Reflection
              ▲▶ 2.1   Maximizing the Organization
                 2.2   Mail Order Marketing




            C:\WP51\LEARN\OUTLINE.WKB                    Doc 1 Pg 1 Ln 1.4" Pos 1"
```

9 Press **Date/Outline**, then select **D**efine.

▢ Select **D**efine from the **T**ools menu.

The settings displayed for "Attach Previous Level" are all set to Yes for the legal style. However, the other three styles (Paragraph, Outline, and Bullets) are set to No.

10 Select **B**ullets (5), then press **Exit** twice to return to the editing screen.

11 Press **Screen**, then press **Enter** to format the outline.

```
                              HALVA International
                            Annual Corporate Report

            ▲▶ •    The First Fifty Years
                 o      The European Connection
                 o      The Roots of Mail Order

               •  A Time for Reflection
            ▲▶ o      Maximizing the Organization
                 o      Mail Order Marketing
```

**Editing a Numbering
Style**

Bullets are a popular way of creating a business presentation from an outline. However, the bullets are sometimes not used for the first level of headings.

1 Press **Date/Outline** (Shift-F5), select **D**efine (6), then select **U**ser-defined (6).

⌨ Select **D**efine from the **T**ools menu.

2 Press **Delete** (Del) twice to remove the bullet for level 1, then press **Exit** (F7) three times to return to the editing screen.

3 Press **Screen** (Ctrl-F3), then press **Enter** to reformat the outline.

The bullets disappear from the level 1 headings ("The First Fifty Years" and "A Time for Reflection") in the outline.

Now that the Bullets style has been set, all the previous Paragraph Number Definition codes should be deleted.

4 Press **Reveal Codes** (Alt-F3).

⌨ Select **R**eveal Codes from the **E**dit menu.

5 Press **Left Arrow** (←), then press **Backspace** three times to delete the first three [Par Num Def] codes.

6 Press **Reveal Codes** to display the normal editing screen.

⌨ Select **R**eveal Codes from the **E**dit menu.

If you are creating a presentation from an outline, you may also want to bold the level 1 headings and add some extra spacing between the headings. For now, let's change the headings back to the original Outline style.

7 Press **Delete** (Del), then type **y** to delete the Paragraph Number Definition code.

Creating an Outline Style

Before typing a heading, you have been pressing ♦**Indent** to separate the paragraph number from the heading. You could save a lot of keystrokes if WordPerfect automatically inserted the indents for you.

1 Press **Date/Outline** (Shift-F5), then select **D**efine (6).

⌨ Select **D**efine from the **T**ools menu.

You have already been introduced to selecting and editing paragraph number styles (Legal, Bullet, etc.). You can also create an *outline* style that formats each level of paragraph numbering for you.

2 Select Outline Style **N**ame (9).

A list is displayed on your screen with a note stating that only paragraph numbers are currently being inserted when you press Enter.

3 Select Create (2) to create the outline style.

A menu is displayed on your screen that lists a name and description with a table of levels.

```
Outline Styles: Edit

  Name:

  Description:


▶ Level   Type        Enter
    1     Open
    2     Open
    3     Open
    4     Open
    5     Open
    6     Open
    7     Open
    8     Open




  1 Name; 2 Description; 3 Type; 4 Enter; 5 Codes: 0
```

4 Select **N**ame (1) and enter **Indented** to give the style a name (like "Bullets" or "Legal" for paragraph numbering styles).

5 Select **D**escription (2) and enter **Indented paragraph numbers** to describe the style.

The table in the middle of the screen includes the level number, type of Outline Style code (open or paired), and what happens when you press Enter (paired style only).

Because you only need to insert the paragraph number and an indent, the open style of code is the correct type. The paired codes are designed for formatting that includes base fonts, attributes, etc.

6 Make sure that the cursor is on level 1 in the table, then select **C**odes (5) to display the Style editing screen for level 1.

The editing screen for outline styles is like the one used for creating headers and footers. The word "Style:" on the status line lets you know which editing screen you are using, and a Paragraph Number code has already been inserted for you.

I.

Style: Press Exit when done   Doc 1 Pg 1 Ln 1" Pos 1"
Ⓑ[
[Par Num:1]

Outline Styles

All you need to do for level 1 is to add the indent.

7 Press **Right Arrow** (→), then press ◆**Indent** (F4) to add an indent to the paragraph number for level 1.

8 Press **Exit** (F7) to return to the Outline Styles Edit menu.

9 Press **Down Arrow** (↓) to highlight level 2 in the table, then select **Codes** (5).

Because level 2 numbering is at the first tab stop from the left margin, you need to add a tab in front of the paragraph number, then an indent after the paragraph number.

10 Press **Tab**, press **Right Arrow** (→), then press ◆**Indent** to add an indent to the paragraph number for level 2.

11 Press **Exit** to return to the Outline Styles Edit menu.

While the outline only has two levels of numbering at this point, the final section of the outline (which you still need to type) includes four levels of numbering.

12 Using steps 9 through 11 as a guide, add two tabs and an indent for level 3, and three tabs and an indent for level 4.

13 When you finish, press **Exit** to return to the list of outline styles.

Selecting an Outline Style

Now that you have finished creating the outline style, it is displayed in the Outline Style list.

⚠ INDENTED STYLE

```
     Name                Description

     -- NONE --          Use paragraph numbers only
  ▶  Indented            Indented paragraph numbers
```

```
   1 Select; 2 Create; 3 Edit; 4 Delete; 5 Save; 6 Retrieve; 7 Update: 1
```

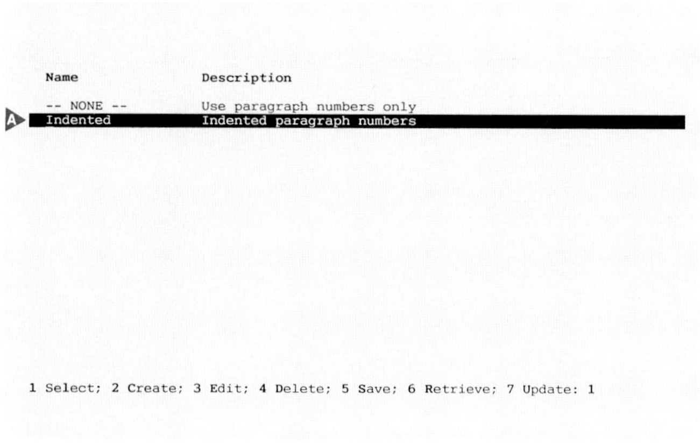

Whenever you want to use the style, all you need to do is select it.

1 Make sure that the "Indented" style is highlighted, then press **Enter** to select the style.

The name of the style is displayed next to "Outline Style Name" in the Paragraph Number Definition menu to let you know that the style has been selected.

2 Press **Exit** (F7) twice to place the Paragraph Number Definition code for the Indented style into the outline.

3 Press **Screen** (Ctrl-F3), then press **Enter** to reformat the screen.

WordPerfect replaces the paragraph numbers already in the outline with Outline Style codes.

4 Press **Reveal Codes** (Alt-F3) to display the codes for the outline styles.

⌨ Select **R**eveal Codes from the **E**dit menu.

Each Outline Style code includes the name (Lvl 1, Lvl 2, etc.) and type (Open) of code.

A STYLE NAME

B TYPE OF CODE

```
                              HALVA International
                            Annual Corporate Report

          I.        The First Fifty Years
               A.        The European Connection
               B.        The Roots of Mail Order

          II.       A Time for Reflection
               A.        Maximizing the Organization
               B.        Mail Order Marketing
          C:\WP51\LEARN\OUTLINE.WKB                Doc 1 Pg 1 Ln 1.4" Pos 1"
          [            ▲    ▲    ▲    ▲    ▲    ▲    ▲    ▲    )   ▲    ▲
          [Par Num Def:][Center][VRY LARGE][BOLD]HALVA International[bold][vry large][HRt]

          [Center][ITALC]Annual Corporate Report[italc][HRt]
          [Par Num Def:Indented][HRt]
          [Outline On][HRt]
          [Outline Lvl 1 Open Style][→Indent]The First Fifty Years[HRt]
          [Outline Lvl 2 Open Style][→Indent]The European Connection[HRt]
          [Outline Lvl 2 Open Style][→Indent]The Roots of Mail Order[HRt]
          [HRt]
          [Outline Lvl 1 Open Style][→Indent]A Time for Reflection[HRt]

          Press Reveal Codes to restore screen
```

5 Place the cursor on the Outline Style code for "The First Fifty Years" heading.

Notice that the code expands to display the contents of the style (a paragraph number and an indent).

A STYLE CONTENTS

```
                              HALVA International
                            Annual Corporate Report

          I.        The First Fifty Years
               A.        The European Connection
               B.        The Roots of Mail Order

          II.       A Time for Reflection
               A.        Maximizing the Organization
               B.        Mail Order Marketing
          Outline                                  Doc 1 Pg 1 Ln 1.73" Pos 1"
          [            ▲    ▲    ▲    ▲    ▲    ▲    ▲    ▲    )   ▲    ▲
          [Center][ITALC]Annual Corporate Report[italc][HRt]
          [Par Num Def:Indented][HRt]
          [Outline On][HRt]
          [Outline Lvl 1 Open Style;[Par Num:1][→Indent]][→Indent]The First Fifty Years[HR
          t]
          [Outline Lvl 2 Open Style][→Indent]The European Connection[HRt]
          [Outline Lvl 2 Open Style][→Indent]The Roots of Mail Order[HRt]
          [HRt]
          [Outline Lvl 1 Open Style][→Indent]A Time for Reflection[HRt]
          [Outline Lvl 2 Open Style][→Indent]Maximizing the Organization[HRt]

          Press Reveal Codes to restore screen
```

Because an indent is already provided in the Outline Style code, the [Indent] code between the style code and the heading needs to be deleted. In fact, all the original Indent codes need to be deleted in the outline.

6 Press **Reveal Codes**, then place the cursor in the line above the first heading ("The First Fifty Years").

7 Press **Block** (Alt-F4), then press **Home,Home,↓** to highlight the entire outline.

8 Press **Replace** (Alt-F2).

⊞ *Select* ***R****eplace from the Search menu.*

9 Type **n** for no confirm, then press **◆Indent** (F4) to look for Indent codes *only in the block.*

10 Press **◆Search** (F2) twice to begin replacing.

Because you did not enter anything for the "Replace with:" message, WordPerfect deletes each Indent code and leaves nothing behind to replace it. And because you used the Replace feature with Block, WordPerfect only replaced Indent codes in the highlighted text.

Finishing the Outline

With the Paragraph Number Definition code in place for the outline styles, you are ready to finish creating the outline.

1 Place the cursor in the line below the "Mail Order Marketing" heading.

2 Press **Enter**, then press **Shift-Tab** to move the paragraph number (and indent) back to level 1.

Notice that you can change the level of the paragraph number in the Outline Style code by using Shift-Tab (or Tab).

3 Type **The Next Fifty Years** for the heading.

4 Press **Enter** to insert another paragraph number and indent (in the Outline Style code), then press **Tab** to move the number to level 2.

5 Type **Expanding Markets** for the heading.

Now that you have been introduced to inserting paragraph numbers and indents with the Outline Styles feature, follow the illustration below to create the rest of the outline on your own.

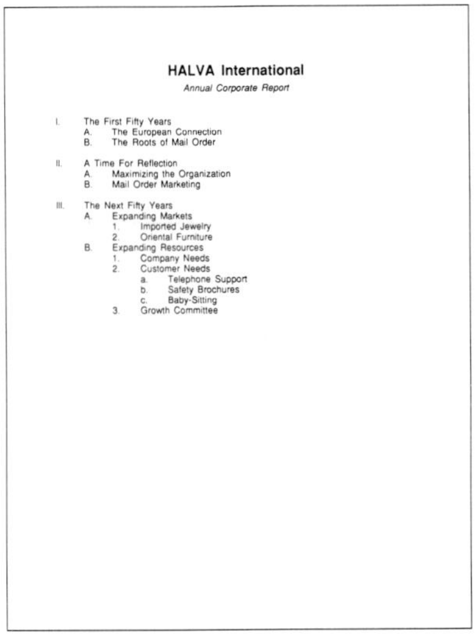

HALVA International
Annual Corporate Report

I.   The First Fifty Years
     A.   The European Connection
     B.   The Roots of Mail Order

II.   A Time For Reflection
     A.   Maximizing the Organization
     B.   Mail Order Marketing

III.   The Next Fifty Years
     A.   Expanding Markets
         1.   Imported Jewelry
         2.   Oriental Furniture
     B.   Expanding Resources
         1.   Company Needs
         2.   Customer Needs
             a.   Telephone Support
             b.   Safety Brochures
             c.   Baby-Sitting
         3.   Growth Committee

Remember that pressing Enter inserts a new paragraph number and indent, and that Tab and Shift-Tab move the paragraph number from level to level in a line. If you make a mistake, use Backspace to delete the Outline Style code and the hard return, then press Enter to start over again.

Saving the Outline

When you finish, you may want to save the outline as an example for future reference.

1   Press **Exit** (F7), type **y** to save the outline, then enter **outline** for the filename.

2   Type **n** to clear the screen and stay in WordPerfect.

Whenever you save an outline, the list of outline styles that you create is also saved with the outline in case you want to edit or delete the styles you have created.

Lesson 19: Corporate Report — Indents and Line Spacing

After creating an outline for the report, the next step is to begin writing it. To save you time, we've already typed the first draft of the report. In this lesson you begin formatting the report by using tabs, indents, and line spacing.

Indenting the First Line of a Paragraph

Let's begin by retrieving the report and indenting the first line of each paragraph with a tab.

1 Press **Retrieve** (Shift-F10) and enter **report.wkb** to retrieve the first draft of the corporate report.

⌨ *Select **Retrieve** from the **File** menu.*

2 Move the cursor to the beginning of the first paragraph, press **Tab**, then press **Down Arrow** (↓) twice.

Notice that the cursor remains at the same position (1.5") as you move down through the remaining lines of text (check the status line).

▲ TAB POSITION
🅱 CURSOR POSITION

```
                      The First Fifty Years

        🅰▶A wise man once said that "Friends come and go, but enemies
     accumulate."1  The same can be said of the relationships that
     develop between a company and its customers.

     The 🅱ar 1989 marks the 50th anniversary of the founding of HALVA
     International.  While many other import/export businesses have
     started in glory and ended in defeat, the HALVA International
     corporation continues to thrive.

     While there are many theories surrounding the success of HALVA
     International, the truth lies in the careful cultivation of
     customer relationships and continued efforts to provide quality
     merchandise at affordable prices.

     In this report, the past, present, and future status of HALVA
     International are reviewed, with an emphasis on these
     characteristics as being vital to the continued survival of the
     company.


     The European Connection
     The year was 1939, and the rumors of war had become a nightmare
     C:\WP51\LEARN\REPORT.WKB                    Doc 1 Pg 1 Ln 1.67" Pos 1.5"
```

For easier editing, WordPerfect tries to keep the same cursor position for each line as you move the cursor up or down through the text.

3 Use **Tab** to indent the first line of the remaining paragraphs in the report.

Important: *Do not indent titles or the table in the middle of the report.*

You may want to use **Reveal Codes** (Alt-F3) while formatting the paragraphs to make sure that any codes at the beginning of a line remain in place, and that only the text of the first line is indented.

4 When you finish, make sure Reveal Codes is off, then press **Home,Home,↑** to return the cursor to the beginning of the report.

Indenting an Entire Paragraph

While the Tab key indented the first line of each paragraph, there are times when you may want to indent the entire paragraph. For example, quotations of three lines or more are often typed as a separate paragraph and indented to give additional emphasis to the quotation.

1 Press **Go To** (Ctrl-Home), then press **Down Arrow** (↓) to move the cursor to the bottom of page 1.

2 Move the cursor to the first line of the quotation near the top of the screen ("Suddenly, the entire face...").

3 Press **Home,←** then press **Delete** (Del) to erase the tab at the beginning of the paragraph.

While you could insert a tab at the beginning of each line, the tabs would move with the text as you edited the paragraph. What you really want to do is create a "temporary" margin that lines up all the text of the paragraph at a tab stop.

4 Press **♦Indent** (F4), then press **Down Arrow** (↓) to reformat the paragraph.

⊞ *Select Align from the Layout menu, then select Indent ♦.*

Notice that the left side of the paragraph is lined up at the 1.5" tab stop (.5 inch from the left margin).

▲ 1.5" TAB STOP

```
virtually severed, intercontinental business was at a standstill.

        "Suddenly, the entire face of economics changed to a
   ▲survival industry.  Manufacturing resources were transformed
    overnight into a war machine.  Sacrifice of conveniences
    became the test of civil loyalty."

        It was an awkward, if not impossible, time for the birth of
    an import/export business.  But, then, Bryan Metcalf was no
    ordinary individual.

    The Roots of Mail Order
        Realizing that crisis times called for an extraordinary
    effort, Metcalf knew that his trade in oriental rugs1 was doomed
    unless he could find a way to secure transportation of the rugs
    to his customers.  Concerning this bleak period, Metcalf
    comments, "It seemed as though there was absolutely no chance for
    economic survival.  However, even in the darkest hour I received
    renewed strength and hope when recalling the sacrifices widowed
    mother was called on to make while raising 5 boys."


    =================================================================
    C:\WP51\LEARN\REPORT.WKB                  Doc 1 Pg 1 Ln 6" Pos 1.5"
```

However, most paragraph quotations need to be indented from the left *and* right.

5 Press **Up Arrow** (↑), then press **Backspace** to delete the **♦**Indent.

6 Press ♦**Indent♦** (Shift-F4), then press **Down Arrow** to reformat the paragraph.

⌨ *Select Align from the Layout menu, then select Indent ♦♦.*

WordPerfect indents the paragraph an equal amount from both the left and right, using the same distance indented from the left margin (.5") to indent the paragraph from the right margin.

7 Move the cursor to the paragraph at the bottom of the page (under the title "The Roots of Mail Order").

The quotation in the middle of the paragraph is long enough to format it as a new paragraph.

8 Place the cursor at the beginning of the quotation ("It seemed as though..."), then press **Backspace** to delete the space after the comma.

9 Press **Enter** twice to create a new paragraph.

10 Press ♦**Indent♦** to indent the quotation from both the left and right margins, then press **Down Arrow** to reformat the paragraph.

⌨ *Select Align from the Layout menu, then select Indent ♦♦.*

▲ INDENTED QUOTATION

```
virtually severed, intercontinental business was at a standstill.

   ▶ "Suddenly, the entire face of economics changed to a
     survival industry.  Manufacturing resources were
     transformed overnight into a war machine.  Sacrifice of
     conveniences became the test of civil loyalty."

     It was an awkward, if not impossible, time for the birth of
an import/export business.  But, then, Bryan Metcalf was no
ordinary individual.

The Roots of Mail Order
     Realizing that crisis times called for an extraordinary
effort, Metcalf knew that his trade in oriental rugsl was doomed
unless he could find a way to secure transportation of the rugs
to his customers.  Concerning this bleak period, Metcalf
comments,

   ▶ "It seemed as though there was absolutely no chance for
     economic survival.  However, even in the darkest hour I
     received renewed strength and hope when recalling the
     sacrifices widowed mother was called on to make while
     raising 5 boys."
C:\WP51\LEARN\REPORT.WKB                    Doc 1 Pg 1 Ln 8.67" Pos 1.5"
```

After indenting the quotation paragraphs, you decide that you want to indent the paragraphs an additional tab stop to add extra emphasis.

11 Move the cursor to the beginning of each quotation paragraph, then press ♦**Indent♦** to indent the text an additional half inch.

⌨ *Select Align from the Layout menu, then select Indent ♦♦.*

By using the Indent keys, you can quickly create new margins for a paragraph with a single keystroke (by using the existing tab stops), and without ever using the Format key to set new left and/or right margins. As soon as you press Enter, the cursor returns to the left margin again.

Changing the Line Spacing

Many reports also add extra spacing between lines to make the text easier to read. Although double spacing is often used, a similar effect can be achieved without taking quite as much space by setting 1.5 line spacing.

1 Press **Home,Home,↑** to move the cursor to the beginning of the report.

2 Press **Format** (Shift-F8) and select **L**ine (1).

⌨ *Select Line from the Layout menu.*

3 Select Line **S**pacing (6).

4 Enter **1.5** for the new line spacing, then press **Exit** (F7) to return to the editing screen.

You can see the actual 1.5 spacing by using the View Document screen.

5 Press **Print** (Shift-F7).

⌨ *Select Print from the File menu.*

6 Select **V**iew Document (6), select Full **P**age (3), then use **Page Up** (PgUp) and **Page Down** (PgDn) to display the report.

7 When you finish, press **Exit** (F7) to return to the editing screen.

Once you set line spacing at 1.5, it remains at that setting from the location of the Line Spacing code to the end the of document. However, the following parts of the report need to be set for single line spacing:

- Paragraph quotations
- Operating Expenses table

8 Using steps 2 through 4 as a guide, format the paragraph quotations and the Operating Expenses table for single line spacing by using the Line Format feature (Shift-F8,1,6).

⌨ *Select Line from the Layout menu.*

Make sure that the cursor is at the beginning of the first line of the quotations and the table title before setting single line spacing. Set line spacing back to 1.5 at the end of the last line in the quotations and table.

9 When you finish, press **Home,Home,↑** to move the cursor to the beginning of the report.

Underlining Tabs

While formatting the table, you may have noticed that the column titles are not underlined.

1 Press **Page Down** (PgDn) three times to display the Operating Expenses table at the top of page 4.

2 Place the cursor at the beginning of the line with the Expense, Quarter, and Change column titles.

3 Press **Block** (Alt-F4), then press **Home,→** to block the titles.

⊞ *Block the titles by holding down the left button on the mouse and dragging the pointer to the end of the line.*

4 Press **Underline** (F8).

⊞ *Select Appearance from the Font menu, then select Underline.*

The individual titles are underlined, but there is no underlining between the titles to help separate them from the table information.

△ NO UNDERLINING

```
                        Operating Expenses
                              1989

    Expense          ▼▼  Fourth    ▼▼  Third     ▼▼
                         Quarter       Quarter       Change

    Payroll              330,485.00   289,800.00      14.04%
    Taxes                 35,500.00    12,075.00     194.00%
    Rent                  29,600.00    29,600.00       0.00%
    Phone                  6,200.00     2,173.50     185.25%
    Mail                   4,980.00     8,780.00     -43.28%
    Utilities              9,060.00     2,500.00     262.40%
    Office Supplies        6,037.50     4,350.00      38.79%


    Totals/Average       421,862.50   349,278.50      20.78%


        While some expenses increased significantly, the overall

    average was well below the 50 percent increase in sales.  This

    remarkable achievement is due, in part, to careful planning and
    C:\WP51\LEARN\REPORT.WKB                   Doc 1 Pg 4 Ln 1.67" Pos 6.9"
```

5 Press **Home,Home,↑** to return to the beginning of the report.

6 Press **Format** (Shift-F8) and select **O**ther (4).

⊞ *Select **O**ther from the **L**ayout menu.*

WordPerfect always underlines text, but gives you a choice of having spaces and/or tabs underlined. The initial setting is to have spaces underlined, but not tabs.

7 Select **U**nderline Spaces/Tabs (7).

8 Press **Enter** for spaces (to keep the Yes setting), then type **y** to underline tabs.

9 Press **Exit** (F7) to return to the editing screen.

10 Press **Page Down** (PgDn) three times to return to the Operating Expenses table.

Now that you have set tabs to be underlined, both text and tabs are underlined in the table.

```
                          Operating Expenses
                                1989
                    ▼▲  Fourth        Third
         Expense        Quarter       Quarter      Change

         Payroll            330,485.00    289,800.00     14.04%
         Taxes               35,500.00     12,075.00    194.00%
         Rent                29,600.00     29,600.00      0.00%
         Phone                6,200.00      2,173.50    185.25%
         Mail                 4,980.00      8,780.00    -43.28%
         Utilities            9,060.00      2,500.00    262.40%
         Office Supplies      6,037.50      4,350.00     38.79%


         Totals/Average     421,862.50    349,278.50     20.78%



             While some expenses increased significantly, the overall

         average was well below the 50 percent increase in sales.  This

         remarkable achievement is due, in part, to careful planning and
         C:\WP51\LEARN\REPORT.WKB                      Doc 1 Pg 4 Ln 1" Pos 1"
```

With the Underline Tabs/Spaces code at the beginning of the document, all tabs in the document are underlined whenever you use the Underline attribute. If, however, you want tab underlining for only part of a document (such as a table), then you can place a code before and after the table (as with line spacing) to set and reset tab underlining.

Viewing and Saving the Report

At this point, you may want to use the View Document screen to display the formatting results for the entire report.

1 Press **Print** (Shift-F7), select **V**iew Document (6), then use **Page Up** (PgUp) and **Page Down** (PgDn) to display the report pages.

2 When you finish, press **Exit** (F7) to return to the editing screen.

3 Press **Exit** again, then type **y** to save the report.

4 Enter **report** for the filename, then press **Enter** to clear the screen and stay in WordPerfect.

Every time you format a document, you need to be aware of the results. This is especially true when trying to format part of a document such as a paragraph.

Some formatting features (like ◆Indent) automatically end at a certain place in the document (at the end of a paragraph).   However, the majority of formatting features (like Line Spacing) change the document until you insert another code that returns the format to its original setting.

Lesson 20: Corporate Report — Tabs

After formatting the text of a document with indents and line spacing, you may decide to add information such as a list or table. In this lesson, you continue editing the corporate report for HALVA International by creating a new table for the report using the Tab features.

Creating a Comparison Table

After checking the report, you decide that a new table, similar to the following, is needed to compare mail order with retail sales during each quarter of 1990.

```
                      Mail Order vs. Retail
                              1990

                            Mail Order              Retail

           First Quarter . . . $2,400,000.00       $500,000.00
           Second Quarter. . . $6,250,000.00     $1,500,000.00
           Third Quarter . . . $4,800,000.00     $1,250,000.00
           Fourth Quarter. . .$12,250,000.00     $6,750,000.00
```

Creating the table involves setting tabs, then typing the table heading, column titles, and information. Current settings such as line spacing may also need to be changed for the table.

Creating the Table Title

Let's begin by retrieving the corporate report and creating a heading for the comparison table.

1 Press **Retrieve** (Shift-F10) and enter **report** to retrieve the corporate report.

⌨ *Select* **Retrieve** *from the* **File** *menu.*

2 Press **Page Down** (PgDn) three times, then press **Go To** (Ctrl-Home) and **Down Arrow** (↓) to move to the bottom of page 4.

3 Press **Center** (Shift-F6), **Bold** (F6), then type **Retail vs. Mail Order** for the table title.

4 Press **Home,→** to move past the Bold off code at the end of the line, then press **Enter** to start a new line.

5 Press **Center**, type **1990** for the year, then press **Enter** twice to end centering and add double spacing.

Setting Decimal Align Tabs

After creating the table heading, you could create the "Retail" and "Mail Order" column titles, then type in the table information. However, to find out exactly where to place the column titles, it would be a good idea to create the rest of the table first.

▲ COLUMN TITLE
Ⓐ QUARTER TITLES
Ⓐ FIGURES

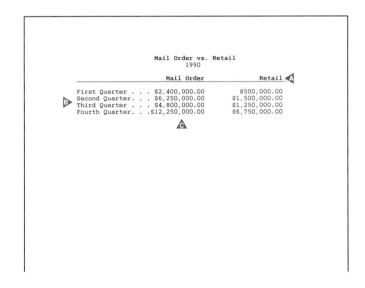

The quarter titles (First Quarter, Second Quarter, etc.) are at the left margin and do not need a tab setting. However, two tabs need to be set for the figures in the table.

1 Press **Format** (Shift-F8) and select **Line** (1).

⊞ *Select **Line** from the **Layout** menu.*

2 Select **Tab Set** (8).

3 Press **Home,←** then press **Delete to End of Line** (Ctrl-End) to clear all tabs from the tab ruler.

Besides setting tabs at any position in a line, a menu at the bottom of the screen lets you select the format of the tab.

```
            Not to be forgotten, however, is the solid base of mail

          order business that continues to provide capital for the retail

          venture.  A comparison of revenues from both mail order and

          retail sales indicates that there is still a solid market of mail

          order customers, despite recent reports of fraud among some mail

          order houses.



                          Retail vs. Mail Order

                                  1990
    ......:...........:.........:.........:.........:.........:........
     !      !          !         !         !         !         !
    -1"     0"        +1"       +2"       +3"       +4"       +5"      +6"
    Delete EOL (clear tabs); Enter Number (set tab); Del (clear tab);
  ▷ Type; Left; Center; Right; Decimal; .= Dot Leader; Press Exit when done.
```

The normal tab is set for Left, which means that the tab stop will be to the left of the text. Also available are Center, Right, and Decimal tabs, which are similar to using the Center, Flush Right, and Tab Align keys to type text.

Because the figures in the table are dollar amounts, it would be a good idea to use the Decimal format to line up all the figures on the decimal point.

4   Enter **3** for a tab stop 3 inches from the left margin, then enter **5** for a tab stop 5 inches from the left margin.

5   Change the two Left tabs to Decimal by placing the cursor on each "L" and typing **d**.

In order to line up the quarter titles with the figures, it would also be helpful to have the first tab insert a dot leader (a line of periods).

6   Place the cursor on the first "D," then type a period (**.**).

The first D is highlighted to let you know that the tab stop is formatted for a dot leader.

7   Press **Exit** (F7) twice to return to the editing screen.

Typing the Table Information

You are now ready to begin typing the table information.

1   Type **First Quarter** for the row title, then press **Tab** and type **$500,000.00** for the retail figure.

When you pressed Tab, WordPerfect automatically inserted a dot leader between "First Quarter" and "$500,000.00." And "$500,000.00" was pushed to the left until you typed the decimal point for decimal alignment.

2 Press **Tab** and type **$2,400,000.00** for the mail order figure, then press **Enter** to start a new line.

Now that you have seen how a dot leader and Decimal tab work in WordPerfect, try typing the rest of the table on your own.

3 Type the following table information using steps 2 and 3 as a guide.

Second Quarter..$1,500,000.00 $6,250,000.00
Third Quarter...$1,250,000.00 $4,800,000.00
Fourth Quarter..$6,750,000.00 $12,250,000.00

Your table should look similar to the following screen:

A TABLE TITLE
B TABLE INFORMATION

```
order customers, despite recent reports of fraud among some mail

order houses.



                        A  Retail vs. Mail Order
                            1990


     First Quarter. . . . .$500,000.00      $2,400,000.00
     Second Quarter . . .$1,500,000.00      $6,250,000.00
   B Third Quarter. . . .$1,250,000.00      $4,800,000.00
     Fourth Quarter . . .$6,750,000.00      $12,250,000.00


     C:\WP51\LEARN\REPORT                   Doc 1 Pg 4 Ln 9.25" Pos 1"
```

Resetting Tabs

After typing the table information, scroll down a couple of lines and notice the beginning of the first paragraph below the table. What happened to the tab at the beginning of the paragraph?

1 Press **Reveal Codes** (Alt-F3) and check the tab at the beginning of the paragraph.

⌨ Select *Reveal Codes* from the *Edit* menu.

The normal Left tab [Tab] has been replaced by a Decimal tab [Align].

▲ DECIMAL TAB

```
First Quarter. . . . .$500,000.00        $2,400,000.00

Second Quarter . . .$1,500,000.00        $6,250,000.00

Third Quarter. . . .$1,250,000.00        $4,800,000.00

Fourth Quarter . . .$6,750,000.00       $12,250,000.00

C:\WP51\LEARN\REPORT           ▼▲          Doc 1 Pg 4 Ln 9.25" Pos 1"
[                                                                    ]
Second Quarter[Dec Tab]$1,500,000.00[Dec Tab]$6,250,000.00[HRt]
Third Quarter[Dec Tab]$1,250,000.00[Dec Tab]$4,800,000.00[HRt]
Fourth Quarter[Dec Tab]$6,750,000.00[Dec Tab]$12,250,000.00[HRt]
[HPg]
[Center][Mark:ToC,1][BOLD]The Next Fifty Years[bold][End Mark:ToC,1][HRt]
[HRt]
[Dec Tab]While the recent upswing in the growth of HALVA International is a[SRt]

welcome indicator, there are also potential problems that need to[SRt]
be addressed.[HRt]

Press Reveal Codes to restore screen
```

WordPerfect is now using the tab format you set for the comparison table. Just like setting line spacing, each time you change the tab setting all tabs in the entire document from the Tab Set code forward use the new setting.

2   Move the cursor to the end of the last line in the table ($12,250,000.00), then press **Enter**.

3   Press **Format** (Shift-F8) and select **Line** (1).

🖳 *Select **Line** from the Layout menu.*

4   Select **Tab Set** (8).

5   Press **Home,←** then press **Delete to End of Line** (Ctrl-End) to erase the two tabs in the tab ruler.

Instead of setting one tab at a time, you can set several tabs by typing the position you want the tabs to start, followed by an interval.

6   Enter **0,.5** to set a tab every half-inch (.5) from the left margin (0).

7   Press **Exit** (F7) twice to return to the editing screen.

8   Press **Down Arrow** (↓) until the paragraph below "The Next Fifty Years" title is displayed.

The [Align] code at the beginning of the paragraph has been replaced by a [Tab] code to reflect the new tab setting.

Setting Absolute Tabs

Now that the table information has been typed, you are ready to create the column titles.

1   Press **Reveal Codes** (Alt-F3) to display the normal editing screen.

🖳 *Select **Reveal Codes** from the Edit menu.*

You are already familiar with Left and Decimal tabs, so let's try using Right tabs to line up the column titles with the right edge of the retail and mail order figures.

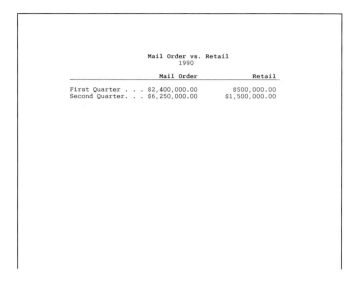

```
                              Mail Order vs. Retail
                                      1990
                              Mail Order            Retail
            _____
            First Quarter . . . $2,400,000.00      $500,000.00
            Second Quarter. . . $6,250,000.00    $1,500,000.00
```

You can find the settings for the tabs by placing the cursor to the right of the last zero in each column, then checking the Position number on the status line.

2 Press **Up Arrow** (↑) until the table is displayed on the screen.

3 Place the cursor to the right of the $500,000.00 figure in the First Quarter line, then write down the Position number on the status line.

4 Place the cursor to the right of the $2,400,000.00 figure in the First Quarter line, then write down the Position number on the status line.

If the cursor was in the correct position for both figures, you should have written down 4.3" for the Retail column, and 6.3" for the Mail Order column. You are now ready to set the tabs.

5 Move the cursor to the empty line below the 1990 subheading.

6 Press **Enter** twice to add some extra spacing, then press **Up Arrow** to move the cursor up one line.

7 Press **Format** (Shift-F8) and select **L**ine (1).

⌨ *Select Line from the Layout menu.*

8 Select **T**ab Set (8).

9 Clear the tabs in the tab ruler by pressing **Home,←** and **Delete to End of Line** (Ctrl-End).

You have been setting tabs as a measurement that is added to the left margin (0 in the tab ruler). This type of tab is called *relative* because the tab changes whenever the left margin changes to keep the same distance between the left margin and the tab.

However, the 4.3" and 6.3" Position numbers are measured from the left edge of the page (not the left margin), and can only be entered as relative tabs if you subtract the left margin (1 inch).

To use the 4.3" and 6.3" measurements, you need to set the tabs as *absolute* by using the Type option on the menu at the bottom of the screen.

10 Type **t** to select the Type option.

WordPerfect displays a menu that lets you select either Absolute or Relative to Margin tabs. Absolute tabs are measured from the left edge of the page and remain in the same location—even when the left margin changes.

11 Select **A**bsolute (1) to set two absolute tabs for the column titles.

Notice that the negative signs (-) and plus signs (+) are gone from the tab ruler, and that the ruler starts numbering at zero (0).

A LEFT EDGE OF PAGE

B DISTANCE FROM LEFT EDGE

```
                              Retail vs. Mail Order
                                      1990



             First Quarter. . . . .$500,000.00      $2,400,000.00
             Second Quarter . . .$1,500,000.00       $6,250,000.00
             Third Quarter. . . .$1,250,000.00       $4,800,000.00
             Fourth Quarter . . .$6,750,000.00      $12,250,000.00
```

The zero represents the left edge of the page, while the numbers represent distances from the left edge of the page.

12 Enter **4.3** for the first tab setting, then enter **6.3** for the second tab setting.

13 Change the tab format to Right by typing an **r** on the two "L's" in the ruler.

14 Press **Exit** (F7) twice to return to the editing screen.

15 Press **Reveal Codes** to display the tab setting codes.

⌨ *Select **R**eveal Codes from the **E**dit menu.*

The Tab Set codes for the titles and the figures include the type of tab to let you know what will happen when the left margin changes.

The settings for the column titles are absolute, and will remain at 4.3" and 6.3" from the left edge of the page. However, the +3" and +5" settings for the figures are always added to the left margin, and will shift the figures to the left or right as the left margin changes in size.

Typing the Column Titles

After setting the tabs, you are ready to type the column titles. Watch what happens in the Reveal Codes screen as you type the column titles.

1 Press **Bold** (F6), then press **Underline** (F8).

2 Press **Tab** and type **Retail** for the first column title, then press **Tab** and type **Mail Order** for the second column title.

As you pressed Tab, WordPerfect inserted an [Align] code to line up the title to the right. There are also [Align] codes separating the figures in the two columns.

When you use Center, Right, or Decimal tabs, WordPerfect inserts a [Center] or [Align] code when you press the Tab key. And like a normal [Tab] code, you can delete the [Center] or [Align] code to erase the tab, or press Tab to insert another [Center] or [Align] code.

Formatting the Table

With the table completed, let's check the results in the View Document screen.

1 Press **Print** (Shift-F7), then select **View Document** (6).

⌨ *Select Print from the File menu.*

Try viewing the table at Full Page and at 100%. While displaying the table in the View Document screen, you may notice that the table needs to be set to single line spacing. The table would also look better on the page if it were centered between the left and right margins.

2 Press **Exit** (F7) to return to the editing screen.

Setting Single Line Spacing

Because you are already familiar with using the Line Spacing feature, the next two steps give you general instructions for formatting the table for single line spacing.

1 Move the cursor to the beginning of the table (Retail vs. Mail Order line), then set single line spacing (Shift-F8,1,6).

⌨ *Select Line from the Layout menu.*

2 Move the cursor to the end of the last line in the table and set the spacing back to 1.5.

3 Press **Reveal Codes** (Alt-F3) to display the normal editing screen.

⌨ *Select **Reveal Codes** from the **Edit** menu.*

Centering the Table

Now that the single line spacing has been completed, how can you quickly (and easily) center the table between the margins?

If you try using the Center key for each line, then the last tab (and text) will be forced to the next line. The Tab key produces the same result (you may want to try it yourself).

Because there is about one inch of space from the right edge of the table to the right margin, an easier way would be to add an extra half inch to the left margin.

1 Move the cursor to the Retail vs. Mail Order heading, then press **Home,Home,←** to place the cursor at the beginning of the line.

2 Press **Format** (Shift-F8) and select **Line** (1).

⌨ *Select **Line** from the **Layout** menu.*

3 Select **Margins Left/Right** (7).

4 Enter **1.5** for the left margin, then press **Enter** to keep the right margin at one inch.

5 Press **Exit** (F7) to return to the editing screen.

6 Press **Down Arrow** (↓) to move the cursor a line at a time through the table.

Notice that the figures shift to the right to adjust for the new left margin (relative tabs), while the column titles remain in the same position (absolute tabs).

Ⓐ COLUMN TITLES

Ⓑ FIGURES

```
                              Retail vs. Mail Order
                                      1990

                               Retail        Mail Order  ◁Ⓐ

                 First Quarter . . . .  $500,000.00       $2,400,000.00
                 Second Quarter. . . $1,500,000.00        $6,250,000.00
             Ⓑ▷  Third Quarter . . . $1,250,000.00        $4,800,000.00
                 Fourth Quarter. . . $6,750,000.00       $12,250,000.00

                 _

       ---------------------------------------------------------------------
                               The Next Fifty Years


                 While the recent upswing in the growth of HALVA

                 International is a welcome indicator, there are also potential

                 problems that need to be addressed.
       C:\WP51\LEARN\REPORT                        Doc 1 Pg 4 Ln 9.08" Pos 1.5"
```

Because the column titles did not shift to the right, they are no longer aligned with the right edge of the figure columns.

7 Press **Reveal Codes** (Alt-F3) to display the tab setting codes in the table.

🖳 *Select **R**eveal Codes from the **E**dit menu.*

8 Move the cursor to the right of the [Tab Set:Abs: 4.3",6.3"] code at the beginning of Retail and Mail Order line.

Let's set two relative tabs for the column titles, then see what happens in the table.

9 Press **Format** and select **L**ine.

🖳 *Select **L**ine from the **L**ayout menu.*

10 Select **T**ab Set (8).

11 Clear the tabs in the tab ruler by pressing **Home,Home,←** and **Delete to End of Line** (Ctrl-End).

12 Type **t** to select Type, then select **R**elative to Margin (2) for the tab type.

The tab ruler is redisplayed with the left margin at zero (0), and with the ruler adjusted for the new 1.5" left margin setting. The relative tab settings for the column titles need to be set at one inch less than the original 4.3" and 6.3" Position numbers.

13 Enter **3.3** and **5.3** for the relative tab settings, then place the cursor on each "L" and type **r** for Right tabs.

14 Press **Exit** twice to return to the editing screen.

15 Press **Left Arrow** (←), then press **Backspace** to delete the Absolute Tab Set code.

16 Press **Reveal Codes** to display the normal editing screen.

🖳 *Select **R**eveal Codes from the **E**dit menu.*

The column titles have shifted to the right to adjust for the left margin, and are now aligned with the right side of the figures.

```
                           Retail vs. Mail Order
                                   1990
                                  Retail           Mail Order

              First Quarter . . . . $500,000.00     $2,400,000.00
              Second Quarter. . . $1,500,000.00     $6,250,000.00
              Third Quarter . . . $1,250,000.00     $4,800,000.00
              Fourth Quarter. . . $6,750,000.00    $12,250,000.00
                                        Ⓑ                 Ⓑ



     ================================================================================
                          The Next Fifty Years


              While the recent upswing in the growth of HALVA

              International is a welcome indicator, there are also

              potential problems that need to be addressed.
     C:\WP51\LEARN\REPORT                               Doc 1 Pg 4 Ln 8" Pos 1.5"
```

With the table set for a 1.5" left margin, you need to set the rest of the report back to a one inch margin.

17 Move the cursor to the beginning of the line below the table, then set the left margin back to one inch (Shift-F8,1,7) for the rest of the report.

While you may not always want the tab settings to adjust to a new left margin, if you are not certain of the final settings for tabbed columns, using relative tabs can save you a lot of time when making changes to a table.

Moving the Tabbed Columns

Now that the table has been created, let's switch the Retail and Mail Order columns so that the Mail Order column is first in the table.

The Move feature includes an option for moving columns separated by tabs, but you need to use Block to indicate which column you want moved.

1 Place the cursor somewhere in the Retail title, press **Block** (Alt-F4), then place the cursor somewhere in the $6,750,000.00 figure for the fourth quarter.

📖 *Select **B**lock From the **E**dit menu to turn on Block. Choose Se**l**ect from the **E**dit menu, then select Tabular **C**olumn. Skip to step 4 below.*

While the highlighted text on the screen includes part of the table that you do not want to move, watch what happens when you tell WordPerfect that you only want to move the column.

2 Press **Move** (Ctrl-F4).

3 Select Tabular **C**olumn (2).

Because WordPerfect knows that you only want to move the column identified by the beginning and ending of the block, the column is automatically highlighted for you to show exactly what will be moved.

4 Select **M**ove (1) to remove the column from the table.

5 Move the cursor to the Mail Order title, press **End** to place the cursor at the very end of the line, then press **Enter** to retrieve the column.

The entire column (including tabs) is inserted exactly where you want the retail figures to appear.

▲ INSERTED COLUMN

```
order customers, despite recent reports of fraud among some mail

order houses.



                          Retail vs. Mail Order
                                1990

          Mail Order               Retail              ▼▲
                                                        ▼

     First Quarter . . . $2,400,000.00        $500,000.00
     Second Quarter. . . $6,250,000.00        $1,500,000.00
     Third Quarter . . . $4,800,000.00        $1,250,000.00
     Fourth Quarter. . .$12,250,000.00        $6,750,000.00




   =========================================================================
                      The Next Fifty Years
     C:\WP51\LEARN\REPORT                      Doc 1 Pg 4 Ln 8" Pos 3"
```

Notice that the dot leader is now being used for the Mail Order column as indicated in the tab setting. Whenever you move a tab to a new place in a line, WordPerfect automatically adjusts the position *and* the format of the tab to match the tab setting.

But what happened to the column titles? They are now at the left margin, instead of over the columns.

6 Press **Reveal Codes** (Alt-F3) to check the column titles line.

▢ *Select **R**eveal Codes from the **E**dit menu.*

Notice the location of the tab setting code.

```
order houses.


                        Retail vs. Mail Order
                                1990

            Mail Order              Retail
C:\WP51\LEARN\REPORT                                Doc 1 Pg 4 Ln 8" Pos 3"
{    ▲   ▲   ▲   ▲   ▲   ▲     ▲   ▲    ▲    ▲    ▲     }    ▲
[Ln Spacing:1][L/R Mar:1.5",1"][Center][BOLD]Retial vs. Mail Order[bold][HRt]
[Center]1990[HRt]
[HRt]                              ▲
[BOLD][UND][Tab]Mail Order[und][bold][Tab Set:Rel: +3.3",+5.3"][BOLD][UND][Rt Ta
b]Retail[bold][und][HRt]
[HRt]
[Tab Set:Rel: +3",+5"]First Quarter[Dec Tab]$2,400,000.00[Dec Tab]$500,000.00[HR
t]
Second Quarter[Dec Tab]$6,250,000.00[Dec Tab]$1,500,000.00[HRt]
Third Quarter[Dec Tab]$4,800,000.00[Dec Tab]$1,250,000.00[HRt]

Press Reveal Codes to restore screen
```

When WordPerfect moved the Retail column, the code was also included, and needs to be moved to the beginning of the line.

7 Make sure that the cursor is on the [Tab Set:Rel: +3.3",+5.3"] code, then press **Delete** (Del) to erase the code.

8 Press **Home,Home,Home,←** to move the cursor to the beginning of the line.

9 Press **Cancel** (F1), then select **R**estore (1) to place the code at the beginning of the line.

While Undelete is a convenient way of moving text and codes in a document, you may want to use Move to avoid losing the text you want moved. Remember that Undelete only holds the last three deletions. If you make three or more deletions before restoring, then the item you wanted to move cannot be restored.

Combining Paired Codes

As a final note, notice the Bold and Underline codes in the column titles line of the table.

A BOLD CODES

B UNDERLINE CODES

```
order houses.




                          Retail vs. Mail Order
                                 1990

                         Mail Order            Retail
C:\WP51\LEARN\REPORT                           Doc 1 Pg 4 Ln 8" Pos 1.5"
[                                              ]
[Ln Spacing:1][L/R Mar:1.5",1"][Center][BOLD]Retial vs. Mail Order[bold][HRt]
[Center]1990[HRt]
[HRt]
[Tab Set:Rel: +3.3",+5.3"][BOLD][UND][Rt Tab]Mail Order[und][bold][BOLD][UND][Rt
 Tab]Retail[bold][und][HRt]
[HRt]
[Tab Set:Rel:  .8",  ."]First Quarter[Dec Tab]$2,400,000.00[Dec Tab]$500,000.00[HR
t]
Second Quarter[Dec Tab]$6,250,000.00[Dec Tab]$1,500,000.00[HRt]
Third Quarter[Dec Tab]$4,800,000.00[Dec Tab]$1,250,000.00[HRt]

Press Reveal Codes to restore screen
```

Whenever you move text that is formatted with Bold or Underline, WordPerfect makes sure that the text will be bolded and underlined when it is retrieved. When you retrieved the Retail column, WordPerfect bolded and underlined the Retail title separately. As a result, there are now two sets of Bold and Underline codes.

Although the two sets of codes will still bold and underline all the text and tabs, you could change the two sets of codes to one set by using Block.

1 Make sure the cursor is on the first [BOLD] code in the line.

2 Press **Block** (Alt-F4), press **End**, then press **Bold** (F6).

Because you blocked the entire line before pressing Bold, WordPerfect made sure that only one set of Bold codes appeared, and that any extra Bold codes were deleted.

▲ BOLD ON CODE
▲ BOLD OFF CODE

```
order houses.




                        Retail vs. Mail Order
                                1990

                        Mail Order              Retail
C:\WP51\LEARN\REPORT                            Doc 1 Pg 4 Ln 8" Pos 6.8"
[
[Ln Spacing:1][L/R Mar:1.5",1"][Center][BOLD]Retial vs. Mail Order[bold][HRt]
[Center]1990[HRt]
[HRt]
[Tab Set:Rel: +3.3",+5.3"][BOLD][UND][Rt Tab]Mail Order[und][UND][Rt Tab]Retail[
und][bold][HRt]
[HRt]
[Tab Set:Rel: +3",+5"]First Quarter[Dec Tab]$2,400,000.00[Dec Tab]$500,000.00[HR
t]
Second Quarter[Dec Tab]$6,250,000.00[Dec Tab]$1,500,000.00[HRt]
Third Quarter[Dec Tab]$4,800,000.00[Dec Tab]$1,250,000.00[HRt]

Press Reveal Codes to restore screen
```

3 Press **Block**, press **Go To** (Ctrl-Home) twice, then press **Underline** (F8).

Once again, WordPerfect makes sure that only one set of Underline codes appears in the line.

▲ UNDERLINE ON CODE
▲ UNDERLINE OFF CODE

```
order houses.




                        Retail vs. Mail Order
                                1990

                        Mail Order              Retail
C:\WP51\LEARN\REPORT                            Doc 1 Pg 4 Ln 8" Pos 1.5"
[
[Ln Spacing:1][L/R Mar:1.5",1"][Center][BOLD]Retial vs. Mail Order[bold][HRt]
[Center]1990[HRt]
[HRt]
[Tab Set:Rel: +3.3",+5.3"][UND][BOLD][Rt Tab]Mail Order[Rt Tab]Retail[bold][und]
[HRt]
[HRt]
[Tab Set:Rel: +3",+5"]First Quarter[Dec Tab]$2,400,000.00[Dec Tab]$500,000.00[HR
t]
Second Quarter[Dec Tab]$6,250,000.00[Dec Tab]$1,500,000.00[HRt]
Third Quarter[Dec Tab]$4,800,000.00[Dec Tab]$1,250,000.00[HRt]

Press Reveal Codes to restore screen
```

Now that the column titles have been cleaned up, the table heading needs to be changed to reflect the new position of the columns.

4 Move the cursor to the first line of the table heading (Retail vs. Mail Order) *between* the Bold codes.

5 Delete the entire heading, then type **Mail Order vs. Retail** for the new heading.

6 Press **Reveal Codes** to display the normal editing screen.

⊞ *Select **R**eveal Codes from the **E**dit menu.*

▲ TABLE TITLE
▲ COLUMN TITLES
▲ TABLE INFORMATION

```
order houses.


                              ▼A▼
                      Mail Order vs. Retail
                           ▼B▼990                ▼B▼
                         Mail Order              Retail

         First Quarter . . . $2,400,000.00      $500,000.00
       ▷ Second Quarter. . . $6,250,000.00    $1,500,000.00
         Third Quarter . . . $4,800,000.00    $1,250,000.00
         Fourth Quarter. . .$12,250,000.00    $6,750,000.00




         ===============================================================
                      The Next Fifty Years
   C:\WP51\LEARN\REPORT                        Doc 1 Pg 4 Ln 7.5" Pos 5.55"
```

The Reveal Codes screen can be very important when editing to help you place the cursor in the correct position before deleting or adding codes or text.

Viewing and Saving the Report

At this point, you may want to use the View Document screen to display the formatting results for the entire report.

1 Press **Print** (Shift-F7), select **V**iew Document (6), then select 100% (1).

2 Press **Go To** (Ctrl-Home), then press **Down Arrow** (↓) to display the Mail Order vs. Retail table.

⊞ *Select **P**rint from the **F**ile menu.*

Try using a variety of cursor keys to move through the report. You may want to continue using the Go To (Ctrl-Home) and Up/Down Arrow keys to move to the top or bottom of a page.

3 When you finish, press **Exit** (F7) to return to the editing screen.

4 Press **Exit** again and type **y** to save the report.

5 Press **Enter** and type **y** to replace the REPORT file, then press **Enter** again to clear the screen.

Tabs have always been important in typing and word processing. As you continue using the Tab features, you will begin to appreciate the many ways WordPerfect helps you to format your text with tabs.

Lesson 21: Corporate Report — Footers, Footnotes, and Endnotes

Reports often include footnotes and endnotes for referencing sources and ideas. In this lesson you are introduced to the Footnotes and Endnotes features that help you document a report, and to a technique for numbering alternating pages with Footers.

Page Numbering with a Footer

Let's begin by numbering the pages of the report with a footer.

1 Press **Retrieve** (Shift-F10) then enter **report** to retrieve the corporate report.

⌨ *Select Retrieve from the File menu.*

2 Press **Format** (Shift-F8), then select **P**age (2).

⌨ *Select Page from the Layout menu.*

3 Select **F**ooters (4), then select Footer **A** (1).

4 Select Every **P**age (2) to have a footer printed on every page of the report.

One way of numbering pages in a report is to include the title of the report and the page number in the same line. The title appears on one end of the line, with the page number on the opposite end.

5 Type **Corporate Report** for the report title.

6 Press **Flush Right** (Alt-F6), then type **Page** and press the **Space Bar**.

7 Press **Format** and select **P**age.

⌨ *Select Page from the Layout menu.*

8 Select Page **N**umbering (6), then select **I**nsert Page Number (3) to insert a ^B into the footer.

9 Press **Exit** (F7) twice to exit the footer editing screen and return to the normal editing screen.

Checking the Footer in View Document

Now that you have created a footer for page numbering, let's check the results in the View Document screen.

1 Press **Print** (Shift-F7), select **V**iew Document (6), then select Full Page (3).

⌨ *Select Print from the File menu.*

2 Use **Page Down** (PgUp) and **Page Up** (PgDn) to scroll through the report.

Besides using Go To with the arrow keys to move to the top or bottom of a page, you can also enter a number to move to a specific page.

3 Press **Go To** (Ctrl-Home) and enter **1** to move to the first page.

4 Select 100% (1), then press **Go To** and **Down Arrow** (↓) to move to the bottom of the first page.

On some screens (e.g., CGA) you may need to use a 200% view before you can actually read the text.

While the footer is at the bottom of the page, what is the sentence immediately above the footer that is separated from the report by a short line?

A FOOTNOTE
B FOOTER

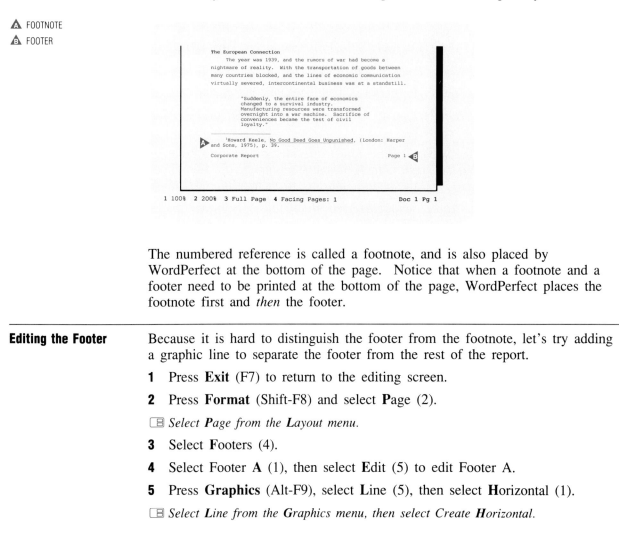

The numbered reference is called a footnote, and is also placed by WordPerfect at the bottom of the page. Notice that when a footnote and a footer need to be printed at the bottom of the page, WordPerfect places the footnote first and *then* the footer.

Editing the Footer

Because it is hard to distinguish the footer from the footnote, let's try adding a graphic line to separate the footer from the rest of the report.

1 Press **Exit** (F7) to return to the editing screen.

2 Press **Format** (Shift-F8) and select **P**age (2).

⬚ *Select Page from the Layout menu.*

3 Select **F**ooters (4).

4 Select Footer **A** (1), then select **E**dit (5) to edit Footer A.

5 Press **Graphics** (Alt-F9), select **L**ine (5), then select **H**orizontal (1).

⬚ *Select Line from the Graphics menu, then select Create Horizontal.*

You have already created a thin, black line for page numbering in the business letter (lesson 14). Let's try creating a thicker horizontal line this time that is shaded gray at 50%.

6 Select **W**idth of Line (4), then enter **1/18** for a thicker line width.

7 Select **G**ray Shading (5), enter **50** for the percentage, then press **Exit** (F7) to return to the footer editing screen.

8 Press **Enter** twice to double space between the line and the footer text, then press **Exit** twice to return to the normal editing screen.

9 Press **Print** (Shift-F7), then select **V**iew Document.

🖥 *Select Print from the File menu.*

10 Press **Go To** (Ctrl-Home), then press **Down Arrow** (↓) to view the bottom of the first page.

You can now distinguish the footer more easily with the graphics line in place.

⚠ GRAPHICS LINE

```
        The European Connection
            The year was 1939, and the rumors of war had become a
        nightmare of reality.  With the transportation of goods between
        many countries blocked, and the lines of economic communication
        virtually severed, intercontinental business was at a standstill.

            "Suddenly, the entire face of economics
            changed to a survival industry.
            Manufacturing resources were transformed
            overnight into a war machine.  Sacrifice of
        _____
        ¹Howard Keele, No Good Deed Goes Unpunished, (London: Harper
        and Sons, 1975), p. 39.

        Corporate Report                                      Page 1


  1 100%  2 200%  3 Full Page  4 Facing Pages: 1             Doc 1 Pg 1
```

If you ever change the left and/or right margin of the report, the line will automatically adjust to the new margin settings as long as the Left/Right Margin code comes *before* the Footer Code.

11 Press **Exit** to return to the editing screen.

Numbering on Alternating Pages

Whenever a document is printed on both sides of the paper (e.g., magazine, book), the page numbers are printed on the outside edge of each page to help you quickly find a particular page.

For example, glance down at the bottom of the pages in the *WordPerfect Workbook*. Notice that the even-numbered pages (left side) have the page number printed at the left margin, while the odd-numbered pages (right page) have the page number printed at the right margin.

Because the report will be printed on both sides of the page, you need to create a footer for the odd-numbered pages and a footer for the even-numbered pages.

1 Press **Home,Home,**↑ to move the cursor to the beginning of the document, then press **Reveal Codes** (Alt-F3).

⌨ *Select **R**eveal Codes from the **E**dit menu.*

2 Press **Backspace** to delete the Footer A code.

Let's begin by creating a new footer A for odd-numbered pages.

3 Press **Format** (Shift-F8) and select **P**age (2).

⌨ *Select **P**age from the **L**ayout menu.*

4 Select **F**ooters (4), select Footer **A** (1), then select **O**dd Pages (3) to create a new footer.

5 Press **Graphics** (Alt-F9), select **L**ine (5) then select **H**orizontal (1).

⌨ *Select **L**ine from the **G**raphics menu, then select **C**reate Horizontal.*

6 Set the line width to **.056"**, the gray shading to **50%**, then press **Exit** (F7) to return to the Footer A editing screen.

7 Press **Enter** twice to double space between the line and the footer text.

8 Type **Corporate Report** and press **Flush Right** (Alt-F6), then type **Page** and press the **Space Bar**.

9 Press **Format** (Shift-F8) and select **P**age (2).

⌨ *Select **P**age from the **L**ayout menu.*

10 Select Page **N**umbering (6), then select **I**nsert Page Number (3) to insert a ^B into the footer.

11 Press **Exit** (F7) twice to return to the normal editing screen.

Now that you have created a footer for odd-numbered pages, display the results in the View Document screen.

12 Press **Print** (Shift-F7), select **V**iew Document, then select Facing Pages (4).

⌨ *Select **P**rint from the **F**ile menu.*

13 Press **Page Down** (PgDn) to view pages 2 and 3 of the report.

When you select Facing Pages, WordPerfect displays the odd-numbered pages on the right and the even-numbered pages on the left (just like a book).

1 100%   2 200%   3 Full Page   4 Facing Pages: 4   Doc 1 Pg 2-3

A footer is displayed for page 3, but there is no footer for page 2 (and all other even-numbered pages in the report).

14 Press **Exit** to return to the editing screen.

15 Press **Reveal Codes** to display the normal editing screen.

⌨ *Select **R**eveal Codes from the **E**dit menu.*

16 Press **Home,Home,↑** to move the cursor to the beginning of the report.

17 Follow steps 3 through 11 to create a Footer B for even-numbered pages (step 4), with the page number at the *left* margin.

18 When you finish creating footer B, press **Print** and select View Document.

19 Press **Page Down** to display pages 2 and 3 of the report.

A footer should be displayed for both pages, with the page numbers on the outside edge of each page.

If there is not a footer for page 2, then you may have created a second footer A or selected "Odd Pages" instead of "Even Pages." Try deleting the Footer code and starting over again.

20 Press **Exit** to return to the editing screen.

Creating a Footnote   Footnotes are a formalized way of documenting sources for quotations, facts, and ideas in a report. While a corporate report may not need footnotes, footnotes are often included in other reports and research papers.

A footnote number is usually placed in the document next to the text that needs to be referenced. The same number appears at the bottom of the page with details about the source of the information.

As long as you know how to type a footnote, WordPerfect makes adding one to your document simple.

1 Move the cursor to the second paragraph on page 1 of the report.

2 Place the cursor to the right of the comma (next to the word defeat) in the second sentence of the paragraph.

3 Press **Footnote** (Ctrl-F7), select **F**ootnote (1), then select **C**reate (1).

⌨ *Select **F**ootnote from the Layout menu, then select Create.*

You are placed in an editing screen that is exactly like the one for headers and footers (except for "Footnote:" in the lower left corner). In fact, most of the features available when editing a footer are also available for footnotes.

A footnote number is already provided for you. All you need to do is type the text of the footnote.

4 Type the following footnote (underline the newsletter title):

Friend Krupke, Times and Seasons Newsletter, (New York: Longfellow Press, 1988), p. 2.

5 Press **Exit** (F7) to return to the normal editing screen.

The Footnote code is represented by a number 2 in the editing screen.

▲ FOOTNOTE NUMBER

```
                        The First Fifty Years


     A wise man once said that "Friends come and go, but enemies
accumulate."1  The same can be said of the relationships that
develop between a company and its customers.


     The year 1989 marks the 50th anniversary of the founding of
HALVA International.  While many other import/export businesses
have started in glory and ended in defeat,2 the HALVA
International corporation continues to thrive.


     While there are many theories surrounding the success of
C:\WP51\LEARN\REPORT                        Doc 1 Pg 1 Ln 3" Pos 5.27"
```

6 Press **Reveal Codes** (Alt-F3), then press **Left Arrow** (←) to highlight the Footnote code.

⌨ *Select **R**eveal Codes from the Edit menu.*

Because the actual footnote can only be seen in the View Document screen, the first part of the footnote is displayed in the Reveal Codes screen to help you find a particular footnote.

A FOOTNOTE CODE

B FOOTNOTE TEXT

```
accumulate."1  The same can be said of the relationships that

develop between a company and its customers.


     The year 1989 marks the 50th anniversary of the founding of

HALVA International.  While many other import/export businesses

have started in glory and ended in defeat,2 the HALVA
C:\WP51\LEARN\REPORT                              Doc 1 Pg 1 Ln 3" Pos 5.2"
[                ▲   ▲    ▲    ▲    ▲    ▲    ▲    ▲    ▲    }    ▲   ▲  ]
[HRt]
[Tab]The year 1989 marks the 50th anniversary of the founding of[SRt]
HALVA International.  While many other import/export businesses[SRt]
have started in glory and ended in defeat,[Footnote:2:[Note Num]Friend Krupke, [
UND]Times and Seaso ... ]] the HALVA[SRt]
International corporation continues to thrive.[HRt]
[HRt]
[Tab]While there are many theories surrounding the success of[SRt]
HALVA International, the truth lies in the careful cultivation of[SRt]
customer relationships[Index:Customer relationships] and continued efforts to pr

Press Reveal Codes to restore screen
```

7 Press **Reveal Codes** to display the normal editing screen.

⌨ *Select **Reveal Codes** from the **Edit** menu.*

Now that you have discovered how simple it can be to add a footnote to a document, try adding another footnote to the report.

8 Move the cursor to the end of the first sentence in the same paragraph.

9 Press **Footnote** (Ctrl-F7), select **F**ootnote (1), then select **C**reate (1).

⌨ *Select **F**ootnote from the **L**ayout menu, then select **C**reate.*

10 Type **Ibid., p. 5.** and press **Exit** to return to the normal editing screen.

Both footnotes you created are numbered with a 2. Now watch what happens as you move the cursor down through the paragraph.

11 Press **Down Arrow** (↓) twice to reformat the second paragraph.

The 2 in the second sentence is automatically updated to 3 by WordPerfect. Automatic updating of footnote numbers is a very convenient feature, especially when editing a report.

12 Press **Print** (Shift-F7), select **V**iew Document, then select 100% (1).

13 Press **Go To** (Ctrl-Home) and **Down Arrow** to display the bottom of the first page.

⌨ *Select **P**rint from the **F**ile menu.*

WordPerfect places the new footnotes at the bottom of the page.

▲ NEW FOOTNOTES

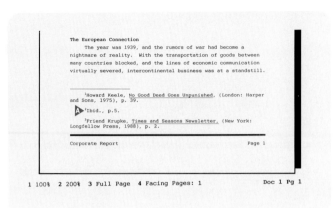

Text that did not fit on the first page has been moved to the second page to make room for the footnotes. Once you type the footnote, all you need to do is sit back and let WordPerfect take care of the formatting.

14 Press **Exit** to return to the editing screen.

Editing a Footnote

After creating a footnote, you can quickly edit the contents of the footnote by letting WordPerfect know the footnote number. For example, the page number reference in the first footnote needs to be changed to 40.

1 Press **Footnote** (Ctrl-F7), select **F**ootnote (1), then select **E**dit (2).

⌨ *Select Footnote from the Layout menu, then select Edit.*

2 Enter **1** for the footnote number.

WordPerfect finds and displays the contents of the footnote.

3 Delete 39 for the page number, type **40**, then press **Exit** (F7) to return to the normal editing screen.

Because you enter a footnote number, you can be anywhere in a document and still edit a footnote. As soon as you exit the footnote, the cursor is placed to the right of the footnote number in the text.

Changing the Endnote Numbering Method

Now that you are familiar with footnotes, let's try searching for an endnote.

1 Press **Home,Home,↑** to move the cursor to the beginning of the report.

2 Press **◆Search** (F2), press **Footnote** (Ctrl-F7), then select **E**ndnote (2).

3 Select **N**ote (1), then press **◆Search** to begin looking for an endnote.

The cursor stops next to a 1 in the text. Like footnotes, the Endnote code is placed in the text next to the item you want to reference.

4 Press **Left Arrow** (←) to place the cursor on the Endnote number, then press **Reveal Codes** (Alt-F3) to display the Endnote code.

▢ *Select **Reveal Codes** from the **Edit** menu.*

Notice that the Endnote code is very similar to the Footnote code. Both contain the number for the note and the text of the note.

5 Press **Right Arrow** (→), then press ♦**Search** twice to find the next endnote.

The cursor stops next to a 2 in the text. But what does the 4 represent in the same paragraph?

▲ ENDNOTE NUMBER
▲ FOOTNOTE NUMBER

```
                    Ⓑ
management.4  To that end, he has worked to give employees a

voice in both their job description and the goals of the

company.2
                    ▲


C:\WP51\LEARN\REPORT                        Doc 1 Pg 3 Ln 5.5" Pos 1.87"
[                                        Ⓑ                      ]
SRt]
management.[Footnote:4;[Note Num]Bryan Metcalf, "Nothing is Imposs ... ]  To tha
t end, he has worked to give employees[Index:Employees] a[SRt]
voice in both their job description and the goals of the[SRt]
company.[Endnote:2;[Note Num] Bryan often takes employees with him on business
.. ][HRt]           ▲
[HRt]
[HRt]
[BOLD]Maximizing the Organization[bold][HRt]
[Tab]However, in all the attention to employees[Index:Employees], the goal to[SR

Press Reveal Codes to restore screen
```

If you check the Reveal Codes screen, you will notice that the 4 is a footnote. Both the footnotes and endnotes are using numbers, which can be very confusing. However, the problem can be solved by changing the method of numbering the endnotes.

6 Press **Reveal Codes** to display the normal editing screen, then press **Home,Home,↑** to return to the beginning of the report.

▢ *Select **Reveal Codes** from the **Edit** menu.*

7 Press **Footnote**, select Endnote, then select Options (4).

▢ *Select **Endnote** from the **Layout** menu, then select **Options**.*

A menu of options is displayed that lets you change such items as endnote spacing, how much of an endnote to keep together on a page, and the method of endnote numbering. A final option also lets you change the numbering method.

8 Select Endnote Numbering **M**ethod (5), select **L**etters (2), then press **Exit** (F7) to return to the editing screen.

9 Press **♦Search** twice to move to the first endnote in the report, then press **♦Search** twice again to move to the second endnote in the report.

The endnotes are now referenced with letters to help distinguish them from the footnotes.

A ENDNOTE LETTER
B FOOTNOTE NUMBER

> Despite advice to the contrary, Metcalf has always
> maintained that employees should be given direction instead of
> management.4 To that end, he has worked to give employees a
> voice in both their job description and the goals of the
> company.b
>
> **Maximizing the Organization**
>   However, in all the attention to employees, the goal to
> provide quality merchandise at discount prices continues to give
> purpose and direction to the company.
> C:\WP51\LEARN\REPORT   Doc 1 Pg 3 Ln 5.5" Pos 1.87"

Creating a Separate Page for Endnotes

While footnotes are placed at the bottom of the same page as the footnote number, where does WordPerfect place the endnotes in a document?

1 Press **Print** (Shift-F7), then select **V**iew Document (6).

⌨ *Select* **P***rint from the* **F***ile menu.*

Although the endnote letter "B" is displayed in the text of the current page, the endnote is not included with footnote 4 at the bottom of the page.

A ENDNOTE LETTER
B FOOTNOTE ONLY

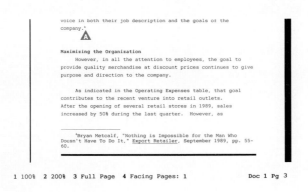

2 Press **Home,Home,↓**.

As you can see, WordPerfect places all the endnotes on the last page of the document. However, they can only be seen in View Document or when you print the document.

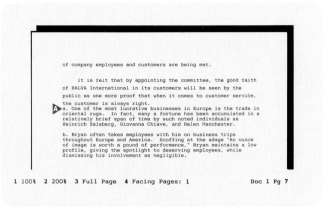

of company employees and customers are being met.

It is felt that by appointing the committee, the good faith of HALVA International in its customers will be seen by the public as one more proof that when it comes to customer service, the customer is always right.

a. One of the most lucrative businesses in Europe is the trade in oriental rugs. In fact, many a fortune has been accumulated in a relatively brief span of time by such noted individuals as Heinrich Salsberg, Giovanna Chiave, and Helen Manchester.

b. Bryan often takes employees with him on business trips throughout Europe and America. Scoffing at the adage "An ounce of image is worth a pound of performance," Bryan maintains a low profile, giving the spotlight to deserving employees, while dismissing his involvement as negligible.

1 100% 2 200% 3 Full Page 4 Facing Pages: 1   Doc 1 Pg 7

Because there is already text on the last page, you can separate the endnotes from the rest of the report by creating a new page.

3 Press **Exit** (F7) to return to the editing screen.

4 Press **Home,Home,↓** then press **Hard Page** (Ctrl-Enter) to create a new page at the end of the report.

5 Press **Center** (Shift-F6), press **Bold** (F6), then type **Endnotes** to title the page.

6 Press **End** to move the cursor to the end of the line, then press **Enter** to add extra spacing between the title and the endnotes.

7 Press **Print**, then select View Document to display the endnotes on the new page.

🖃 *Select* ***Print*** *from the* ***F****ile menu.*

You may have noticed that the endnotes use single line spacing, while the line spacing for the report text is 1.5.

Because headers, footers, footnotes, and endnotes are created in a separate editing screen, WordPerfect assumes that you want to use the initial formats (such as single line spacing) until you change them in the header, footer, footnote, or endnote. This can be especially useful when you want to create a different format for a header, footer, footnote, or endnote.

Protecting a Block of Text

Now that you are in the View Document screen, you may want to check the rest of the report to see if there are any additional changes that could be made to the format.

1 Select Facing Pages (4) then press **Home,Home,↑** to return to the beginning of the report.

2 Press **Page Down** (PgDn) to display pages 2 and 3, then press **Page Down** again to display pages 4 and 5.

Some more space could be added above and below the Operating Expenses table. A page break is also dividing the Mail Order vs. Retail table.

△ OPERATING EXPENSES TABLE

△ PAGE BREAK

1 100% 2 200% 3 Full Page 4 Facing Pages: 4   Doc 1 Pg 4-5

3 Press **Exit** (F7) to return to the editing screen.

4 Move the cursor to the empty line above the Operating Expenses table and press **Enter** to add extra spacing.

5 Move the cursor to the empty line below the Operating Expenses table and press **Enter** to add extra spacing.

6 Press **Go To** (Ctrl-Home), then press **Down Arrow** (↓) to display the Mail Order vs. Retail table at the bottom of page 4.

You could use a Hard Page break to move the table to the top of page 5. However, because you always want the table to stay together *no matter where it is placed in the report*, you need a way to protect it from all soft page breaks.

7 Move the cursor to the Mail Order vs. Retail heading, then press **Home,Home,Home,←** to move the cursor in front of all the codes at the very beginning of the line.

⌨ *Move the mouse pointer to the beginning of the Mail Order vs. Retail line.*

8 Press **Block** (Alt-F4), then move the cursor to the line below the table.

⌨ *Block the table by holding down the left button on the mouse and dragging the mouse pointer to the line below the table.*

9 Press **Format** (Shift-F8), then type **y** to have WordPerfect protect the block.

⌨ *Select Protect Block from the Edit menu.*

WordPerfect places a soft page break above the table to keep it all on the same page.

10 Press **Up Arrow** (↑) until the cursor is above the soft page break, then press **Reveal Codes** (Alt-F3).

Notice that the text is protected by a Block Protect On code at the beginning of the subheading and a Block Protect Off code at the end of the table (you need to scroll down to display the Off code).

A BLOCK PROTECT ON CODE
B BLOCK PROTECT OFF CODE

Any text added between the codes is also protected.

11 Press **Print** (Shift-F7), then select **V**iew Document (6).

⌨ *Select Print from the File menu.*

Now that the Mail Order vs. Retail table is protected from a page break, it looks awkward by itself on page 5.

1 100%   2 200%   3 Full Page   4 Facing Pages: 4   Doc 1 Pg 4-5

Let's include the paragraph at the bottom of page 4 with the table, then add a subheading with the paragraph.

12 Press **Exit** to return to the editing screen.

13 Place the cursor in the paragraph at the bottom of page 4.

14 Press **Move** (Ctrl-F4), select **P**aragraph (2), then select **M**ove (1).

⌨ *Choose Select from the Edit menu, select **P**aragraph, then select **M**ove (1).*

The paragraph is deleted from the screen and is ready to move to a new location.

Because the paragraph needs to stay with the table, it should be included between the Block Protect On and Off codes.

The cursor should be on the Block Protect On code. If you press Enter to retrieve the paragraph now, the paragraph will be outside the block protection codes.

However, the paragraph also needs to come *before* the line spacing and margin codes or it will be formatted for single line spacing and a left margin of 1.5".

15 Press **Right Arrow** (→), then press **Enter** to retrieve the paragraph.

16 Press **Reveal Codes** to display the normal editing screen.

⊞ *Select* ***R****eveal Codes from the* ***E****dit menu.*

The paragraph is now included with the table at the top of page 5.

17 Press **Bold** (F6), type **Mail Order Marketing** for a subheading above the paragraph, then press **Bold** and **Enter** to end the line.

18 Press **Print**, then select **View Document** to display pages 4 and 5.

⊞ *Select* ***P****rint from the* ***F****ile menu.*

The subheading is at the top of page 5 because it is included between the block protection codes with the paragraph and table.

19 Press **Exit** to return to the editing screen.

Saving the Report

You may want to use the View Document screen again to page through the entire document. Try displaying the report in both Full Page and Facing Pages views. When you finish, return to the editing screen to save the edited report.

1 Press **Exit** (F7), type **y**, then press **Enter** to use the Report filename.

2 Type **y** to replace the report on disk with the edited version, then type **n** to clear the screen.

In this lesson you have been introduced to features that help you reference pages, sources, and ideas, as well as protecting blocks of text. As you continue on through the lessons, you will discover many other features that can save you time and effort when creating larger documents with WordPerfect.

Lesson 22: Corporate Report — Table of Contents and Index

After formatting and editing a report (or any larger document), you may want to add a table of contents or index. In this lesson you discover how easy it can be to create a table of contents or index with WordPerfect, then finish the report by adding a title page.

Marking Text for the Table of Contents

Whenever you want to create a table of contents, all you need to do is mark the headings in your document, then WordPerfect builds (generates) the table of contents for you.

1 Press **Retrieve** (Shift-F10), then enter **report** to retrieve the formatted corporate report from lesson 21.

⬛ *Select Retrieve from the File menu.*

To save you time, the headings for the first and the last sections of the report have been marked for the table of contents. All you need to do is mark the headings for the "A Time for Reflection" section.

2 Press **Page Down** (PgDn) twice, then press **Right Arrow** (→) to place the cursor at the beginning of "A Time for Reflection" at the top of page 3.

⬛ *Move the mouse pointer to the beginning of "A Time for Reflection."*

3 Press **Block** (Alt-F4), then press **Home,**→ to highlight the heading.

⬛ *Block the heading by holding down the left button and dragging the mouse pointer across the heading.*

4 Press **Mark Text** (Alt-F5), select ToC (1), then enter **1** (one) for the heading level.

⬛ *Select Table of Contents from the Mark menu.*

You can have up to five levels of headings in a table of contents. The first level is generated at the left margin, with levels 2 through 5 at tab stops.

5 Press **Reveal Codes** (Alt-F3) to display the codes that mark the heading for the table of contents.

⬛ *Select Reveal Codes from the Edit menu.*

A [Mark:ToC,1] code indicates the beginning of the text for the table of contents, while an [End Mark:Toc,1] indicates the end of the text for the table of contents.

```
                              A Time For Reflection_


        While the past provides understanding, the present provides
     reality.  In this part of the report, we hope to give an overview
     of HALVA International that provides a moment of insight into the
     current direction of the company.
     C:\WP51\LEARN\REPORT                              Doc 1 Pg 3 Ln 1" Pos 5.3"
     ▬▬▬▬▬▬▬▬▬▬▬▬▬▬▬▬▬▬▬▬▬▬▬▬▬▬▬▬▬▬▬▬▬▬▬▬▬▬▬▬▬▬▬▬▬▬▬▬▬▬▬▬▬▬▬▬▬
     make while raising 5 boys."[Ln Spacing:1.5][HRt]
     [HRt]
     [HPg]    ▼                                         ▼
     [Center][Mark:ToC,1][BOLD]A Time For Reflection[bold][End Mark:ToC,1][HRt]
     [HRt]
     [Tab]While the past provides understanding, the present provides[SRt]
     reality.  In this part of the report, we hope to give an overview[SRt]
     of HALVA International that provides a moment of insight into the[SRt]
     current direction of the company[Index:Company direction].[HRt]
     [HRt]

     Press Reveal Codes to restore screen
```

Any text or codes between the Mark Text codes is used in the table of contents. Because the [BOLD] and [bold] codes are included, the heading "A Time for Reflection" will be bolded when WordPerfect generates the table of contents.

6 Press **Down Arrow** (↓) until the cursor is on the "Direction vs. Management" heading.

7 Press **Home,←** to move the cursor to the beginning of the heading.

The "Direction vs. Management" heading is a subheading to the section, and needs to be marked for level 2. Because level 2 headings are not bolded in the table of contents for the report, the Bold codes do not need to be included with the marked text.

8 Press **Block**, press **Home,→**, then press **Left Arrow** (←) to place the cursor at the end of the heading (on the [bold] code).

9 Press **Mark Text** (Alt-F5), select ToC (1), then enter **2** for the heading level.

⌨ *Select Table of Contents from the Mark menu.*

The heading is surrounded by [Mark:ToC,2] and [End Mark:ToC,2] codes that include the table of contents level number (2). The Mark Text codes do not affect the way the text is displayed or printed, but simply let WordPerfect know what text in the document to use for the table of contents.

Now that you have marked two headings in the section, there are still two more headings that need to be marked for the table of contents.

10 Mark the following two headings for the second level of the table of contents (use steps 7 and 8 as a guide).
Maximizing the Organization
Mail Order Marketing

11 When you finish, press **Reveal Codes** to display the normal editing screen.

⊟ *Select **R**eveal Codes from the **E**dit menu.*

Creating a Page for the Table of Contents

Now that the text is marked for the table of contents, the next step is to create a separate page for the table at the beginning of the report.

1 Press **Home,Home,Home,↑** to move the cursor to the very beginning of the report (before any codes).

2 Press **Hard Page** (Ctrl-Enter), then press **Up Arrow** (↑) to place the cursor on the new page.

3 Press **Center** (Shift-F6), press **Bold** (F6), then type **Table of Contents** for the title.

4 Press **Right Arrow** (→) to move past the Bold Off code, then press **Enter** twice for double spacing.

Defining the Table of Contents

With a page created for the table of contents, you are ready to define the format for the table.

1 Press **Mark Text** (Alt-F5), select **D**efine (5), then select Define Table of Contents (1).

⊟ *Select **D**efine from the **M**ark menu, then select Table of Contents.*

A menu is displayed that includes the number of levels in the table of contents, as well as the page numbering style for each level in the table.

The page numbering style is set to "Flush right with leader," which means that page numbers will be placed at the right margin with a dot leader placed between the headings and the numbers.

2 Select **N**umber of Levels (1), then type **2** for two levels of headings in the table of contents.

3 Press **Exit** (F7) to return to the editing screen.

4 Press **Reveal Codes** (Alt-F3) to display the definition code for the table of contents.

⊟ *Select **R**eveal Codes from the **E**dit menu.*

The definition code not only includes information about the format of the table, but also marks the place where WordPerfect will generate the table of contents.

A TABLE OF CONTENTS FORMAT

B GENERATED AT CODE

```
                          Table of Contents


-------------------------------------------------------------------
                         The First Fifty Years


         A wise man once said that "Friends come and go, but enemies

     accumulate."1  The same can be said of the relationships that
C:\WP51\LEARN\REPORT                           Doc 1 Pg 1 Ln 1.33" Pos 1"

[Center][BOLD]Table of Contents[bold][HRt]
[HRt]
[Def Mark:ToC,2:5,5][HPg]
[HRt]
[Ln Spacing:1.5][Undrln:Spaces,Tabs][Footer A:Odd pages; ... ][Footer B:Even pag
es; ... ][End Opt][Center][Mark:ToC,1][BOLD]The First Fifty Years[bold][End Mark
:ToC,1][HRt]
[HRt]
[Tab]A wise man once said that "Friends come and go, but enemies[SRt]
accumulate."[Footnote:1;[Note Num]Howard Keele, [UND]No Good Deed Goe ... ]  The
 same can be said of the relationships that[SRt]

Press Reveal Codes to restore screen
```

5 Press **Reveal Codes** to display the normal editing screen.

⊟ Select **Reveal Codes** from the **Edit** menu.

Generating the Table of Contents

Once the text is marked and the table defined, all you need to do is give the signal, and WordPerfect will generate a table of contents complete with headings, dot leaders, and page numbers.

1 Press **Mark Text** (Alt-F5) and select **G**enerate (6).

⊟ Select **Generate** from the **Mark** menu.

2 Select **G**enerate Tables, Indexes, Auto References, etc. (5).

A "Continue?" message is displayed to remind you that any existing tables, lists, or indexes will be replaced. Whenever WordPerfect generates text in a document, the original text is replaced by the new table, list, or index. The "Continue?" message gives you a chance to back out before continuing with the process.

3 Type **y** to generate the table of contents.

A "Generation in Progress" message is displayed that keeps you informed of the progress being made in generating the table of contents.

When the generating is completed, the table is displayed on your screen at the position of the definition code.

▲ TABLE OF CONTENTS

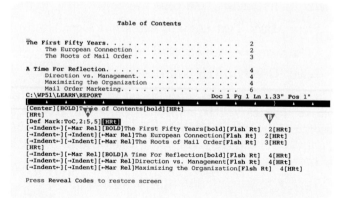

4 Press **Reveal Codes** (Alt-F3) to display the codes in the table of contents.

☐ *Select **R**eveal Codes from the **E**dit menu.*

Notice that Indent, Margin Release, and Flush Right codes have been added to format the text you marked for the table of contents, and that page numbers for the table are displayed at the right margin.

▲ FORMATTING CODES
▲ PAGE NUMBERS

The definition code for the table of contents is still in the same place to mark the beginning of the table of contents.

5 Press **Go To** (Ctrl-Home), then press **Down Arrow** (↓) to move to the bottom of the table.

An [End Def] code has also been added to mark the end of the table of contents. If you edit the document, and need to generate the table of contents again, WordPerfect uses the two definition marks to identify the text that needs to be replaced with the new table of contents.

If you mistakenly type text between the two definition codes, then the text will be deleted if the table is regenerated. By placing the table of contents on a separate page, you should have no trouble with losing text when using the Generate feature.

6 Press **Reveal Codes**, then press **Home,Home,↑** to display the entire table of contents on the screen.

⌨ *Select **R**eveal Codes from the **E**dit menu.*

Editing the Table of Contents

The numbering in the table of contents begins at page 2 because the table of contents is now on page 1 of the report. The endnotes heading is also missing from the table of contents and needs to be included.

⚠ PAGE NUMBERS

⚠ MISSING ENDNOTES HEADING

```
                          Table of Contents
 _                                                   ▼▼

The First Fifty Years. . . . . . . . . . . . . . .    2
        The European Connection . . . . . . . . . . .  2
        The Roots of Mail Order . . . . . . . . . . .  3

A Time For Reflection. . . . . . . . . . . . . . . .  4
        Direction vs. Management. . . . . . . . . . .  4
        Maximizing the Organization . . . . . . . . .  4
        Mail Order Marketing. . . .`. . . . . . . . .  6

The Next Fifty Years . . . . . . . . . . . . . . . .  7
        Expanding Markets . . . . . . . . . . . . . .  7
        Expanding Resources . . . . . . . . . . . . .  7
 ▣
============================================================================
                          The First Fifty Years


      A wise man once said that "Friends come and go, but enemies

accumulate."1  The same can be said of the relationships that
C:\WP51\LEARN\REPORT                         Doc 1 Pg 1 Ln 1" Pos 1"
```

While you could edit the generated text to change the page numbers and add the endnotes heading, all your changes would be replaced if you ever generated the table of contents again. You should always edit the document, not the table of contents, then have WordPerfect generate the table again with the editing changes.

For example, instead of typing in new page numbers for the table of contents, let's use the Format key to start numbering at 1 on the first page of the report.

1 Press **Page Down** (PgDn) to move the cursor to the top of the first page of the report (page 2 on the status line).

2 Press **Format** (Shift-F8) and select **P**age (2).

⊞ *Select **P**age from the **L**ayout menu.*

3 Select Page **N**umbering (6).

4 Select New Page Number (1), then enter **1** (one) to start page numbering at 1 on the first page of the report.

5 Press **Exit** (F7) to return to the editing screen.

The page number on the status line is now set to 1, even though the page is actually the second one in the report.

6 Press **Home,Home,↓** to move the cursor to the end of the report.

7 Place the cursor at the beginning of the Endnotes heading and use **Block** (Alt-F4) to highlight the heading (include the [BOLD] and [bold] codes).

8 Press **Mark Text** (Alt-F5), select ToC (1), then enter **1** (one) for the level number.

⊞ *Select **T**able of **C**ontents from the **M**ark menu.*

With the numbering changed and the endnotes heading marked, you are ready to regenerate the table of contents.

9 Press **Mark Text**, select **G**enerate (6), then select **G**enerate Tables, Indexes, Auto References, etc. (5).

⊞ *Select **G**enerate from the **M**ark menu, then select **G**enerate Tables, Indexes, Auto References, etc. (5).*

10 Type **y** to continue and have WordPerfect replace the old table with a new table of contents.

When the generating is completed, the table of contents numbering begins at 1, and a new "Endnotes" heading has been added to the table of contents.

Ⓐ PAGE NUMBERING

Ⓑ ENDNOTES HEADING

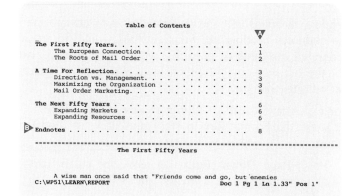

```
                          Table of Contents           ▼Ⓐ

The First Fifty Years. . . . . . . . . . . . . . . . . . 1
          The European Connection . . . . . . . . . . . . . 1
          The Roots of Mail Order . . . . . . . . . . . . . 2

A Time For Reflection. . . . . . . . . . . . . . . . . 3
          Direction vs. Management. . . . . . . . . . . . 3
          Maximizing the Organization . . . . . . . . . . 3
          Mail Order Marketing. . . . . . . . . . . . . . 5

The Next Fifty Years . . . . . . . . . . . . . . . . . 6
          Expanding Markets . . . . . . . . . . . . . . . 6
          Expanding Resources . . . . . . . . . . . . . . 6

Ⓑ Endnotes . . . . . . . . . . . . . . . . . . . . . . 8

=========================================================
                      The First Fifty Years


      A wise man once said that "Friends come and go, but enemies
C:\WP51\LEARN\REPORT                        Doc 1 Pg 1 Ln 1.33" Pos 1"
```

Because WordPerfect generates the table of contents at the definition code, you can be anywhere in the document to start generating a new table.

Marking Text for the Index

Generating an index with WordPerfect is very similar to generating a table of contents. You provide the text for the index and a definition code, and WordPerfect takes care of creating the index.

Because you may not always want to use the text in a document for the index, you can either create your own index heading, or use Block to mark existing text for a heading.

For example, let's include the word "survival" as an index heading. The word appears three times in the report.

1 Press ♦**Search** (F2), type **survival** then press ♦**Search** again to find the first occurrence of the word.

⌨ *Select **Forward** from the Search menu, type **survival**, then click the right-hand mouse button.*

The cursor stops next to "survival" in the phrase "survival of the company."

2 Press ♦**Search** twice to find the second occurrence of the word.

⌨ *Select **Next** from the Search menu.*

The cursor stops next to "survival" in the phrase "survival industry."

3 Press ♦**Search** twice to find the last occurrence of the word.

⌨ *Select **Next** from the Search menu.*

The cursor stops next to "survival" in the phrase "economic survival."

There are three types of survival included in the report—company, industrial, and economic survival. It would probably be best to list "Survival" in the index as a heading, with Company, Industrial, and Economic, as subheadings. However, the phrases are not written as Survival Company, Survival Industrial, and Survival Economic.

In this case, you need to type the text for the index headings.

4 Press **Mark Text** (Alt-F5), then select **Index** (3)

If you are using the Mark Text function key, WordPerfect displays the word closest to the cursor as a suggested index heading.

If you use the Index option on the Mark pull-down menu, WordPerfect will not automatically display a suggested heading. You must First block the word you want to mark.

⌨ *Block the word "survival," then select **Index** from the **Mark** menu.*

5 Delete the period (.) at the end of the word "Survival." (if you used the function key), then press **Enter**.

The same word is also displayed for the subheading.

6 Type **economic** for the subheading, then press **Enter**.

7 Press **Reveal Codes** (Alt-F3) to display the Index code.

⌨ *Select* **Reveal Codes** *from the* **Edit** *menu.*

Notice that the Index code includes the text for the heading and the subheading.

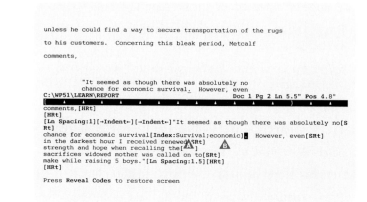

▲ HEADING
Ⓑ SUBHEADING

When you generate the index, WordPerfect uses the text in the code and the page number where the code is located for the index. As long as the index code stays next to the text that needs to be referenced (like a Footnote code), the page number in the index will be correct.

8 Press **Reveal Codes** to display the normal editing screen.

⌨ *Select* **Reveal Codes** *from the* **Edit** *menu.*

9 Press **Word Left** (Ctrl-←), then press ◆**Search** (Shift-F2) twice to move the cursor to the second occurrence of "survival."

⌨ *Select* **Backward** *from the* **Search** *menu, then click the right-hand mouse button.*

10 Press **Mark Text** (Alt-F5), select Index (3), then press **Enter** to use the word "Survival" for the heading.

⌨ *Block the word "survival," then select* **Index** *from the* **Mark** *menu.*

Because you used the word "Survival" without editing it, WordPerfect does not display a word for the subheading.

11 Enter **industrial** for the subheading.

12 Press **Word Left**, then press ◆**Search** twice to move the cursor to the first occurrence of "survival."

⊞ *Select Next from the Search menu.*

13 Press **Mark Text**, select Index, press **Enter** to use the word "Survival" for the heading, then enter **company** for the subheading.

⊞ *Block the word "survival," then select Index from the Mark menu.*

Sometimes you may be able to use the text in a document for an index heading. For example, besides listing economic survival as a subheading, you may also want to list it as a heading in the index.

14 Press ◆**Search** twice, then press ◆**Search** twice again to move the cursor to the phrase "economic survival."

⊞ *Select Forward from the Search menu and click the right-hand mouse button. Then select Next from the Search menu.*

15 Press **Block** (Alt-F4), then press **Word Left** twice to highlight the phrase.

16 Press **Mark Text**, select Index, press **Enter** to use the phrase as a heading, then press **Enter** again for no subheading.

⊞ *Block the phrase, then select Index from the Mark menu.*

If you do not want a subheading for an index marking code, then simply press Enter (if no text appears), or delete any suggested text and press Enter.

17 Press **Reveal Codes** to display the index codes for the "economic survival" phrase.

⊞ *Select Reveal Codes from the Edit menu.*

Notice that there are two index marking codes. WordPerfect will use both codes to create two entries in the index with the same page number.

▲ INDEX MARKING CODES

```
unless he could find a way to secure transportation of the rugs

to his customers.  Concerning this bleak period, Metcalf

comments,

              "It seemed as though there was absolutely no
              chance for economic survival.  However, even
C:\WP51\LEARN\REPORT                          Doc 1 Pg 2 Ln 5.5" Pos 3.1"
[                                                                           ]
comments,[HRt]
[HRt]
[Ln Spacing:1][→Indent←][→Indent←]"It seemed as though there was absolutely no[S
Rt]
chance for [Index:Economic survival]economic survival[Index:Survival;economic].
 However, even[SRt]
in the darkest hour I received renewed[SRt]
strength and hope when recalling the[SRt]
sacrifices widowed mother was called on to[SRt]
make while raising 5 boys."[Ln Spacing:1.5][HRt]

Press Reveal Codes to restore screen
```

18 Press **Reveal Codes** to display the normal editing screen.

⬛ *Select Reveal Codes from the Edit menu.*

Creating a Page for the Index

With the text marked, you need to create a separate page for the index at the very end of the report (after the endnotes).

1 Press **Home,Home,↓** to move the cursor to the end of the report.

2 Press **Hard Page** (Ctrl-Enter) to create a new page at the end of the report.

3 Press **Center** (Shift-F6), press **Bold** (F6), then type **Index** for the title.

4 Press **Bold** to turn off bolding, then press **Enter** twice for double spacing.

The index title also needs to be marked for the table of contents.

5 Press **Up Arrow** (↑) twice, then press **Right Arrow** to place the cursor at the beginning of the index title.

6 Press **Block** (Alt-F4), then press **End** to highlight the title.

7 Press **Mark Text** (Alt-F5), select **ToC** (1), then enter **1** (one) for the level number.

⬛ *Select Table of Contents from the Mark menu.*

Defining the Index

Like the table of contents, you also need to define a format for the index.

1 Press **Home,Home,↓** to move the cursor to the end of the index page.

2 Press **Mark Text** (Alt-F5), select **Define** (5), then select Define **Index** (3).

⬛ *Select Define from the Mark menu, then select Index.*

3 Press **Enter** for no concordance file (only headings from the index codes).

A menu is displayed that includes five different styles of page numbering for the index. The numbering style is usually the same for an entire index (and there are only headings and subheadings), no numbering levels are included. All you need to do is select a style.

4 Select **P**age Numbers Follow Entries (2) for the numbering style.

The definition code for the index (like the one for table of contents) also marks the place where WordPerfect will generate the index.

Generating the Index

Let's try generating the index for the report from the index codes you created, and those already provided for you in the report.

1 Press **Mark Text** (Alt-F5), select Generate (6), then select Generate Tables, Indexes, Auto References, etc. (5).

▢ *Select Generate from the Mark menu, then select Generate Tables, Indexes, Auto References, etc. (5).*

2 Type **y** to generate both the index and a new table of contents.

The "Generation in Progress" message is displayed to keep you informed of the progress. When the generating is completed, the index is displayed on your screen at the position of the definition code.

▲ INDEX

```
==============================================
                   Endnotes

==============================================
                    Index
▲
Company  1

Company direction  3

Customer relationships  1

Customers  1

Economic

       communication  1

Economic survival  2
C:\WP51\LEARN\REPORT                    Doc 1 Pg 9 Ln 1.5" Pos 1"
```

Indent and Margin Release codes have been added to format the index headings, and page numbers are listed after each heading or subheading. An [End Def] code has also been included to mark the end of the index.

Because the end of the report is formatted for 1.5 line spacing, the index is also formatted for the same line spacing.

3 Press **Go To** (Ctrl-Home), then press **Up Arrow** (↑) to move the cursor to the top of the page.

4 Press **Format** (Shift-F8), select Line (1), then select Line Spacing (6).

▢ *Select Line from the Layout menu, then select Line Spacing (6).*

5 Enter **1** (one) for the line spacing, then press **Exit** (F7) to return to the editing screen.

The Line Spacing code is outside of the index definition codes at the top of the page so that the index will continue to be formatted for single line spacing, even when the index is regenerated.

Creating an Index Concordance

Some words or phrases that you want included in the index may occur several times in a document. You could mark each occurrence, or you could create a concordance.

A concordance is a list of words that you want WordPerfect to include as headings in the index. When an index is generated, WordPerfect searches for the words in the document and provides page numbers for them in the index.

Let's try creating a concordance, including the concordance filename in the index definition, then regenerating the index.

1 Press **Switch** (Shift-F3) to display the second editing screen.

⌨ *Select Switch Document from the Edit menu.*

2 Type **Retail** and press **Enter**, then type **Mail Order** and press **Enter**.

3 Press **Exit** (F7), type **y** to save the headings, then enter **concord** for the filename.

4 Type **y** to exit the second editing screen and return to the report.

As you can see, the concordance is simply a WordPerfect document with a list of headings you want to use in the index. Each heading should be on a separate line that ends with a hard return. You can use any filename you want for the concordance.

5 Press **Reveal Codes** (Alt-F3).

⌨ *Select Reveal Codes from the Edit menu.*

6 Place the cursor on the [Def Mark:Index,2] code below the Index heading, then press **Delete** (Del) to delete the code.

7 Press **Mark Text** (Alt-F5), select **Define** (5), then select Define **I**ndex (3).

⌨ *Select Define from the Mark menu, then select Index.*

8 Enter **concord** for the name of the concordance, then select **P**age Numbers Follow Entries (2).

With the concordance filename included in the index definition code, let's try generating the index again.

9 Press **Reveal Codes** to display the normal editing screen.

⌨ *Select Reveal Codes from the Edit menu.*

10 Press **Mark Text**, select **G**enerate (6), then select **G**enerate Tables, Indexes, Auto References, etc. (5).

⌨ *Select Generate from the Mark menu, then select Generate Tables, Indexes, Auto References, etc. (5).*

11 Type **y** to generate a new index and a new table of contents.

When the generating is completed, the index is displayed on your screen at the position of the definition code.

12 Press **Page Down** (PgDn) to display the bottom of the index on your screen.

The Retail and Mail Order headings are listed alphabetically in the index with page numbers where the words can be found in the report.

⚠ MAIL ORDER HEADING

⚠ RETAIL HEADING

```
      Company  1
      Company direction  3
      Customer relationships  1
      Customers  1
      Economic
            communication  1
      Economic survival  2
      Employees  3
 Ⓐ▸  Mail Order  2, 5
      Merchandise
            imported jewelry  6
            music boxes  6
            oriental furniture  6
            oriental rugs  2, 6
 Ⓑ▸  Retail  5, 3, 5, 3, 5, 6, 5
      Survival
            company  1
            economic  2
            industrial  2
      War machine  2
      World War II  1


      C:\WP51\LEARN\REPORT                        Doc 1 Pg 9 Ln 4.83" Pos 1"
```

While using a concordance may seem to be an easy way to generate an entire index *without* marking text, you may not want each occurrence of a word referenced in the index. In addition, the number of words you can have in a concordance is limited by the amount of memory you have available when generating the tables, lists, and/or index in a document.

Moving the Endnotes

Now that you have completed the table of contents and index, let's take a moment to check for any formatting problems by using the View Document screen.

1 Press **Print** (Shift-F7), select **V**iew Document (6), then select Full Page (3).

⌨ *Select Print from the File menu.*

The index is displayed on the last page, but what is the text below the index headings?

2 Select 100% (1), then press **Go To** (Ctrl-Home) and **Down Arrow** (↓) for a closer look at the text.

Because the index is now the last page of the report, WordPerfect is displaying the endnotes at the end of the index.

▲ ENDNOTES

```
        Employees  3
        Mail Order   2, 5
        Merchandise
              imported jewelry  6
              music boxes  6
              oriental furniture  6
              oriental rugs  2, 6
        Retail  5, 3, 5, 3, 5, 6, 5
        Survival
              company  1
              economic  2
              industrial  2
        War machine  2
        World War II  1

        a. One of the most lucrative businesses in Europe is the trade in
 ⒜      oriental rugs.  In fact, many a fortune has been accumulated in a
        relatively brief span of time by such noted individuals as
        Heinrich Salsberg, Giovanna Chiave, and Helen Manchester.

        b. Bryan often takes employees with him on business trips
 ⒜      throughout Europe and America.  Scoffing at the adage "An ounce
        of image is worth a pound of performance," Bryan maintains a low
        profile, giving the spotlight to deserving employees, while
        dismissing his involvement as negligible.


 1 100%  2 200%  3 Full Page  4 Facing Pages: 1                Doc 1 Pg 9
```

Is there a way to make sure that the endnotes are printed on their own page?

3 Press **Exit** (F7) to return to the editing screen.

4 Press **Page Up** (PgUp), then press **Down Arrow** (↓) to move the cursor to the line below the Endnotes title.

5 Press **Footnote** (Ctrl-F7), then select Endnote **P**lacement (3).

⌨ *Select Endnote from the Layout menu, then select **P**lacement.*

6 Type **n** when you see the "Restart Endnote Numbering?" message (there is only one set of endnotes in the report).

A comment is displayed on the screen to let you know that you need to generate before WordPerfect can determine how much space the endnotes will take in the report.

▲ ENDNOTES COMMENT

```
                                Endnotes
            ▼
            ⒜
  ┌──────────────────────────────────────────────────────────────────┐
  │ Endnote Placement                                                  │
  │ It is not known how much space endnotes will occupy here.          │
  │ Generate to determine.                                             │
  └──────────────────────────────────────────────────────────────────┘


  ============================================================================
  Economic
        communication  1
  Economic survival  2
  Employees  3
  Mail Order  2, 5
  Merchandise
        imported jewelry  6
        music boxes  6
        oriental furniture  6
        oriental rugs  2, 6
  Retail  5, 3, 5, 3, 5, 6, 5
  Survival
        company  1
  C:\WP51\LEARN\REPORT                        Doc 1 Pg 9 Ln 1" Pos 1"
```

The comment represents an Endnote Placement code that can be seen in Reveal Codes.

7 Press **Reveal Codes** (Alt-F3) to display the Endnote Placement code.

⊟ *Select Reveal Codes from the Edit menu.*

The endnotes will be printed at the location of the Endnote Placement code, just as an index or table of contents is generated at a definition code.

8 Press **Reveal Codes** to display the normal editing screen.

⊟ *Select Reveal Codes from the Edit menu.*

9 Press **Backspace** to delete the extra hard page that WordPerfect placed in the document to protect the endnotes.

10 Press **Mark Text** (Alt-F5), select **Generate** (6), then select **Generate Tables, Indexes, Auto References, etc.** (5).

⊟ *Select Generate from the Mark menu, then select Generate Tables, Indexes, Auto References, etc. (5).*

11 Type **y** to generate the index, table of contents, and the space needed for the endnotes.

When the generating is completed, a new comment is displayed for the Endnote Placement code.

12 Press **Print**, select **View Document**, then select **Full Page**.

⊟ *Select Print from the File menu.*

Because you are using an Endnote Placement code, the endnotes are no longer placed at the end of the report with the index.

13 Press **Page Up** (PgUp) to display the endnotes.

The endnotes are displayed below the Endnotes title at the location of the Endnote Placement code.

Discontinuing Footers

The bottom of the index page includes page numbering, which is normally not included in an index.

▲ PAGE NUMBERING

1 100%   2 200%   3 Full Page   4 Facing Pages: 3   Doc 1 Pg 8

1 Press **Exit** (F7) to return to the editing screen.

2 Make sure the cursor is at the top of the Index page, then press **Format** (Shift-F8) and select **P**age (2).

⌨ *Select Page from the Layout menu.*

You could select Suppress from the Page Format menu to prevent the footer from being printed on the current page, but if the index becomes larger than a page, you would need to place another suppress code at the top of each page of the index.

3 Select **F**ooters (4), select Footer **A** (1), then select **D**iscontinue (1).

4 Select **F**ooters, select Footer **B** (2), then select **D**iscontinue.

5 Press **Exit** to return to the editing screen, then press **Reveal Codes** (Alt-F3).

⌨ *Select Reveal Codes from the Edit menu.*

Discontinue codes for footer A and footer B are displayed on the screen. Neither footer will be printed from the beginning of the index to the end of the report until you create another footer A or footer B.

Creating a Title Page

As a final touch, let's add a title page to the report using a graphics box.

1 Press **Home,Home,Home,↑** to move the cursor to the very beginning of the report.

2 Press **Hard Page** (Ctrl-Enter) to create a new page, then press **Page Up** (PgUp) to place the cursor on the new page.

3 Press **Graphics** (Alt-F9), select **F**igure (1), then select **C**reate (1).

⊟ *Select* **F***igure from the Graphics menu, then select* **C***reate.*

4 Select Anchor **T**ype (4), select **P**age (2), then press **Enter** to keep the box on the title page.

5 Select **V**ertical Position (5), then select **F**ull Page (1).

Now that the box has been created for the title page, you can edit the contents of the box to include the report title.

6 Select **E**dit (9) to include the report title inside the box.

The editing screen for graphics boxes is very similar to the one used for footers, endnotes, etc., and is just as powerful.

⚠ BOX MESSAGE

```
⬆ Box:  Press Exit when done, Graphics to rotate text       Ln 0" Pos 0"
[


  Press Reveal Codes to restore screen
```

7 Press **Format** (Shift-F8), select **O**ther (4), then select **A**dvance (1).

⊟ *Select* **O***ther from the Layout menu, then select* **A***dvance.*

You can use the Advance feature in a variety of ways to move text to an exact location on the page.

8 Select **D**own (2), then enter **2.5** to move the text 2½ inches down the page.

9 Press **Exit** (F7) to return to the box editing screen.

10 Press **Center** (Shift-F6) to center the title.

11 Press **Font** (Ctrl-F8), select **S**ize (1), then select **V**ery Large (6).

12 Type **HALVA International** for the title, press **End** to move past the [vry large] code.

13 Press **Enter** twice to double space.

14 Press **Center** to center the subtitle.

15 Press **Font**, select **Size**, then select **Large** (5).

16 Press **Font** again, select **Appearance** (2), then select **Italic** (4).

17 Type **Corporate Report** for the subtitle, then press **Exit** twice to return to the normal editing screen.

18 Press **Print** (Shift-F7), select **View Document** (6), then select **Full Page** (3).

⌨ *Select Print from the File menu.*

A border is drawn around the page with the titles 2½ inches down inside the border.

A BORDER
B TITLES

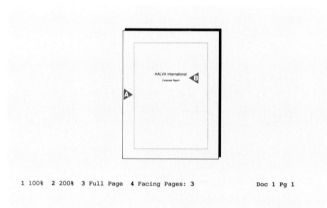

It is important to remember that the titles are actually contained in the figure box, and can only be edited by editing the box. A border was used in the newsletter in lessons 16 and 17, but the text of the newsletter was in the normal editing screen, with the figure box printed on top of the text.

19 Select **100%** (1) for a closer look, then press **Exit** to return to the editing screen.

Changing the Graphics Box Border

While the single-line border is a good choice for a title page, there are other types of borders available for graphics boxes.

1 Press **Left Arrow** (←) to place the cursor on the Figure code.

2 Press **Graphics** (Alt-F9), select **Figure** (1), then select **Options** (4).

⌨ *Select Figure from the Graphics menu, then select Options.*

A menu with several options for changing the format of a figure box is displayed on the screen.

3 Select **B**order Style (1) to change the style of the left, right, top, and bottom borders.

Another menu is displayed at the bottom of the screen that lets you select from several styles of borders such as double, dashed, thick, etc. You can select a different style for each side of the border, or format all four sides with the same style.

4 Type **3** four times to set a double style for all four sides of the border, then press **Exit** (F7) to return to the editing screen.

5 Press **Print** (Shift-F7), select **V**iew Document (6), then select Full Page (3).

⌨ *Select Print from the File menu.*

A double border surrounds the title, which you can change to another style at any time by using the Figure Options menu.

6 Press **Exit** to return to the editing screen.

Spell-Checking the Report

Now that the report is finished, you may want to check the text for any misspelled words.

1 Press **Spell** (Ctrl-F2), then select **D**ocument (3).

⌨ *Select Spell from the Tools menu, then select Document.*

During the spell-checking, WordPerfect not only checks the main text of the report, but also stops in footers, footnotes, endnotes, graphics boxes, etc. if a word cannot be found.

2 Press **Exit** (F7) when spell-checking is completed to exit the word count message.

If you find spelling errors in a table of contents or index, you should correct the misspelling in the text marked for the table of contents, create new codes for the misspelled index words, then regenerate the document.

Saving and Printing the Report

If you want to keep the formatted report for future reference, then you need to save the final draft on disk.

1 Press **Exit** (F7), type **y** and press **Enter** to save the report, then type **y** again to replace the report on disk.

If you want to send the report to your printer, then you can press Cancel to prevent WordPerfect from clearing the screen.

2 Press **Cancel** (F1) to stay in WordPerfect and keep the report on your screen.

3 Use the Print menu (Shift-F7) to select your own printer (s), view the report (6), then send the report to the printer (1).

⌨ *Select* **Print** *from the* **File** *menu.*

Lessons 13 through 22 have introduced you to several basic features of WordPerfect that can help you format and organize documents. At this point, you can continue on with lessons 23 and 24 to learn about merging documents, skip to lesson 25 for some additional insights into the program, or select a feature from the lessons in the Special Features section.

You may also want to review one or more of the lessons you have already completed, try some of the exercises you may have skipped, or apply some of the skills you have learned to enhance your own WordPerfect documents.

Lesson 23: Merge Fundamentals

As the word suggests, merging is the process of combining at least two items to make a third. For example, the water from a stream and a spring may flow together into a pond. Although the pond is neither a stream nor a spring, it contains water from both sources.

In word processing, merging refers to the process of combining information from at least two sources to produce an entirely new document.

Merging with Retrieve

A simple merge can be done by using Retrieve to combine a file on disk with the document on your screen.

1 Press **Retrieve** (Shift-F10), then enter **retail.wkb** to retrieve a letter.

▣ Select **R**etrieve from the **F**ile menu.

The letter on your screen is complete except for the inside address and salutation. Instead of typing the information, you can retrieve it from another file on disk.

2 Make sure that the cursor is at the beginning of the letter.

3 Press **Retrieve**, then enter **address.wkb** to insert an address and salutation into the letter.

▣ Select **R**etrieve from the **F**ile menu.

By using Retrieve, you have merged the document on the screen with a file on disk to create a letter to Robin.

A NAME AND ADDRESS

B LETTER

```
        Robin Pierce
        InterChange, Inc.
▷       544 Westminster Circle NW
        Atlanta, GA 30327

        Dear Robin,

        We are proud to announce the grand opening of several HALVA
▷       International retail stores throughout the country.  Stores are
        scheduled to open in the following cities during the first
        quarter of the year:

            New York, New York         January 18
            Boston, Massachusetts      January 26
            San Francisco, California  February 10
            Los Angeles, California    February 24
            Atlanta, Georgia           March 9
            Chicago, Illinois          March 17

        As a preferred customer, you will be receiving a special
        invitation, and I personally look forward to meeting you at the
        opening.

        Sincerely,
        C:\WP51\LEARN\RETAIL.WKB                    Doc 1 Pg 1 Ln 1" Pos 1"
```

4 Press **Exit** (F7) and type **n** twice to clear the screen.

Primary and Secondary Files

Saving the inside address and salutation in a file and then retrieving it into a letter is one way of merging. However, if you wanted to send the same letter to several people, you would need an address file for each individual.

It would be much easier if all the names and addresses could be kept in a single list, and you could indicate the places in the letter where you wanted the name and address inserted.

A NAMES AND ADDRESSES

B PLACES TO INSERT INFORMATION

Robin Pierce
InterChange, Inc.
544 Westminster Circle NW
Atlanta, GA 30327
Robin
(404) 359-2828

Jayna Wilder-Smith
8611 Market St.
San Francisco, CA 94102
Jayna
(415) 987-4598

Joseph Corrales, Jr.
Kensington House, #312
176 West 45th
New York, NY 10036
Joe

NAME **B**
ADDRESS

Dear FIRST NAME, **B**

We are proud to announce the grand opening of several HALVA
International retail stores throughout the country. Stores are
scheduled to open in the following cities during the first
quarter of the year:

New York, New York   January 18
Boston, Massachusetts   January 26
San Francisco, California February 10
Los Angeles, California February 24
Atlanta, Georgia   March 9
Chicago, Illinois   March 17

As a preferred customer, you will be receiving a special
invitation, and I personally look forward to meeting you at the
opening.

Sincerely,

Bryan Metcalf
President
HALVA International

ccc
Enclosures (2)

By merging the same letter with each individual in the list, a personalized letter could then be created for each person.

A INSERTED INFORMATION

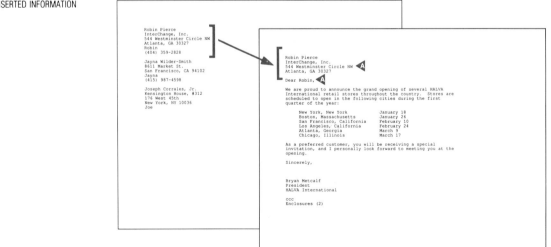

Robin Pierce
InterChange, Inc.
544 Westminster Circle NW
Atlanta, GA 30327
Robin
(404) 359-2828

Jayna Wilder-Smith
8611 Market St.
San Francisco, CA 94102
Jayna
(415) 987-4598

Joseph Corrales, Jr.
Kensington House, #312
176 West 45th
New York, NY 10036
Joe

Robin Pierce
InterChange, Inc.
544 Westminster Circle NW **A**
Atlanta, GA 30327

Dear Robin, **A**

We are proud to announce the grand opening of several HALVA
International retail stores throughout the country. Stores are
scheduled to open in the following cities during the first
quarter of the year:

New York, New York   January 18
Boston, Massachusetts   January 26
San Francisco, California February 10
Los Angeles, California February 24
Atlanta, Georgia   March 9
Chicago, Illinois   March 17

As a preferred customer, you will be receiving a special
invitation, and I personally look forward to meeting you at the
opening.

Sincerely,

Bryan Metcalf
President
HALVA International

ccc
Enclosures (2)

The Merge feature in WordPerfect is designed to work in this way. The letter for the merge is called the *primary file*, while the list of names and addresses is called the *secondary file*.

▲ SECONDARY FILE
▲ PRIMARY FILE

```
Robin Pierce
InterChange, Inc.
544 Westminster Circle NW
Atlanta, GA 30327
Robin
(404) 359-2828

Jayna Wilder-Smith
8611 Market St.
San Francisco, CA 94102
Jayna
(415) 987-4598

Joseph Corrales, Jr.
Kensington House, #312
176 West 45th
New York, NY 10036
Joe
```

```
NAME
ADDRESS

Dear FIRST NAME,

We are proud to announce the grand opening of several HALVA
International retail stores throughout the country.  Stores are
scheduled to open in the following cities during the first
quarter of the year:

    New York, New York        January 18
    Boston, Massachusetts     January 26
    San Francisco, California February 10
    Los Angeles, California   February 24
    Atlanta, Georgia          March 9
    Chicago, Illinois         March 17

As a preferred customer, you will be receiving a special
invitation, and I personally look forward to meeting you at the
opening.

Sincerely,


Bryan Metcalf
President
HALVA International

ccc
Enclosures (2)
```

After the merging is completed, a personalized letter has been created for each individual in the secondary file. A page break between each letter makes it convenient to send the merged document to the printer and have each letter printed on a separate piece of paper.

Merging with Merge

For example, let's try merging a list of customers with a letter announcing the opening of several retail stores for HALVA International.

1 Press **Merge/Sort** (Ctrl-F9) and select **M**erge (1).

⌨ *Select **M**erge from the **T**ools menu.*

2 Enter **stores.wkb** for the name of the primary file, and then enter **customer.wkb** for the name of the secondary file.

WordPerfect begins merging the two files, and, when the merging is completed, your cursor is at the end of all the merged letters.

3 Press **Home,Home,↑** to move to the beginning of the merged letters.

```
Robin Pierce
InterChange, Inc.
544 Westminster Circle NW
Atlanta, GA 30327

Dear Robin,

We are proud to announce the grand opening of several HALVA
International retail stores throughout the country.  Stores are
scheduled to open in the following cities during the first
quarter of the year:

      New York, New York        January 18
      Boston, Massachusetts     January 26
      San Francisco, California February 10
      Los Angeles, California   February 24
      Atlanta, Georgia          March 9
      Chicago, Illinois         March 17

As a preferred customer, you will be receiving a special
invitation, and I personally look forward to meeting you at the
opening.

Sincerely,
                              Doc 1 Pg 1 Ln 1" Pos 1"
```

There should be one letter for each customer in the secondary file.

4 Press **Page Down** (PgDn) several times to scroll through the letters created during the merge.

5 When you finish, press **Exit** (F7) and type **n** twice to clear the screen.

Merge Codes and the Secondary File

Indicating which information you want from the secondary file (the list), and where you want it placed in the primary file (the letter) is done by using special merge codes.

1 Press **Retrieve** (Shift-F10) and enter **customer.wkb** to retrieve the list of names and addresses.

⌨ *Select **R**etrieve from the **F**ile menu.*

Notice that two different merge codes are used in the secondary file.

```
Robin Pierce{END FIELD} ◀▲
InterChange, Inc.
544 Westminster Circle NW
Atlanta, GA 30327{END FIELD}
Robin{END FIELD}
(404) 359-2828{END FIELD}
{END RECORD} ◀▲
==========================================================
Jayna Wilder-Smith{END FIELD}
8611 Market St.
San Francisco, CA 94102{END FIELD}
Jayna{END FIELD}
(415) 987-4598{END FIELD}
{END RECORD}
==========================================================
Anna Lee Pierce{END FIELD}
P.O. Box 1392
Central Park Station
Buffalo, NY 14215{END FIELD}
Anna{END FIELD}
(716) 453-5678{END FIELD}
{END RECORD}
==========================================================
Joseph Corrales, Jr.{END FIELD}
Field: 1                      Doc 1 Pg 1 Ln 1" Pos 1"
```

The group of information about each customer is called a *record*. As you can see, each record ends with an {END RECORD} merge code and is separated from the other records with a hard page break.

2 Press **Page Down** (PgDn) twice, then check the page (Pg) number on the status line.

The status line should display page 3, which is the third record in the primary file.

You can move from record to record by using the Page Up and Page Down keys. Because there is only one record on each page, the page number on the status line becomes the record number.

If you want to know how many records there are in a secondary file,

3 Press **Home,Home,↓**, press **Page Up** (PgUp), then check the page number on the status line.

There should be eleven records in this secondary file.

4 Press **Home,Home,↑** to return to the beginning of the secondary file.

Each record is divided into smaller units of information called *fields*. Each field ends with an {END FIELD} merge code, and is separated from the other fields by a hard return after the {END FIELD} code.

5 Press **Down Arrow** (↓), then press **Up Arrow** (↑).

Notice the "Field:" message on the left side of the status line.

Ⓐ FIELD MESSAGE

```
Robin Pierce{END FIELD}
InterChange, Inc.
544 Westminster Circle NW
Atlanta, GA 30327{END FIELD}
Robin{END FIELD}
(404) 359-2828{END FIELD}
{END RECORD}
============================================================================
Jayna Wilder-Smith{END FIELD}
8611 Market St.
San Francisco, CA 94102{END FIELD}
Jayna{END FIELD}
(415) 987-4598{END FIELD}
{END RECORD}
============================================================================
Anna Lee Pierce{END FIELD}
P.O. Box 1392
Central Park Station
Buffalo, NY 14215{END FIELD}
Anna{END FIELD}
(716) 453-5678{END FIELD}
{END RECORD}
============================================================================
Joseph Corrales, Jr.{END FIELD}
Ⓐ▶ Field: 1                                    Doc 1 Pg 1 Ln 1" Pos 1"
```

The message lets you know that your cursor is in field 1 of the first record (page 1).

6 Press **Down Arrow** and check the "Field:" message.

Because you have moved the cursor past the {END FIELD} code on the first line, the message is updated to "Field: 2."

7 Press **Down Arrow** again and check the "Field:" message.

The message still displays "2" for the field because there is no {END FIELD} code at the end of the second line in the record.

8 Press **Down Arrow** twice to move the cursor to the word Robin.

Now the message has been updated to display 3 on the status line. The updating only happens when you move the cursor past an {END FIELD} code.

The first field in the record is the customer's name, the second field is the customer's address, the third field is the customer's first name, and the fourth field is the customer's phone number.

Ⓐ NAME
Ⓑ ADDRESS
Ⓒ FIRST NAME
Ⓓ PHONE NUMBER

```
Ⓐ▸ Robin Pierce{END FIELD}
    InterChange, Inc.
Ⓑ▸ 544 Westminster Circle NW
    Atlanta, GA 30327{END FIELD}
Ⓒ▸ Robin{END FIELD}
Ⓓ▸ (404) 359-2828{END FIELD} ◀Ⓓ
    {END RECORD}
========================================================================
    Jayna Wilder-Smith{END FIELD}
    8611 Market St.
    San Francisco, CA 94102{END FIELD}
    Jayna{END FIELD}
    (415) 987-4598{END FIELD}
    {END RECORD}
========================================================================
    Anna Lee Pierce{END FIELD}
    P.O. Box 1392
    Central Park Station
    Buffalo, NY 14215{END FIELD}
    Anna{END FIELD}
    (716) 453-5678{END FIELD}
    {END RECORD}
========================================================================
    Joseph Corrales, Jr.{END FIELD}
    Field: 3                          Doc 1 Pg 1 Ln 1.67" Pos 1"
```

You can have as many lines of text as you want in a field (e.g., address), and as many records as you want in the secondary file. However, for a simple merge to work properly, the following must be done:

- Each field should end with an {END FIELD} code and a hard return.
- Each record should end with an {END RECORD} code and a hard page.
- Each record should have the same number of fields with the information arranged in the same order.

Opening a Window   Records and fields let you organize the information in the list, but how do you indicate where and what information to include in the letter from the secondary file?

1 Press **Page Up** (PgUp) to move the cursor back to the beginning of the first record.

2 Press **Switch** (Shift-F3) to display the second document screen.

⌨ *Select Switch Document from the Edit menu.*

3 Press **Retrieve** (Shift-F10) and enter **stores.wkb** to retrieve the primary file.

⌨ *Select Retrieve from the File menu.*

Let's compare the primary file with the secondary file by using Window to split the screen.

4 Press **Screen** (Ctrl-F3), then select Window (1).

⌨ *Select Window from the Edit menu.*

5 Enter **12** to split the screen evenly between the two windows.

The secondary file in the document 1 editing screen is displayed in the top half, while the primary file in the document 2 editing screen is displayed in the bottom half.

A SECONDARY FILE
B PRIMARY FILE

```
Robin Pierce{END FIELD}
InterChange, Inc.
544 Westminster Circle NW        ◄B
Atlanta, GA 30327{END FIELD}
Robin{END FIELD}
(404) 359-2828{END FIELD}
{END RECORD}
====================================================================
Jayna Wilder-Smith{END FIELD}
8611 Market St.
Field: 1                                    Doc 1 Pg 1 Ln 1" Pos 1"
[▼    ▼     ▼     ▼     ▼     ▼     ▼     ▼   ]   ▼    ▼
{FIELD}1¯
{FIELD}2¯

Dear {FIELD}3¯,

A We are proud to announce the grand opening of several HALVA
  International retail stores throughout the country.  Stores are
  scheduled to open in the following cities during the first
  quarter of the year:

       New York, New York          January 18
       Boston, Massachusetts       January 26
C:\WP51\LEARN\STORES.WKB                   Doc 2 Pg 1 Ln 1" Pos 1"
```

Both windows are independent of each other and can be used for editing. You can press Switch, as you normally would, to move back and forth between the editing screens.

Because the two windows are completely independent of each other, the messages for the document 1 editing screen are displayed at the bottom of the top window, instead of at the bottom of the screen.

Merge Codes and the Primary File

Wherever information is needed from the secondary file, a {FIELD} merge code is placed in the primary file.

```
Robin Pierce{END FIELD}
InterChange, Inc.
544 Westminster Circle NW
Atlanta, GA 30327{END FIELD}
Robin{END FIELD}
(404) 359-2828{END FIELD}
{END RECORD}
================================================================
Jayna Wilder-Smith{END FIELD}
8611 Market St.
Field: 1                                    Doc 1 Pg 1 Ln 1" Pos 1"
[  ▼   ▼    ▼    ▼   ▼   ▼   ▼   ▼   ▼    ▼   ▼   )   ▼    ▼    ▼
▲{FIELD}1~
 {FIELD}2~

Dear {FIELD}3~,

We are proud to announce the grand opening of several HALVA
International retail stores throughout the country.  Stores are
scheduled to open in the following cities during the first
quarter of the year:

     New York, New York        January 18
     Boston, Massachusetts     January 26
C:\WP51\LEARN\STORES.WKB                    Doc 2 Pg 1 Ln 1" Pos 1"
```

The {FIELD} codes include a number that indicates the field which should be inserted into the letter. A tilde ($\sim$) is placed after the field number to help WordPerfect know that the number is part of the {FIELD} code, and not part of the text in the letter.

The position of the {FIELD} code, field number, and tilde indicates the place where the information from the field should be inserted into the letter.

For example, {FIELD}1~ tells WordPerfect to insert the first field at the beginning of the letter.

```
Robin Pierce{END FIELD}
InterChange, Inc.
544 Westminster Circle NW
Atlanta, GA 30327{END FIELD}
Robin{END FIELD}
(404) 359-2828{END FIELD}
{END RECORD}
================================================================
Jayna Wilder-Smith{END FIELD}
8611 Market St.
▲Field: 1                                   Doc 1 Pg 1 Ln 1" Pos 1"
[  ▼   ▼    ▼    ▼   ▼   ▼   ▼   ▼   ▼    ▼   ▼   )   ▼    ▼    ▼
{FIELD}1~
{FIELD}2~

Dear {FIELD}3~,

We are proud to announce the grand opening of several HALVA
International retail stores throughout the country.  Stores are
scheduled to open in the following cities during the first
quarter of the year:

     New York, New York        January 18
     Boston, Massachusetts     January 26
C:\WP51\LEARN\STORES.WKB                    Doc 2 Pg 1 Ln 1" Pos 1"
```

The first field in each record contains the full name of the customer. During the merge, the customer's full name is inserted at the position of the

{FIELD}1~.

The {FIELD}2~ in the letter inserts the information from the second field of the record (the address), while {FIELD}3~ inserts information from the third field (the first name).

Because the word "Dear" is used in every letter, you do not need to include it as part of the information in the third field. Only the information that changes from letter to letter (name, address, etc.) should be included in the secondary file.

The fourth field contains the customer's phone number, but a {FIELD}4~ is not placed in the primary file because the phone number does not need to be inserted into the letter. However, the phone number may be important to include in other documents that you create with Merge.

For an example of using a phone number in a primary file, turn to Merging a List *in the* Special Techniques *lesson of* Fundamentals II.

Editing the Secondary File

Dividing the secondary file into records and fields is a common way of organizing information for many software programs. You may want to think of each record as an address card in a desktop card file.

The information to be filled in (name, address, phone number, etc.) is always in the same place on each card, even though the information may be longer or shorter. Even if there is no information for an item (e.g., a phone number), a place is still kept open for the information to be filled in later.

What is true for address cards is also true for the secondary file. The name, address, and first name are always in the same place in the record. And while some addresses are longer than others, there is always a field for an address, even if the field is empty.

1 Press **Switch** (Shift-F3) to place the cursor in the document 1 editing screen (top half).

⌨ *Select Switch Document from the* **E***dit menu. You can also switch documents by placing the mouse pointer in the desired window and clicking the left mouse button.*

2 Press **Page Down** (PgDn) until you reach the record for Ted Mortinthal.

Notice that Ted Mortinthal's address is missing. However, an {END FIELD} code and a hard return hold the field open until an address can be entered.

3 Place the cursor at the beginning of the empty address field (to the left of the {END FIELD} code).

4 Type the following address:

**1380 Georgia Ave.
Silver Springs, MD 20910**

The record for Ted Mortinthal should now include his address as well as his full name, first name, and phone number.

```
Ted Mortinthal{END FIELD}
1380 Georgia Ave.
Silver Springs, MD 20910{END FIELD}
Ted{END FIELD}
(301) 522-8700{END FIELD}
{END RECORD}
================================================================================


Field: 2                                     Doc 1 Pg 11 Ln 1.33" Pos 3.4"
[                                                       )
{FIELD}1~
{FIELD}2~

Dear {FIELD}3~,

We are proud to announce the grand opening of several HALVA
International retail stores throughout the country.  Stores are
scheduled to open in the following cities during the first
quarter of the year:

     New York, New York        January 18
     Boston, Massachusetts     January 26
C:\WP51\LEARN\STORES.WKB                     Doc 2 Pg 1 Ln 1" Pos 1"
```

5 Press **Exit** (F7), type **y**, and enter **customer** to save the list in a new file.

6 Type **n** to clear the document 1 editing screen.

Closing a Window

When you want to clear an editing screen, you normally use Exit.

1 Press **Switch** (Shift-F3) to place the cursor in the bottom window.

⌨ *Select Switch Document from the Edit menu. You can also switch documents by placing the mouse pointer in the desired window and clicking the left mouse button.*

2 Press **Exit** (F7), and then type **n** twice to clear the document 2 editing screen.

However, to close a window, you need to use Window on the Screen menu.

3 Press **Switch** to place the cursor in the document 1 editing screen.

⌨ *Select Switch Document from the Edit menu. You can also switch documents by placing the mouse pointer in the desired window and clicking the left mouse button.*

4 Press **Screen** (Ctrl-F3), select Window (1), and then enter **0** for the number of lines.

⌨ *Select Window from the Edit menu.*

WordPerfect closes the bottom window (document 2) and returns the document 1 editing screen to its full size.

Reviewing the Fundamentals

Let's review some of the basic concepts of merging documents with WordPerfect.

Ⓐ END OF FIELD
Ⓑ END OF RECORD
Ⓒ INSERT FIELDS

```
Robin Pierce{END FIELD}  ◄Ⓐ
InterChange, Inc.
544 Westminster Circle NW
Atlanta, GA 30327{END FIELD}
Robin{END FIELD}
(404) 359-2828{END FIELD}
{END RECORD}  ◄Ⓑ
=====================================
Jayna Wilder-Smith{END FIELD}
8611 Market St.
San Francisco, CA 94102{END FIELD}
Jayna{END FIELD}
(415) 987-4598{END FIELD}
{END RECORD}
=====================================
Joseph Corrales, Jr.{END FIELD}
Kensington House, #312
176 West 45th
New York, NY 10036{END FIELD}
Joe{END FIELD}
(212) 687-1203{END FIELD}
{END RECORD}
```

```
{FIELD}1~  ◄Ⓒ
{FIELD}2~

Dear {FIELD}3~,  ◄Ⓒ

We are proud to announce the grand opening of several HALVA
International retail stores throughout the country.  Stores are
scheduled to open in the following cities during the first
quarter of the year:

        New York, New York          January 18
        Boston, Massachusetts       January 26
        San Francisco, California   February 10
        Los Angeles, California     February 24
        Atlanta, Georgia            March 9
        Chicago, Illinois           March 17

As a preferred customer, you will be receiving a special
invitation, and I personally look forward to meeting you at the
opening.

Sincerely,


Bryan Metcalf
President
HALVA International

ccc
Enclosures (2)
```

The idea of merging can be as simple as retrieving one document into another with Retrieve. However, most merging in WordPerfect is done by using a primary file (such as a letter) and a secondary file (such as an address list) with Merge.

The secondary file contains a record of information for each individual. The record is divided into fields so that parts of the information can be inserted at various locations in the primary file. The inserting is done in the primary file by using {FIELD} merge codes to indicate which fields you want from the record.

It is important to make sure that each record contains the same number of fields with the same type of information in each field. If not, you may get a name where you need an address, or a phone number where you need a name.

Lesson 24: Mass Mailings

One of the most common uses of the Merge feature is for sending a customized version of a letter to tens, hundreds, or thousands of people (a mass mailing). In this lesson you continue learning about the basics of Merge by editing a primary and secondary file for a mass mailing of letters to HALVA International customers.

Merging the Customer Letters

Let's begin the lesson by merging the retail store announcement letter with the customer list you edited in lesson 23.

1 Press **Merge/Sort** (Ctrl-F9) and select **Merge** (1).

⊟ *Select Merge from the Tools menu.*

2 Enter **stores.wkb** for the name of the primary file, then enter **customer** for the name of the secondary file.

As soon as you enter the name of the secondary file, the merge begins, and a "* Merging *" message appears at the bottom of the screen.

⚠ MERGING MESSAGE

▶ * Merging *_

The length of time it takes WordPerfect to perform the merge depends on the number of {FIELD} codes in the primary file, the size of the primary file, and the number of records in the secondary file.

Computers also process information at different rates of speed. The faster the processing chip you have in your computer, the faster the merging is done in WordPerfect.

Because there are only 11 records in the customer list, the merge should go quickly. When the merging is completed, the letter for the last customer in the secondary file should be on your screen.

3 Press **Go To** (Ctrl-Home) then **Up Arrow** (↑) to move the cursor to the top of the last letter.

After merging, the letters are ready to send to the printer. It is not necessary to save the merged letters because they can always be created again by simply merging the primary and secondary files.

4 Press **Exit** (F7), and then type **n** twice to clear the screen without saving the letters.

Adding a Record

As the number of HALVA International customers increases, a new record for each customer is added to the secondary file.

1 Press **Retrieve** (Shift-F10) and enter **customer** to retrieve the secondary file.

⌨ *Select **R**etrieve from the **F**ile menu.*

2 Press **Home** twice and then **Down Arrow** (↓) to move the cursor to the end of the list to add a new customer.

The first field in each record contains the full name of the customer. The {END FIELD} code at the end of the field can be inserted by using End Field.

3 Type **Samantha Dance** then press **End Field** (F9) to create the first field.

An {END FIELD} merge code *and* a hard return are inserted for you when you press End Field.

4 Type the following address and press **End Field** (F9) at the end of the second line:

1487 Lockwood Dr.
New Bedford, MA 02743

5 Type **Samantha** and press **End Field** to end the first name field.

6 Type **(617) 687-5321** and press **End Field** to end the phone number field.

Now that the record information has been typed, you are ready to insert an {END RECORD} merge code.

7 Press **Merge Codes** (Shift-F9) to display a list of additional merge codes.

⌨ *Select Merge Codes from the **T**ools menu.*

There are five merge codes available on the menu with a sixth option that lets you display a list of even more merge codes.

▲ MERGE CODES MENU

```
(916) 878-4550{END FIELD}
{END RECORD}
==================================================================================
Scott L. Ziegler{END FIELD}
Merchants Exchange
450 S. Flower St.
Los Angeles, CA 90014{END FIELD}
Scott{END FIELD}
(213) 937-3370{END FIELD}
{END RECORD}
==================================================================================
Ted Mortinthal{END FIELD}
1380 Georgia Ave.
Silver Springs, MD 20910{END FIELD}
Ted{END FIELD}
(301) 522-8700{END FIELD}
{END RECORD}
==================================================================================
Samantha Dance{END FIELD}
1487 Lockwood Dr.
New Bedford, MA 02743{END FIELD}
Samantha{END FIELD}
(617) 687-5321{END FIELD}
```
▲1 Field, 2 End Record, 3 Input, 4 Page Off, 5 Next Record; 6 More: 0

8 Select **E**nd Record (2).

An {END RECORD} code *and* a page break are inserted for you.

The record you have created for Samantha Dance should look exactly like the one on the screen below.

```
==================================================================================
Scott L. Ziegler{END FIELD}
Merchants Exchange
450 S. Flower St.
Los Angeles, CA 90014{END FIELD}
Scott{END FIELD}
(213) 937-3370{END FIELD}
{END RECORD}
==================================================================================
Ted Mortinthal{END FIELD}
1380 Georgia Ave.
Silver Springs, MD 20910{END FIELD}
Ted{END FIELD}
(301) 522-8700{END FIELD}
{END RECORD}
==================================================================================
Samantha Dance{END FIELD}
1487 Lockwood Dr.
New Bedford, MA 02743{END FIELD}
Samantha{END FIELD}
(617) 687-5321{END FIELD}
{END RECORD}
==================================================================================

Field: 1                                    Doc 1 Pg 13 Ln 1" Pos 1"
```

Remember that an {END FIELD} merge code is not needed at the end of each line, only at the end of a field. For example, {END FIELD} should appear after the ZIP code in Samantha's record, but *not after* the street address. If you have placed an {END FIELD} code after the street address, erase it by using Backspace or Delete.

Merging the Customer Letters

With the new record added, you can save the edited list and start another merge.

1 Press **Exit** (F7), type **y**, press **Enter**, and then type **y** again to replace the CUSTOMER secondary file.

2 Type **n** to clear the screen for the merge (always merge from a clear screen).

3 Press **Merge/Sort** (Ctrl-F9) and select **Merge (1)**.

⌨ *Select Merge from the Tools menu.*

4 Enter **stores.wkb** for the name of the primary file, and then enter **customer** for the name of the secondary file.

When the merge finishes, you should have a new letter for Samantha added to the end of all the merged letters.

5 Press **Go To** (Ctrl-Home) and then **Up Arrow** (↑) to move to the top of the letter to Samantha.

Adding a Field to the Primary File

Now that the secondary file has been edited, let's try editing the primary file to add a date and another first name.

1 Press **Exit** (F7) and type **n** twice to clear the screen.

2 Press **Retrieve** (Shift-F10) and enter **stores.wkb** to retrieve the primary file.

⌨ *Select Retrieve from the File menu.*

3 Move the cursor to the last paragraph, and place the cursor on the "y" of the word "you" after the phrase "As a preferred customer, . . .".

The customer's first name can be inserted at this point in the letter by using the {FIELD} merge code.

4 Press **Merge Codes** (Shift-F9) to display the menu of merge codes.

⌨ *Select Merge Codes from the Tools menu.*

5 Select **Field (1)**, then enter **3** to insert field three (the first name) into the letter during a merge.

6 Type a comma (,), press the **Space Bar**, and then press **Down Arrow** (↓).

Your primary file should now look like the one illustrated below.

```
{FIELD}1~
{FIELD}2~
Dear {FIELD}3~,

We are proud to announce the grand opening of several HALVA
International retail stores throughout the country.  Stores are
scheduled to open in the following cities during the first
quarter of the year:

        New York, New York          January 18
        Boston, Massachusetts       January 26
        San Francisco, California   February 10
        Los Angeles, California     February 24
        Atlanta, Georgia            March 9
        Chicago, Illinois           March 17

As a preferred customer, {FIELD}3, ~you will be receiving a special
invitation, and I personally look forward to meeting you at the
opening.

Sincerely,


C:\WP51\LEARN\STORES.WKB                    Doc 1 Pg 1 Ln 3.83" Pos 3.9"
```

{FIELD} is a very flexible merge code, and can be used to insert the same field wherever and whenever you want in a primary file.

Adding a Date to the Primary File

Before saving the edited primary file, let's insert one more merge code into the letter.

1 Press **Home,Home,Home,↑** to move the cursor to the very beginning of the letter.

2 Press **Enter** four times to add extra spacing, then press **Home,↑** to move the cursor above the spacing.

3 Press **Merge Codes** (Shift-F9), then select **M**ore (6).

⌨ *Select Merge Codes from the **T**ools menu, then select **M**ore.*

A window appears in your screen that displays a list of additional merge codes (commands) available in WordPerfect.

▲ LIST OF MERGE CODES

```
                                          ┌──────────────────────────────────────┐
                                        ▲ │{ASSIGN}var˜expr˜                       │
                                          │{BELL}                                  │
                                          │{BREAK}                                 │
                                          │{CALL}label˜                            │
   {FIELD}1˜                              │{CANCEL OFF}                            │
   {FIELD}2˜                              │{CANCEL ON}                             │
                                          │{CASE}expr˜cs1˜lb1˜...csN˜lbN˜˜         │
   Dear {FIELD}3˜,                        │{CASE CALL}expr˜cs1˜lb1˜...csN˜lbN˜˜    │
                                          │{CHAIN MACRO}macroname˜         (˜G)    │
   We are proud to announce the grand openi│{CHAIN PRIMARY}filename˜               │
   International retail stores throughout t└──────────────────────────────────────┘
   scheduled to open in the following citie
   quarter of the year:

        New York, New York        January 18
        Boston, Massachusetts     January 26
        San Francisco, California February 10
        Los Angeles, California   February 24
        Atlanta, Georgia          March 9
        Chicago, Illinois         March 17

   As a preferred customer, {FIELD}3, ˜you will be receiving a special
   invitation, and I personally look forward to meeting you at the
   opening.
                             (Name Search; Enter or arrows to Exit)
```

You can move through the list by using the Home and arrow keys, or by simply typing the name of a particular code.

4 Type **d** to move the cursor to the {DATE} code, then press **Enter** to place the code in the letter.

▲ {DATE} CODE

```
 ▲ {DATE}_

   {FIELD}1˜
   {FIELD}2˜

   Dear {FIELD}3˜,

   We are proud to announce the grand opening of several HALVA
   International retail stores throughout the country.  Stores are
   scheduled to open in the following cities during the first
   quarter of the year:

        New York, New York        January 18
        Boston, Massachusetts     January 26
        San Francisco, California February 10
        Los Angeles, California   February 24
        Atlanta, Georgia          March 9
        Chicago, Illinois         March 17

   As a preferred customer, {FIELD}3, ˜you will be receiving a special
   invitation, and I personally look forward to meeting you at the
   opening.
   C:\WP51\LEARN\STORES.WKB              Doc 1 Pg 1 Ln 1" Pos 1"
```

The {DATE} merge code does the same thing as the Date Code feature on the Text In/Out key. Whenever you merge the primary file, WordPerfect automatically inserts the current date at the position of the {DATE} code.

5 Press **Exit** (F7), type **y** to save the edited letter, then enter **stores** to create a new primary file.

6 Type **n** to clear the screen and stay in WordPerfect.

Naming the Fields

Field numbers can be confusing when trying to create or edit a primary file. Is the address in field 1 or field 2? What about the first name or the phone number?

To help you remember how your records are organized, you can use a special merge code to name the fields in the secondary file.

1 Press **Retrieve** (Shift-F10), then enter **customer** to retrieve the secondary file.

⊞ Select **Retrieve** from the **File** menu.

The CUSTOMER secondary file has four fields in each record—a name, an address, a first name, and a phone number.

2 Press **Merge Codes** (Shift-F9), then select **More** (6).

⊞ Select **Merge Codes** from the **Tools** menu, then select **More**.

The list of additional merge codes is displayed on your screen with the cursor highlighting the {DATE} code (the one you just selected).

3 Press **Down Arrow** (↓) until the cursor highlights the {FIELD NAMES} code.

Of all the codes in the list, the {FIELD NAMES} code looks like it might be the most difficult one to use.

▲ {FIELD NAMES} CODE

```
Robin Pierce{END FIELD}
InterChange, Inc.                           {DATE}                        (^D)
544 Westminster Circle NW                   {DOCUMENT}filename~
Atlanta, GA 30327{END FIELD}                {ELSE}
Robin{END FIELD}                            {END FIELD}                   (^R)
(404) 359-2828{END FIELD}                   {END FOR}
{END RECORD}                                {END IF}
==========================================  {END RECORD}                  (^E)
Jayna Wilder-Smith{END FIELD}               {END WHILE}
8611 Market St.                             {FIELD}field~                 (^F)
San Francisco, CA 94102{END FIELD}  ▶  {FIELD NAMES}name1~...nameN~
Jayna{END FIELD}
(415) 987-4598{END FIELD}
{END RECORD}
==========================================
Anna Lee Pierce{END FIELD}
P.O. Box 1392
Central Park Station
Buffalo, NY 14215{END FIELD}
Anna{END FIELD}
(716) 453-5678{END FIELD}
{END RECORD}
==========================================
Joseph Corrales, Jr.{END FIELD}
                    (Name Search; Enter or arrows to Exit)
```

However, WordPerfect makes it easy by guiding you step-by-step through naming the fields.

4 Press **Enter** to select the {FIELD NAMES} code.

An "Enter Field 1:" message is displayed at the bottom of your screen on the status line.

5 Enter **name** for the name of the first field in each record.

The message is updated to "Enter Field 2:" for the name of the second field. All you need to do is continue entering a name for each field.

6 Enter **address** for the name of the second field.

7 Enter **first name** for the name of the third field.

8 Enter **phone** for the name of the fourth field.

An "Enter Field 5:" message is displayed on the screen. Because there are only four fields in each record, you do not need to enter a name for a fifth field.

9 Press **Enter** to end naming the fields.

The {FIELD NAMES} code is inserted at the top of the secondary file with all the information necessary to name the fields.

A {FIELD NAMES} CODE

```
{FIELD NAMES}name~address~first name~phone~~{END RECORD}
================================================================================
Robin Pierce{END FIELD}
InterChange, Inc.
544 Westminster Circle NW
Atlanta, GA 30327{END FIELD}
Robin{END FIELD}
(404) 359-2828{END FIELD}
{END RECORD}
================================================================================
Jayna Wilder-Smith{END FIELD}
8611 Market St.
San Francisco, CA 94102{END FIELD}
Jayna{END FIELD}
(415) 987-4598{END FIELD}
{END RECORD}
================================================================================
Anna Lee Pierce{END FIELD}
P.O. Box 1392
Central Park Station
Buffalo, NY 14215{END FIELD}
Anna{END FIELD}
(716) 453-5678{END FIELD}
{END RECORD}
Field: name                              Doc 1 Pg 2 Ln 1" Pos 1"
```

Notice that the "Field:" message at the bottom of the screen is followed by the word "name" instead of a field number.

```
{FIELD NAMES}name~address~first name~phone~~{END RECORD}
=========================================================================
Robin Pierce{END FIELD}
InterChange, Inc.
544 Westminster Circle NW
Atlanta, GA 30327{END FIELD}
Robin{END FIELD}
(404) 359-2828{END FIELD}
{END RECORD}
=========================================================================
Jayna Wilder-Smith{END FIELD}
8611 Market St.
San Francisco, CA 94102{END FIELD}
Jayna{END FIELD}
(415) 987-4598{END FIELD}
{END RECORD}
=========================================================================
Anna Lee Pierce{END FIELD}
P.O. Box 1392
Central Park Station
Buffalo, NY 14215{END FIELD}
Anna{END FIELD}
(716) 453-5678{END FIELD}
{END RECORD}
A▶Field: name                                  Doc 1 Pg 2 Ln 1" Pos 1"
       B
```

10 Press **Down Arrow** (↓) a line at a time and watch the "Field:" message on the status line.

As you move from field to field, the field name is displayed instead of a number. Not only can field names help you when creating a primary file, but they can also be useful when trying to find a particular field in a record.

11 Press **Exit** (F7), type **y**, press **Enter**, and then type **y** again to replace the CUSTOMER secondary file.

12 Type **n** to clear the screen.

Editing the Primary File

After naming the fields in the secondary file, you may be wondering if the {FIELD} codes in the primary file also need names (instead of numbers) for the letters to merge correctly.

1 Press **Retrieve** (Shift-F10), then enter **stores** to retrieve the edited primary file.

⌨ *Select Retrieve from the File menu.*

Let's try adding a name to one of the {FIELD} codes, leave field numbers for the rest, then try merging the letters to see what happens.

2 Move the cursor to the beginning of the salutation (on the "D" in "Dear"), then press **Delete to End of Line** (Ctrl-End) to erase the text and {FIELD} code in the line.

3 Press **Merge Codes** (Shift-F9), select **Field** (1), then enter **first name** for the name of the field.

⌨ *Select Merge Codes from the Tools menu, then select Field.*

4 Type a comma (,) to end the salutation.

Your merge letter should now look like the one illustrated below with a field name for the salutation, and field numbers for all the other {FIELD} codes.

⚠ FIELD NAME
⚠ FIELD NUMBERS

```
{DATE}


{FIELD}1~
{FIELD}2~

{FIELD}first name~,_

We are proud to announce the grand opening of several HALVA
International retail stores throughout the country.  Stores are
scheduled to open in the following cities during the first
quarter of the year:

        New York, New York        January 18
        Boston, Massachusetts     January 26
        San Francisco, California February 10
        Los Angeles, California   February 24
        Atlanta, Georgia          March 9
        Chicago, Illinois         March 17

As a preferred customer, {FIELD}3, ~you will be receiving a special
invitation, and I personally look forward to meeting you at the
opening.
C:\WP51\LEARN\STORES                    Doc 1 Pg 1 Ln 2.17" Pos 2.2"
```

5 Press **Exit** (F7), type **y**, press **Enter**, then type **y** again to replace the STORES primary file.

6 Type **n** to clear the screen.

Merging the Customer Letters

Let's merge the letters one last time and see what happens with the field numbers and field names.

1 Press **Merge/Sort** (Ctrl-F9) and select **Merge** (1).

⌨ *Select **M**erge from the **T**ools menu.*

2 Enter **stores** for the primary file, then enter **customer** for the secondary file.

3 When the merge is completed, press **Home,Home,↑** to display the first merged letter on the screen.

The current date is inserted at the beginning of the letter, with all the other information (name, address, first name) inserted correctly at the {FIELD} codes.

Even if you are using field names in the secondary file, you can still use field numbers in the primary file for merging documents.

Printing the Letters

The letters are ready to send to the printer. However, because the primary file was created using the Workbook Printer, the merged letters are also assigned to the Workbook Printer.

1 Press **Print** (Shift-F7), and type **s** to display the list of printers.

⬛ *Select **Print** from the **File** menu.*

2 Highlight the name of your printer, and then press **Enter** to select the printer.

After you select your printer, you are returned to the Print menu.

3 Select **P**age (2) to print the letter on your screen.

4 Press **Exit** (F7), then type **n** twice to clear the screen.

When merging hundreds (or thousands) of documents, many companies choose to have each letter automatically sent to the printer *as soon as it is merged*. For details on merging to the printer, turn to the *Merging to the Printer* heading in the *Special Techniques* lesson at the end of *Fundamentals II.*

Lesson 25: Special Techniques

Now that you have completed *Fundamentals II*, there are some additional features and insights in this lesson that you might find helpful when creating a document with WordPerfect.

Each feature (e.g., Advance, Decimal Alignment) is written as a separate exercise. Simply select a feature you want to learn about, then read through the material and complete the steps. You do not need to finish the entire lesson from beginning to end.

Advance

Advance gives you the flexibility of printing text at a specific place on the page. For example, if you are using letterhead paper, and you want the letter to begin printing exactly 2 15/16 inches down from the top of the page, you can use Advance Down.

1 Press **Retrieve** (Shift-F10) and enter **musicbox.wkb** to retrieve a letter.

⌨ *Select Retrieve from the File menu.*

The Line number on the status line lets you know that the letter is already set to print 1" down from the top edge of the page (one-inch top margin). What you need to do is move the text down another 1 15/16" for a total of 2 15/16".

2 Press **Format** (Shift-F8), select **O**ther (4), then select **A**dvance (1).

⌨ *Select Other from the Layout menu, then select Advance.*

3 Select **D**own (2), enter **1 15/16** for the distance you want to move the text, then press **Exit** (F7) to return to the editing screen.

Although the text has not moved down on the editing screen, the Line number on the status line now displays 2.94" (2 15/16").

4 Press **Reveal Codes** (Alt-F3).

⌨ *Select Reveal Codes from the Edit menu.*

5 Press **Left Arrow** (←) to place the cursor on the Advance Down code.

The Line number displays 1" for the top margin setting.

6 Press **Right Arrow** (→) to place the cursor to the right of the Advance Down code.

The measurement in the Advance Down code is added to the top margin, and 2.94" is displayed on the status line.

Displaying the Results

While you can use the status line to find out the exact position of the cursor, the actual results of Advance codes can only be seen in the View Document screen.

1 Press **Reveal Codes** (Alt-F3) to display the normal editing screen.

🔲 *Select **Reveal Codes** from the **Edit** menu.*

2 Press **Print** (Shift-F7), select **V**iew Document (6), then select 100% (1).

🔲 *Select **Print** from the **F**ile menu.*

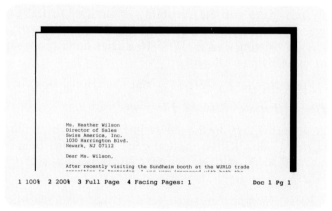

```
Ms. Heather Wilson
Director of Sales
Swiss America, Inc.
1030 Harrington Blvd.
Newark, NJ 07112

Dear Ms. Wilson,

After recently visiting the Sundheim booth at the WURLD trade
```

1 100% 2 200% 3 Full Page 4 Facing Pages: 1   Doc 1 Pg 1

3 Press **Exit** (F7) to return to the editing screen.

Relative and Absolute

The amount you entered (1 15/16") to advance down is a *relative* distance. If you add text *before* the Advance Down code, then WordPerfect still moves the inside address 1 15/16" down the page from the Advance Down code.

1 Press **Home,Home,Home,**↑ to move the cursor to the very beginning of the letter, before any codes.

2 Press **Date/Outline** (Shift-F5), then select Date **T**ext (1).

🔲 *Select **Date T**ext from the **T**ools menu.*

3 Press **Enter** four times to add extra spacing between the date and the inside address.

The Line number lets you know that the cursor is now 1.67" down the page.

4 Press **Right Arrow** (→) to move the cursor past the Advance Down code.

WordPerfect adds the 1.94" in the code to the 1.67" from the extra spacing, then displays 3.61" for the position at which the inside address will be printed.

5 Press **Backspace** and type **y** to delete the Advance Down code.

6 Press **Home,Home,↑** to place the cursor at the beginning of the letter.

7 Press **Format**, select **Other**, then select **Advance**.

⌨ *Select **Other** from the Layout menu, then select **Advance**.*

Besides the Up, Down, Left, and Right options that let you move text a relative amount, you can also select Line or Position to make sure that the text is *always* printed at the same place on the page.

8 Select **Line** (3), then enter **2 15/16** for the distance you want the text moved down the page.

9 Press **Exit** (F7) to return to the editing screen.

The Line number displays 2.94" on the status line. However, because the Advance Line code is an *absolute* measurement, WordPerfect will print the date 2 15/16" from the top edge of the page even if text is added before the code.

10 Press **Left Arrow** (←) and check the Line number on the status line (it should read 1").

11 Press **Enter** fourteen times to add extra spacing at the beginning of the letter.

The Line number displays 3.33". Now watch what happens when you press the right arrow to move past the Advance Line code.

12 Press **Right Arrow** (→) and check the Line number on the status line.

WordPerfect moves the date back up to the exact line indicated in the Advance Line code (2.94").

13 Press **Exit**, then type **n** twice to clear the screen.

As you create letters, reports, newsletters, etc., you will begin to find ways that the Advance feature can be used to place text at an exact position on the page.

Remember that relative Advance codes (Up, Down, Left, and Right) add an exact distance to the current cursor position, while absolute Advance codes (Line and Position) place the text at an exact distance from the top or left edge of the page (independent of the cursor position).

Cross-References

Whenever you include tables, illustrations, graphs, etc., in a document, you may refer to them from time to time in the text by including a "see page" phrase followed by a page number.

As you edit the document, the page numbers for some of the "see page" references may need to be changed.

Creating a Cross-Reference

To help you keep the page numbers updated, WordPerfect provides a Cross-Reference feature that ties the page number in your references to the appropriate table or illustration. If, in the process of editing, the table or illustration moves to a new page, the page number in the cross-reference is automatically updated.

1 Press **Retrieve** (Shift-F10), then enter **report.wkb** to retrieve the HALVA International corporate report.

⊟ *Select Retrieve from the File menu.*

2 Press ◆**Search** (F2), type **expenses table**, then press ◆**Search** again.

⊟ *Select Forward from the Search menu.*

The cursor stops next to the phrase "As indicated in the Operating Expenses table,...". Below the paragraph is the table. Let's try using the Cross-Reference feature to create a "see page" reference that is tied to the table.

3 Press the **Space Bar**, type **(see page)** for the phrase, then press **Left Arrow** (←) and the **Space Bar**.

A SEE ALSO REFERENCE

```
Despite advice to the contrary, Metcalf has always maintained
that employees should be given direction instead of management.2
To that end, he has worked to give employees a voice in both
their job description and the goals of the company.2

Maximizing the Organization
However, in all the attention to employees, the goal to provide
quality merchandise at discount prices continues to give purpose
and direction to the company.
                              ▲
As indicated in the Operating Expenses table (see page ), that
goal contributes to the recent venture into retail outlets.
After the opening of several retail stores in 1989, sales
increased by 50% during the last quarter.  However, as
demonstrated by the table figures, operating expenses were often
more than twice those of the third quarter.
                       Operating Expenses
                             1989

                        Fourth        Third
Expense                 Quarter       Quarter      Change

D:\WP51\LEARN\REPORT.WKB                     Doc 1 Pg 2 Ln 5.17" Pos 6.5"
```

You are now ready to insert a page number that automatically references the Operating Expenses table.

4 Press **Mark Text** (Alt-F5), select Cross-**R**eference (1), then select Mark **B**oth Reference and Target (3).

⌨ *Select Cross-**R**eference from the **M**ark menu, then select **B**oth.*

The *reference* is the place you want the page number to appear in the text ("see page..."). The *target* is the item you want to reference (e.g., Operating Expenses table).

After selecting Mark Both Reference and Target, a menu is displayed on your screen that lets you select the type of cross-reference you want to create. All you need to do for this cross-reference is to refer to the page number of the table.

5 Select **P**age Number (1).

You are returned to the report to move the cursor to the item (target) you want referenced.

6 Place the cursor on the "Operating Expenses" title at the top of the table, then press **Enter** to mark the target.

7 Enter **expenses** for the target name.

You are returned to the report, where the number "2" is displayed for the cross-reference.

8 Press **Down Arrow** (↓) twice, then press **Reveal Codes** (Alt-F3).

⌨ *Select Reveal Codes from the Edit menu.*

Ⓐ PAGE NUMBER
Ⓑ REFERENCE CODE
Ⓒ TARGET CODE
Ⓓ TARGET NAME

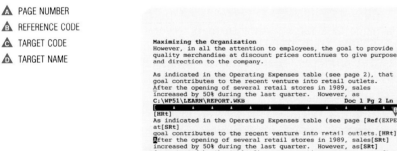

A Reference code displays the page number, while a Target code (inserted at the table title) keeps the number updated. The two codes are tied together because they both contain the "expenses" target name that you entered.

Updating a Cross-Reference

Whenever you make editing changes to a document, all you need to do is generate to update the reference numbers.

1 Press **Reveal Codes** (Alt-F3) to display the normal editing screen.

⊟ *Select Reveal Codes from the Edit menu.*

2 Place the cursor on the "Operating Expenses" title, then press **Home,Home,Home,←** to move the cursor to the very beginning of the line.

3 Press **Hard Page** (Ctrl-Enter) to place the table on a new page.

The table is now on page 3 and the cross-reference is on page 2 of the report.

4 Press **Mark Text** (Alt-F5), then select **Generate** (6).

⊟ *Select Generate from the Mark menu.*

5 Select **Generate** Tables, Indexes, Cross-References, etc. (5), then type **y** to start generating.

A message is displayed that keeps you informed of the progress while WordPerfect is generating new references.

6 When generating is completed, press **Page Down** (PgDn) twice, then press **Up Arrow** (↑) until the paragraph with the "see page" reference is displayed on the screen.

WordPerfect updated the "see page" cross-reference to page 3.

7 Press **Exit** (F7), then type **n** twice to clear the screen.

After giving a name to a target, you can mark several cross-references in the document by selecting Mark Reference. You can also reference items such as graphics boxes and footnotes. For details on these and other features, turn to the *Cross-Reference* heading in the *WordPerfect Reference Manual*.

Decimal Alignment

The Tab Align key and Decimal tabs let you line up numbers at a decimal point (.) as you type.

1 Make sure the editing screen is clear, then press **Enter** twice.

2 Type the following list of numbers. Press **Tab,** then press **Tab Align** (Ctrl-F6) before typing each number.

⊟ *Select Align from the Layout menu, then select Tab Align.*

185.30
3,500.10
12,500.00

The numbers should all be lined up on the decimal point, with a comma separating the thousands.

While a decimal point is commonly used in the United States to separate the integer (21) from the decimal value (.5), in many countries (and for some types of accounting), the decimal point is used to separate the thousands, and a comma is used instead of the decimal point.

3   Press **Enter** twice, press **Format** (Shift-F8), then select **O**ther (4).

⊟ *Select* **O**ther *from the Layout menu.*

4   Select **D**ecimal/Align Character (3), enter a comma (,) for the decimal character, then enter a period (.) for the thousands' separator.

5   Press **Exit** (F7) to return to the editing screen.

6   Press **Tab**, then press **Tab Align** (Ctrl-F6).

⊟ *Select* **A**lign *from the Layout menu, then select* **T**ab Align.

Notice that the "Align char =" message now displays a comma for the decimal alignment character.

⚠ COMMA

```
              185.30
            3,500.10
           12,500.00
           ⚠ _




Align char = ,                        Doc 1 Pg 1 Ln 2" Pos 2"
```

7   Type **21.500,00** and press **Enter**.

8   Type the following list of numbers, pressing **Tab** then **Tab Align** at the beginning of each number.

⊟ *Select* **A**lign *from the Layout menu, then select* **T**ab Align.

930,00
27.800,50
1.500.890,00

Setting the decimal alignment character and the thousands' separator not only changes the way numbers are formatted when you use Tab Align, but also affects numbers typed (and calculated) in Math columns and in Tables. You may even want to set an alignment character (such as a space) for text.

9 Press **Exit**, then type **n** twice to clear the screen.

For additional details on setting a decimal alignment character or thousands' separator, turn to the *Other Format* section in the *WordPerfect Reference Manual*.

Extended Search

The Search keys can be used for finding a word or phrase in the main text of a document, but what about text in places such as endnotes or headers?

1 Press **Retrieve** (Shift-F10), then enter **report.wkb** to retrieve the corporate report.

⬚ *Select Retrieve from the File menu.*

2 Press **♦Search** (F2), type **fortune**, then press **♦Search** again.

⬚ *Select Forward from the Search menu.*

WordPerfect briefly displays a "* Not found *" message. However, the word "fortune" is included in an endnote.

3 Press **Home**, then press **♦Search** (F2).

⬚ *Select Extended from the Search menu, then select Forward.*

An "-> Extended srch:" message is displayed on the status line.

4 Press **♦Search** to begin the extended search.

The word is found in the first endnote in the corporate report.

▲ WORD FOUND

```
1. One of the most lucrative businesses in Europe is the trade in
oriental rugs.  In fact, many a fortune has been accumulated in a
relatively brief span of time by such noted individuals as
Heinrich Salsberg, Giovanna Chiave, and Helen Manchester.
```

```
Endnote:  Press Exit when done                    Ln 1.17" Pos 4.9"
```

5 Press **♦Search** again.

⬚ *Select Extended from the Search menu, then select Next.*

This time the normal "-> Srch:" message is displayed on the screen. To continue an extended search, you need to press Home each time.

6 Press **Cancel** (F1) to back out of the Search message.

7 Press **Home**, then press **◆Search** twice to continue looking for "fortune."

⌨ *Select Extended from the Search menu, then select Forward.*

A "* Not found *" message lets you know that the word is not found in any other place in the report.

8 Press **Exit** (F7) to return to the editing screen.

9 Press **Exit** again, then type **n** twice to clear the screen.

Besides endnotes, an extended search also includes footnotes, headers, footers, captions for graphic boxes, and text typed in graphics boxes. You can use Home with **◆Search** or **◆Search**, or select from the Extended submenu on the Search pull-down menu, to do an extended search of your document.

Hyphenation

When you finish editing a document, you can improve the appearance of some lines when the document is printed by using Hyphenation.

1 Press **Retrieve** (Shift-F10), then enter **report.wkb** to retrieve the corporate report.

⌨ *Select Retrieve from the File menu.*

Turning On Hyphenation
WordPerfect is initially set to hyphenate words using the hyphenation found in the Speller dictionary WP{WP}US.LEX file and the hyphenation rules found in the WP{WP}US.HYC file. All you need to do is turn on Hyphenation, and WordPerfect does the rest.

1 Press **Format** (Shift-F8), then select Line (1).

⌨ *Select Line from the Layout menu.*

2 Select Hyphenation (1), then type **y** to turn on Hyphenation.

3 Press **Exit** (F7) to return to the editing screen.

4 Press **Home,↓** to reformat the text on the screen.

The word "characteristics" in the fourth paragraph is hyphenated.

▲ HYPHENATED WORD

```
                    The First Fifty Years

A wise man once said that "Friends come and go, but enemies
accumulate."1  The same can be said of the relationships that
develop between a company and its customers.

The year 1989 marks the 50th anniversary of the founding of HALVA
International.  While many other import/export businesses have
started in glory and ended in defeat, the HALVA International
corporation continues to thrive.

While there are many theories surrounding the success of HALVA
International, the truth lies in the careful cultivation of
customer relationships and continued efforts to provide quality
merchandise at affordable prices.

In this report, the past, present, and future status of HALVA
International are reviewed, with an emphasis on these character- ◀
istics as being vital to the continued survival of the company.


The European Connection
The year was 1939, and the rumors of war had become a nightmare
of reality.  With the transportation of goods between many
C:\WP51\LEARN\REPORT.WKB                      Doc 1 Pg 1 Ln 4.83" Pos 1"
```

5 Press **Page Down** (PgDn), then press **Home,**↓ to reformat the second page of the report.

The words "personality" and "International" in the second paragraph on the page are hyphenated.

6 Press **Home,Home,**↑ to return to the beginning of the report.

7 Press **Reveal Codes** (Alt-F3).

⌨ *Select **R**eveal Codes from the **E**dit menu.*

A [Hyph On] code is placed in the document whenever you turn on Hyphenation.

▲ [HYPH ON] CODE

```
                    The First Fifty Years

A wise man once said that "Friends come and go, but enemies
accumulate."1  The same can be said of the relationships that
develop between a company and its customers.

The year 1989 marks the 50th anniversary of the founding of HALVA
International.  While many other import/export businesses have
started in glory and ended in defeat, the HALVA International
corporation continues to thrive.

C:\WP51\LEARN\REPORT.WKB                      Doc 1 Pg 1 Ln 1" Pos 1"
[Hyph On][Center][Mark:ToC,1][BOLD]The First Fifty Years[bold][End Mark:ToC,1][H
Rt]
[HRt]
A wise man once said that "Friends come and go, but enemies[SRt]
accumulate."[Footnote:1;[Note Num]Howard Keele, [UND]No Good Deed Goe ... ]  The
 same can be said of the relationships that[SRt]
develop between a company[Index:Company] and its customers[Index:Customers].[HRt
]
[HRt]
The year 1989 marks the 50th anniversary of the founding of HALVA[SRt]

Press Reveal Codes to restore screen
```

Turning Off Hyphenation

If you return to the Line Format menu and type **n** for no hyphenation, WordPerfect places a [Hyph Off] code in your document.

1 Press **Page Down** to move the cursor to the top of the second page.

2 Press **Format** (Shift-F8), then select **L**ine (1).

⌨ *Select Line from the Layout menu.*

3 Select Hyphenation (1), then type **n** to turn off Hyphenation.

4 Press **Exit** (F7) to return to the editing screen.

A [Hyph Off] code has been placed in the text to turn off Hyphenation from the code to the end of the report. However, the words "personality" and "International" are still hyphenated.

5 Delete the hyphen in the word "personality," then press **Down Arrow** (↓).

Both "personality" and "International" wrap to the left margin, but "International" still has a hyphen in the middle of the word. Although you can see the hyphen in the Reveal Codes screen, it is not displayed in the editing screen.

▲ HYPHEN IN REVEAL CODES

```
While the past provides understanding, the present provides
reality.  In this part of the report, we hope to give an overview
of HALVA International that provides a moment of insight into the
current direction of the company.

Direction vs. Management
The nature of an organization is often determined by the
personality of its founder.  In focusing on the nature of HALVA
International, one immediately recognizes the influence of Bryan
C:\WP51\LEARN\REPORT.WKB                    Doc 1 Pg 2 Ln 2.83" Pos 6.6"
[                                                                        ]
[BOLD]Direction vs. Management[bold][HRt]
The nature of an organization is often determined by the[SRt]
personality of its founder.  In focusing on the nature of HALVA[SRt]
Intern-ational, one immediately recognizes the influence of Bryan[SRt]
Metcal▲ the man.[HRt]
[HRt]
Despite advice to the contrary, Metcalf has always maintained[SRt]
that employees[Index:Employees] should be given direction instead of management.
[Footnote:2;[Note Num]Bryan Metcalf, "Nothing is Imposs ... ] [SRt]
To that end, he has worked to give employees[Index:Employees] a voice in both[SR

Press Reveal Codes to restore screen
```

This type of hyphen is called a Soft Hyphen, and is only used by WordPerfect if the word needs to be hyphenated at the end of a line. Otherwise, it is not displayed in the editing screen, nor is it printed.

You can insert a Soft Hyphen into a word by holding down Ctrl and typing a dash (hyphen).

6 Press **Reveal Codes** (Alt-F3) to display the normal editing screen.

⌨ *Select Reveal Codes from the Edit menu.*

7 Press **Exit**, then type **n** twice to clear the screen.

By using the Hyphenation On and Off codes, you can format parts of a document for hyphenation, or simply place a Hyphenation On code at the beginning of the document to have WordPerfect hyphenate the entire document.

Hyphenation Notes

If WordPerfect needs help hyphenating a word, a message is displayed that prompts you to place the hyphen between syllables.

By letting WordPerfect hyphenate words, the lines can be adjusted to print a more exact number of characters in the line. This adjustment produces more evenly-spaced text when the document is printed—especially when Full Justification is on.

You can adjust the frequency of hyphenation by increasing or decreasing the size of the Hyphenation Zone in the Line Format menu. Turn to the *Hyphenation Zone* heading in the *WordPerfect Reference Manual* for details.

Merge Input

The Pause macro command (lesson 15) can be used to help guide you through filling in a form such as a memo (lesson 5). However, as soon as you press the Enter key, the macro continues.

Inserting an {INPUT} Code

If you like the Pause command, but need to press Enter while typing text (e.g., a list of names), try using the Input merge code instead of the Pause macro command.

1 Press **Retrieve** (Shift-F10), then enter **memo.wkb** to retrieve a memo form.

⊟ *Select **R**etrieve from the **F**ile menu.*

2 Press **Down Arrow** (↓) twice, then press **End** to move the cursor to the end of the To line.

3 Press **Merge Codes** (Shift-F9), then select **I**nput (3).

⊟ *Select **M**erge Codes from the **T**ools menu, then select **I**nput.*

An "Enter Message:" prompt appears on the status line. When you merge the memo, WordPerfect pauses at the Input code and displays the message that you enter.

4 Enter **Type name(s); Press F9 to continue** for the message.

The Input code and the message are inserted into the memo.

▲ INPUT CODE AND MESSAGE

```
                         Corporate Memo
        To:          ▷(INPUT}Type name(s); Press F9 to continue¯_
        From:
        Date:        September 29, 1989
        Subject:

                     =======================================



C:\WP51\LEARN\MEMO.WKB                    Doc 1 Pg 1 Ln 1.33" Pos 6"
```

5 Press **Down Arrow** (↓) twice to move the cursor to the end of the From line.

6 Press **Merge Codes** (Shift-F9), select Input (3), then enter **Type name(s); Press F9 to continue** for the message.

⌨ *Select Merge Codes from the Tools menu, then select Input.*

7 Press **Down Arrow** four times to move the cursor to the end of the Subject line.

8 Press **Merge Codes**, select Input, then enter **Type subject; Press F9 to continue** for the message.

⌨ *Select Merge Codes from the Tools menu, then select Input.*

When you finish, there should be three input codes in the memo form.

```
                          Corporate Memo
        To:       ▷ {INPUT}Type name(s); Press F9 to continue˜

        From:     ▷ {INPUT}Type name(s); Press F9 to continue˜

        Date:        September 29, 1989

        Subject:  ▷ {INPUT}Type subject; Press F9 to continue˜_

                  =========================================




        C:\WP51\LEARN\MEMO.WKB                 Doc 1 Pg 1 Ln 2.33" Pos 6"
```

Merging with the Primary File and Keyboard

With the merge codes added, the memo form is now a primary file. Let's save the memo form, then try using it with the Merge feature.

1 Press **Exit** (F7), type **y**, enter **memo.25** for the filename, then type **n** to clear the screen.

2 Press **Merge/Sort** (Ctrl-F9), then select **Merge** (1).

▱ *Select Merge from the Tools menu.*

3 Enter **memo.25** for the name of the primary file.

Because there are no {FIELD} codes in MEMO.25, you do not need a secondary file. All the information will by typed from the keyboard.

4 Press **Enter** for the secondary file.

WordPerfect pauses at the To title and displays the message you created for the Input code on the status line.

```
                              Corporate Memo
         To:                  _




 ▷ Type name(s); Press F9 to continue            Doc 1 Pg 1 Ln 1.33" Pos 2.5"
```

5   Type **Sean Gyll** then press **Enter**.

Pressing Enter returns the cursor to the left margin (instead of continuing with the merge), and you can enter another name.

6   Press **Tab**, type **Dale Boman** then press **End Field** (F9) to continue the merge.

The merge pauses at the From title and displays the message you created for the Input code on the status line.

7   Type your own name, then press **End Field** to continue the merge.

8   Type your subject, then press **End Field** to continue.

As soon as you press End Field, the cursor moves to the end of the memo form, and the merge is completed (there are no more merge codes left in the memo).

9   Type your message.

Besides pressing Enter when the merge pauses, you can also use the editing and format features of WordPerfect (including Reveal Codes) to help you create a document.

10 Press **Exit** (F7), then type **n** twice to clear the screen.

If you want to stop the merge while it is at a pause (or any time a merge is running), press **Merge Codes** (Shift-F9) and select **Q**uit (1).

Merging a List

There are many types of primary files that you can create to merge information from a secondary file. For example, a phone list can be created from a secondary file by using the {FIELD} and {PAGE OFF} merge codes in a primary file.

Creating the Primary File

Let's use the CUSTOMER.WKB secondary file for the merge, and place the customer names (field 1) at the left margin and the phone numbers (field 4) at a 3" tab stop in a primary file.

1 Press **Format** (Shift-F8), then select **L**ine (1).

⌨ *Select Line from the Layout menu.*

2 Select **T**ab Set (8).

3 Press **Delete to End of Line** (Ctrl-End) to erase the tab settings, then enter **3** to set a tab stop 3" from the left margin.

4 Press **Exit** (F7) twice to return to the editing screen.

Now that the tab is set for the column of phone numbers, let's add the {FIELD} codes for field 1 (name) and field 4 (phone number).

5 Press **Merge Codes** (Shift-F9), select **F**ield (1), then enter **1** for the field number.

⌨ *Select Merge Codes from the Tools menu, then select Field.*

6 Press **Tab** to move the cursor to the phone number column.

7 Press **Merge Codes**, select **F**ield, then enter **4** for the field number.

⌨ *Select Merge Codes from the Tools menu, then select Field.*

For each name and phone number to be placed on a separate line, you need to add a hard return after the {FIELD}4~ code.

8 Press **Enter** to place each name and phone number on a separate line.

When you merged the business letters (lessons 23 and 24), WordPerfect placed a hard page break between letters to keep them on separate pages. However, you do not need a page break between each customer in the phone list.

9 Press **Merge Codes**, then select **P**age Off (4).

⌨ *Select Merge Codes from the Tools menu, then select Page Off.*

Your primary file should now look like the one illustrated on the screen below.

```
{FIELD}1~              {FIELD}4~
{PAGE OFF}_
```

Doc 1 Pg 1 Ln 1.17" Pos 1"

10 Press **Exit** (F7), type **y**, enter **phones.25** for the name of the primary file, then type **n** to clear the screen.

Merging the Primary File

Let's try merging the primary file with the list of customers to build a phone list.

1 Press **Merge/Sort** (Ctrl-F9), then select **Merge** (1).

⊟ *Select **Merge** from the **T**ools menu.*

2 Enter **phones.25** for the primary file, then enter **customer.wkb** for the secondary file.

When the merge is completed, you should have a list of names and phone numbers displayed on your screen.

Ⓐ NAMES

Ⓑ PHONE NUMBERS

```
  Ⓐ                        Ⓑ
Robin Pierce             (404) 359-2828
Jayna Wilder-Smith       (415) 987-4598
Anna Lee Pierce          (716) 453-5678
Joseph Corrales, Jr.     (212) 687-1203
Kathleen O'Hara          (617) 789-2027
Mary Anna Pickford       (502) 224-7273
Paul Magleby             (312) 377-3980
Rosanne Jacobsen         (718) 492-7770
Samuel A. Roberts        (916) 878-4550
Scott L. Ziegler         (213) 937-3370
Ted Mortinthal           (301) 522-8700
 _
```

Doc 1 Pg 1 Ln 2.83" Pos 1"

However, because you placed the Tab Set code with the other Merge codes in the primary file, WordPerfect included a Tab Set code at the beginning of each line.

3 Press **Home,Home,↑**, then press **Reveal Codes** (Alt-F3) to display the Tab Set codes.

⬚ *Select **Reveal Codes** from the **Edit** menu.*

Document Initial Codes and the Primary File

A much better way of including formatting codes in a primary file is to use the Initial Codes feature.

1 Press **Reveal Codes** (Alt-F3) to display the normal editing screen.

⬚ *Select **Reveal Codes** from the **Edit** menu.*

2 Press **Exit** (F7), then type **n** twice to clear the screen.

3 Press **Retrieve** (Shift-F10), then enter **phones.25** to retrieve the primary file.

⬚ *Select **Retrieve** from the **File** menu.*

4 Press **Left Arrow** (←), then press **Backspace** and type **y** to delete the Tab Set code.

5 Press **Format** (Shift-F8), then select **Document** (3).

⬚ *Select **Document** from the **Layout** menu.*

6 Select Initial Codes (2).

An Initial Codes editing screen is displayed. Any formatting codes that you place in the screen are saved with the document, but are not included as part of the text and codes displayed in the Reveal Codes screen.

7 Press **Format**, then select **Line** (1).

⬚ *Select **Line** from the **Layout** menu.*

8 Select Tab Set (8).

9 Press **Delete to End of Line** (Ctrl-End) to erase the existing tab stops, then enter **2.75** to set a tab stop for the phone numbers.

10 Press **Exit** (F7) four times to return to the normal editing screen.

11 Press **Reveal Codes** to display the codes in the primary file.

⬚ *Select **Reveal Codes** from the **Edit** menu.*

Only the Merge codes are displayed. The Tab Set code is stored as a format for the document with any other initial codes you may have set.

12 Press **Exit**, type **y**, press **Enter**, type **y** again to replace the PHONES.25 file, then type **n** to clear the screen.

13 Press **Merge/Sort** (Ctrl-F9), then select **Merge** (1).

▭ *Select* **Merge** *from the* **Tools** *menu.*

14 Enter **phones.25** for the primary file, then enter **customer.wkb** for the secondary file.

15 When the merge is completed, press **Home,Home,↑**, then press **Word Right** (Ctrl-→) twice to move to the first phone number in the list.

There are no Tab Set codes displayed in Reveal Codes, but the phone numbers are lined up at 3.75" from the left edge of the page (check the status line) because the Tab Set code is with the document initial codes.

16 Press **Exit**, then type **n** twice to clear the screen.

Whenever you need to set a format for a primary file, it is a good idea to place the format code with the document initial codes. The format code will affect the entire primary file *without* inserting a code for each record in the secondary file.

Merging to the Printer

During a merge, WordPerfect stores all the merged documents in your computer's memory. If there is not enough room in memory, then temporary files are created on disk to hold the rest of the documents.

When merged documents run into the hundreds or thousands, many companies choose to handle a merge by having each document sent to the printer as it is merged by WordPerfect.

The process of merging to the printer saves memory and disk space because only one document (e.g., a business letter) is in memory at a time. In addition, valuable printer time and employee hours can be saved by having WordPerfect merge and print documents during off hours (i.e., evenings and weekends).

You can merge to the printer by adding a {PRINT} code and a {PAGE OFF} code to the end of a primary file.

1 Press **Retrieve** (Shift-F10), then enter **stores.wkb** to retrieve a primary file business letter.

▭ *Select* **Retrieve** *from the* **File** *menu.*

2 Press **Home,Home,↓** to place the cursor at the end of the letter.

3 Press **Enter** to start a new line.

4 Press **Merge Codes** (Shift-F9), then select **M**ore (6) to display the list of merge codes.

⌨ *Select Merge Codes from the **T**ools menu, then select **M**ore.*

5 Type **print** to move the cursor to the {PRINT} code in the list, then press **Enter** to insert the code into the letter.

6 Press **Merge Codes**, then select **P**age Off (4) to insert a {PAGE OFF} code into the letter.

⌨ *Select Merge Codes from the **T**ools menu, then select **P**age Off.*

You should now have both a {PRINT} and a {PAGE OFF} code on the last line of the letter.

▲ MERGE CODES

```
We are proud to announce the grand opening of several HALVA
International retail stores throughout the country.  Stores are
scheduled to open in the following cities during the first
quarter of the year:

          New York, New York        January 18
          Boston, Massachusetts     January 26
          San Francisco, California February 10
          Los Angeles, California   February 24
          Atlanta, Georgia          March 9
          Chicago, Illinois         March 17

As a preferred customer, you will be receiving a special
invitation, and I personally look forward to meeting you at the
opening.

Sincerely,


Bryan Metcalf
President
HALVA International
{PRINT}{PAGE OFF}
C:\WP51\LEARN\STORES.WKB                 Doc 1 Pg 1 Ln 5.67" Pos 1"
```

The {PRINT} code tells WordPerfect to send the merged letter to the printer and clear the screen (memory). The {PAGE OFF} code makes sure that a hard page break is not inserted between letters.

If you want to test the letter by merging it with the CUSTOMER.WKB secondary file, you need to select your own printer before saving the edited letter (save it as LETTER.25).   Whatever printer is selected when the primary file is saved is the same printer that will be used when WordPerfect merges the letters to the printer.

If you save the letter *without* selecting your printer, then WordPerfect will try using the Workbook Printer, which is not designed to print with any printer.

When you finish the exercise,

7 Press **Exit** (F7), then type **n** twice to clear the screen.

Parallel Columns

You have already used Newspaper columns to place a list of marketing representatives (lesson 13) and a newsletter (lesson 16) into columns. Text in Newspaper columns flows from the bottom of one column to the top of the next column.

Defining Parallel Columns

However, sometimes a group of items needs to be placed in columns across the page *without* the text flowing from one column to the next. For example, a script for a video production may include directions for a camera shot in the left column, and the narration for the camera shot in the right column.

Not only do the camera shot and the narration need to be kept together across the page, but each time you finish typing the narration, you need to have WordPerfect start a new column 1 for the next camera shot. In this case, you can use Parallel columns to solve both problems.

1   Press **Columns/Table** (Alt-F7), select **C**olumns (1), then select **D**efine (3).

⌨ *Select **C**olumns from the **L**ayout menu, then select **D**efine.*

2   Select **T**ype (1) from the Text Column Definition menu.

A menu is displayed at the bottom of the screen with two types of Parallel columns available. The Parallel type simply turns columns off and then back on again each time you end the last column across the page. The Parallel with Block Protect type adds Block Protect codes around the Column On and Off codes to make sure that none of the columns are split by a soft page break.

The camera shot directions and the narration are short enough in most video scripts that it would be a good idea to have them protected from a soft page break. However, in other scripts the dialogue or narration could be quite long. In this case, it would be better to use Parallel columns without Block Protect codes so that the narration could be split by a page break.

3   Select Parallel with **B**lock Protect (3), then press **Exit** to leave the Text Column Definition menu.

4   Select **O**n (1) to turn on the parallel columns, then press **Reveal Codes** (Alt-F3).

⌨ *Select **R**eveal Codes from the **E**dit menu.*

A [Block Pro:On] code is inserted before the [Col On] code to protect the columns from a page break.

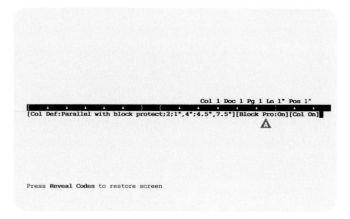

```
                                        Col 1 Doc 1 Pg 1 Ln 1" Pos 1"
[Col Def:Parallel with block protect;2;1",4";4.5",7.5"][Block Pro:On][Col On]
                                                          ⚠

Press Reveal Codes to restore screen
```

Typing the First Camera Shot
You are now ready to begin creating the first camera shot with narration.

1 Press **Reveal Codes** (Alt-F3) to display the normal editing screen.

⊟ *Select **Reveal Codes** from the **Edit** menu.*

2 Press **Left Arrow** (←) twice, press **Enter** four times, then press **Up Arrow** (↑) twice.

3 Press **Font** (Ctrl-F8), select **Appearance** (2), then select **Italic** (4).

⊟ *Select **Appearance** from the **Font** menu, then select **Italic**.*

4 Type **Fade In** then press **Home,Home,↓** to move to the right of the Column On code.

5 Type **1.** and press ◆**Indent** (F4).

6 Press **Caps Lock** to type uppercase letters, then type **scottish countryside with mist on moor in background** for the description.

7 Press **Caps Lock** to turn off the feature.

8 Press **Hard Page** (Ctrl-Enter) to start the narration at the top of the second column.

9 Press **Center** (Shift-F6), type **Narrator:** then press **Enter** twice for double spacing.

10 Type the following narration:

In the dawn of time, before the pipes sounded from the highlands, ancients warred, or Spirits listed through the glen, a clan of terrible Giants arose from the mists of the earth.

11 Press **Hard Page** (Ctrl-Enter) to end the second column.

12 Press **Reveal Codes** to display the codes in the script.

⌨ *Select **Reveal Codes** from the Edit menu.*

When you pressed Hard Page at the end of the second column, WordPerfect inserted a Block Protect Off and Column Off code, a hard return to double space between the sets of columns, then a Block Protect On and Column On code to start the next camera shot and narration.

▲ BLOCK PROTECT CODES
▲ COLUMN CODES

```
    1.    SCOTTISH COUNTRYSIDE WITH          Narrator:
          MIST ON MOOR IN
          BACKGROUND                   In the dawn of time, before
                                       the pipes sounded from the
                                       highlands, ancients warred, or
                                       Spirits listed through the
                                       glen, a clan of terrible Giants
                                       arose from the mists of the
                                       earth.

    _
                                       Col 1 Doc 1 Pg 1 Ln 3.33" Pos 1"
[       ▲   ▲   ▲   ▲   ▲   ]    {      ▲   ▲   ▲   ▲   ▲   }    ▲
arose from the mists of the[SRt]
earth.[Block Pro:Off][Col Off]
[HRt]
[Block Pro:On][Col On]█

Press Reveal Codes to restore screen
```

Typing the Second Camera Shot

You are now ready to type the second camera shot with narration.

1 Press **Left Arrow** (←) twice, press **Enter** twice, then press **Up Arrow** (↑) twice.

2 Press **Font** (Ctrl-F8), select **Appearance** (2), then select **Italic** (4).

⌨ *Select **Appearance** from the Font menu, then select **Italic**.*

3 Type **Cut To** then press **Home,Home,↓** to move to the right of the Column On code.

You are now ready to create the second camera shot with narration.

4 Press **Reveal Codes** (Alt-F3) to display the normal editing screen.

⌨ *Select **Reveal Codes** from the Edit menu.*

5 Type **2.** and press **◆Indent** (F4).

6 Press **Caps Lock** to type uppercase letters, then type **close up of screaming woman running from flaming cottage** for the description.

7 Press **Caps Lock** to turn off the feature.

8 Press **Hard Page** (Ctrl-Enter) to start the narration at the top of the second column.

9 Press **Center** (Shift-F6), type **Narrator:** then press **Enter** twice for double spacing.

10 Type the following narration:

Descending from enormous caverns in the rocks, the giants plundered entire villages, leaving but a few children and old ones to weave legends of primeval horror.

11 Press **Hard Page** (Ctrl-Enter) to end the second column.

Finishing the Script

Now that you have started the video script, you may want to continue with the story or simply end the exercise.

1 When you finish, you may want to print the script or preview it in View Document. Afterwards, press **Exit** (F7), then type **n** twice to clear the screen.

With all the Block Protect and Column codes inserted at the beginning and end of each set of columns, editing in parallel columns can be difficult. However, for some applications (such as writing scripts), parallel columns can be an important help when creating a document that requires a set of columns across a page.

For additional details on parallel columns, turn to the Columns, Parallel *heading in the* WordPerfect Reference Manual.

Reveal Codes Screen Size

Whenever you press Reveal Codes, the lower half of the screen displays the codes in your document. If you would like to see more of the normal editing screen, and less of the Reveal Codes screen, you can change the size of both.

1 Press **Reveal Codes** (Alt-F3) to display the Reveal Codes screen.

⌨ *Select* **Reveal Codes** *from the* **Edit** *menu.*

2 Press **Screen** (Ctrl-F3), then select **W**indow (1).

⌨ *Select* **Window** *from the* **Edit** *menu.*

A message is displayed in the middle of the screen that lets you indicate the number of lines you want displayed in the editing screen (window).

The lines are currently set for "11," but can be changed by entering a new number, or simply by pressing Up Arrow or Down Arrow to change the size of the editing screen.

3 Press **Down Arrow** (↓) six times to increase the size of the editing screen.

As the editing screen becomes larger, the Reveal Codes screen becomes smaller.

4   Press **Enter** to set the size of the editing screen and the Reveal Codes screen.

5   Press **Retrieve** (Shift-F10), then enter **report.wkb** to retrieve the corporate report.

⊟ *Select **Retrieve** from the **File** menu.*

Try moving through the report and making some editing changes. You may decide that you like a smaller Reveal Codes screen.

6   When you finish, press **Screen** (Ctrl-F3), select **Window** (1), then enter **11** to return the editing screen to its normal size.

⊟ *Select **Window** from the **Edit** menu.*

7   Press **Reveal Codes** to display the normal editing screen.

⊟ *Select **Reveal Codes** from the **Edit** menu.*

8   Press **Exit** (F7), then type **n** twice to clear the screen.

By using the Window feature you can change the size of the Reveal Codes screen while you are in WordPerfect. However, the next time you start WordPerfect, the Reveal Codes screen returns to its normal size.

If you want to change the initial setting for the Reveal Codes screen size, use the Setup key (Shift-F1,2,6,6). After changing the initial setting, the Reveal Codes screen will be displayed with the new size each time you start WordPerfect.

For the lessons to work properly, you need to have the Reveal Codes screen size set at 10 (Setup key), or the editing screen size set at 11 (Screen key).

Lesson 26: Characters and Keyboards

In this lesson you learn how to create special characters with Compose and how to create customized keyboards with Keyboard Layout. Both features help you expand the possibilities of your computer, your printer, and WordPerfect.

Typing Characters with Compose

A standard computer keyboard includes the letters of the alphabet (uppercase and lowercase), numbers, and a few symbols and punctuation marks.

While these may be all the characters you need for typing most documents, there may be times when you need to type a foreign word, symbols in a math formula, Greek characters, or other special characters that are *not* on the keyboard. To help you insert these characters into a document, WordPerfect provides a Compose feature.

For example, if you want to type a bullet (•) in front of each item in a list, you can use Compose to insert the bullet if it isn't on the keyboard.

1 Press **Exit** (F7), then type **n** twice to make sure the screen is cleared.

2 Press **Compose** (Ctrl-2), type an asterisk (*), then type a period (.).

⬚ *Select Characters from the Font menu, then enter* ***.** *at the Key= prompt.*

Make sure you press Ctrl-2 instead of Ctrl-F2, or you will be pressing Spell instead of Compose.

3 Press **Tab**, type **Small Filled Bullet**, then press **Enter** to start a new line.

By using the Compose key and typing two characters, you were able to insert a small bullet into the list.

4 Press **Compose** (Ctrl-2), then type an asterisk (*) twice.

⬚ *Select Characters from the Font menu, then enter* ****** *at the Key= prompt.*

This time a larger bullet is displayed on the screen.

5 Press **Tab**, type **Medium Filled Bullet**, then press **Enter** to start a new line.

For examples of all the special characters you can insert by using the Compose key and typing two characters, turn to the Compose *heading in the* WordPerfect Reference Manual.

Character Sets and Compose

Both the small and medium bullets are part of a large group of over 1700 characters that are available in WordPerfect. The characters are divided into *character sets*, with a number assigned to each character in the set. The

WordPerfect character sets include all the characters on your keyboard, plus hundreds of other characters.

For example, the small bullet (·) is in character set 4, and is number 3 in the character set.

1 Press **Reveal Codes** (Alt-F3) to turn on the Reveal Codes screen.

🖳 *Select **Reveal Codes** from the **Edit** menu.*

The small bullet character is displayed in both the normal editing screen and the Reveal Codes screen.

2 Press **Home,Home,↑** to place the cursor on the small bullet.

The small bullet expands in the Reveal Codes screen to display the character set numbers for the bullet.

A SMALL BULLET
B CHARACTER SET
C NUMBER IN CHARACTER SET

If you know the character set numbers for a special character, then you can type the numbers when using the Compose key.

A table of all the characters in the WordPerfect character sets is available in Appendix P: WordPerfect Characters *of the* WordPerfect Reference Manual.

3 Press **Compose** (Ctrl-2), type **4,3** for the character set numbers of the small bullet, then press **Enter**.

🖳 *Select **Characters** from the **Font** menu, then enter **4,3** at the Key= prompt.*

4 Press **Left Arrow** (←) to place the cursor on the new bullet.

A small bullet (exactly like the first) is displayed on your screen, with the same character set numbers in Reveal Codes.

5 Press **Delete** (Del) to delete the bullet at the cursor.

6 Press **Reveal Codes** to display the normal editing screen.

⌨ *Select **R**eveal Codes from the **E**dit menu.*

Characters in the Editing Screen

Let's type a few more special characters with the Compose key, then display them in the View Document screen.

1 Press **Home,↓** to place the cursor in the empty line at the bottom of the list.

2 Press **Compose** (Ctrl-2), type a slash (/), then type **2** to insert a ½ character.

⌨ *Select **C**haracters from the **F**ont menu, then enter /2 at the Key= prompt.*

3 Press **Tab**, type **One Half**, then press **Enter** to start a new line.

4 Press **Compose**, then type **AE** to insert an Æ diagraph.

⌨ *Select **C**haracters from the **F**ont menu, then enter **AE** at the Key= prompt.*

5 Press **Tab**, type **AE Digraph**, then press **Enter** to start a new line.

6 Press **Compose**, type **e** for the first character, then type **'** (on the same key as ") for the second character.

⌨ *Select **C**haracters from the **F**ont menu, then enter **e'** at the Key= prompt.*

7 Press **Tab**, type **e Acute**, then press **Enter** to start a new line.

While some characters (such as a bullet or an e acute) can be inserted with Compose by typing two characters already on your keyboard, most of the WordPerfect characters can only be inserted by typing the character set numbers.

8 Press **Compose** (Ctrl-2), type **8,36** for a Sigma (a character from the Greek alphabet), then press **Enter** to insert the character.

⌨ *Select **C**haracters from the **F**ont menu, then enter **8,36** at the Key= prompt.*

9 Press **Tab**, type **Sigma**, then press **Enter** to start a new line.

10 Press **Compose**, type **4,23** for a copyright symbol, then press **Enter** to insert the character.

⌨ *Select **C**haracters from the **F**ont menu, then enter **4,23** at the Key= prompt.*

11 Press **Tab**, type **Copyright**, then press **Enter** to start a new line.

Notice that a reverse video rectangle is displayed on the screen (on most computers) instead of the copyright symbol.

```
   ·         Small Filled Bullet
   •         Medium Filled Bullet
   ½         One Half
   Æ         AE Digraph
   é         e Acute
   Σ         Sigma
 ▲ ▪         Copyright
   ‾
```

Doc 1 Pg 1 Ln 2.17" Pos 1"

Although there are over 1700 characters available in the WordPerfect sets, most computers can display only 256 or 512 characters in the normal editing screen. If a character is not available for display on the editing screen, then WordPerfect displays the rectangle.

Characters in the View Document Screen

To see all the characters in the WordPerfect character sets, you need to use the View Document screen.

1 Press **Print** (Shift-F7), select **V**iew Document (6), then select 200% (2).

⌨ *Select **Print** from the **File** menu.*

A list similar to the following should be displayed on your View Document screen.

```
   Ⓐ    Ⓑ
   ·
   ·         Small Filled Bullet
   •         Medium Filled Bullet
   ½         One Half
   Æ         AE Digraph
   é         e Acute
   Σ         Sigma
   ©         Copyright
```

1 100% 2 200% 3 Full Page 4 Facing Pages: 2   Doc 1 Pg 1

If one or more of the special characters is *not* displayed, then you know that WordPerfect cannot print the characters using your printer.

2 Press **Exit** (F7) to return to the normal editing screen.

Displaying the CHARACTR.WKB File

One of the best ways to find out which WordPerfect characters your printer can print is to retrieve the CHARACTR.WKB file and display it in the View Document screen.

1 Press **Exit** (F7), then type **n** twice to clear the screen.

2 Press **Retrieve** (Shift-F10), then enter **charactr.wkb** to retrieve the test file.

▭ *Select Retrieve from the File menu.*

The CHARACTR.WKB file contains all the WordPerfect characters, with a table created for each character set.

3 Press **Page Down** (PgDn) to display the second page of character sets.

Let's check the character sets (maps) in the View Document screen to see which of the characters are available at your printer.

4 Press **Print** (Shift-F7), select **View Document** (6), then select **100%** (1).

▭ *Select Print from the File menu.*

If your printer is like most printers, then many of the characters will be missing in character sets 4, 5, and 6.

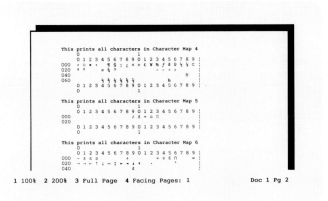

However, if your printer does not have the characters available, WordPerfect still may be able to print the characters for you.

5 Press **Exit** to return to the editing screen.

Printing Graphic Characters

If your printer can print graphics, then WordPerfect can print *all* the characters in the WordPerfect character sets that are missing by graphically creating them at the printer.

1 Press **Home,Home,↑** to move the cursor to the beginning of the document.

A note at the beginning of the test file lets you know that the graphics quality has been set to "Do Not Print" to display only those characters available at your printer. However, if you set the graphics quality to Medium (or High) then WordPerfect will graphically create each missing character for you.

2 Press **Print** (Shift-F7), type **g** to select Graphics Quality, then select **M**edium (3).

⌨ *Select* Print *from the* File *menu.*

3 Select **V**iew Document (6), then press **Page Down** (PgDn) to display character sets 4, 5, and 6 on the screen.

If your printer can print graphics, then you should see all three tables filled with characters (it may take a moment to display them all on the screen).

4 Press **Cancel** (F1) to return to the Print menu.

Although setting the graphics quality (or text quality) to Do Not Print determines whether or not WordPerfect will print all the characters in the character sets, the actual quality of the printed graphics characters depends on the resolution settings for text quality and graphics quality.

If you set the text quality to High, then WordPerfect will print both the graphics characters and the rest of the characters in your document at the highest resolution available at your printer. If the text quality is set to Medium or Draft, then the setting for the graphics quality is used.

For most documents, you may want to select Medium for both text and graphics quality as it normally takes much longer to print graphics characters when the text quality is set at High.

5 Press **Exit** (F7) to return to the editing screen.

6 Press **Exit**, then type **n** twice to clear the screen.

For additional details about the graphic characters that WordPerfect can print for you, turn to the Compose *and* Print Quality *headings in the* WordPerfect Reference Manual.

Creating a Keyboard

Even if you frequently use a special character when typing documents, you may forget what character set numbers (or two characters) to type to insert the character into a document.

To help you solve the problem, you can use the Keyboard Layout feature to assign the special character to a convenient keystroke on the keyboard.

For example, you may use the small bullet each time you type a list in a document. By creating your own keyboard, you can assign the small bullet to a key like Alt-b.

If you are running WordPerfect from two disk drives, replace the Learning diskette in drive B with the Macros/Keyboards diskette.

1 Press **Setup** (Shift-F1), then select **K**eyboard Layout (5).

⌨ *Select Setup from the File menu, then select Keyboard Layout.*

A list of keyboards that come with your WordPerfect package is displayed on your screen.

```
Setup: Keyboard Layout
     ALTRNAT
     ENHANCED
     EQUATION
     MACROS
     SHORTCUT













1 Select; 2 Delete; 3 Rename; 4 Create; 5 Copy; 6 Original;
7 Edit; 8 Map; N Name search: 1
```

The ALTRNAT and MACROS keyboards will be introduced at the end of the lesson. For now, let's create our own keyboard for the small bullet character.

2 Select **C**reate (4), then enter **special** for the name of the new keyboard.

WordPerfect creates a SPECIAL.WPK (**W**ord**P**erfect **K**eyboard) file on disk for storing the new keystrokes and displays the name of the keyboard in the list.

3 Select **M**ap (8) to map (assign) the small bullet to the Special keyboard.

Mapping Characters
to a Keyboard

A menu is displayed that not only lets you map characters and keystrokes to the Ctrl, Alt, and normal typing keys on the keyboard, but also gives you an overview of the keyboard mapping.

A KEYBOARD NAME
B KEYS
C ACTION

```
Keyboard: Map

A▶ Name: SPECIAL

B▶ Alt  Key       ABCDEFGHIJKLMNOPQRSTUVWXYZ1234567890-=\`[];',./
         Action  C▶CCCCCCCCCCCCCCCCCCCCCCCCCCCCCCCCCCCCCCC

     Ctrl Key       ABCDEFGHIJKLMNOPQRSTUVWXYZ[\]_          C = Command
         Action  CCCCCCCCCCCCCCCCCCCCCCCCCCCCCC            M = Keyboard Macro

         Key       !"#$%&'()*+,-./0123456789:;<=>?@
         Action    !"#$%&'()*+,-./0123456789:;<=>?@

         Key       ABCDEFGHIJKLMNOPQRSTUVWXYZ[\]^_`
         Action    ABCDEFGHIJKLMNOPQRSTUVWXYZ[\]^_`

         Key       abcdefghijklmnopqrstuvwxyz{|}~
         Action    abcdefghijklmnopqrstuvwxyz{|}~


     Key         Action          Description
     Alt-A       (ALT A)


1 Key; 2 Macro; 3 Description; 4 Original; 5 Compose; N Key Name Search: 1
```

There are five sets of rows—one for the Alt keys, one for the Ctrl keys, and three for the normal typing keys. Each set is divided into a row of keys that you can map (top row) with a row of characters below that represents the action of each key.

If a single keystroke has been mapped to the key, then a **C** is displayed for the action. If a macro has been mapped to the key, then an **M** is displayed for the action. If a single character has been mapped to the key, then the character (unbolded) is displayed for the action.

You can move the cursor through the keyboard map by using the Home and arrow keys.

1 Press **Right Arrow** (→) until the cursor stops under the "T" in the Alt key row.

⌨ *You can move the cursor through the keyboard map by placing the mouse pointer under the desired character and clicking the left button.*

Information about the ALT-t key is displayed at the bottom of the keyboard map under the Key, Action, and Description titles.

2 Press **Down Arrow** (↓) twice to move the cursor to the first row of normal typing keys.

The cursor stops under the 3 in the line, and information about the "3" key is displayed at the bottom of the screen.

3 Press **Home,**← to move the cursor to the beginning of the row, then press **Home,**↑ to move the cursor back to the beginning of the Alt key row.

Now that you have been introduced to the keyboard map, let's assign the small bullet to Alt-b.

4 Press **Right Arrow** to place the cursor under the B in the Alt key row.

5 Select **K**ey (1) from the menu at the bottom of the screen.

A "Key:" message is displayed on the screen. At this point you can press any key on the keyboard. If you press Compose, then you can map any of the WordPerfect characters to the Alt-b key.

6 Press **Compose** (Ctrl-2), type **4,3** for the small bullet, then press **Enter**.

The small bullet is displayed in the Alt key row, with the character set numbers for the bullet under the Action title at the bottom of the screen.

A SMALL BULLET

B CHARACTER SET NUMBERS

```
Keyboard: Map

  Name: SPECIAL

  Alt  Key       ABCDEFGHIJKLMNOPQRSTUVWXYZ1234567890-=\`[];',./
       Action    C·CCCCCCCCCCCCCCCCCCCCCCCCCCCCCCCCCCCCC

  Ctrl Key       ABCDEFGHIJKLMNOPQRSTUVWXYZ[\]_           C = Command
       Action    CCCCCCCCCCCCCCCCCCCCCCCCCCCCCC           M = Keyboard Macro

       Key       !"#$%&'()*+,-./0123456789:;<=>?@
       Action    !"#$%&'()*+,-./0123456789:;<=>?@

       Key       ABCDEFGHIJKLMNOPQRSTUVWXYZ[\]^_`
       Action    ABCDEFGHIJKLMNOPQRSTUVWXYZ[\]^_`

       Key       abcdefghijklmnopqrstuvwxyz{|}~
       Action    abcdefghijklmnopqrstuvwxyz{|}~


  Key            Action          Description
  Alt-B          [·:4,3]
                 B

  1 Key; 2 Macro; 3 Description; 4 Original; 5 Compose; N Key Name Search: 1
```

7 Select **D**escription (3), then enter **Small Bullet** to describe the Alt-b keystroke.

Before leaving the keyboard map, let's assign one more character to the keyboard.

8 Press **Down Arrow** (↓) three times, then press **Home,**→ to move the cursor to the end of the second row of normal typing characters.

9 Press **Left Arrow** (←) twice to place the cursor under the up caret (^) character.

If you are only mapping a character to the keyboard, you can use the Compose option (instead of the Key option) from the menu at the bottom of the screen.

10 Select Compose (5), type **4,23** for the copyright symbol, then press **Enter**.

A reverse video rectangle (on most computers) is displayed under the up caret, with the character set numbers at the bottom of the screen.

11 Select **Description** (3), then enter **Copyright** to describe the character.

12 Press **Exit** (F7) to return to the list of keyboards.

Selecting and Using a Keyboard

Before you can use the new mapping for the Alt-b and Up Caret keys, you need to select the Special keyboard.

1 Make sure the SPECIAL keyboard is highlighted, then press **Enter** to select the keyboard.

The filename of the keyboard (SPECIAL.WPK) is displayed in the Setup menu.

2 Press **Exit** (F7) to return to the normal editing screen.

Let's try using the new keyboard mapping to create a new list of characters.

3 Press **Alt-b** to type a small bullet on the screen.

4 Press **Tab**, type **Small Bullet**, then press **Enter** to start a new line.

5 Press the Up Caret key (Shift-6) to insert a reverse video rectangle for the copyright symbol.

6 Press **Tab**, type **Copyright**, then press **Enter** to start a new line.

7 Press **Print** (Shift-F7), select **View Document** (6), then select 200% (2) to display the characters.

⌨ *Select Print from the File menu.*

8 When you finish, press **Exit** to return to the editing screen.

Mapping Keystrokes to a Keyboard

Besides mapping characters to a keyboard, you can also map keystrokes. For example, let's assign the Block feature to the Ctrl-b key.

1 Press **Setup** (Shift-F1), then select **Keyboard Layout** (5).

⌨ *Select Setup from the File menu, then select Keyboard Layout.*

2 Make sure the cursor is on the SPECIAL keyboard, then select **Map** (8) to display the keyboard map.

3 Press **Down Arrow** (↓) to move the cursor to the Ctrl key row, then press **Right Arrow** (→) to place the cursor under the B in the row.

4 Select **Key** (1), then press **Block** (Alt-F4).

The Block feature is still mapped to Alt-F4, but it is also assigned to Ctrl-b (check the Action at the bottom of the screen).

5 Select **Description** (3), then enter **Block Feature** to describe the keystroke.

Using the Macro Editor

Mapping a character or single keystroke may take care of most of your needs, but what if you want to assign more than one keystroke to the keyboard?

1   Press **Up Arrow** (↑) to move the cursor to the small bullet (·) in the Alt key row.

2   Select **M**acro (2) from the menu at the bottom of the screen.

An editing window is displayed that lets you assign more than one keystroke to a key.

A KEYSTROKE

B EDITING WINDOW

```
Key: Action
     Key              Alt-B
     Description

  ┌────────────────────────────────────────────────┐
  │ ·                                                │
  │ A                                                │
  │                                                  │
  │ B                                                │
  │                                                  │
  │                                                  │
  │                                                  │
  │                                                  │
  └────────────────────────────────────────────────┘

  Ctrl-PgUp for macro commands;  Press Exit when done
```

The editing window is part of the *Macro Editor*, and is used to edit existing macros that you have already created from the normal editing screen, or to create (or edit) a keyboard macro with the Keyboard Layout feature.

For details on using the Macro Editor, see Macros, Macro Editor *in the* WordPerfect Reference Manual.

3   Press **Right Arrow** (→) to move the cursor to the right of the small bullet.

4   Press ◆**Indent** (F4) to insert an {Indent} command into the editing window.

5   Press **Exit** (F7) to return to the keyboard map.

An **M** has replaced the **C** in the row of Alt keys, and a {KEY MACRO 1} message is displayed under the Action title at the bottom of the keyboard map.

The {KEY MACRO 1} message is used to reference the ALT-b keyboard mapping if you happen to press ALT-b when creating a macro with the Special keyboard selected. For details on the {KEY MACRO} references, turn to Keyboard Layout, Map *in the* WordPerfect Reference Manual.

Whenever you use the Macro Editor to assign more than one character or keystroke to a key, WordPerfect recognizes the mapping as a macro and displays an **M** in the keyboard map. If you used the Macro Editor again to delete the indent, then the **M** in the map would be replaced by a small bullet because there would be only one character assigned to Ctrl-b.

6 Select **D**escription (3), then enter **Small Bullet with Indent** to describe the macro.

7 Press **Exit** twice to return to the normal editing screen.

Using the Edited Keyboard

Let's use the new mapping for the Alt-b and Ctrl-b keys to add another item in the list.

1 Press **Alt-b** to insert a small bullet and an indent.

2 Type **Small Bullet (Bolded)**, then press **Enter** to start a new line.

3 Press **Up Arrow** (↑) to place the cursor on the small bullet.

4 Press **Ctrl-b** to turn on Block, then press **Home,**→ to highlight the entire line.

5 Press **Bold** (F6) to bold the line.

Creating a Macro

Although using Ctrl-b might be easier to remember (B = Block) than the original Alt-F4 mapping, it does not save you any keystrokes, and may even be more difficult to access on some keyboards.

However, if Ctrl-b blocked and bolded an entire line, instead of just turning on Block, then Ctrl-b would be a much more valuable keystroke.

Because you are already in the normal editing screen, let's create the macro using Macro Define, then retrieve the macro into the Special keyboard.

1 Press **Up Arrow** (↑) to place the cursor at the end of the copyright symbol line.

2 Press **Macro Define** (Ctrl-F10), enter **bold** for the name of the macro, then enter **Bold a Line** for the description.

⬚ *Select Macro from the Tools menu, then select Define.*

A "Macro Def" message is displayed to let you know that WordPerfect is ready to record your keystrokes in a BOLD.WPM file.

3 Press **Home,**← to place the cursor at the beginning of the line.

4 Press **Block** (Alt-F4), then press **End** to highlight the entire line.

5 Press **Bold** (F6) to bold the text in the line.

6 Press **Macro Define** (Ctrl-F10) to end defining the macro.

⬚ *Select Macro from the Tools menu, then select Define.*

Retrieving a Macro into a Keyboard

Now that the BOLD.WPM is defined, let's retrieve it into the Special keyboard.

1 Press **Setup** (Shift-F1), then select **K**eyboard Layout (5).

⌨ *Select Setup from the **F**ile menu, then select **K**eyboard Layout.*

2 Make sure the cursor is on the SPECIAL keyboard, then select **E**dit (7).

A list is displayed that includes all the keystrokes from the keyboard map.

⚠ ALT-B KEYSTROKE

```
Keyboard: Edit

Name: SPECIAL

Key            Action          Description

Alt-B          {KEY MACRO 1}   Small Bullet with Indent
Ctrl-B         {Block}         Block Feature
˜              [■:4,23]        Copyright




1 Action; 2 Dscrptn; 3 Original; 4 Create; 5 Move; Macro: 6 Save; 7 Retrieve: 1
```

Although the keyboard map gives an excellent overview of the Ctrl and Alt key assignments, the list of keystrokes lets you quickly see only those keys that you have mapped in the keyboard.

If you do not enter a description for a key in the keyboard map, then it is not displayed in the list of keystrokes.

3 Select **R**etrieve (7) from the menu at the bottom of the screen.

4 Press **Ctrl-b** to assign the macro to the Ctrl-b keystroke.

5 Type **y** to replace the existing keystroke (Block) with the keystrokes from the BOLD macro.

6 Enter **bold** for the name of the macro you want to retrieve.

The BOLD macro is retrieved into the Special keyboard file (SPECIAL.WPK), then mapped to the Ctrl-b keystroke. The description you already created (Bold a Line) is displayed in the list.

When you retrieve an existing macro into a keyboard, only a copy of the macro is retrieved. The original macro is still available on disk. You can also use the Save option to save a copy of a keyboard macro as a separate macro file.

7 Select **A**ction (1) to display the keystrokes assigned to Ctrl-b in the Macro Editor.

Besides the keys you pressed from the keyboard while defining the macro, a {DISPLAY OFF} command has been included by WordPerfect.

```
Key: Action
     Key          Ctrl-B
     Description   Bold a Line
    ┌─────────────────────────────────────────────────────────────┐
    │{DISPLAY OFF}{Home}{Left}{Block}{End}{Bold}                    │
    │   ⚠                                                           │
    │                                                               │
    │                                                               │
    │                                                               │
    │                                                               │
    └─────────────────────────────────────────────────────────────┘
    Ctrl-PgUp for macro commands;  Press Exit when done
```

The {DISPLAY OFF} command makes sure that you do not see the actual keystrokes being performed when you press Ctrl-b. Only the "* Please Wait *" message will be displayed.

8 Press **Exit** (F7) twice to return to the list of keyboards.

9 Select **M**ap (8) to see the keyboard map for the Special keyboard.

Now that you have assigned a macro to Ctrl-b, an **M** is displayed for Ctrl-b in the keyboard map.

10 Press **Down Arrow** (↓), then press **Right Arrow** (→) to place the cursor under the B in the Ctrl key row.

11 Select **M**acro (2) to display the keystrokes for Ctrl-b.

The Macro Editor appears again with the same keystrokes you already viewed from the list of mapped keystrokes. When a key is mapped as a macro, you can use the Macro Editor from the keyboard map (Macro option) or from the list of keystrokes (Action) to edit the same keystrokes.

Because you are editing the same macro, whatever editing you do from the keyboard map also affects the macro in the list of keyboard macros (and vice versa).

Creating a Macro in a Keyboard

Before leaving the list of keystrokes, let's create a macro for the Ctrl-r key that blocks the same text again.

1 Press **Exit** (F7) twice to return to the list of Keyboards, then select **E**dit (7) to display the Keyboard Edit menu.

2 Select **C**reate (4), press **Ctrl-r** to map the Ctrl-r keystroke, then enter **Reblock Text** for the description.

3 Press **Delete** (Del) to delete the {^R} code.

4 Press **Block** (Alt-F4) to insert a {Block} command, then press **Go To** (Ctrl-Home) twice to insert two {Go To} commands into the macro editing window.

5 Press **Exit** (F7) to return to the list of keystrokes.

Using the Edited Keyboard

Let's return to the editing screen and try using Alt-b, Ctrl-b, and Ctrl-r to create, bold, and italicize a new item in the list.

1 Press **Exit** (F7) twice to return to the normal editing screen.

2 Press **Home,↓** to place the cursor in the empty line at the bottom of the list.

3 Press **Alt-b** to insert a small bullet and an indent.

4 Type **Small Bullet (Bolded and Italicized)**, then press **Ctrl-b** to bold the line.

5 Press **Ctrl-r** to reblock the same line.

6 Press **Font** (Ctrl-F8), select **A**ppearance (2), then select **I**talic (4) to italicize the line.

⌨ *Select Appearance from the Font menu, then select Italics.*

By using the Keyboard Layout features, you can quickly build a keyboard that helps you customize your keyboard by adding special characters, remapping existing features, creating macros in the macro editor, and organizing your existing macros by retrieving them into the keyboard file.

Selecting the Original Keyboard

Before finishing the lesson, let's return your keyboard to its original mapping, then look at a couple of keyboards that are shipped with the WordPerfect package.

1 Press **Setup** (Shift-F1), then select **K**eyboard Layout.

⌨ *Select Setup from the File menu, then select Keyboard Layout.*

2 Select **O**riginal (6) to return WordPerfect to its original keyboard mapping.

You can also press Ctrl-6 from the normal editing screen to select the original keyboard mapping for the current editing session only.

You are returned to the Setup menu where a keyboard is no longer displayed next to the Keyboard Layout option.

3 Select **K**eyboard Layout (5) to return to the list of keyboards.

4 Make sure that the ALTRNAT keyboard is highlighted, then select **E**dit (7) to display the keyboard macros available.

Many people prefer to have the Escape key work like the Cancel key, and the Help key mapped to F1. These features have already been remapped on the ALTRNAT keyboard for you. All you need to do is select the keyboard.

5 Press **Exit** (F7) to return to the list of keyboards.

6 Highlight the MACROS keyboard with the cursor, then select **E**dit to display the keyboard macros available.

The Macros keyboard includes keys that make editing, printing, and many other features of WordPerfect quicker and easier to use.

7 Press **Exit** to return to the list of keyboards.

Deleting a Keyboard

You may want to try selecting and using these keyboards at the end of the lesson. For now, let's delete the Special keyboard you have created (if you want it deleted), then clear the editing screen.

1 Highlight the SPECIAL keyboard with the cursor.

2 Select **D**elete (2), then type **y** to delete the keyboard file (SPECIAL.WPK) from your disk and remove the keyboard from the list.

3 Press **Exit** (F7) to return to the editing screen.

4 Press **Exit** and type **n** twice to clear the screen.

What you have learned about special characters and keyboards in this lesson may be all you need to start using the WordPerfect characters and Keyboard Layout features. If you are interested in learning more about these features, turn to the *Compose*, *Keyboard Layout*, and *Macros* headings in the *WordPerfect Reference Manual*.

If you are running WordPerfect from two disk drives, you need to replace the Macros/Keyboards diskette in drive B with the Learning diskette before continuing on to the next lesson.

Lesson 27: Document Management

From creating document summaries to adding password protection to files, WordPerfect provides a variety of features that make managing your documents easier and more productive.

In this lesson, you are introduced to several of these features. To discover all the document management possibilities, turn to the suggested headings in the *WordPerfect Reference Manual* that are listed in the lesson.

Creating a Comment

When creating or editing a document, you may want to make a note in the text, but only want the note displayed on the screen—not printed with the document.

To insert a non-printing note in a document, you can use the Comment feature. For example, let's add a comment to a newsletter article that indicates where a graph should be placed in the article.

1 Press **Retrieve** (Shift-F10), then enter **newstext.wkb** to retrieve three newsletter articles.

⊞ *Select Retrieve from the File menu.*

2 Press **Down Arrow** (↓) five times to place the cursor in the empty line between the first and second paragraphs.

3 Press **Text In/Out** (Ctrl-F5), select **Comment** (4), then select **Create** (1).

⊞ *Select Comment from the Edit menu, then select Create.*

An editing window is displayed on your screen that lets you type characters and spaces, and bold and underline text.

4 Press **Bold** (F6), type **Roger**, then press **Bold** again to end bolding.

5 Press **Enter** to start a new line.

6 Type the following comment:

We need a graphic line chart here that shows the predicted increase in music box sales from 1990 to 1995. Gloria has the exact music box sales figures.

7 Press **Exit** (F7) to exit the editing window for the comment.

8 Press **Reveal Codes** (Alt-F3) to display the Reveal Codes screen.

⊞ *Select Reveal Codes from the Edit menu.*

The comment is displayed in the editing screen as a box that stretches from the left margin to the right margin. However, the comment is displayed as a single code in the Reveal Codes screen.

Record sales of the new line of music boxes has boosted first quarter revenues t
the tune of 2 million dollars. It is expected that by the year 1995, one out of
3 people in the United States and Canada will own a music box.

```
    Roger
A▷  We need a graphic line chart here that shows the predicted increase in
    music box sales from 1990 to 1995.  Gloria has the exact music box sales
    figures.
```

C̄:\WP51\LEARN\NEWSTEXT.WKB   Doc 1 Pg 1 Ln 1.83" Pos 1"
[▮   ▲   ▲   ▲   ▲   ▲   ▲   ▲   ▲   ▲   ▲   ▲)   ▲   ▲   ▲]
Record sales of the new line of music boxes has boosted first quarter revenues t
o[SRt]
the tune of 2 million dollars. It is expected that by the year 1995, one out of
every[SRt]
3 people in the United States and Canada will own a music box.[HRt]
B▷[Comment][**HRt**]
On the drawing boards are music box watches, dash[-]board models for cars,[SRt]
waterproof boxes for showers, ultra[-]light boxes for backpackers, and even an[S
Rt]
amplified music box that plays a disco version of "Que Sera Sera."[HRt]

Press **Reveal Codes** to restore screen

The comment is not displayed in the View Document screen because comments are not printed with the document.

9 Press **Print** (Shift-F7), select **V**iew Document (6), then select 100% (1).

⌨ *Select **P**rint from the **F**ile menu.*

The newsletter article is displayed as if there were no comment at all in the text.

10 Press **Exit** to return to the editing screen.

Converting a Comment to Text

If you *do* want the comment to print with the document, you can convert the comment to normal text.

1 Make sure the cursor is below the comment on the screen.

When you want to edit or convert a comment to text, WordPerfect searches *backward* through the document for the first comment. If you place the cursor below the comment you want to edit or convert, then the correct comment will be selected.

If a comment cannot be found by searching backward through the document, then WordPerfect searches forward through the document for the first comment available.

2 Press **Text In/Out** (Ctrl-F5), select **C**omment (4), then select Convert to Text (3).

⌨ *Select **C**omment from the **E**dit menu, then select Convert to **T**ext.*

WordPerfect takes the text out of the comment box, and inserts it directly into the newsletter article.

If you decide that you want to convert text to a comment, then you can use the Block and Text In/Out keys.

3 Press **Block** (Alt-F4).

⌨ *Select **Block** from the **Edit** menu.*

4 Press **Enter** twice, then press **Left Arrow** (←) to highlight the original comment text.

5 Press **Text In/Out** (Ctrl-F5), then type **y** to convert the text to a comment.

⌨ *Select **Comment** from the **Edit** menu, then select **Create**.*

The highlighted text is placed in a comment box, and will not be printed with the document.

6 Press **Reveal Codes** (Alt-F3) to display the normal editing screen.

⌨ *Select **Reveal Codes** from the **Edit** menu.*

If you want to turn off the display of comments of all documents while editing in WordPerfect, you can use the Setup key (Shift-F1,2,6,2,n). For additional details on the Comments feature, turn to the Document Comments *heading in the* WordPerfect Reference Manual.

Creating a Document Summary

A document summary is a list of information that is stored with the document. The document summary can include such items as the names of the author and typist, keywords to help find the file, and an abstract (a brief summary) of the document's contents.

Because the newsletter articles are already on the screen, let's create a document summary for the newsletter.

1 Press **Format** (Shift-F8), select **D**ocument (3), then select **S**ummary (5) to display the Document Summary menu on the screen.

⌨ *Select **Document** from the **Layout** menu, then select **Summary**.*

A revision date (when the newsletter was last saved) and a creation date (when the summary was first created) are displayed on the screen.

```
Document Summary              ▼A

              Revision Date   12-22-89 11:34a
         1 - Creation Date    01-01-90 10:31a
         2 - Document Name     ▲B
             Document Type
         3 - Author
             Typist
         4 - Subject
         5 - Account
         6 - Keywords
         7 - Abstract


         Selection: 0               (Retrieve to capture; Del to remove summary)
```

There are several items of information that could be included in the document summary. However, let's simply enter an author, a couple of keywords, and an abstract for the newsletter.

2   Select Author (3), type **Rebecca Hartshorn** for the author's name, then press **Enter**.

3   Press **Enter** to skip by the typist's name.

4   Select **K**eywords (6), type **July Newsletter** for the keywords, then press **Enter**.

When you are in the List Files screen, you can search for the newsletter by the keywords in the document summary (you will do that later in the lesson).

You can either type in the abstract yourself, or have WordPerfect insert the first 400 characters of the document for you by using Retrieve.

5   Press **Retrieve** (Shift-F10), then type **y** to retrieve the first part of the newsletter for the abstract.

WordPerfect may also retrieve other information into the document summary when you press Retrieve. For details on the Retrieve key and the Document Summary options, turn to the Document Summary *heading in the* WordPerfect Reference Manual.

6   Select **A**bstract (7), then place the cursor at the end of the first sentence (... 2 million dollars.).

7   Press **Delete to End of Page** (Ctrl-PgDn) to delete the rest of the abstract.

8   Press **Exit** (F7) twice to return to the editing screen.

9 Press **Save** (F10), then enter **newsltr.jul** to save the edited newsletter.

⌨ *Select Save from the File menu.*

Looking into a File

The only place you can edit a document summary is from the Document Summary menu. However, you can view the contents of the document summary when using Look in the List Files screen.

1 Press **List** (F5), then press **Enter** to display all the files in the LEARN directory (or on your Learn diskette).

⌨ *Select List Files from the File menu.*

Besides using the cursor keys and Name Search to locate a file in a directory, you can also use the Search keys.

2 Press ♦**Search** (F2), type **newsltr.jul** for the filename, then press **Enter** to start the search.

WordPerfect looks through the filenames (and subdirectory names), then stops at the NEWSLTR.JUL file.

3 Select **Look** (6) to display the contents of the file.

Because a document summary has been created for the NEWSLTR.JUL file, WordPerfect displays the summary before displaying the contents of the file.

🔺 HEADER INFORMATION
🅱 LOOK SCREEN
🅲 LOOK MENU

```
🔺 File: C:\WP51\LEARN\NEWSLTR.JUL          WP5.1        Revised: 12-22-89 11:34a
   Name:                                                 Created: 01-01-90 10:31a

   Subject

   Account

   Keywords    July Newsletter

   Author      Rebecca Hartshorn
   Typist
   Abstract
       Sales Up by Two Million; Record sales of the new line of music boxes has
       boosted first quarter revenues to the tune of 2 million dollars.


                                        🅱



🅲 Look Doc Summ: 1 Next; 2 Prev; 3 Look at text; 4 Print Summ; 5 Save to File: 0
```

The header information at the top of the screen includes the revision and creation dates of the document summary. The rest of the document summary information is displayed in the Look screen.

A menu at the bottom of the screen lets you move to the next or previous file in the directory, look at the text of the file, print the document summary, or save the summary in a file on disk.

4 Select **L**ook at Text (3) to display the contents of the newsletter.

You can scroll through the document with the cursor keys. However, some of the keys work a little differently in the Look screen.

5 Press **End** to shift the newsletter to the left to see the ends of the lines.

6 Press **End** again to shift the newsletter back to the left margin.

7 Press **Page Down** (PgDn) twice to scroll through the newsletter a screen at a time.

8 Press **Home,Home,**↑ to return to the beginning of the newsletter, then press **Down Arrow** (↓) twice to place the cursor at the beginning of the first paragraph.

9 Press **Right Arrow** (→) four times to shift the newsletter to the left five characters at a time.

10 Press **Home,**← to return to the left margin.

While in the Look screen, you can also use the Search keys to find a particular word in the text. For details on all the features available in the Look screen, turn to the Look *heading in the* WordPerfect Reference Manual.

The Look menu at the bottom of the screen includes options for looking at the previous or next file in the List Files screen, and an option for returning to the document summary.

11 Select **P**revious Document (2), then select **P**revious Document again to view the contents of the two files before the NEWSLTR.JUL file.

The header information is updated as you move from file to file to reflect the filename and revision date.

12 Select **N**ext Document (1) twice to return to the NEWSLTR.JUL file (check the header information for the filename).

You are returned to the document summary of the newsletter (instead of the newsletter text).

13 Press **Exit** (F7) to return to the List Files screen.

Long Document Names   The List Files screen is divided into a header at the top of the screen, the file list itself, and a menu of options at the bottom of the screen.

Normally, the file list is divided into two columns with the subdirectories
<Dir> listed in alphabetical order, followed by an alphabetical listing of the
files in the current directory.

A SUBDIRECTORIES

B COLUMNS

```
01-28-90  05:30p              Directory C:\WP51\LEARN\*.*
Document size:          0  Free: 13,944,832 Used:    312,705    Files:       76

.     Current   <Dir>              ..     Parent   <Dir>
WORK           <Dir>  01-25-90 08:11a   ADDRESS .WKB      415  01-03-90 02:48p
ADVANCED.TUT       3  01-25-90 01:11p   ARROW-22.WPG      116  01-07-90 03:04p
BALLOONS.WPG   2,806  01-07-90 03:04p   BANNER  .TUT      631  01-25-90 01:11p
BANNER-3.WPG     648  01-07-90 03:04p   BEGIN   .TUT       11  01-25-90 01:11p
BICYCLE .WPG     607  01-07-90 03:04p   BKGRND-1.WPG   11,391  01-07-90 03:04p
BORDER-8.WPG     144  01-07-90 03:04p   BULB    .WPG    2,030  01-07-90 03:04p
BURST-1 .WPG     748  01-07-90 03:04p   BUTTRFLY.WPG    5,278  01-15-90 09:38a
CALENDAR.WPG     300  01-07-90 03:04p   CERTIF  .WPG      608  01-07-90 03:04p
CHARACTR.WKB  13,458  01-03-90 03:04p   CHKBOX-1.WPG      582  01-07-90 03:04p
CLOCK   .WPG   1,811  01-07-90 03:04p   CNTRCT-2.WPG    2,678  01-07-90 03:04p
CONCORD .         334  01-27-90 09:04a   CUSTOMER.       2,256  01-28-90 11:10p
CUSTOMER.WKB   1,986  01-03-90 02:49p   DEVICE-2.WPG      657  01-07-90 03:04p
DIPLOMA .WPG   2,342  01-07-90 03:04p   ENVELOPE.          854  01-05-90 09:44a
ENVELOPE.MLT     635  01-05-90 09:48a   EQUATION.WKB    5,780  01-03-90 02:49p
FLOPPY-2.WPG     404  01-07-90 03:04p   GAVEL   .WPG      887  01-07-90 03:04p
GLOBE2-M.WPG   7,785  01-07-90 03:04p   GRAPH   .WPG      889  01-28-90 09:51a
HANDS-3 .WPG   1,046  01-07-90 03:04p   INTRO   .TUT   29,936  01-25-90 01:11p
INTRO_1 .TUT   9,408  01-25-90 01:11p   INVOICE .       2,815  01-07-90 09:00p

1 Retrieve; 2 Delete; 3 Move/Rename; 4 Print; 5 Short/Long Display;
6 Look; 7 Other Directory; 8 Copy; 9 Find; N Name Search: 6
```

This style of list is called the *short display*, and is limited in the amount of
information that can be used to name and organize the files.

Besides the short display, you can also select a *long display* style that
displays the subdirectories and files in alphabetical order, but with only one
subdirectory or file per line.

1 Select **S**hort/**L**ong Display (5), select **L**ong Display (2), then press **Enter**.

A "* Please Wait *" message is displayed while WordPerfect sorts through
the files. When you select long display, only WordPerfect files (documents
that you can retrieve into WordPerfect) are included in the list.

When the sorting is completed, the long display file list appears on the
screen. Each file is on a separate line, a row of column titles is added to the

header, and two new columns are added for a descriptive name and a document type.

▲ COLUMN TITLES
▲ DESCRIPTIVE NAME
▲ DOCUMENT TYPE

```
01-22-90  12:21p              Directory C:\WP51\LEARN\*.*
Document size:      3,742   Free: 14,018,560 Used:    226,182   Files:       27
Descriptive Name                      Type     Filename     Size   Revision Date

Current Directory                              .  <Dir>
Parent Directory                               .. <Dir>
                                        ADDRESS .TUT      978  01-20-90 01:11p
                                        ADDRESS .WKB      415  01-03-90 02:48p
                                        CONCORD .         334  01-19-90 09:04a
                                        CUSTOMER.        2,256  01-21-90 06:10p
                                        CUSTOMER.WKB     1,986  01-03-90 02:49p
                                        ENVELOPE.MLT      635  01-05-90 09:48a
                                        EQUATION.WKB     5,780  01-03-90 02:49p
                                        INTRO_1 .TUT     9,408  01-15-90 01:11p
                                        LETTER  .TUT      653  01-17-90 01:11p
                                        LETTER_F.TUT      679  01-05-90 01:11p
                                        LETTER_P.TUT      652  01-18-90 01:11p
                                        LETTER1 .TUT      778  01-14-90 01:11p
                                        MEMO    .25       914  01-22-90 10:31a
                                        MEMO    .WKB      785  01-03-90 02:50p
                                        MUSICBOX.WKB     3,338  01-03-90 02:50p
                                        NEWSLTR .WKB    15,239  01-03-90 02:15p

 1 Retrieve; 2 Delete; 3 Move/Rename; 4 Print; 5 Short/Long Display;
 6 Look; 7 Other Directory; 8 Copy; 9 Find; N Name Search: 6
```

A descriptive name can be up to 68 characters long, with the first 30 of those characters displayed in the List Files screen.. The document type can be up to 20 characters long (9 displayed on the screen), and can be used to organize and find files that are in the same category (i.e., letters, reports, newsletters).

The descriptive name can include both an alias directory and a long document name. An alias directory is simply a description that you can add to a directory on your disk to let you know what the directory contains. For details on creating alias directories, turn to the *Directories* heading in the *WordPerfect Reference Manual*.

Adding a Long Document Name

The long document name is an additional name that you can give a file to better describe the file contents, and can be added to a document in the Document Summary menu.

For example, let's return to the editing screen and add a long document name to the NEWSLTR.JUL file.

1 Press **Exit** (F7) to return to the editing screen.

2 Press **Format** (Shift-F8), select **D**ocument (3), then select **S**ummary (5).

⌨ *Select Document from the Layout menu, then select Summary.*

3 Select Document **N**ame (2), type **July Newsletter -- Second Draft** for the long document name, then press **Enter**.

While in the Document Summary Edit menu you can also add a document type.

4 Type **News** for the document type, then press **Enter**.

5 Press **Exit** to return to the editing screen.

6 Press **Exit** again, type **y**, press **Enter**, then type **y** to replace the NEWSLTR.JUL file on disk with the edited version on the screen.

7 Type **n** to clear the screen.

Document Summary on Save/Exit

WordPerfect provides a feature that automatically displays the Document Summary menu if you are saving a document that does not have a document summary. This feature can be especially useful if you are using the long display style for List Files, and want to make sure that each file you save has a long document name and/or type attached to it.

1 Press **Setup** (Shift-F1), then select **E**nvironment (3).

⊟ *Select Setup from the File menu, then select Environment.*

2 Select **D**ocument Management/Summary (4).

A menu is displayed that lets you set several items for document management. For details on these items, turn to the *Environment Setup* heading in the *WordPerfect Reference Manual*.

3 Select **C**reate Summary on Save/Exit (1), then type **y** for Yes.

4 Press **Exit** (F7) to return to the editing screen.

Let's retrieve the NEWSTEXT.WKB file, then save it as NEWSTEXT.JUL and see what happens.

5 Press **Retrieve** (Shift-F10), then enter **newstext.wkb** to retrieve the original newsletter articles.

⊟ *Select Retrieve from the File menu.*

6 Press **Exit**, then type **y** to save the newsletter.

A Document Summary menu is displayed for the newsletter.

7 Press **Retrieve**, then type **y** to insert text from the newsletter into the abstract.

Not only is text added for the abstract, but WordPerfect also inserts the latest author (Rebecca Hartshorn) saved in a document summary during the editing session (in the NEWSLTR.JUL file).

For details on what information WordPerfect inserts into a document summary when you press Retrieve, turn to the Document Summary *heading in the* WordPerfect Reference Manual.

8 Select Document Name (2), type **July Newsletter -- First Draft** for the long document name, then press **Enter**.

9 Type **News** for the document type, then press **Enter**.

10 Select **K**eywords (6), type **July Newsletter** for the keywords, then press **Enter**.

11 Select **A**bstract (7), place the cursor at the end of the first sentence (. . . 2 million dollars.), then press **Delete to End of Page** (Ctrl-PgDn) to delete the rest of the text.

12 Press **Exit** (F7) twice to exit the Document Summary menu.

13 Enter **newstext.jul** for the filename, then type **n** to clear the screen.

A Document Summary Edit menu is displayed when saving a document only if a summary does not already exist for the document. Once the document summary is created, you can only change it by going to the Document Summary menu.

Displaying Long Document Names

Let's return to the List Files screen to see the long document names and document types for the NEWSTEXT.JUL and NEWSLTR.JUL files.

1 Press **List** (F5), then press **Enter** to display the List Files screen.

⊡ *Select List Files from the File menu.*

After a moment, the WordPerfect document files in the LEARN directory (or on the Learn diskette) are displayed on the screen.

2 Press **◆Search** (F2), type **second draft** to find the NEWSLTR.JUL file, then press **Enter** to begin the search.

With the long display on, WordPerfect searches through the descriptive names, document types, and filenames to find "second draft." WordPerfect displays the word "draft" in the long document name without a "t" because only 30 characters can be displayed at a time for the descriptive name.

The long document name and document type are displayed for both the NEWSTEXT.JUL and NEWSLTR.JUL files. In addition, the files are alphabetically sorted by their *long document name* instead of the filename.

3 Press **Enter** to display the document summary in the Look screen.

The Header for the file now includes the long document name and document type, along with the file dates.

4 Press **Exit** (F7) twice to return to the editing screen.

Before continuing the lesson, let's set the Create Summary on Save/Exit option back to No.

5 Press **Setup** (Shift-F1), select **E**nvironment (3), then select **D**ocument Management/Summary (4).

⊡ *Select Setup from the File menu, then select Environment.*

6 Select Create Summary on Save/Exit (1), then type **n** for No.

7 Press **Exit** to return to the editing screen.

Adding a Password

A password can be added to a file to prevent other people from printing or retrieving the file. To add a password, the document needs to be displayed in the normal editing screen.

1 Press **Retrieve** (Shift-F10), then enter **newsltr.jul** to retrieve the second draft of the newsletter.

⌨ *Select **Retrieve** from the **F**ile menu.*

2 Press **Text In/Out** (Ctrl-F5), select **P**assword (2), then select Add/Change (1).

⌨ *Select **P**assword from the **F**ile menu, then select Add/Change.*

For security reasons, the password is *not* displayed on the screen as you type it. To make sure that you have typed the password correctly, WordPerfect has you enter the password twice.

3 Enter **july** for the password, then re-enter **july** a second time.

If you do not type "july" the same way both times, then WordPerfect lets you try again.

Now that a password has been added, the newsletter needs to be saved so that the password is saved with the document.

4 Press **Exit** (F7), type **y**, press **Enter** to use the same filename, then type **y** to replace the file on disk with the password-protected version.

5 Type **n** to clear the screen.

Retrieving a Locked Document

Let's retrieve the newsletter and see what happens.

1 Press **Retrieve** (Shift-F10), then enter **newsltr.jul** for the filename.

⌨ *Select **Retrieve** from the **F**ile menu.*

WordPerfect asks for a password before retrieving the file.

2 Enter **july** for the password to retrieve the newsletter.

A locked document should be retrieved onto a clear screen or the text may not be locked when you Save or Exit.

After you retrieve a locked document, all files associated with the current editing of the document (backup files, etc.) are also locked.

Looking at a Locked Document	Not only do you need to enter a password before retrieving the file, but you also need to enter a password before looking at the file in the List Files screen.

1 Press **List** (F5), then press **Enter** to display the List Files screen.

⊟ *Select List Files from the File menu.*

2 Press ♦**Search** (F2), type **newsltr.jul** for the second draft filename, then press **Enter** to start the search.

When the cursor stops on the NEWSLTR.JUL file, notice that the long document name and document type have been replaced by a "[Locked]" message.

3 Press **Enter** to display the Look screen for the NEWSLTR.JUL file.

4 Enter **july** for the password.

The document summary for the newsletter is displayed on the screen.

5 Press **Exit** (F7) twice to return to the normal editing screen.

Removing a Password

Whenever you want to remove a password from a document, make sure the document is retrieved to the normal editing screen, then use Text In/Out.

1 Press **Text In/Out** (Ctrl-F5), select **P**assword (2), then select **R**emove (2).

⊟ *Select Password from the File menu, then select **R**emove.*

Once the password is removed, you need to replace the file on disk with the edited version on your screen.

2 Press **Exit** (F7), type **y**, press **Enter** to use the same filename, then type **y** to replace the file on disk with the unprotected version.

3 Type **n** to clear the screen.

WordPerfect Corporation has no method of unlocking your files if you forget the password.

Finding a File

Whenever you want to locate a particular file, but can't remember the name of the file, you can use the Find option on the List Files menu to search through the contents of the files in the current directory.

1 Press **List** (F5) twice to display the List Files screen.

⊟ *Select List Files from the File menu, then click the right-hand button.*

By pressing List twice, you can return to the same screen that was displayed when you last exited List Files. The NEWSLTR.JUL file is still displayed as locked because the screen is not updated when you press List twice.

2 Press **List** (F5), then press **Enter** to update the list of files and place the cursor on Current Directory.

3 Select **F**ind (9) from the List Files menu.

A menu is displayed that lets you search for a file by entering part or all of a filename or text from the document summary, the first page of the document, or from anywhere in the document. You can also set certain conditions for the search.

4 Select **D**ocument Summary (2), then enter **draft** for the word pattern.

WordPerfect begins matching the word "draft" against the text in all document summaries of the files displayed in the current directory.

A counter is displayed at the bottom of the screen to keep you updated on the search. When the search is completed, only those files with the word "draft" in their document summary are displayed on the screen. If your current directory is LEARN, then only the NEWSTEXT.JUL and NEWSLTR.JUL files should appear on the screen.

5 Press **List**, then press **Enter** to redisplay all the files in the directory and place the cursor on Current Directory.

6 Select **F**ind (9), then select **C**onditions (5) to display the Conditions menu.

There are several options available in the Conditions menu for directing the search for a file. Details on all these options can be found under the *Find, Conditions* heading in the *WordPerfect Reference Manual*.

Let's try using the Document Summary option to look for the newsletter files by the document type (news) and the keywords (July Newsletter).

7 Select Document Summary (5), then press **Enter** three times to place the cursor to the right of Document Type.

8 Type **news** for the type, then press **Enter** five times to place the cursor to the right of Keywords.

9 Type **july newsletter** for the keywords, then press **Exit** to finish filling in the search conditions for the document summary.

10 Select **P**erform Search (1) to begin the search.

The file counter is displayed at the bottom of the screen to keep you updated on the progress of the search. When the search is completed, the NEWSTEXT.JUL and NEWSLTR.JUL files are displayed in the file list.

At this point, you may want to continue using the Find options to search for particular files in the current directory or another directory on your disk (use the Other Directory option to change directories).

11 When you finish, press **Exit** (F7) to return to the editing screen.

The more you discover about the features introduced in this lesson, the more you will appreciate the many ways WordPerfect can help you to protect and manage your WordPerfect documents.

Lesson 28: Envelopes and Labels

Addressing envelopes for mailing is one of the most common word processing jobs. Whether you are addressing a single envelope or printing hundreds of address labels for mass mailings, WordPerfect can make the job easier for you.

Creating an Envelope Definition

Whenever you are printing on something other than a standard 8.5" x 11" sheet of paper, you need to define the size, shape, and type of paper for WordPerfect. This definition (sometimes called a *form*) can be used once for special needs and then deleted, or it can be saved and used over and over again.

If you want an address printed directly on an envelope, you need to create a paper size/type definition for it.

1 Press **Format** (Shift-F8), select **P**age (2), then select Paper Size/Type (7).

⌨ *Select **P**age from the Layout menu, then select Paper Size/Type.*

A short list of paper definitions is displayed on your screen. This list is specific to the printer that you have selected.

Initially, there will only be two or three items on the list, including the standard 8.5" x 11" definition and a definition called *ALL OTHERS*. If you were creating a special definition for a one-time use, you would use the ALL OTHERS definition. See *Paper Size/Type* in the *WordPerfect Reference Manual* for details on how and when to use the ALL OTHERS definition.

You will probably want to create definitions for frequently used forms (e.g., envelopes and labels) and add them permanently to the list.

Some laser printers include a standard envelope definition on the list. In this lesson you will learn how to create one yourself.

2 Select **A**dd (2) from the menu at the bottom of the screen to create a new definition.

A list of paper types appears, letting you indicate the type of paper on which you will be printing. Selecting a paper type ensures that any special instructions for printing that type are sent to the printer.

3 Select **E**nvelope (5) for the paper type.

You are returned to the Edit Paper Definition menu. Notice that the paper type is designated as envelope, but the paper size is still 8.5" x 11".

4 Select Paper **S**ize (1).

A list of standard paper sizes is displayed on your screen.

5 Select **E**nvelope (5) to set the size for a standard 9.5" x 4" business correspondence envelope.

*If you are creating a definition for an envelope of a different size, all you need to do is select **O**ther (o) and enter the correct width and height.*

Let's assume for the purposes of this lesson that you will be manually feeding a single envelope into a laser printer.

Most Dot Matrix printers print envelopes in standard Portrait orientation.

Most laser printers require you to feed envelopes from the end, rather than from the top. This means that the printer is printing the lines of text *down* the paper (i.e., perpendicular to the leading edge), rather than *across* it (i.e., parallel to the leading edge), as it normally does. Therefore, you need to change the font from the standard *portrait* (parallel) to *landscape* (perpendicular).

6 Select **F**ont Type (3), then select **L**andscape (2).

For more details on Font Type, see Printing, Landscape *in the* WordPerfect Reference Manual.

When loading manually, it is often convenient to have the computer signal you when it is time to put the envelope into the printer.

7 Select **P**rompt to Load (4), then type **y** to select **Y**es.

For details on Prompt to Load, see Paper Size/Type *in the* WordPerfect Reference Manual.

8 Select **L**ocation (5), then select **M**anual (3).

For details on Location, see Paper Size/Type *and* Sheet Feeder *in the* WordPerfect Reference Manual.

The Edit Paper Definition menu should now look like the one illustrated below.

A PAPER SIZE
B PAPER TYPE

```
Format: Edit Paper Definition

          Filename                    WORKBOOK.PRS
A  1 - Paper Size                     9.5" x 4"
B  2 - Paper Type                     Envelope - Wide
     3 - Font Type                    Landscape
     4 - Prompt to Load               Yes
     5 - Location                     Manual
     6 - Double Sided Printing        No
     7 - Binding Edge                 Left
     8 - Labels                       No
     9 - Text Adjustment - Top        0"
                           Side       0"

   Selection: 0
```

9 Press **Enter** to return to the list of paper definitions.

The new definition you created for envelopes is highlighted at the head of the list.

*If your printer already had an envelope definition, select **D**elete (4) to delete the one you just created and use the definition that came with your package.*

10 Choose **S**elect (1) to designate the envelope definition, then press **Exit** (F7) to return to the normal editing screen.

Positioning the Address

With the envelope definition selected, you are ready to type the address. A standard position for typing the address on a 9.5" x 4" envelope is 4.5" in from the left edge of the envelope, and 2" down from the top edge of the envelope.

Advance could be used to print the address 4.5" in from the left margin, but an Advance code would need to be placed at the beginning of each address line. A simpler way is to set a new left margin.

1 Press **Format** (Shift-F8), select **L**ine (1), then select **M**argins Left/Right (7).

⊟ *Select **L**ine from the Layout menu, then select **M**argins Left Right.*

2 Enter **4.5** for the left margin.

It would also be a good idea to set the right margin to "0" so that there will be plenty of room for the address lines.

3 Enter **0** for the right margin, then press **Enter** to return to the main Format menu.

Some laser printers have a minimum allowable margin. If you enter 0 and get a result such as 0.2, that is the minimum.

Besides setting the left and right margins, the top and bottom margins should be set to "0" to avoid any problems with advancing the envelope in some printers (top margin), and to make sure there are enough lines available for longer addresses (bottom margin).

4 Select **P**age (2) then select **M**argins Top/Bottom (5).

5 Enter **0** for the top margin, then enter **0** for the bottom margin.

6 Press **Enter** to return to the main Format menu.

With the margins set, you can use Advance to place the address exactly 2" down from the top of the envelope.

7 Select **O**ther (4), then select **A**dvance (1).

8 Select Line (3) and enter **2** to have WordPerfect advance 2" down the envelope.

9 Press **Exit** (F7) to return to the editing screen.

10 Press **Reveal Codes** (Alt-F3) to see the formats you have set for the envelope.

⌨ *Select Reveal Codes from the Edit menu.*

Your screen should display the same codes as those illustrated below.

```
                                        Doc 1 Pg 1 Ln 2" Pos 4.5"
        ▲   ▲    (    ▲    ▲    ▲    ▲    ▲    ▲    ▲
[Paper Sz/Typ:9.5" x 4",Envelope][L/R Mar:4.5",0"][T/B Mar:0",0"][AdvToLn:2"]
```

11 Press **Reveal Codes** (Alt-F3) to display the normal editing screen.

⌨ *Select Reveal Codes from the Edit menu.*

12 Press **Exit** (F7), type **y**, and enter **envelope** to save the settings in a file.

13 Type **n** to clear the screen.

Printing the Address   The envelope file can now be retrieved, filled in, and printed any time you want to print the forwarding address on an envelope.

1 Press **Retrieve** (Shift-F10) and enter **envelope** to retrieve the envelope formats.

⌨ *Select Retrieve from the File menu.*

2 Type the following address:

Robin Pierce
InterChange, Inc.
544 Westminster Circle NW
Atlanta, GA 30327

3 Press **Print** (Shift-F7), select **V**iew Document (6), then select Full Page (3).

⌨ *Select Print from the File menu.*

Although the normal editing screen looks the same as it does with a standard 8.5" x 11" document, View Document displays the addressed envelope in its true shape and placement.

4 Press **Exit** to return to the editing screen.

5 Press **Exit**, then type **n** twice to clear the screen.

Creating a Primary File

Once the formats for the envelope file are set, you can create a primary file for merging and printing several envelopes at the same time.

When you place formatting codes like paper size/type, margins, and advance in a primary file, those codes get merged to each record. This can slow down the operation of the merge. It's a good idea, therefore, to put formatting codes for a primary file in document initial codes.

1 Press **Format** (Shift-F8), select **D**ocument (3), then select Initial Codes (2).

⌨ *Select Document from the Layout menu, then select Initial Codes.*

2 Press **Format** (Shift-F8), select **P**age (2), then select Paper Size/Type (7).

⌨ *Select Page from the Layout menu, then select Paper Size/Type.*

3 Highlight the Envelope definition, choose **S**elect (1), then press **Exit** (F7) to return to the initial codes editing screen.

4 Press **Format** (Shift-F8), select **L**ine (1), then select **M**argins Left/Right (7).

⌨ *Select Line from the Layout menu, then select Margins Left Right.*

5 Enter **4.5** for the left margin.

6 Enter **0** for the right margin, then press **Enter** to return to the main Format menu.

7 Select **P**age (2) then select **M**argins Top/Bottom (5).

8 Enter **0** for the top margin, then enter **0** for the bottom margin.

9 Press **Exit** (F7) 3 times to return to the normal editing screen.

10 Press **Format** (Shift-F8), select **O**ther (4), then select **A**dvance (1).

⌨ *Select Other from the Layout menu, then select Advance.*

11 Select **L**ine (3) enter **2** to have WordPerfect advance 2" down the envelope, then press Exit to return to the editing screen.

CUSTOMER.WKB can serve as a secondary file. The full name and address of each customer are in the first and second fields of each record.

12 Press **Merge Codes** (Shift-F9), select **F**ield (1), then enter **1** to insert a {Field}1~ for the first field.

⌨ *Select Merge Codes from the **T**ools menu, select **F**ield, then enter **1**.*

13 Press **Enter** to start a new line.

14 Press **Merge Codes** (Shift-F9), select **F**ield (1), then enter **2** to insert a {Field}2~ for the second field.

⌨ *Select Merge Codes from the **T**ools menu, select **F**ield, then enter **2**.*

15 Press **Exit** (F7), type **y**, enter **envelope.mlt** to name the primary file used for multiple envelopes, then type **n** to clear the screen.

Merging the Addresses

With ENVELOPE.MLT saved as a primary file, you can merge with a secondary file to create addresses for printing on envelopes.

1 Press **Merge/Sort** (Ctrl-F9) and select **M**erge (1).

⌨ *Select Merge from the **T**ools menu.*

2 Enter **envelope.mlt** for the primary file, then enter **customer.wkb** for the secondary file.

3 When the merging is completed, press **Home** twice then press **Up Arrow** (↑) to move to the first address.

An address for each envelope is ready to be printed.

4 Press **Print** (Shift-F7), then select **V**iew Document (6).

⌨ *Select Print from the **F**ile menu.*

Cycle through the addressed envelopes using Page Up and Page Down, then exit to the editing screen.

5 Press **Exit** (F7) and type **n** twice to clear the screen.

Remember that when you actually print envelopes, you may need to reset the Font Type, Location, and Prompt to Load options on the Edit Paper Definitions menu to fit your own printer.

For details on how to set these options for your situation, see the *Paper Size/Type*, *Sheet Feeder*, and *Printing, Landscape* sections in the *WordPerfect Reference Manual*.

Creating a Label Definition

Rather than printing directly on envelopes, you may want to print addresses on sheets of adhesive labels. Just as when printing on envelopes, you need to define the size, shape, and type of paper for WordPerfect to print your labels correctly.

1 Press **Format** (Shift-F8), select **P**age (2), then select Paper Size/Type (7).

⊞ *Select **P**age from the Layout menu, then select Paper Size/Type.*

2 Select **A**dd (2) from the menu at the bottom of the screen to create a new definition for labels.

3 Select **L**abels (4) for the paper type.

You are returned to the Edit Paper Definition menu.

4 Select **L**abels (8), then type **y** to get to the labels menu.

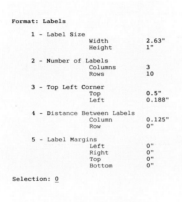

```
Format: Labels

     1 - Label Size
                    Width          2.63"
                    Height         1"

     2 - Number of Labels
                    Columns        3
                    Rows           10

     3 - Top Left Corner
                    Top            0.5"
                    Left           0.188"

     4 - Distance Between Labels
                    Column         0.125"
                    Row            0"

     5 - Label Margins
                    Left           0"
                    Right          0"
                    Top            0"
                    Bottom         0"

Selection: 0
```

In order to place text correctly on the labels, WordPerfect uses a series of measurements. This information includes the size of the sheet, the size of the labels, and the number and placement of labels on the sheet.

Other critical information is how far the top left corner of the first label is from the top and left edges of the sheet, as well as the dimensions of any space between rows or columns of labels.

The default settings on the menu are for a common arrangement of labels on an 8.5" x 11" sheet, shown in the illustrations below.

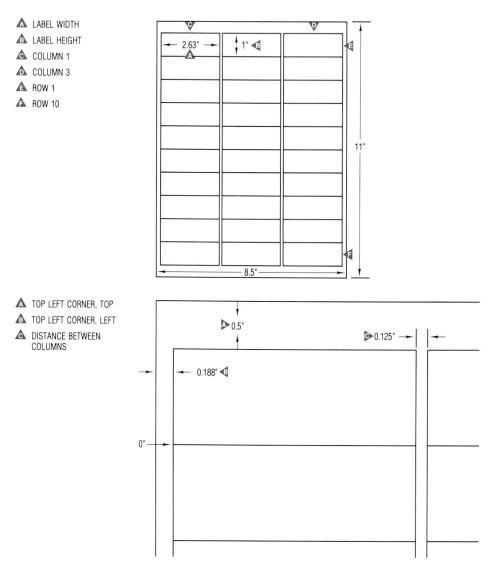

A LABEL WIDTH
B LABEL HEIGHT
C COLUMN 1
D COLUMN 3
E ROW 1
F ROW 10

A TOP LEFT CORNER, TOP
B TOP LEFT CORNER, LEFT
C DISTANCE BETWEEN
    COLUMNS

Any of these settings can be changed as necessary to fit the kind of labels that you have.

5 Select **D**istance Between Labels (4).

6 Press **Enter** to accept the default setting for Column, enter **1/8** for Row, then press **Enter** to return to the Edit Paper Definition menu.

An "Error: Labels will not fit on paper size" message appears briefly at the bottom of the screen. WordPerfect calculates that ten 1" labels, plus .5" empty space on top of the sheet, plus 1.125" total space between the rows of labels will not fit on an 11" sheet of paper. This aspect of the Labels feature can help you avoid mistakes in your measuring.

7 Select **D**istance Between Labels (4), press **Enter** to accept the default setting for Column, then enter **0** (zero) for Row.

Notice also that you can set margins that will apply to each label (rather than to the whole sheet). With labels this small, however, margins would probably not leave sufficient room for long addresses.

8 Press **Enter** to return to the Edit Paper Definition menu.

The sheet of labels is designed for portrait orientation, so you don't have to change the Font Type.

9 Select **P**rompt to Load (4), then select **Y**es.

For details on Prompt to Load, see Paper Size/Type *in the* WordPerfect Reference Manual.

10 Select **L**ocation (5), then select **M**anual (3).

For details on Location, see Paper Size/Type *and* Sheet Feeder *in the* WordPerfect Reference Manual.

11 Press **Exit** to return to the list of paper definitions.

The new definition you created for labels is highlighted on the list.

12 Press **Exit** (F7) twice to return to the normal editing screen.

13 Press **Exit**, then type **n** twice to clear the screen.

Creating a Primary File

Now you can create a primary file for merging and printing the labels. Once again, the paper definition code *must* be included in the document initial codes for the primary file.

Important*: If the paper definition is not in the initial codes, WordPerfect will only print one address on each sheet of labels.*

1 Press **Format** (Shift-F8), select **D**ocument (3), then select Initial Codes (2).

⌨ *Select **D**ocument from the Layout menu, then select Initial Codes.*

2 Press **Format** (Shift-F8), select **P**age (2), then select Paper Size/Type (7).

⌨ *Select **P**age from the Layout menu, then select Paper Size/Type.*

3 Highlight the Labels definition, choose **S**elect (1), then press **Exit** (F7) three times to return to the normal editing screen.

The full name and address of each customer in the CUSTOMER.WKB secondary file are in the first and second fields of each record.

4 Press **Merge Codes** (Shift-F9), select **F**ield (1), then enter **1** to insert a {Field}1~ for the first field.

⊟ *Select* **Merge Codes** *from the* **Tools** *menu, then select* **Field**.

5 Press **Enter** to start a new line.

6 Press **Merge Codes** (Shift-F9), select **F**ield (1), then enter **2** to insert a {Field}2~ for the second field.

⊟ *Select* **Merge Codes** *from the* **Tools** *menu, then select* **Field**.

7 Press **Exit** (F7), type **y**, enter **labels.30** to name and save the file, then type **n** to clear the screen.

Merging the Addresses

With LABELS.30 saved as a primary file, you can merge with a secondary file to create addresses for printing on labels.

1 Press **Merge/Sort** (Ctrl-F9) and select **M**erge (1).

⊟ *Select* **Merge** *from the* **Tools** *menu.*

2 Enter **labels.30** for the primary file, then enter **customer.wkb** for the secondary file.

3 When the merging is completed, press **Home** twice then press **Up Arrow** (↑) to move to the first address.

An address for each label is ready to be printed.

Notice that each address is separated by a hard page break, just like when you merged addresses for printing onto envelopes. If you move the cursor from one address to the next, you will see the Page number on the status line change.

When you are printing standard sheets or envelopes, you want each page to print on a separate sheet. However, with this label definition you want thirty "pages" to print on one sheet.

WordPerfect solves this dilemma by distinguishing between *logical pages* and *physical pages* in a labels definition. With the labels definition in the primary file's document initial codes, WordPerfect knows that there are thirty labels (i.e., logical pages) on each 8.5" x 11" sheet (i.e., physical page).

4 Press **Print** (Shift-F7), select **V**iew Document (6), then select **1**00% (1).

⊟ *Select* **Print** *from the* **File** *menu.*

Notice how the logical pages are arranged on the physical page. WordPerfect places the logical pages on the physical page from left to right and from top to bottom, as shown in the screen below.

⚠ LOGICAL PAGE #1
⚠ LOGICAL PAGE #3
⚠ LOGICAL PAGE #7

Because there were fewer than thirty records in this secondary file, the remainder of the labels (logical pages) created by this paper definition are left blank.

5 Press **Exit** to return to the editing screen.

Remember that when you actually print labels you may need to reset the Font Type, Location, and Prompt to Load options on the Edit Paper Definitions menu to fit your own printer.

For details on how to set these options for your situation, see the *Paper Size/Type*, *Sheet Feeder*, and *Printing, Landscape* sections in the *WordPerfect Reference Manual*.

6 Press **Exit** (F7) and type **n** twice to clear the screen.

The LABELS Macro

Included with your WordPerfect package is a macro file called LABELS.WPM. This macro will automatically create definitions for several of the most commonly used kinds of labels. This macro and the Merge feature can automate office filing tasks and save you time.

For example, every office maintains filing cabinets full of labeled file folders. You could use Merge to put the full name field from a client list onto adhesive labels for the file folders. The LABELS macro can create the label definition for you.

If you are running WordPerfect from two disk drives, replace the learning diskette in drive B with the Macros/Keyboards diskette before continuing the lesson.

1 Press **Macro** (Alt-F10).

🖳 *Select Macro from the Tools menu, then select Execute.*

2 Enter **labels** to begin the macro.

A list of Label Page/Size definitions is displayed. Notice that the first item on the list (A) is similar to the labels definition you created earlier in this lesson.

A 1/2" x 1 3/4" label is the right size for file folders.

3 Type **g** to move the cursor to the 1/2" x 1 3/4" option, then press **Enter** to select it.

The macro pauses for you to set the location for your printer.

4 Select **Manual** (3) to indicate that you will manually feed the label sheets into your printer.

The macro pauses to ask if you want a prompt to load. This is generally a good idea when manually feeding labels into the printer.

5 Select **Yes**.

You are returned to the list of definitions. You could create another definition at this time if you needed to, but for the purposes of this lesson we will quit here.

6 Press **Exit** (F7) to terminate the macro and return to the normal editing screen.

If you are running WordPerfect from two disk drives, replace the Macros/Keyboards diskette in drive B with the Learning diskette before continuing the lesson.

7 Press **Format** (Shift-F8), select **Page** (2), then select **Paper Size/Type** (7).

⌨ *Select **Page** from the **Layout** menu, then select Paper Size/Type.*

Notice that the new labels definition appears on the list of paper definitions, and is ready to be included in the document initial codes of a primary file.

Now that you have learned how to create paper definitions, you will probably want to create definitions for any envelopes, labels, or other forms that you use on your own printer.

Delete the definitions you created for this lesson. Use this lesson and the appropriate sections in the *WordPerfect Reference Manual* as a guide to create the definitions you need for your own situation.

8 Press **Exit** twice to return to the editing screen.

Lesson 29: Equations

Whenever you need to include a mathematical or scientific equation in a report, research paper, or any other document, you can use the Equation feature to help you create a simple or complex equation.

If you do not have a graphics card in your computer, it is difficult to use the Equation feature for building equations because the equation is not displayed on the screen (just a pattern of dots). However, you still may want to try doing the lesson to see what is possible without a graphics card.

Creating an Equation

Trying to create an equation in the normal editing screen can be difficult, even when creating a simple one. For example, the following formula (equation) is often used to help calculate depreciation on an asset.

$$\frac{(bv \times 2)}{n}$$

You could create the formula by typing and underlining "(bv x 2)" on one line, then centering the "n" with spaces on a second line. However, an easier way would be to use the Equation feature.

1 Press **Graphics** (Alt-F9) to display the Graphics menu.

⌨ *Select the Graphics pull-down menu.*

Besides creating a Figure, Table, Text, or User Box, you can also create a box for an equation.

2 Select **E**quation (6), then select **C**reate (1).

A menu is displayed that is exactly like the definition menu for all graphic boxes. You can change the size of the box, the horizontal and vertical position, the anchor type, and even add a caption.

An Equation box is set to Full (Horizontal Position) and Yes (Wrap Text Around Box), which means that text will only be printed above and below the formula (no text to the right or left).

Because "Equation" is selected for the contents, a special Equation Editor is available with the Edit option.

3 Select **E**dit (9) to display the Equation Editor.

The Equation Editor fills the screen and is divided into three main areas.

△A EDITING WINDOW
△B DISPLAY WINDOW
△C EQUATION PALETTE

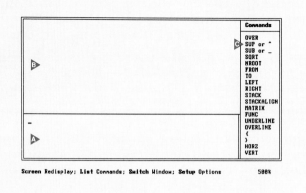

The Editing window is where you type the text to create a formula. The Display window is where you view the results. The Equation Palette provides lists of commands and symbols for building an equation.

In most cases, you can type an equation just as you would say it aloud. For example, to describe the depreciation formula you might say "bv times 2 over n."

4 Type (**bv times 2**) **over n** to create the formula.

The text you typed is displayed in the Editing window, but nothing appears in the Display window.

5 Press **Screen** (Ctrl-F3 or F9) to display the formula.

⊟ *Select Screen from the menu at the bottom of the Equation Editor.*

If you do not see a formula in the Display window, then you probably do not have a graphics card installed in your computer. If you do have a graphics card, then you may not have the correct graphics driver selected on the Setup key (Shift-F1,2,2).

The formula appears in the Display window, but not exactly the way you wanted it created. Only the right parenthesis ")" is over the "n," not the entire (bv x 2) set of characters.

▲ RIGHT PARENTHESIS

```
                  ▼▲
               )             │ Commands
 (bv×2 ───           │ OVER
         n           │ SUP or ^
                     │ SUB or _
                     │ SQRT
                     │ NROOT
                     │ FROM
                     │ TO
                     │ LEFT
                     │ RIGHT
                     │ STACK
                     │ STACKALIGN
                     │ MATRIX
                     │ FUNC
 (bv times 2) over n_ │ UNDERLINE
                     │ OVERLINE
                     │ {
                     │ }
                     │ HORZ
                     │ VERT

 Screen Redisplay; List Commands; Switch Window; Setup Options        500%
```

The word *over* is a command that places the character to the left of the command over the character to the right. For WordPerfect to recognize (bv x 2) as a single character (expression) to the left of the command, you need to place braces { } around the characters.

6 Press **Home,←** and type { at the beginning of the formula text.

7 Press **Word Right** (Ctrl-→) twice, press **Right Arrow** (→) twice, then type } to enclose (bv times 2) in braces.

After editing an equation, you can display the results by pressing the Screen key again.

8 Press **Screen** (Ctrl-F3 or F9) to display the edited formula.

⊟ *Select Screen from the menu at the bottom of the Equation Editor.*

If you placed the braces in the correct position (check the Editing window in the screen below), then the formula displays the "(bv times 2)" characters over the "n."

A DISPLAYED FORMULA

B EDITED FORMULA TEXT

$$\frac{(bv\times 2)}{n}$$

```
Commands

OVER
SUP or ^
SUB or _
SQRT
NROOT
FROM
TO
LEFT
RIGHT
STACK
STACKALIGN
MATRIX
FUNC
UNDERLINE
OVERLINE
{
}
HORZ
VERT
```

{(bv times 2)}_over n

Screen Redisplay; List Commands; Switch Window; Setup Options   500%

Viewing the Equation

By typing an equation in the Editing window, you are using commands, characters, and symbols to describe exactly how you want the formula to appear.

However, to see exactly what your printer can do to duplicate the equation in the Display window, you need to see the equation in the View Document screen.

1 Press **Exit** (F7) twice to return to the normal editing screen.

An Equation box appears in the normal editing screen to let you know that the formula is in a graphic box.

2 Press **Print** (Shift-F7), select **V**iew Document (6), then select 100% (1).

⌨ *Select **Print** from the **File** menu.*

The formula is centered between the margins at the top of the page.

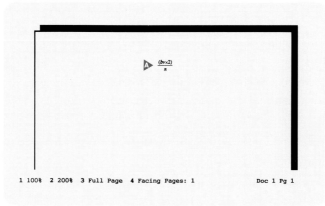

It is also much smaller than the one displayed in the Equation Editor. Equations in the editor are displayed at approximately 500% (depending on your monitor and the size of the equation) to give you a closer look when editing or creating an equation.

The size of the printed equation is the size of your initial base font.

3 Press **Exit** to return to the editing screen.

4 Press **Format** (Shift-F8), then select **D**ocument (3) to display the Document Format menu.

Select **D**ocument from the Layout menu.

The size of the initial base font in the Document Format menu is included in the font name. For example, the initial base font for a printer might be Times Roman 12pt (points).

```
Format: Document

      1 - Display Pitch - Automatic  Yes
                          Width       0.1"

      2 - Initial Codes
                                          🅑
      3 - Initial Base Font    ▲ Times Roman 12pt

      4 - Redline Method         Printer Dependent

      5 - Summary




      Selection: 0
```

5 Press **Exit** to return to the editing screen.

Printing an Equation

When you send an equation to your printer, WordPerfect uses the features and characters available at the printer to reproduce the formula you see in the View Document screen.

If your printer can print graphics, then you should have no problem printing any character in an equation. However, if you printer cannot print graphics, then there may be some characters that cannot be printed. In this case, a space is printed instead of the character.

1 Press **Print** (Shift-F7), then select **F**ull Document (1).

⌨ *Select Print from the File menu.*

2 Press **Print** again to display the Print menu.

⌨ *Select Print from the File menu.*

There are two options on the Print menu that control the quality of printing.

⚠ GRAPHICS QUALITY
⚠ TEXT QUALITY

```
         Print

             1 - Full Document
             2 - Page
             3 - Document on Disk
             4 - Control Printer
             5 - Multiple Pages
             6 - View Document
             7 - Initialize Printer


         Options

             S - Select Printer                 Workbook Printer
             B - Binding Offset                 0"
             N - Number of Copies               1
             U - Multiple Copies Generated by   WordPerfect
       ▶ A  G - Graphics Quality                Medium
             T - Text Quality                   High
         B



         Selection: 0
```

You can set each option to Draft, Medium, or High quality (or Do Not Print). Because the equation is printing as a graphics image, you may want to try adjusting the Graphics Quality option to a higher resolution (Medium or High), then try printing again.

If the print quality is better, then your printer can print graphics at different resolutions. However, the higher the resolution (quality), the more time it normally takes for your printer to print graphics images (and your document).

The Text Quality option only affects an equation if you set the text quality to "High". If the text quality is set to "High," then WordPerfect prints the equation in a high graphics resolution; otherwise, the graphics quality setting is used.

Printing an equation as text will be covered later in the lesson.

3   Press **Exit** (F7) to return to the editing screen.

4   Press **Exit**, then type **n** twice to clear the screen.

Using the Equation Palette

Now that you have been introduced to creating, displaying, and printing an equation, let's retrieve a document that includes some equations (formulas).

1   Press **Retrieve** (Shift-F10), then enter **equation.wkb** to retrieve the document.

⌨ *Select **R**etrieve from the **F**ile menu.*

A list is displayed on your screen that includes a description of several functions for a spreadsheet. Each description needs a formula created to indicate how information in the spreadsheet is calculated.

The functions and descriptions in the document on your screen are found in the Function List *of the* PlanPerfect 5.0 Reference Manual. PlanPerfect *is a spreadsheet package available from WordPerfect Corporation.*

For example, let's create a formula for the NPV (Net Present Value) function.

$$\sum \frac{V_i}{(1 + int)_i}$$

The NPV formula is a little more complex than the depreciation formula, but can still be easy to create with the Equation Editor. An equation box has already been set up. All you need to do is create the formula.

2   Press **Graphics** (Alt-F9), select **E**quation (6), select **E**dit (2), then enter **2** to display the Definition menu for the second equation box.

⌨ *Select **E**quation from the **G**raphics menu, select **E**dit, then enter **2**.*

3   Select **E**dit (9) to display the Equation Editor.

The scientific and mathematical symbols you need for creating most formulas are available on the Equation Palette.

▲ EQUATION PALETTE

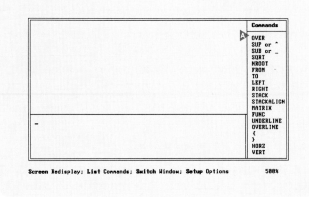

4 Press **List** (F5) to move the cursor to the Equation Palette.

⌨ *Select List from the menu at the bottom of the Equation Editor.*

A menu of commands, several menus of symbols, and a menu of functions can be displayed in the palette by pressing the Page Up or Page Down key.

5 Press **Page Down** (PgDn) eight times to rotate through all the palette menus until you return to the Commands menu.

⌨ *Place the mouse pointer on PgDn in the lower right corner of the screen and click the left button.*

The name of the menu is displayed at the top of the palette, while the name (and a short description) of the highlighted command or symbol in the palette is displayed at the bottom of the screen.

▲ MENU NAME
⒝ COMMAND OR SYMBOL
NAME

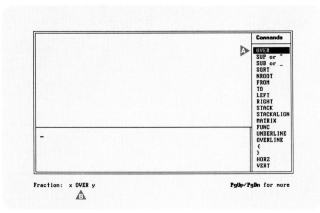

The SUM symbol (Σ) in the NPV formula is included in the Large menu.

6 Press **Page Down** to display the Large menu, then press **Enter** to insert the SUM symbol into the Editing window.

▣ *Place the mouse pointer on the SUM symbol and double-click to insert it into the Editing window.*

A SUM keyword is displayed that represents the symbol in the formula.

7 Press **Screen** (Ctrl-F3 or F9) to see the symbol in the Display window.

▣ *Select Screen from the menu at the bottom of the Equation Editor.*

You can also insert the actual symbol character into the Editing window by pressing Ctrl-Enter.

8 Press **List** (F5) to switch to the palette, then press **Ctrl-Enter** to insert the symbol into the Editing window.

▣ *Select List from the menu at the bottom of the Equation Editor.*

If the SUM symbol cannot be displayed by your computer, then a reverse video rectangle appears on the screen that represents the symbol.

9 Press **Screen** (Ctrl-F3 or F9) to see both symbols in the Display window.

▣ *Select Screen from the menu at the bottom of the Equation Editor.*

10 Press **Backspace** twice to delete the symbol character (but leave the SUM keyword).

11 Press **Screen** to redisplay the formula.

▣ *Select Screen from the menu at the bottom of the Equation Editor.*

As you become more familiar with some of the commands and symbols in the Equation Palette, you will probably want to type them directly from the keyboard. However, the palette is always available in case you need to find an unfamiliar command or symbol.

By using Compose, you can access any of the characters in the WordPerfect Character Sets (you cannot use Ctrl-v, only Ctrl-2). For details on using the Compose feature, turn to the Compose *heading in the* WordPerfect Reference Manual.

Completing the NPV Formula

△ SUBSCRIPTED i

The V in the formula includes a subscripted "i" which can be formatted by using the SUB command.

$$\sum \frac{V_i \triangleleft}{(1 + int)_i \triangleleft}$$

1 Type **V** for the first character, then press **List** (F5) to return to the palette.

▭ *Select List from the menu at the bottom of the Equation Editor.*

2 Press **Page Up** (PgUp) to display the Commands menu, then press **Down Arrow** (↓) until the cursor is on the SUB command.

▭ *Place the mouse pointer on PgUp and click the left button.*

3 Press **Enter** to insert the command into the Editing window.

▭ *Place the mouse pointer on the SUB command and double-click to insert it into the Editing window.*

4 Type **i** for the subscripted character, then press the **Space Bar**.

Subscripted and superscripted characters are printed at 2/3 the size of the base font if the formula is printed as a graphics image. If the formula is printed as text, then the font(s) assigned to the Subscript and Superscript attributes are used.

You are already familiar with the OVER command and braces { } to place one character or expression over another. The only other command you need to use for the formula is the SUP command to superscript the second "i" in the formula.

5 Type **over {(1 + int)}** to begin the second expression.

Commands such as SUB and OVER can be typed in uppercase or lowercase letters.

6 Press **List** (F5) to return to the palette.

▭ *Select List from the menu at the bottom of the Equation Editor.*

7 Make sure that the SUB command is highlighted, then press **Enter** to place the command in the Editing window.

▭ *Place the mouse pointer on the SUP command and double-click to insert it into the Editing window.*

8 Type **i** to complete the formula.

9 Press **Screen** (Ctrl-F3 or F9) to see the formula in the Display window.

▭ *Select Screen from the menu at the bottom of the Equation Editor.*

Because the "Vi" is tied together by a SUB command, it is seen as a single character by WordPerfect and is placed on top of the formula.

Notice that the "int" characters in the Editing window are being used as a keyword by WordPerfect to display an integral in the Display window.

$$\sum \frac{V_i}{(1+ \int)_i}$$

SUM V SUB i over {(1 + int)} SUB i_

Commands

OVER
SUP or ^
SUB or _
SQRT
NROOT
FROM
TO
LEFT
RIGHT
STACK
STACKALIGN
MATRIX
FUNC
UNDERLINE
OVERLINE
{
}
HORZ
VERT

Screen Redisplay; List Commands; Switch Window; Setup Options   474%

Whenever you want characters to be displayed exactly as they appear in the Editing window (instead of being used as a keyword), you can place a backslash (\) in front of the characters.

10 Place the cursor on the "i" in "int," then type a backslash (\).

11 Press **Screen** to see the results in the Display window.

Select Screen from the menu at the bottom of the Equation Editor.

After typing a backslash, only the characters up to a space or another command are displayed exactly as they appear in the Editing window. WordPerfect then continues converting commands and keywords to formats and symbols.

Adding Space to an Equation

Spaces are necessary to separate commands and keywords in an equation, but they do not add space to an equation.

For example, a space is needed between the SUB and "i" for WordPerfect to recognize SUB as a command.

1 Delete the space between the SUB command and the "i" in the V SUB i expression.

2   Press **Screen** (Ctrl-F3 or F9) to see the results in the Display window.

⊟ *Select Screen from the menu at the bottom of the Equation Editor.*

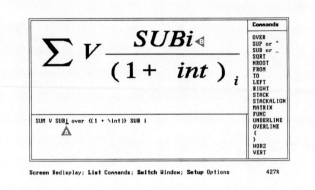

The characters SUBi are displayed in the formula, instead of the "i" being subscripted.

3   Place the cursor on the "i" in SUBi, then press the **Space Bar** to add a space.

4   Press **Screen** to see the results in the Display window.

⊟ *Select Screen from the menu at the bottom of the Equation Editor.*

Now that SUB is separated by a space to the left and right, it is recognized as a command again and displayed correctly in the Display window.

Whenever you select a command from the Equation Palette, spaces are placed around the command for you. However, if you are typing a command from the keyboard, you need to make sure that you enter your own spaces to format the command correctly.

If you are using a symbol such as a plus sign, spaces are not needed to display the equation correctly.

5   Delete the spaces to the left and right of the plus sign (+) in the (1 + \int) expression.

6   Press **Screen** to see the results in the Display window.

⊟ *Select Screen from the menu at the bottom of the Equation Editor.*

The spacing is still the same to the left and right of the plus sign (+), even without the spaces in the Editing window.

The space inserted by the Space Bar only affects the way the formula is displayed in the Editing window; it does not affect the way the formula is displayed in the View Document screen or printed. You can increase the actual amount of space in a printed equation by typing a tilde (~) for a normal space or a backward accent (`) for a thin space (1/4 of a normal space).

The tilde and backward accent are both on the same key on your keyboard.

7 Place the cursor to the right of the "M" in the SUM keyword, then type a tilde (~).

8 Place the cursor on the plus sign (+) in the (1+\int) expression, then type two backward accents (`).

9 Press **Screen** (Ctrl-F3 or F9) to see the results in the Display window.

⌨ *Select Screen from the menu at the bottom of the Equation Editor.*

The space between the SUM character and the rest of the formula has been increased, as well as the space between the 1 and the plus sign (+).

Ⓐ INCREASED SPACE
Ⓑ TILDE
Ⓒ BACKWARD ACCENTS

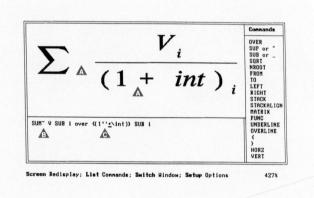

Hard Returns in the Editing Window

Besides using spaces, you can also use hard returns in the Editing window to make a formula easier to read. For example, let's use hard returns to place the two sets of characters on separate lines.

1 Place the cursor to the right of SUM~ in the formula, then press **Enter**.

2 Place the cursor to the right of the "i" in the V SUB i expression, press **Delete** (Del) to delete the space, then press **Enter**.

3 Place the cursor to the right of the "r" in the OVER command, then press **Enter**.

4 Press **Screen** (Ctrl-F3 or F9) to see the results of the formatting.

⌨ *Select Screen from the menu at the bottom of the Equation Editor.*

Although the formula in the Editing window is broken up into several lines, WordPerfect still sees the formula as one line of characters and does not change the way the formula is displayed.

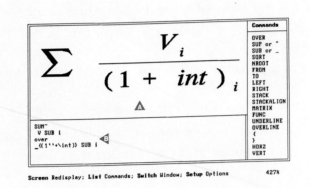

5 Press **Exit** (F7) twice to return to the normal editing screen.

Creating a Larger Formula

There are three more formulas in the function list. Two of them (equations 3 and 5) have already been created for you and are available as examples of how to build a formula.

A third formula (equation 4) needs to be created for the TERM function, and is illustrated below.

$$ \frac{ln\left(\dfrac{\dfrac{PMT(1 + i * t)}{i} - FV}{\dfrac{PMT(1 + i * t)}{i} + PV}\right)}{ln\,(i + 1)} $$

Whenever you are creating a larger equation, it is a good idea to start with an expression at the center of the equation, then build the rest of the equation around it.

For example, you already know how to place one expression over another, so you can start by placing the PMT(1+i*t) expression over the i.

1 Press **Graphics** (Alt-F9), select **E**quation (6), select **E**dit (2), then enter **4** to select the fourth Equation box.

▢ *Select **E**quation from the Graphics menu, select **E**dit, then enter **4**.*

2 Select **E**dit (9) to display the Equation Editor.

3 Type the following formula:

{PMT(1"+i*t)} over i ~-~FV

4 Press **Screen** (Ctrl-F3 or F9) to view the formula in the Display window.

⌨ *Select Screen from the menu at the bottom of the Equation Editor.*

The braces make sure that the entire PMT(1+i*t) expression is placed over "i." However, now you need to place the entire formula over another PMT expression.

5 Press **Home,←** to place the cursor at the beginning of the line, then type a left brace {.

6 Press **Home,→** to place the cursor at the end of the line, then type a right brace }.

By starting with a smaller part of the formula, then building out, it is easier to use braces for indicating the parts of the formula that need to be kept together.

Saving and Retrieving an Equation

The PMT expressions in the formula are identical, except for the –FV and the +PV characters.

⚠ PMT EXPRESSIONS

$$\ln \left(\frac{\dfrac{PMT(1+i*t)}{i} - FV}{\dfrac{PMT(1+i*t)}{i} + PV} \right)$$
$$\overline{}$$
$$\ln(i+1)$$

To save time typing a larger formula, you can use Save and Retrieve.

1 Press **Save** (F10), then enter **pmt** for the filename.

2 Press **Enter** to start a new line in the Editing window.

3 Press **Retrieve** (Shift-F10), then enter **pmt** to retrieve the PMT equation file.

A copy of the first PMT expression is inserted into the Editing window. All you need to do is edit the copy to create the second PMT expression.

4 Press **Delete** (Del) to delete the space at the beginning of the line.

5 Delete the minus sign (–) and type a plus sign (+) in the retrieved text, then delete the ~FV and type **PV** in its place.

6 Press **Up Arrow** (↑), then press **End** to place the cursor at the end of the first line in the Editing window.

7 Press the **Space Bar** to insert a space, then type **over** to place the first line in the Editing window over the second line.

8 Press **Screen** (Ctrl-F3 or F9) to see the results in the Display window.

Your formula should now look like the one displayed below:

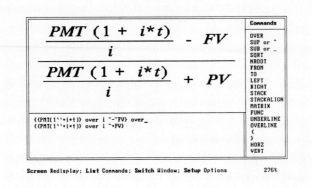

Select Screen from the menu at the bottom of the Equation Editor.

By using the Save and Retrieve keys, you have been able to quickly create a major section of the TERM formula.

An equation can be created in the normal editing screen (text, spaces, and hard returns only), saved as a file, then retrieved into an Equation box using the Filename option on the Equation Definition menu or the Retrieve key in the Equation Editor.

You can also retrieve an equation saved from the Equation Editor into the normal editing screen, edit it, save it, then retrieve it back into an Equation box with the Filename option or Retrieve key.

Equations and the Display Window

▲ VIEW PERCENTAGE

After displaying the formula, the percentage in the lower right corner of the screen may change to a smaller number.

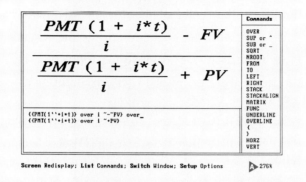

$$\frac{PMT\ (1\ +\ i*t)}{i}\ -\ FV$$
$$\frac{\dfrac{PMT\ (1\ +\ i*t)}{i}\ -\ FV}{\dfrac{PMT\ (1\ +\ i*t)}{i}\ +\ PV}$$

Commands

OVER
SUP or ^
SUB or _
SQRT
NROOT
FROM
TO
LEFT
RIGHT
STACK
STACKALIGN
MATRIX
FUNC
UNDERLINE
OVERLINE
{
}
HORZ
VERT

{{PMT(1`+i*t)} over i ~-~FV} over_
{{PMT(1`+i*t)} over i ~+PV}

Screen Redisplay; **List** Commands; **Switch** Window; **Setup** Options   ▲ 276%

As you create and display an equation, WordPerfect tries to keep the image in the Display window as large as possible. You can adjust the view of the equation in the Display window by using the cursor keys.

1 Press **Switch** (Shift-F3) to move into the Display window.

A double border on the right side of the Display window tells you that the window is active, and that you can change the view of the image.

▲ DISPLAY WINDOW
▲ DOUBLE BORDER

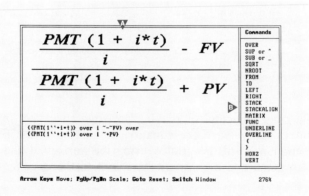

$$\frac{PMT\ (1\ +\ i*t)}{i}\ -\ FV$$
$$\frac{PMT\ (1\ +\ i*t)}{i}\ +\ PV$$

Commands

OVER
SUP or ^
SUB or _
SQRT
NROOT
FROM
TO
LEFT
RIGHT
STACK
STACKALIGN
MATRIX
FUNC
UNDERLINE
OVERLINE
{
}
HORZ
VERT

{{PMT(1`+i*t)} over i ~-~FV} over
{{PMT(1`+i*t)} over i ~+PV}

Arrow Keys Move; **PgUp/PgDn** Scale; **Goto** Reset; **Switch** Window   276%

Pressing the Page Up or Page Down key enlarges or reduces the view by 25% at a time.

2 Press **Page Down** (PgDn) six times to reduce the view of the formula.

As you reduce the view, WordPerfect tries to keep the equation in the upper left corner of the Display window. You can move the equation to another place in the window by using the Home and arrow keys.

3 Press **Down Arrow** (↓) five times, then press **Home,**→ to place the formula in the center of the display window.

You can even move an equation outside the window.

4 Press **Home,**← twice to move the formula to the left.

If you decide that you want to restore the original view of the equation, you can use the Go To key.

5 Press **Go To** (Ctrl-Home) to redisplay the original view of the formula.

6 Press **Switch** (Shift-F3) to exit the Display window and return to the Editing window.

The double border returns to the right side of the Editing window, and you can continue editing the equation.

A EDITING WINDOW

B DOUBLE BORDER

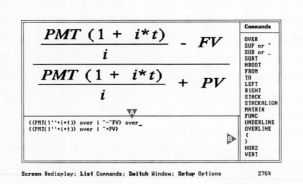

Enlarging, reducing, or moving an equation in the Display window only changes the view of the equation for editing in the Equation Editor. The equation will still be printed using the horizontal and vertical alignment in the Setup menu and the current base font in the document.

LEFT and RIGHT Commands

⚠ PARENTHESES

The next step in creating the TERM formula is to enclose the two PMT expressions in parentheses.

$$\ln \left(\frac{\dfrac{PMT\,(1 + i * t)}{i} - FV}{\dfrac{PMT\,(1 + i * t)}{i} + PV} \right)$$
$$\overline{\qquad\qquad\qquad\qquad\qquad}$$
$$\ln\,(i + 1)$$

1 Press **Home,Home,↑** to move the cursor to the beginning of the formula.

2 Type a left parenthesis (.

3 Press **Home,Home,↓** to move the cursor to the end of the formula.

4 Type a right parenthesis).

5 Press **Screen** (Ctrl-F3 or F9) to see the results in the Display window.

▭ *Select Screen from the menu at the bottom of the Equation Editor.*

The parentheses only surround the line in the middle of the formula.

⚠ PARENTHESES

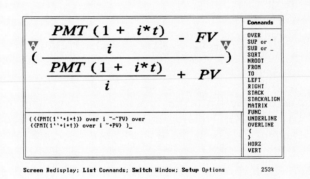

You need parentheses that can expand to enclose the entire displayed formula.

6 Press **Home,Home,↑** to move the cursor to the beginning of the formula.

7 Type **left** for the LEFT command, then press the **Space Bar**.

8 Press **Right Arrow** (→), then press **Enter** to place the command on its own line.

While placing the LEFT command on its own line is not necessary, it helps when reading the formula in the Editing window.

9 Press **Home,Home,↓** to move the cursor to the end of the formula.

10 Press **Left Arrow** (←) to place the cursor on the right parenthesis, then press **Enter**.

11 Type **right** for the RIGHT command, then press the **Space Bar**.

The LEFT and RIGHT commands expand a character so that it encloses an expression in an equation.

12 Press **Screen** to see the results in the Display window.

⌨ *Select Screen from the menu at the bottom of the Equation Editor.*

The parentheses have expanded to enclose the entire formula.

▲ EXPANDED PARENTHESES

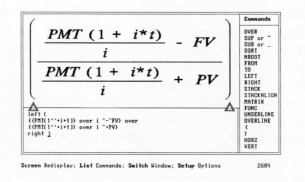

For a complete list of the characters and symbols that can be used with the LEFT and RIGHT commands, turn to the *LEFT* heading under *Equations, Commands Syntax* in the *WordPerfect Reference Manual*.

Completing the TERM Formula

Let's finish creating the TERM formula by providing you with an example of the completed formula as it should appear in the Editing window.

1 Finish creating the TERM formula in the Editing window by following the example below:

{ln~ left (
{{PMT(1"+i*t)} over i ~-~FV} over
{{PMT(1"+i*t)} over i ~+PV}
right)}
over
{ln~(i~+1)}

2 Press **Screen** (Ctrl-F3 or F9) to see the results in the Display window.

⊟ *Select Screen from the menu at the bottom of the Equation Editor.*

The TERM formula should now look like the one in the screen below.

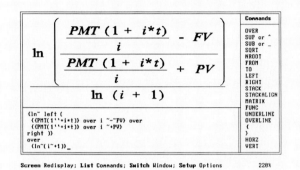

If the formula is displayed incorrectly, or you see an "ERROR: Incorrect format" message displayed and the Display window goes blank, try comparing your formula to the one in step 1. You may have forgotten a brace, or a tilde may be in the wrong place.

The error message is designed to help you find an error in the way you have typed an equation. For example, let's try adding some more space between "RIGHT)" and the expressions in the formula.

3 Place the cursor on the right parenthesis in the "RIGHT)}" section of the formula, then type a tilde (~) to add a normal space.

4 Press **Screen** to see the results in the Display window.

⊟ *Select Screen from the menu at the bottom of the Equation Editor.*

The "ERROR: Incorrect format" message is briefly displayed, and the cursor is placed in the formula at the beginning of the formatting error.

▲ ERROR MESSAGE

▲ INCORRECT FORMAT

```
                                                    Commands

                                                    OVER
                                                    SUP or  ^
                                                    SUB or  _
                                                    SQRT
                                                    NROOT
                                                    FROM
                                                    TO
                                                    LEFT
                                                    RIGHT
                                                    STACK
                                                    STACKALIGN
                                                    MATRIX
                                                    FUNC
  {ln~ left (                                       UNDERLINE
    {{PMT(1``+i*t)} over i ~-~FV} over              OVERLINE
    {{PMT(1``+i*t)} over i ~+PV}                    (
  right ~)}                                         )
  over                                              HORZ
    {ln~( i~+1)}                                    VERT
```

▲ ERROR: Incorrect format

The cursor is at the tilde, which means that the tilde is probably in the wrong place in the formula.

5   Press **Delete** (Del) to erase the tilde, then press **Home,←** to move the cursor to the beginning of the line.

6   Type a tilde (~) in front of the RIGHT command.

7   Press **Screen** to see the results in the Display window.

⌨ *Select Screen from the menu at the bottom of the Equation Editor.*

If you placed the tilde in front of the RIGHT command (and the rest of the formula is formatted correctly), there should be more space between the right parenthesis and the expressions.

8   Press **Exit** (F7) twice to return to the normal editing screen.

Changing the Equation Options

Now that you have created the equations needed for the function list, let's try formatting the depreciation formula on the first page of the list.

1   Press **Home,Home,↑** to move the cursor to the beginning of the document.

2   Press **Print** (Shift-F7), select **V**iew Document (6), then select 100% (1) to display the first page of the function list.

⌨ *Select **P**rint from the **F**ile menu.*

A depreciation formula like the one you already created at the beginning of the lesson is included with the DDB (double declining balance) function.

⚠ DDB FUNCTION
⚠ DEPRECIATION FORMULA

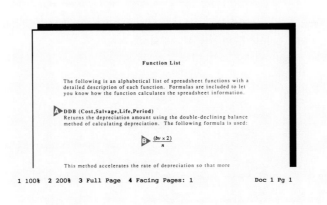

Function List

The following is an alphabetical list of spreadsheet functions with a detailed description of each function. Formulas are included to let you know how the function calculates the spreadsheet information.

A▶DDB (Cost,Salvage,Life,Period)
Returns the depreciation amount using the double-declining balance method of calculating depreciation. The following formula is used:

$$B▷ \frac{(bv \times 2)}{n}$$

This method accelerates the rate of depreciation so that more

1 100% 2 200% 3 Full Page 4 Facing Pages: 1   Doc 1 Pg 1

The "bv" and "n" in the formula are known as *variables*. The "bv" represents a book value, and the "n" represents the life of an asset.

Variables in an equation are printed in italics if an italics font or method of creating italics is available at your printer.

It would help the person reading about the function if you included a description of each variable. To keep the descriptions with the formula, let's include them as a caption for the Equation box.

3 Press **Exit** (F7) to return to the editing screen.

4 Press **Graphics** (Alt-F9), select **E**quations (6), then select **E**dit (2).

⌨ *Select Equation from the Graphics menu, then select Edit.*

5 Enter **1** (one) to display the definition menu for the depreciation formula.

6 Select **C**aption (3), then press **Backspace** to delete the equation number.

7 Press **Font** (Ctrl-F8), select **A**ppearance (2), then select **I**talic (4).

⌨ *Select Appearance from the Font menu, then select Italic.*

8 Type the following for the variable descriptions:

bv = book value in that period; n = life of the asset

9 Press **Exit** twice to return to the normal editing screen.

Captions for equations are set to print on the right side of the Equation box. You can change the position of the caption by using the equation options.

10 Press **Reveal Codes** (Alt-F3) to display the codes in the function list.

⌨ *Select Reveal Codes from the Edit menu.*

11 Press **Left Arrow** (←) to place the cursor on the Equation Box code.

12 Press **Graphics** (Alt-F9), select **E**quation (6), then select **O**ptions (4).

⌨ *Select* **E**quation *from the* **G**raphics *menu, then select* **O**ptions.

The equation options are initially set for no borders around the box, and for captions printed on the right side.

▲ NO BORDERS

Ⓑ CAPTIONS ON RIGHT SIDE

```
Options: Equation

    1 - Border Style                      ▼▲
           Left                         None
           Right                        None
           Top                          None
           Bottom                       None
    2 - Outside Border Space
           Left                         0.083"
           Right                        0.083"
           Top                          0.083"
           Bottom                       0.083"
    3 - Inside Border Space
           Left                         0.083"
           Right                        0.083"
           Top                          0.083"
           Bottom                       0.083"
    4 - First Level Numbering Method     Numbers
    5 - Second Level Numbering Method    Off
    6 - Caption Number Style             [BOLD](1)[bold]
    7 - Position of Caption          Ⓑ▶Right side
    8 - Minimum Offset from Paragraph    0"
    9 - Gray Shading (% of black)        0%

    Selection: 0
```

13 Select **P**osition of Caption (7), select **B**elow Box (1), then press **Exit** to return to the editing screen.

14 Press **Print**, then select **V**iew Document to display the caption.

⌨ *Select* **P**rint *from the* **F**ile *menu.*

Changing the Equation Size

The caption looks fine underneath the formula, but the formula needs to be printed a little larger (like the NPV formula) to help it stand out on the page.

1 Press **Exit** (F7) to return to the editing screen.

2 Press **Graphics** (Alt-F9), select **E**quation (6), then select **E**dit (2).

⌨ *Select* **E**quation *from the* **G**raphics *menu, then select* **E**dit.

3 Enter **1** (one) to edit the depreciation formula.

4 Select **E**dit (9) to display the formula in the Equation Editor.

Several keys are listed at the bottom of the Equation Editor, including the Setup key.

5 Press **Setup** (Shift-F1) to display the Setup options for the Equation Editor.

⌨ *Select* **S**etup *from the menu at the bottom of the Equation Editor.*

The first option in the menu lets you indicate if you want the formula printed as a graphics image or as text.

```
Equation: Options
  ▶1 - Print as Graphics         Yes
    2 - Graphical Font Size       Default
    3 - Horizontal Alignment      Center
    4 - Vertical Alignment        Center




Selection: 0
```

The option is set to Yes, which means that WordPerfect uses one of three graphic font styles (Helvetica, Times Roman, or Courier) to print the equation as a graphics image.

WordPerfect tries to match the default base font in the document with one of the three graphic font styles. For example, if the default base font is New Century Schoolbook 12pt, then the Times Roman font style (the one most similar to New Century Schoolbook) is used to print the equation.

If you are printing the equation as a graphics image, the second option lets you print the equation the same size as the default base font, or lets you enter your own point size.

6 Select **G**raphical Font Size (2), select **S**et Point Size (2), then enter **18** for the point size.

One point is equal to 1/72 of an inch.

7 Press **Exit** three times to return to the normal editing screen.

8 Press **Print** (Shift-F7), then select **V**iew Document (6) to see the edited formula.

⌨ *Select Print from the File menu.*

The formula is now larger, and will be printed with the Times Roman graphic font style (to match the Roman 12 pt base font) at 18 points.

▲ LARGER FORMULA

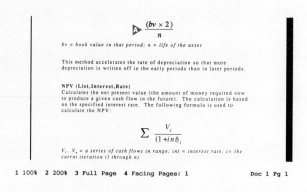

$$\blacktriangle \frac{(bv \times 2)}{n}$$

bv = book value in that period; n = life of the asset

This method accelerates the rate of depreciation so that more depreciation is written off in the early periods than in later periods.

NPV (List,Interest,Rate)
Calculates the net present value (the amount of money required now to produce a given cash flow in the future). The calculation is based on the specified interest rate. The following formula is used to calculate the NPV:

$$\sum \frac{V_i}{(1 + int)_i}$$

$V_i...V_s$ = a series of cash flows in range; int = interest rate; i = the currnt iteration (I through n)

1 100%   2 200%   3 Full Page   4 Facing Pages: 1   Doc 1 Pg 1

The Setup options available from the Equation Editor only affect the current formula being created. If you want to set the options for all formulas, then use the Setup key from the normal editing screen (Shift-F1,4,3).

Changing the Base Font

If you want to print an equation using one of the fonts at your printer (instead of the graphic fonts in WordPerfect), you need to print the formula as text rather than as a graphic image.

1 Press **Exit** (F7) to return to the editing screen.

2 Press **Graphics** (Alt-F9), select **E**quation (6), select **E**dit (2), then enter **1** (one) to edit the Equation box.

⌨ *Select Equation from the Graphics menu, select Edit, then enter 1.*

3 Select **E**dit (9) to display the formula in the Equation Editor.

4 Press **Setup** (Shift-F1), select **P**rint as Graphics (1), then type **n** for No.

⌨ *Select Setup from the menu at the bottom of the Equation Editor.*

5 Press **Exit** three times to return to the normal editing screen.

If you are printing an equation as text, then WordPerfect uses the initial base font of the document (Shift-F8,3,3) to print the formula. However, if an Equation Options code is included with the Equation box, then you can insert a Base Font code *before* the option code to print the equation in any font available at your printer.

6 Press **Left Arrow** (←) to place the cursor at the beginning of the line (on the Equation Options code).

The Base Font code needs to come before the Equation Options code for the equation to use the new font.

Let's try printing the depreciation formula using the Helvetica 18pt font.

7 Press **Font** (Ctrl-F8), then select Base **F**ont (4).

⊟ *Select Base **F**ont from the **F**ont menu.*

8 Press **Up Arrow** (↑) until the cursor highlights the Helvetica 18pt font, then press **Enter** to select the font.

9 Press **Down Arrow** twice to reformat the text below the Equation box.

The lines in the paragraphs below the equation are reformatted for the Helvetica 18pt font, but need to be printed with the initial base font (Roman 12 pt).

10 Press **Up Arrow** to place the cursor at the beginning of the paragraph below the box (This method accelerates...).

11 Press **Font** (Ctrl-F8), then select Base **F**ont (4).

⊟ *Select Base **F**ont from the **F**ont menu.*

12 Press **Down Arrow** until the cursor highlights the Roman 12pt font, then press **Enter** to select the font.

Now that the formula is set for a larger font, with the rest of the list formatted for the Roman 12pt font, let's display the results in the View Document screen.

13 Press **Print** (Shift-F7), then select **V**iew Document (6).

⊟ *Select **P**rint from the **F**ile menu.*

Although printing an equation as text can be important when you want an exact font style, printing an equation as a graphics image is acceptable for most applications.

If WordPerfect can't find or produce a character when printing an equation as text, then a space is printed instead of the character.

Changing the Font for a Caption

The paragraphs below the formula are in the Courier 10cpi font, but the caption is still using the same base font as the formula (Helvetica 15pt).

△ HELVETICA 18pt

△ ROMAN 12pt

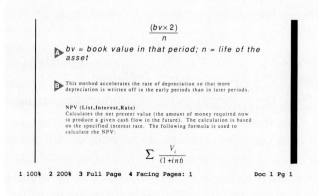

1 Press **Exit** (F7) to return to the editing screen.

2 Press **Graphics** (Alt-F9), select **Equation** (6), select **Edit** (2), then enter **1** (one) to edit the depreciation formula.

⊟ *Select Equation from the Graphics menu, select Edit, then enter 1.*

3 Select **Caption** (3) to add a Base Font code to the caption.

4 Press **Font** (Ctrl-F8), select **Base Font** (4), press **Down Arrow** (↓) until you highlight the Roman 12pt font, then press **Enter** to select the font.

⊟ *Select Base Font from the Font menu.*

5 Press **Exit** twice to return to the normal editing screen.

6 Press **Print** (Shift-F7), then select **View Document** (6).

⊟ *Select Print from the File menu.*

Both the caption and the text below the formula are now in the same font.

A ROMAN 12pt

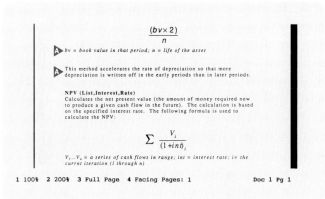

Aligning the Equation
in the Box

The Setup menu includes Horizontal Alignment and Vertical Alignment options to help you move the equation around inside the box.

The depreciation formula is initially set to be centered horizontally in the equation box. Let's try printing the formula on the left side of the box.

1 Press **Exit** (F7) to return to the editing screen.

2 Press **Graphics** (Alt-F9), select **E**quation (6), select **E**dit (2), then enter **1** (one).

⌨ *Select Equation from the Graphics menu, select Edit, then enter 1.*

3 Select **E**dit (9), then press **Setup** (Shift-F1) to display the Setup Options menu for the depreciation formula.

⌨ *Select Setup from the menu at the bottom of the Equation Editor.*

4 Select **H**orizontal Alignment (3), then select **L**eft (1) to move the formula to the left inside the box.

5 Press **Exit** three times to return to the normal editing screen.

6 Press **Home,Home,**↑ to move the cursor to the beginning of the document.

7 Press **Print** (Shift-F7), then select **V**iew Document (6) to display the list.

⌨ *Select Print from the File menu.*

The formula is now aligned at the left side of the box (near the left margin).

▲ LEFT ALIGNED

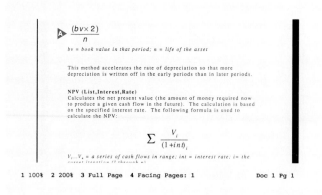

$$\frac{(bv \times 2)}{n}$$

bv = book value in that period; n = life of the asset

This method accelerates the rate of depreciation so that more
depreciation is written off in the early periods than in later periods.

NPV (List,Interest,Rate)
Calculates the net present value (the amount of money required now
to produce a given cash flow in the future). The calculation is based
on the specified interest rate. The following formula is used to
calculate the NPV:

$$\sum \frac{V_i}{(1+int)_i}$$

$V_1...V_x$ = a series of cash flows in range; int = interest rate; i = the

1 100%   2 200%   3 Full Page   4 Facing Pages: 1   Doc 1 Pg 1

To indent the formula a little more to the right, you can use the equation
options to increase the size of the space inside the box.

*You can also use the HORZ command in a formula to shift the formula to the right
in the graphics box (e.g., HORZ 240 {(bv*2)} over n).*

8 Press **Exit** to return to the editing screen, then scroll down the page until
you place the cursor on the [Equ Box:1;; ...] code.

9 Press **Graphics** (Alt-F9), select **E**quation (6), then select **O**ptions (4).

⊟ *Select **E**quation from the **G**raphics menu, then select **O**ptions.*

10 Select **I**nside Border Space (3), then enter **.25** to increase the space on the
left inside the box.

11 Press **Enter** three times to leave the Right, Top, and Bottom inside
borders at .083", then press **Exit** to return to the editing screen.

12 Press **Left Arrow** (←), then press **Backspace** to delete the first (original)
Equation Options code.

13 Press **Home,Home,**↑ to move the cursor to the beginning of the function
list.

14 Press **Print**, then select **V**iew Document to display the list.

⊟ *Select **P**rint from the **F**ile menu.*

The depreciation formula is indented ¼ of an inch from the left margin.

▲ ¼ INCH INDENT

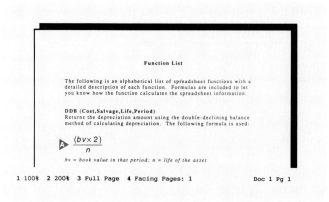

Viewing and Printing the Function List

Now that the formatting is completed, you may want to display the rest of the function list in the View Document screen.

1 Scroll through the function list using the cursor keys.

All the other formulas in the function list have been formatted like the depreciation formula. Because the STDEV (standard deviation) formula uses a large square root symbol, the formula is formatted to print as graphics (instead of text).

2 Press **Exit** (F7) to return to the editing screen.

3 Press **Reveal Codes** (Alt-F3) to display the normal editing screen.

⬚ *Select **R**eveal Codes from the **E**dit menu.*

You may want to finish the lesson by viewing equations 3 and 5 in the Equation Editor, printing and/or saving the function list (you need to select your own printer first), or by creating your own formula.

4 When you are finished with the lesson, make sure you clear the normal editing screen by pressing **Exit** and typing **n** twice.

The Equations lesson has introduced you to some of the basic editing features of the Equation Editor. For details on all the features available, turn to the three *Equations* headings in the *WordPerfect Reference Manual*.

If you frequently use several characters from the Equation Palette or type them with Compose, you may want to assign them to a special Equation keyboard. Turn to the Equation Keyboard *heading under* Equations *in the* WordPerfect Reference Manual *for details.*

Lesson 30: Forms Fill-in

Pre-printed forms are one of the most reliable and economical ways of gathering or sending information. Most forms are professionally printed, then filled in by hand or with a typewriter.

However, if you fill in the same form frequently, you may want to use WordPerfect to help you print the information. In this lesson, the Advance, Comment, Table, and Merge features are used to help print information on an invoice form.

Check the feature tables in the Workbook Appendix for lessons that introduce the Advance, Comments, Table, and Merge features.

Advancing Text

The following is an invoice for HALVA International that was filled in using the Advance, Comment, and Table features in WordPerfect to type and print the information on the form.

Let's retrieve a document that contains these features to see how they are used.

1   Press **Retrieve** (Shift-F10), then enter **invoice.wkb** to retrieve the document.

⬚ *Select **R**etrieve from the **F**ile menu.*

The document you retrieved does not look like the invoice form. Instead, there are comments on the page (in double-walled boxes) that indicate the information you need to type to fill in the invoice.

⚠ COMMENTS

```
   ┌─────────────────────────────────────────────────────────────────┐
 ▷ │ Bill To                                                           │
   │ Type the name and address of the person or company being billed for the │
   │ merchandise.                                                      │
   └─────────────────────────────────────────────────────────────────┘

   ┌─────────────────────────────────────────────────────────────────┐
   │ Ship To                                                           │
   │ Type the name and address of the person or company to whom the merchandise │
 ▷ │ should be shipped.                                                │
   │                                                                   │
   │ WARNING!  Do not press Down after typing a line.  Press Down Arrow (↓) to │
   │ move to the empty lines provided.                                 │
   └─────────────────────────────────────────────────────────────────┘

   ┌─────────────────────────────────────────────────────────────────┐
 ▷ │ Date                                                              │
   │ The date the invoice is printed.                                  │
   C:\WP51\LEARN\INVOICE.WKB                         Doc 1 Pg 1 Ln 3" Pos 1"
```

Below each comment is an empty line (or lines) where the information is typed. Advance codes at the beginning of each line tell WordPerfect exactly where to print the information on the form.

For example, the empty line for the Bill To information includes Advance codes to print the information 3" from the top edge of the form and 1" from the left edge of the form.

2   Press **Reveal Codes** (Alt-F3) to see the Advance codes in the document.

⬚ *Select **R**eveal Codes from the **E**dit menu.*

Besides the Advance codes, each comment displayed in the editing screen is a single WordPerfect code in the Reveal Codes screen. The comment appears on the screen, but is not printed.

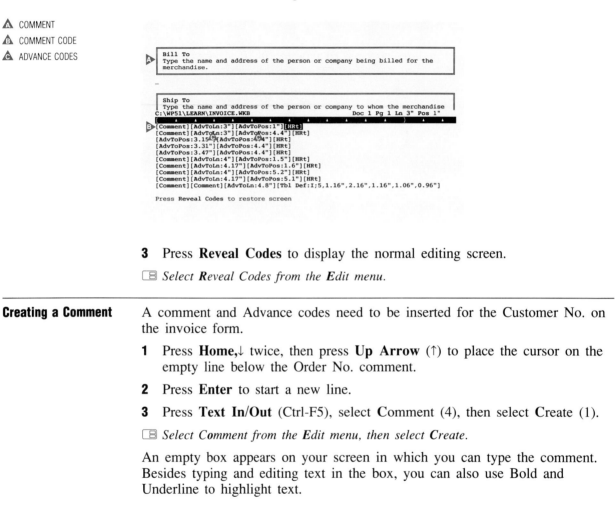

A COMMENT

B COMMENT CODE

C ADVANCE CODES

3 Press **Reveal Codes** to display the normal editing screen.

🖵 *Select **Reveal Codes** from the **Edit** menu.*

Creating a Comment

A comment and Advance codes need to be inserted for the Customer No. on the invoice form.

1 Press **Home,↓** twice, then press **Up Arrow** (↑) to place the cursor on the empty line below the Order No. comment.

2 Press **Enter** to start a new line.

3 Press **Text In/Out** (Ctrl-F5), select **Comment** (4), then select **Create** (1).

🖵 *Select **Comment** from the **Edit** menu, then select **Create**.*

An empty box appears on your screen in which you can type the comment. Besides typing and editing text in the box, you can also use Bold and Underline to highlight text.

4 Press **Bold** (F6), type **Customer No.** for the comment, then press **Exit** (F7) to return to the information document.

Your comment should look like the one illustrated on the screen below.

```
┌─────────────────────────────────────────────────────────────────┐
│  Invoice No.                                                      │
└─────────────────────────────────────────────────────────────────┘


┌─────────────────────────────────────────────────────────────────┐
│  Order No.                                                        │
└─────────────────────────────────────────────────────────────────┘

 ▷┌─────────────────────────────────────────────────────────────────┐
   │  Customer No.                                                    │
   └─────────────────────────────────────────────────────────────────┘


   ┌─────────────────────────────────────────────────────────────────┐
   │  Merchandise Ordered Table                                       │
   │  Press Tab after typing each item in a line (Shift-Tab takes     │
   │  you back one item).  You do not need to press Enter when you    │
   │  reach the end of a line.                                        │
   │                                                                  │
   │  When you finish, calculate the amounts, delete any empty rows,  │
   │  then remove all the borders in the table.                       │
   └─────────────────────────────────────────────────────────────────┘
```

C:\WP51\LEARN\INVOICE.WKB   Doc 1 Pg 1 Ln 4.34" Pos 1"

Adding the Advance Codes

Now that the comment has been created, the Advance codes need to be added to print the customer number in the blank line provided on the invoice form.

The blank line is 4.5" down from the top of the form, and 5.3" in from the left edge of the form.

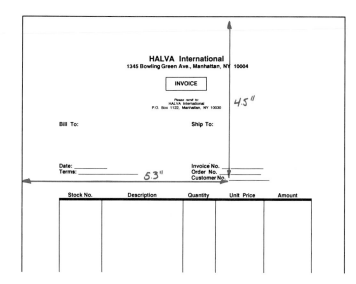

Once you measure the distance from the top of the form to the blank line, you need to subtract the line height for one line from the measurement, or the text will print just below the line instead of above the line.

You can find out the current line height by using the Format key.

1 Press **Format** (Shift-F8), then select **L**ine (1).

⌨ *Select Line from the Layout menu.*

2 Select Line **H**eight (4), then select **F**ixed (2).

A line height of .167" is displayed for the current font in the Workbook Printer (Courier 10cpi font). By rounding the .167" measurement to .17", then subtracting .17" from the vertical measurement (4.5"), you get a measurement of 4.33" for the Advance code.

3 Press **Cancel** (F1) twice to return to the main Format menu.

4 Select **O**ther (4), then select **A**dvance (1).

5 Select **L**ine (3), then enter **4.33** for the adjusted vertical measurement.

6 Select **A**dvance (1), select **P**osition (6), then enter **5.3** for the horizontal measurement.

7 Press **Exit** (F7) to return to the invoice document.

By using the Advance Line and Advance Position options, you can make sure that the text will be printed in the correct position.

Filling In the Invoice

Now that the customer number has been added, let's fill in the invoice information, then send the document on your screen to the printer.

1 Press **Home,Home,**↑ to place the cursor on the empty line below the Bill To comment.

2 Type the following name and address for the Bill To information, pressing **Enter** after each line:

Robin Pierce
InterChange, Inc.
544 Westminster Circle NW
Atlanta, GA 30327

3 Press **Down Arrow** (↓) to place the cursor on the empty line below the Ship To comment.

Notice the warning in the comment box about Enter.

```
┌─────────────────────────────────────────────────────────────────┐
│ Bill To                                                           │
│ Type the name and address of the person or company being billed for the │
│ merchandise.                                                      │
└─────────────────────────────────────────────────────────────────┘
Robin Pierce
InterChange, Inc.
544 Westminster Circle NW
Atlanta, GA 30327

┌─────────────────────────────────────────────────────────────────┐
│ Ship To                                                           │
│ Type the name and address of the person or company to whom the merchandise │
│ should be shipped.                                                │
│ WARNING!  Do not press Enter after typing a line.  Press Down Arrow (↓) to │
│ move to the empty lines provided.                                 │
└─────────────────────────────────────────────────────────────────┘
_

C:\WP51\LEARN\INVOICE.WKB                    Doc 1 Pg 1 Ln 3" Pos 4.4"
```

Because the Bill To address is printed at the left margin, only one set of Advance codes is needed to print the address in the correct place. However, because the Ship To address is in the middle of the page, each line of the Ship To address in INVOICE.WKB starts with a set of Advance codes.

The Advance codes need to stay at the beginning of each line. If you press Enter when typing a line in the Ship To address, the Advance codes are pushed below the text you type (instead of staying at the beginning of the text), and the address will not print properly on the invoice form.

4 Type the following address in the empty lines below the Ship To comment, using **Down Arrow** (↓) to move from line to line:

InterChange, Inc.
Old Dominion Drive
Atlanta, GA 30338

If you press Enter while typing, simply press Backspace, then press Down Arrow to move to the next empty line.

5 Press **Down Arrow** twice to place the cursor on the empty line below the Date comment, then type **09/25/1990** for the date.

If you want the current date printed on a form, you can use the Date Code feature (Shift-F5,2) to insert a code in the form you fill in that automatically prints the current date.

6 Press **Down Arrow** to place the cursor on the empty line below the Terms comment, then type **90 days** for the payment terms.

7 Press **Down Arrow** to place the cursor on the empty line below the Invoice No. comment.

8 Type the following invoice, order, and customer numbers, pressing **Down Arrow** after each number:

A105678 (invoice number)
00254890 (order number)
P135009 (customer number)

Typing the Ordered Merchandise

The final information to be filled out is the merchandise ordered.

1 Press **Down Arrow** (↓) five times to display the merchandise ordered table.

You should see two comments on your screen followed by a table that looks similar to the one in the invoice form.

Ⓐ TABLE COMMENT
Ⓑ TITLES COMMENT
Ⓒ MERCHANDISE ORDERED TABLE

Ⓐ **Merchandise Ordered Table**
Press **Tab** after typing each item in a line (**Shift-Tab** takes you back one item). You do not need to press **Enter** when you reach the end of a line.

When you finish, calculate the amounts, delete any empty rows, then remove all the borders in the table.

Ⓑ | Stock No. | Description | Quantity | Unit Price | Amount |

Ⓒ

C:\WP51\LEARN\INVOICE.WKB   Cell A5 Doc 1 Pg 1 Ln 6.03" Pos 1.1"

The table has been created with the Tables feature in WordPerfect and lets you quickly enter the information for the ordered merchandise, then calculate the prices in the Amounts column.

Tables are introduced in lessons 34 and 35 of the workbook. You can also turn to the various Table *headings in the* WordPerfect Reference Manual *for additional details on the Table feature.*

The first comment gives you special instructions for typing information in a table; the second comment places titles above the table columns.

Each item you type in the table is placed in a cell. When you are in the table, a cell message is added to the status line to let you know in which cell the cursor is currently located.

2 Press **Up Arrow** (↑) until you see "Cell A1" displayed on the status line.

3 Type **09133** for the stock number, then press **Tab** to move the cursor to the Description column.

4 Type **Spring Music Box** for the description, then press **Tab** to move the cursor to the Quantity column.

5 Type **10** for the quantity, then press **Tab** to move the cursor to the Unit Price column.

6 Type **15.00** for the unit price, then press **Tab** to move the cursor to the Amount column.

A formula is displayed on the status line (C1*D1) to let you know that you can calculate the amount instead of typing it in the cell.

7 Press **Tab** to move the cursor to the beginning of the second line (row) in the table (under the Stock No. column title).

Now that you have been introduced to typing information in a table, let's finish filling in the invoice by adding two more items to the table.

8 Using steps 3 through 7 as a guide, type the following information in the table:

09187 (stock no.)
Goatherd Music Box (description)
2 (quantity)
30.00 (unit price)

09114 (stock no.)
Grandfather Clock (description)
3 (quantity)
550.00 (unit price)

Calculating the Amounts

Now that you have finished typing the ordered merchandise, the amounts can be calculated by using the Table Edit menu.

1 Make sure the cursor is in the table (check for the Cell message on the status line), then press **Columns/Table** (Alt-F7).

▭ *Select **Tables** from the Layout menu, then select **Edit**.*

2 Select **M**ath (5), then select **C**alculate (1).

▭ *While you are in the Table Editor, you can select menu options with the mouse by placing the mouse pointer on the option and clicking the left button.*

Each time you select the Calculate option, WordPerfect calculates all the formulas in the table. Because the formulas for the empty rows were also calculated, zeros are displayed in the Amount column for the rows.

Once you fill in the merchandise, you can delete the empty rows by using the Delete key.

3 Press **Home,Home,↑** to move the cursor to cell A1 of the table, then press **Down Arrow** (↓) three times to place the cursor in cell A4.

4 Press **Delete** (Del), select **R**ows (1), then enter **3** to delete the three empty rows.

Removing the Table Borders

Your finished table should now look like the one below.

```
┌──────────────────────────────────────────────────────────┐
│ When you finish, calculate the amounts, delete any empty rows, │
│ then remove all the borders in the table.                      │
└──────────────────────────────────────────────────────────┘

┌──────────┬───────────────────┬──────────┬────────────┬──────────┐
│ Stock No. │   Description     │ Quantity │ Unit Price │ Amount   │
├──────────┼───────────────────┼──────────┼────────────┼──────────┤
│ 09133    │ Spring Music Box  │    10    │   15.00    │  150.00  │
│ 09187    │ Goatherd Music Box│     2    │   30.00    │   60.00  │
│ 09114    │ Grandfather Clock │     3    │  550.00    │ 1,650.00 │
└──────────┴───────────────────┴──────────┴────────────┴──────────┘

=C3*D3                              Cell E3 Doc 1 Pg 1 Ln 5.5" Pos 7.4"

Ctrl-Arrows Column Widths; Ins Insert; Del Delete; Move Move/Copy;
1 Size; 2 Format; 3 Lines; 4 Header; 5 Math; 6 Options; 7 Join; 8 Split: 0
```

The lines in the table have been provided to help you see a table on the screen that looks like the one on the pre-printed invoice.

However, because the invoice form already has pre-printed lines, you need to remove the lines from the table on your screen or they will be printed on the invoice form.

1 Press **Home,Home,**↑ to place the cursor in cell A1.

2 Press **Block** (Alt-F4), then press **Home,Home,**↓ to highlight all the cells in the table.

3 Select **Lines** (3), select **All** (7), then select **None** (1) to remove all the lines from the table.

4 Press **Exit** (F7) to return to the normal editing screen.

Printing the Invoice Information

Now that you have filled in the invoice information, let's display the page in the View Document screen.

1 Press **Print** (Shift-F7), select **View** Document (6), then select Full Page (3).

⌨ *Select Print from the File menu.*

Each item of information is placed on the page exactly where it should be printed on the actual invoice form.

1 100%   2 200%   3 Full Page   4 Facing Pages: 3   Doc 1 Pg 1

2 Press **Exit** (F7) to return to the editing screen.

At this point, you may want to save the invoice and try printing it on your own printer.

3 Press **Save** (F10), then enter invoice for the filename.

⬛ *Select Save from the File menu.*

4 Press **Print** (Shift-F7).

⬛ *Select Print from the File menu.*

5 Choose Select Printer, highlight the name of your printer, then press **Enter** to select the printer.

6 Select **F**ull Document (1) to send the invoice information to the printer.

7 Press **Exit**, then type **n** twice to clear the screen.

You need to select a smaller font if some of the lines overlap when printing the invoice information. However, each item should print in the place indicated by the Advance codes no matter which font you use to print the information.

Merging to a Form

The Merge feature can be used to help print out multiple invoices, billings, receipts, checks, and other pre-printed forms.

For example, if the information for HALVA International customers were kept in a secondary merge file, a customer record might include the following information for printing invoice forms:

- Ship To address
- Bill To address
- Terms
- Customer Number

By placing {FIELD} codes in a document similar to the INVOICE file edited in this lesson, you could create a primary file that would retrieve the above information for each customer in the secondary file (instead of typing it in yourself).

A FIELD CODE

B SHIP TO ADDRESS

```
  Bill To
  Type the name and address of the person or company being billed for the
  merchandise.

{FIELD}1~
{FIELD}2~

  Ship To
  Type the name and address of the person or company to whom the merchandise
  should be shipped.

  WARNING!  Do not press Enter after typing a line.  Press Down Arrow (↓) to
  move to the empty lines provided.

{FIELD}3~
{FIELD}4~
{FIELD}5~
{FIELD}6~

  Date
C:\WP51\LEARN\INVOICE.PF                          Doc 1 Pg 1 Ln 1" Pos 1"
```

Notice that each line of the Ship To address has a different {FIELD} code. Because of the Advance codes at the beginning of each empty line in the INVOICE file, each line in the Ship To address needs to be placed in a different field of the secondary file so that the lines are merged individually.

B SHIP TO ADDRESS

```
Robin Pierce{END FIELD}
InterChange, Inc.
544 Westminster Circle NW
Atlanta, GA 30327{END FIELD}
Interchange, Inc.{END FIELD}
Flannery Building - Suite #3A{END FIELD}
Old Dominion Drive{END FIELD}
Atlanta, GA 30338{END FIELD}
90 days{END FIELD}
P135009{END FIELD}
Robin{END FIELD}
(404) 359-2828{END FIELD}
{END RECORD}
===================================================================
Jayna Wilder-Smith{END FIELD}
8611 Market St.
San Francisco, CA 94102{END FIELD}
Hildebrant/Meyers Corp.{END FIELD}
P.O. Box 188-125{END FIELD}
Oakland, CA 94104{END FIELD}
{END FIELD}
90 days{END FIELD}
P245109{END FIELD}
Jayna{END FIELD}
Field: 1                                          Doc 1 Pg 1 Ln 1" Pos 1"
```

During the merge, you could have WordPerfect insert the current date by using the {DATE} merge command, then pause the merge by using the {INPUT}~ command to let you type the invoice number, the order number, and the merchandise ordered from the keyboard.

▲ {DATE} COMMAND
▲ {INPUT}~ COMMAND

```
   ┌─────────────────────────────────────────────────────────────────────┐
   │ Date                                                                  │
   │ The date the invoice is printed.                                      │
   └─────────────────────────────────────────────────────────────────────┘
▷{DATE}_

   ┌─────────────────────────────────────────────────────────────────────┐
   │ Terms                                                                 │
   │ One of the following terms should be typed on the line:               │
   │        90 days                                                        │
   │        Monthly Payments                                               │
   │        Cash Discount (15%)                                            │
   └─────────────────────────────────────────────────────────────────────┘
   {FIELD}7~

   ┌─────────────────────────────────────────────────────────────────────┐
   │ Invoice No.                                                           │
   └─────────────────────────────────────────────────────────────────────┘
▷{INPUT}~

   ┌─────────────────────────────────────────────────────────────────────┐
   │ Order No.                                                             │
   └─────────────────────────────────────────────────────────────────────┘
   {INPUT}~
   C:\WP51\LEARN\INVOICE.WKB                      Doc 1 Pg 1 Ln 4.17" Pos 1.6"
```

The {INPUT}~ command for the table should be inserted at the end of the table to have WordPerfect completely create the table before pausing the merge. You can then move back up into the table to enter the information. When you finish, press F9 to continue the merge.

▲ {INPUT}~ COMMAND

```
   ┌─────────────────────────────────────────────────────────────────────┐
   │ When you finish, calculate the amounts, delete any empty rows,        │
   │ then remove all the borders in the table.                             │
   └─────────────────────────────────────────────────────────────────────┘

   ┌──────────────┬──────────────┬──────────┬────────────┬──────────┐
   │ Stock No.    │ Description  │ Quantity │ Unit Price │ Amount   │
   ├──────────────┼──────────────┼──────────┼────────────┼──────────┤
   │              │              │          │            │          │
   │              │              │          │            │          │
   │              │              │          │            │          │
   │              │              │          │            │          │
   └──────────────┴──────────────┴──────────┴────────────┴──────────┘
▷{INPUT}~

   C:\WP51\LEARN\INVOICE.WKB                      Doc 1 Pg 1 Ln 6.53" Pos 1"
```

When the merge is completed, the empty rows in each merged table will need to be deleted, the table calculated (if there are any formulas), and any borders that you do not want printed will need to be set to "None."

You may want to create a macro that completes part or all of these tasks for each merged table. Turn to the Macros *headings in the* WordPerfect Reference Manual *for details on creating macros.*

Lessons 23, 24 and 25 in the workbook introduce you to the Merge feature and the Merge codes and commands described above. If you have questions about the Merge feature, you may want to try doing those lessons first, then turn to the *Merge* heading in the *WordPerfect Reference Manual* for additional details.

Lesson 31: Graphics

You have already been introduced to graphic lines and figures in lessons 14, 16, 17, and 22 in the workbook. In this lesson you are introduced to several ideas and techniques that can be very helpful when using the Graphics feature to format a document.

Creating a Character Box

When creating a graphics box, WordPerfect needs to know if you want the box anchored (attached) to a particular paragraph or page, or if you want the box treated like any other character in a line of text.

Let's retrieve a newsletter that has already been created, then add a graphics box that is anchored in a line like a normal character.

1 Press **Retrieve** (Shift-F10), then enter **newsltr.wkb** to retrieve a HALVA International newsletter.

⌨ *Select **R**etrieve from the **F**ile menu.*

2 Press **Print** (Shift-F7), select **V**iew Document (6), then select 100% (1).

⌨ *Select **P**rint from the **F**ile menu.*

If you do not have a graphics card installed in your computer, you will not be able to display any of the graphic images. However, if your printer can print graphics, you may want to complete the lesson, then send the newsletter to your printer to see the results.

The newsletter masthead (HALVA Herald) has already been formatted with horizontal lines, the volume number, and the date of publication, but could use a graphics image with the title.

3 Press **Exit** (F7) to return to the editing screen.

4 Press **Reveal Codes** (Alt-F3) to display the codes in the newsletter.

⌨ *Select **R**eveal Codes from the **E**dit menu.*

5 Press **Down Arrow** (↓) three times to move the cursor to the HALVA Herald line, then press **Home,←** to make sure the cursor is at the beginning of the line.

6 Press **Graphics** (Alt-F9), select **F**igure (1), then select **C**reate (1).

⌨ *Select **F**igure from the **G**raphics menu, then select **C**reate.*

7 Select Anchor **T**ype (4), then select **C**haracter (3).

The graphics box is currently set to vertically align the bottom border of the box with the bottom of the HALVA Herald title. Let's leave the vertical alignment set at "Bottom" and finish formatting the box.

8 Select **S**ize (7), then select Set **W**idth/Auto Height (1).

9 Enter **.4** to set a width of 4/10 of an inch for the box.

A set of parentheses around the word "high" lets you know that WordPerfect will automatically adjust the height so that the image keeps it original proportions.

A set of parentheses around the word "wide" also indicates that WordPerfect will adjust the width measurement for you.

The graphics box is currently set at .4" wide by .4" high. Watch what happens to the height as soon as you retrieve the graphics image.

10 Select **F**ilename (1), then enter **star-5.wpg** to retrieve the graphics image.

The width remains at .4" (the setting you entered), but the height has been adjusted to .296" for the star image.

11 Select **W**rap Text Around Box (8), then type **n** for No to make sure that the graphics box stays in the same line as the HALVA Herald title.

12 Press **Exit** to return to the editing screen.

13 Press **Print** (Shift-F7), then select View Document (6).

⌨ *Select **P**rint from the **F**ile menu.*

The bottom border of the star graphics box is lined up with the bottom of the HALVA Herald line.

Ⓐ BOTTOM BORDER

Ⓑ BOTTOM OF
TITLE LINE

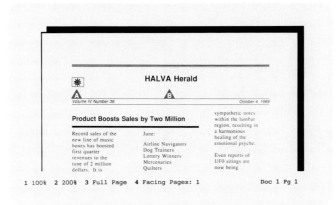

Changing the Box Style

Although the star is in the correct position, the single line border around the star is not needed in the masthead. Also, another graphics image might also look better than the star.

1 Press **Exit** (F7) to return to the editing screen.

The box type is currently set for Figure. However, you can select another type of box while in the Graphics Definition menu.

2 Press **Graphics** (Alt-F9), select **F**igure (1), select **E**dit (2), then enter **1** (one) to display the Graphics Definition menu for the star.

⊟ *Select **F**igure from the **G**raphics menu, select **E**dit, then enter **1**.*

The word "Figure" is displayed next to "Definition:" at the top of the menu to let you know the current box type.

3 Press **Graphics** (Alt-F9), then select **U**ser Box (4).

The words "User Box" now appear at the top of the menu. A User Box does not print any borders around the graphics image.

Before leaving the Graphics Definition menu, let's replace the star image with a butterfly.

4 Select Filename (1), enter **buttrfly.wpg** for the filename of the new image, then type **y** to replace the star with the butterfly.

5 Press **Exit** to return to the editing screen.

Copying a Graphics Image

Because the butterfly is at the left margin, it is the first "character" printed in the line. Let's add another butterfly to the end of the line, and use Flush Right to place it at the right margin.

1 Press **Block** (Alt-F4), then press **Left Arrow** (←) twice to highlight the butterfly graphics box.

2 Press **Move** (Ctrl-F4), select **B**lock (1), then select **C**opy (2).

3 Press **Home,**→ to move the cursor to the end of the line.

4 Press **Flush Right** (Alt-F6), then press **Enter** to retrieve the copy of the butterfly graphics box.

5 Press **Print** (Shift-F7), then select **V**iew Document (6).

⊟ *Select **P**rint from the **F**ile menu.*

Now there are two butterflies in the masthead. However, the butterfly on the right is displayed out in the right margin because WordPerfect is lining up the left border of the box with the right margin.

▲ RIGHT MARGIN

▲ LEFT BORDER OF BOX

HALVA Herald

Volume IV Number 36   October 4, 1989

Product Boosts Sales by Two Million

Record sales of the
new line of music
boxes has boosted
first quarter
revenues to the
tune of 2 million
dollars. It is

June:

Airline Navigators
Dog Trainers
Lottery Winners
Mercenaries
Quilters

sympathetic notes
within the lumbar
region, resulting in
a harmonious
healing of the
emotional psyche.

Even reports of
UFO sitings are
now being

1 100%   2 200%   3 Full Page   4 Facing Pages: 1   Doc 1 Pg 1

6 Press **Exit** (F7) to return to the editing screen.

7 Press **Home,**→ to move the cursor to the end of the HALVA Herald line, then press **Left Arrow** (←) to place the cursor on the [Usr Box:2;BUTTRFLY.WPG;] code.

8 Press **Format** (Shift-F8), select **O**ther (4), then select **A**dvance (1).

9 Select **L**eft (4), enter **.4** to move the graphics box to the left 4/10 of an inch, then press **Exit** (F7) to return to the editing screen.

10 Press **Print**, then select **V**iew Document.

⌨ Select **P**rint from the **F**ile menu.

The butterfly has moved to the left so that the right border of the box now lines up with the right margin.

11 Press **Exit** to return to the editing screen.

By using features like Flush Right and Advance, you can horizontally adjust the position of a character graphics box in a line.

Creating a Drop Cap

An article may sometimes start with the first character printed much larger than the rest of the article. The character is called a *drop cap*. You can quickly create a drop cap in WordPerfect by using a graphics box.

1 Press **Home,**← then press **Down Arrow** (↓) until the cursor is on the "R" in the first line of the article (Record sales of the...).

2 Press **Delete** (Del) to delete the R.

3 Press **Graphics** (Alt-F9), select **Figure** (1), then select **Create** (1).

⊞ *Select* **Figure** *from the Graphics menu, then select* **Create**.

4 Select **Horizontal Position** (6), then select **Left** (1) to have the "R" placed on the left side of the column.

5 Select **Edit** (9), press **Bold** (F6), then type **R** for the drop cap.

6 Press **Left Arrow** (←) twice to place the cursor on the [BOLD] code.

7 Press **Font** (Ctrl-F8), then select Base **Font** (4).

8 Press **Home,Home,**↓ then press **Up Arrow** (↑) to highlight the Roman 25pt font.

9 Press **Enter** to select the font.

10 Press **Exit** (F7) to return to the Graphics Definition menu.

Now that you have formatted the drop cap R in the graphics box, you can have WordPerfect automatically set the correct width and height for the box.

11 Select **Size** (7), then select **Auto Both** (4).

12 Press **Exit** to return to the editing screen.

13 Press **Print** (Shift-F7), then select **View** Document (6).

⊞ *Select* **Print** *from the* **File** *menu.*

The drop cap R is aligned to the left at the top of the paragraph (the correct position), but a single border is not necessary, and the space outside the border needs to be adjusted.

🅐 OUTSIDE BORDER SPACE

🅑 SINGLE LINE BORDER

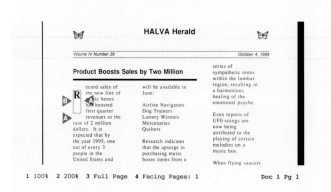

Changing the Figure Options

You could switch to a User Box to get rid of the border, but to change both the border style and the outside border space you need to use the Figure Options menu.

1 Press **Exit** (F7) to return to the editing screen.

2 Press **Left Arrow** (←) to place the cursor on the [Figure:1;;] graphics box code.

The Figure Option code needs to be inserted *before* the figure box for the changes to affect the box.

3 Press **Graphics** (Alt-F9), select **F**igure (1), then select **O**ptions (4).

*Select **F**igure from the **G**raphics menu, then select **O**ptions.*

4 Select **B**order Style (1), then type **1** (one) four times to set the border style to None for all four borders.

5 Select **O**utside Border Space (2), enter **0** (zero) for the left border, then enter **.1** for the right border.

6 Enter **0** (zero) for the top and bottom borders, then press **Exit** to return to the editing screen.

7 Press **Print** (Shift-F7), then select **V**iew Document (6).

*Select **P**rint from the **F**ile menu.*

The border is no longer displayed around the drop cap R, and the outside border space has been adjusted.

A TOP OF DROP CAP

B FIRST LINE OF PARAGRAPH

Creating a Callout

Not only does a graphics box let you place a border around the text, but you can print the box across two or more columns.

For example, a popular way to highlight text in an article is to print it in a larger font. This technique is know as a *callout* (or pull quote), and can be done by using a graphics box.

Let's use a Text Box style to create a callout that overlaps columns 2 and 3 for the article on the first page of the newsletter. The Text Box style is initially set for a thick top and bottom border (no side borders) and lightly shaded (10%)—an ideal combination for a callout.

1   Press **Exit** (F7) to return to the editing screen.

Because the callout will be printed across columns 2 and 3, the Page anchor type needs to be used.

2   Press **Home,Home,↑** to place the cursor at the top of the first page.

Important: *When creating a graphics box that is a page anchor type, it is a good idea to place the graphics box code at the top of the page, or the graphics box may print on the next page. If you want the graphics box to work correctly in text columns, the graphics box code needs to be placed after the Column Definition code.*

3   Press **Graphics** (Alt-F9), select Text **B**ox (3), then select **C**reate (1).

☐ *Select Text **B**ox from the **G**raphics menu, then select **C**reate.*

4   Select Anchor **T**ype (4), select **P**age (2), then press **Enter** to have the callout printed on the current page.

5   Select **V**ertical Position (5), select **S**et Position (5), then enter **6** to have the callout printed six inches down from the top edge of the page.

6   Select **H**orizontal Position (6), select **C**olumns (2), then enter **2-3** to have the callout printed across columns 2 and 3.

7   Select **F**ull (4) to have the callout printed from the left margin of column 2 to the right margin of column 3.

The width of the box is set for the full width of columns 2 and 3 (4.17"). The height will be adjusted by WordPerfect for the height of the text in the box.

8   Select **E**dit (9) to create the text for the callout.

9   Press **F**ont (Ctrl-F8), select Base **F**ont (4), highlight the Roman 15pt Italic font, then press **Enter** to select the font.

10   Press **Bold** (F6), then type the following sentence for the callout:

By the year 1995, one out of every three people in the United States and Canada will own a music box.

11   Press **Exit** twice to return to the normal editing screen.

12   Press **P**rint (Shift-F7), select **V**iew Document (6), then select **F**ull Page (3).

☐ *Select **P**rint from the **F**ile menu.*

The callout is displayed six inches down the page, and across columns 2 and 3. However, there is no top border and no shading for the graphics box (the initial settings for a Text Box).

13 Press **Exit** to return to the editing screen.

Changing the Text Box Options

Whenever a box style is not printing with the initial settings, then an option code has been placed in the document that is affecting the graphics box.

In this case, both the Product Boosts Sales by Two Million headline and the callout are in Text Boxes, with a Text Box Options code before the headline graphic box to eliminate the top border and shading.

Ⓐ TEXT BOX OPTIONS CODE
Ⓑ HEADLINE TEXT BOX
Ⓒ CALLOUT TEXT BOX

```
                              HALVA Herald

        Volume IV Number 36                    October 5, 1989

        ┌TXT 1───────────TXT 1─────────┐   tonal physicist,
          ecord sales of the    June:          claims that the
        C:\WP51\LEARN\NEWSLTR.WKB              Doc 1 Pg 1 Ln 1" Pos 1"

        [Header A:Every page; ... ][Footer A:Every page; ... ][Suppress:HA][Col Def:News
        paper;3;1",2.83";3.33",5.Ⓐ";5.67",7.5"][Txt Opt][Text Box:1;;][HLine:Full,Basel
        ine,6.5",0.028",100%][Text Box:2;;][HRt]  Ⓑ    Ⓒ
        [AdvDn:0.028"][HLine:Full,Baseline,6.5",0.014,100%][HRt]
        [Font:Helvetica 18pt][HRt]
        [Usr Box:1;BUTTRFLY.WPG;][CENTER][BOLD]HALVA Herald[bold][Flsh Rt][AdvLft:0.4"][
        Usr Box:2;BUTTRFLY.WPG;][HRt]
        [HRt]
        [Font:*Roman 12pt][HLine:Full,Baseline,6.5",0.013",100%][HRt]
        [Font:Helvetica 10pt Italic][AdvDn:0.028"]Volume IV Number 36[Flsh Rt][Date:3 1,

        Press Reveal Codes to restore screen
```

You can change the settings for the callout graphics box back to the initial settings by inserting another Text Box Options code.

1 Press **Left Arrow** (←) to place the cursor on the [Text Box:2;;] code.

2 Press **Graphics** (Alt-F9), select Text **B**ox (3), then select **O**ptions (4).

🖥 *Select Text **B**ox from the Graphics menu, then select **O**ptions.*

3 Select **B**order Style (1), then press **Enter** twice to keep the Left and Right borders set to None.

4 Select **T**hick (6) for the top border, then press **Enter** to keep the bottom border set at Thick.

5 Select **G**ray Shading (9), then enter **10** for ten percent gray shading in the box.

Besides setting a top border and shading, it would also be a good idea to set an equal amount of space above and below the box.

6 Select **O**utside Border Space (2), then press **Enter** twice to keep the Left and Right borders set to 0".

7 Enter **.1** for a 1/10 inch top border space, then press **Enter** to keep the bottom border space at 1/10 inch.

8 Press **Exit** (F7) to return to the editing screen.

9 Press **Print** (Shift-F7), then select **View Document** (6) to display the. results.

⌨ *Select **Print** from the **File** menu.*

A top border and gray shading are now included with the callout graphics box.

10 Press **Exit** to return to the editing screen.

Vertical Lines Between Columns

A popular way of visually separating columns on a page is to use vertical lines between the columns.

1 Press **Down Arrow** (↓) until the cursor is in the first column of the article (check for Col 1 on the status line).

By placing the cursor at the top of a column, you can quickly create a vertical line that prints between columns.

2 Press **Go To** (Ctrl-Home), then press **Up Arrow** (↑) to place the cursor at the top of the column.

3 Press **Graphics** (Alt-F9), select **Line** (5), then select **Vertical** (2).

⌨ *Select **Line** from the **Graphics** menu, then select **Create Vertical**.*

4 Select **Horizontal Position** (1), select **Between Columns** (3), then press **Enter** to have the line printed to the right of column 1.

5 Select **Vertical Position** (2), select **Set Position** (5), then press **Enter** to use the displayed setting.

Whenever you select the Set Position option for Vertical Position, WordPerfect displays the current position of the cursor from the top edge of the page. Because you placed the cursor at the top of the column, the displayed setting gives you the correct position for the beginning of the line.

As soon as you enter a vertical position for the beginning of the line, WordPerfect calculates the length of the line to the bottom of the column, then displays the length in the menu.

6 Press **Exit** (F7) to return to the editing screen.

Let's create another vertical line between columns 2 and 3. Because the third column is longer than column 2, you need to move the cursor to the top of column 3 before creating the line.

7 Press **Go To** (Ctrl-Home), press **Home**, then press **Right Arrow** (→) to place the cursor in column 3.

8 Press **Go To**, then press **Up Arrow** to place the cursor at the top of column 3.

9 Press **Graphics** (Alt-F9), select **Line** (5), then select **Vertical** (2).

⌨ *Select **Line** from the **Graphics** menu, then select **Create Vertical**.*

10 Select **H**orizontal Position (1), select **B**etween Columns (3), then enter **2** to have the line printed to the right of column 2.

11 Select **V**ertical Position (2), select **S**et Position (5), then press **Enter** to use the current vertical position of the cursor (top of the column).

12 Press **Exit** to return to the editing screen.

Let's check the vertical lines in the View Document screen to see if they are placed between the columns, and are the correct length.

13 Press **Print** (Shift-F7), then select **V**iew Document (6).

⌨ *Select **Print** from the **File** menu.*

Splitting a Vertical Line	Both lines are the correct length and between the columns. However, the line to the right of column 2 is printing on top of the callout graphics box.

▲ VERTICAL LINE

▲ GRAPHICS BOX

1 100%   2 200%   3 Full Page   4 Facing Pages: 3   Doc 1 Pg 1

To avoid printing a vertical line through a graphics box, you need to create *two* vertical lines—one above the box and one below the box.

1 Press **Exit** (F7) to return to the editing screen

By using the cursor and the Line number on the status line, you can find out what the vertical position needs to be for both lines, as well as the length of the line above the box. The length of the line below the box will be calculated for you by WordPerfect.

2 Write down the Line number (e.g. 2.32") from the status line for the position of the cursor at the top of the column.

3 Press **Down Arrow** (↓) until the cursor is in the line above Text Box 2, then write down the Line number (e.g., 5.62") on the status line.

4 Press **Down Arrow** to place the cursor in the line below Text Box 2, then write down the Line number (e.g., 7.37").

With these three measurements, you are ready to create the vertical lines above and below the graphics box.

Instead of deleting the current vertical line in column 3, let's edit the length of the line so that it prints above the box.

5 Press **Graphics** (Alt-F9), select **L**ine (5), then select **V**ertical (4) to edit the vertical line at the top of the third column.

⌨ *Select Line from the Graphics menu, then select Edit Vertical.*

The Horizontal Position (Column) and the Vertical Position (e.g., 2.32") are already set correctly. All you need to do is adjust the length of the line.

The length of the line above the box can be found by subtracting the position of the cursor at the top of the column (e.g., 2.32") from the position of the cursor in the line above the graphics box (e.g., 5.62").

6 Select **L**ength of Line (3), then enter **3.3** for the length of the line above the box (e.g., 5.62" − 2.32").

7 Press **Exit** to return to the editing screen.

The line below the box is easier to create because you do not need to calculate the length of the line.

8 Press **Graphics** (Alt-F9), select **L**ine (5), then select **V**ertical (2).

⌨ *Select Line from the Graphics menu, then select Create Vertical.*

9 Select **H**orizontal Position (1), select **B**etween Columns (3), then enter **2** to have the line below the box placed to the right of column 2.

10 Select **V**ertical Position (2), select **S**et Position (5), then enter **7.37** to have the line begin below the graphics box.

WordPerfect calculates the distance from the position you enter to the bottom of the column, then displays the correct line length in the menu.

11 Press **Exit** to return to the editing screen.

12 Press **Print** (Shift-F7), then select **V**iew Document (6) to see the lines above and below the graphics box.

⌨ *Select **P**rint from the **F**ile menu.*

The vertical lines are placed to the right of column 2, with the lines in the correct position.

△ LINE ABOVE GRAPHICS BOX

△ LINE BELOW GRAPHICS BOX

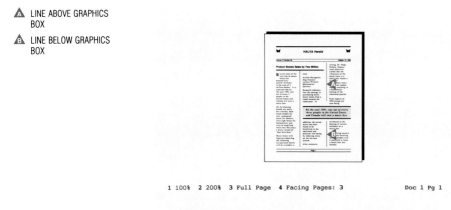

1 100% 2 200% 3 Full Page 4 Facing Pages: 3   Doc 1 Pg 1

Once you have created the vertical lines, you may want to adjust the length of one or both of the lines by editing the vertical lines (Alt-F9,5,4).

Overlaying Figures

Although you may not want a graphics line to print on top of a graphics box, there may be times when you want to print two or more graphics images on top of each other to create a single image on the page.

1 Press **Page Down** (PgDn) to display the second page of the newsletter.

A butterfly is being used to illustrate an article that includes a training class in Hawaii. However, an actual scene of a tropical beach with the butterfly would look much nicer on the page.

Because the butterfly is already in the document, all you need to do is retrieve the tropical beach into a second graphics box. For the two boxes (butterfly and beach) to print on top of one another, you need to make sure that the first box (in this case the butterfly) is set to No for wrapping text around the box.

If the setting is Yes for the first box, then the second box will print below the first box on the page.

2 Press **Exit** (F7) to return to the editing screen.

3 Press **Graphics** (Alt-F9), select **F**igure (1), select **E**dit (2), then enter **2** to edit the box with the butterfly.

⌨ *Select **F**igure from the **G**raphics menu, select **E**dit, then enter **2**.*

4 Select **W**rap Text Around Box (8), type **n** for No, then press **Exit** (F7) to return to the editing screen.

Instead of creating a new Figure graphics box for the tropical beach, let's copy the butterfly box, then replace the butterfly in the copied box with the tropical beach.

5 Press **Block** (Alt-F4), then press **Left Arrow** (←) twice to highlight the [Figure:2;BUTTRFLY.WPG;] code.

6 Press **Save** (F10), then press **Enter** to save a copy of the graphics box.

7 Press **Right Arrow** (→), press **Retrieve** (Shift-F10), then press **Enter** to retrieve the copy of the graphics box.

8 Press **Graphics**, select **F**igure, select **E**dit, then press **Enter** to edit figure 3 (the new graphics box).

⌨ *Select **F**igure from the **G**raphics menu, select **E**dit, then enter 3.*

Whenever you can't remember the name of a graphics file, you can use the List Files feature to retrieve the file.

9 Select **F**ilename (1), press **List** (F5), then type ***.wpg** and press **Enter** to list the WordPerfect graphics files in your LEARN directory.

The graphics files in your WordPerfect package (.WPG extension) were created using the DrawPerfect business presentation graphics package. DrawPerfect should be available from WordPerfect Corporation in the first quarter of 1990.

10 Place the cursor on the BKGRND-1.WPG file, select **R**etrieve (1), then type **y** to replace the butterfly with the BKGRND-1.WPG graphics image.

The text wrapping for the butterfly graphics box is set to No so that the graphics images will print on top of each other. However, to wrap the text in the newsletter article below the graphics boxes, the second graphics box needs to be set to Yes.

11 Select **W**rap Text Around Box (8), type **y** for Yes, then press **Exit** to return to the editing screen.

12 Press **Print** (Shift-F7), then select **V**iew Document (6) to display the graphics images.

⌨ *Select **P**rint from the **F**ile menu.*

Editing a Graphics Image

The tropical beach is printing on top of the butterfly. However, it looks like the butterfly is sinking into the ocean.

🔺 BUTTERFLY
🔺 TROPICAL BEACH

1 100%   2 200%   3 Full Page   4 Facing Pages: 3   Doc 1 Pg 2

What you need to do is change the size and position of the butterfly so that it looks like it is part of the scenery.

1 Press **Exit** (F7) to return to the editing screen.

2 Press **Graphics** (Alt-F9), select **F**igure (1), select **E**dit (2), then enter **2** to edit the butterfly graphics box.

⌨ *Select **F**igure from the **G**raphics menu, select **E**dit, then enter **2**.*

3 Select **E**dit (9) to edit the butterfly graphics image.

The butterfly is displayed on your screen with a row of editing keys and a menu of editing options at the bottom of the screen.

🔺 GRAPHICS IMAGE
🔺 EDITING KEYS
🔺 EDITING OPTIONS

The editing keys can be used to do the initial editing of the graphics image, while the menu options can be used to "fine tune" the editing changes.

If you want to change the graphics image back to its original size and proportion, you can press the Go To key (Ctrl-Home).

4   Press **Page Down** (PgDn) nine times to reduce the size (scale) of the butterfly.

5   Select **S**cale (2) to slightly decrease the size of the butterfly.

6   Enter **7** for Scale X (width), then enter **7** for Scale Y (height).

By entering a different number for each scale, you can stretch the image horizontally (scale X is greater than scale Y) or vertically (scale Y is greater than scale X).

7   Press **Up Arrow** (↑) eight times to move the butterfly near the top of the box.

8   Select **R**otate (3) from the editing options menu, then enter **45** to rotate the butterfly 45 degrees to the left.

A message is displayed that lets you create a mirror image (left is right and right is left) of the graphics figure.

9   Press **Enter** to keep the same image of the butterfly.

10   Press **Left Arrow** (←) eight times to move the butterfly to the upper left corner of the box.

11   Press **Exit** twice to return to the normal editing screen.

12   Press **Print** (Shift-F7), then select **V**iew Document (6) to see the results of the editing.

⌨ *Select Print from the File menu.*

The butterfly is displayed in the upper left corner of the picture, as if it were flying away from the palm tree.

At this point, you may want to return to the butterfly graphics box to experiment with editing the graphics image. When you finish, make sure that you are on page 2 of the newsletter in the View Document screen before continuing the lesson.

Retrieving a Table into a Box

Whenever you create a table with the Table feature in WordPerfect, you can include it in text columns by placing the table in a graphics box.

For example, let's add a table to the last article in the newsletter.

1   Press **Exit** (F7) to return to the editing screen.

2   Press **Page Down** (PgDn) to move to the top of page 3.

3 Press **Down Arrow** (↓) until the cursor is at the beginning of the third paragraph (The above table lists...).

4 Press **Graphics** (Alt-F9), select **F**igure (1), then select **C**reate (1).

⊟ Select **Figure** from the **Graphics** menu, then select **Create**.

5 Select **F**ilename (1), then enter **table.wkb** for the name of the table.

6 Select **H**orizontal Position (6), then select **F**ull (4).

7 Press **Exit** to return to the editing screen.

8 Press **Print** (Shift-F7), then select **V**iew Document (6).

⊟ Select **Print** from the **File** menu.

Creating a Drop Shadow

The table fits inside the graphics box, but it could be shifted to the right to center it horizontally. A drop shadow could also be added to "lift" the box off the page.

1 Press **Exit** (F7) to return to the editing screen.

2 Press **Left Arrow** (←) to place the cursor on the [Figure:4;TABLE.WKB] code.

3 Press **Graphics** (Alt-F9), select **F**igure (1), then select **O**ptions (4).

⊟ Select **Figure** from the **Graphics** menu, then select **Options**.

4 Select **I**nside Border Space (3), enter **.15** for the left border, then press **Enter** three times to leave the other borders set at zero (0).

Whenever you have a border style selected for all four borders, you can create a drop shadow for a graphics box by selecting a Thick or Extra Thick style for any two sides that make a corner of the box.

5 Select **B**order Style (1), then press **Enter** to leave the left border style set at Single.

6 Select **E**xtra Thick (7) for the right border, press **Enter** for the top border, then select **E**xtra Thick for the bottom border.

7 Press **Exit** to return to the editing screen.

8 Press **Print** (Shift-F7), then select **V**iew Document (6).

⊟ Select **Print** from the **File** menu.

The table is now horizontally centered in the graphics box, with a drop shadow that "lifts" the box off the page.

1 100%   2 200%   3 Full Page   4 Facing Pages: 3   Doc 1 Pg 3

9 Press **Exit** to return to the editing screen.

Saving and Printing the Newsletter

Before finishing the lesson, you may want to save the formatted newsletter as a sample document to follow the next time you want to create graphic lines or boxes.

1 Press **Reveal Codes** (Alt-F3) to display the normal editing screen.

🖳 Select **R**eveal Codes from the **E**dit menu.

2 Press **Save** (F10), then enter **newsltr** for the name of the formatted document.

If you want to print the newsletter, you will need to select your own printer. However, after selecting your printer, you will probably need to make several adjustments to the newsletter (such as selecting different fonts) before it looks like the one you formatted with the Workbook Printer.

3 When you finish, press **Exit** (F7), then type **n** twice to clear the screen.

For additional details about the Graphics feature, turn to the various Graphics *headings in the* WordPerfect Reference Manual.

Lesson 32: Sorting Records

You can use the Sort feature to sort lines, paragraphs, or merge records. You have already been introduced to sorting lines in lesson 10. In this lesson, you are given an overview of the Sort feature by sorting (and selecting) records in a secondary merge file.

For additional details on the Sort feature, turn to the various Sort *headings in the* WordPerfect Reference Manual.

Sorting Records by ZIP Code

Merged documents are created in the same order as the records in the secondary file. But what if you want to change the order in which the documents are merged?

For example, when mailing hundreds of letters at a time, the post office normally offers a discount bulk rate if the letters are pre-sorted by ZIP Code.

1   Press **Retrieve** (Shift-F10), then enter **customer.wkb** to display the customer records.

⊟ *Select Retrieve from the File menu.*

2   Press **Page Down** (PgDn) several times to check the ZIP Codes in the customer list.

As you can immediately see, the records are *not* listed by ZIP Code. In fact, they seem to have been entered randomly, instead of in any particular order.

By using the Sort feature, you can list the records by ZIP Code, to take advantage of the bulk rate discount.

3   Press **Home,Home,↑** to move the cursor to the beginning of the secondary file.

4   Press **Merge/Sort** (Ctrl-F9), then select **S**ort (2).

⊟ *Select Sort from the Tools menu.*

A message at the bottom of the screen requests the name of the input file to sort, with the word "(Screen)" following the request.

WordPerfect is asking for the name of the file on disk you would like to sort. However, because the records you want sorted are already retrieved, you can use the name "(Screen)" to tell WordPerfect that the file is on the screen.

5   Press **Enter** to use the "(Screen)" name.

A second message requests an output file for the sorted document. If you press Enter to use the "(Screen)" name, WordPerfect will replace the records currently on the screen with the sorted records. Entering a filename leaves the records on the screen undisturbed, and saves the sorted records on disk.

6 Press **Enter** to have WordPerfect save the sorted records to the screen.

Selecting a Sort Type

The screen is now divided in half with the records displayed in the top half of the screen, and the Sort menu displayed in a window in the bottom half of the screen.

◬ MERGE RECORDS
◬ MENU TITLE
◬ SORT MENU

```
▷Robin Pierce{END FIELD}
 InterChange, Inc.
 544 Westminster Circle NW
 Atlanta, GA 30327{END FIELD}
 Robin{END FIELD}
 (404) 359-2828{END FIELD}
 {END RECORD}
 ==================================================
▷Jayna Wilder-Smith{END FIELD}
 8611 Market St.
                              Doc 2 Pg 1 Ln 1" Pos 1"
[    ▲    ▲    ▲    ▲    ▲    ▲    ▲    ▲    )  ▲    ▲
--------------------------▷ Sort by Line --------------------------
Key Typ Field Word    Key Typ Field Word    Key Typ Field Word
 1   a    1    1        2                      3
 4                      5                      6
 7                      8                      9
Select

Action                Order                 Type
Sort                  Ascending             Line sort
▷1 Perform Action; 2 View; 3 Keys; 4 Select; 5 Action; 6 Order; 7 Type: 0
```

Sort is quite flexible and includes several options for sorting *and* selecting records. The title at the top of the menu lets you know the type of sorting that WordPerfect will be doing.

1 Select **T**ype (7), then select **M**erge (1) to indicate that you want to sort a secondary merge file.

Creating a Key

Directly below the title are the keys (up to 9) that you can use for sorting the records. A *key* identifies the information by which you want the records sorted.

For example, to sort the records by ZIP Code, you need to create a key that tells WordPerfect where the ZIP Code is located in each record. A key for a secondary merge file includes the type, field, line, and word.

1 Select **K**eys (3) to create a key for sorting the records by ZIP Code.

The cursor moves up to the "a" in the first key under the Type title. A message at the bottom of the screen indicates that you can type "a" or "n" to select an alphanumeric or numeric sort.

The only time you need to do a numeric sort is if you are sorting numbers of unequal lengths such as dates (e.g., 12/1/89, 5/6/89). Most of the time, you will be doing an alphanumeric sort.

2 Press **Right Arrow** (→) to leave the "a" and move to the field number.

Because the fields in each record are counted from top to bottom, the ZIP Code is at the end of the second field.

```
Robin Pierce{END FIELD}
InterChange, Inc.
544 Westminster Circle NW
Atlanta, GA 30327{END FIELD}
Robin{END FIELD}
(404) 359-2828{END FIELD}
{END RECORD}
=====================================================================
Jayna Wilder-Smith{END FIELD}
8611 Market St.
                                          Doc 2 Pg 1 Ln 1" Pos 1"
[     ▲    ▲    ▲    ▲    ▲    ▲    ▲    ▲    ▲    ▲    )    ▲    ▲    ]
------------------------- Sort Secondary Merge File -------------------------

Key Typ Field Line Word     Key Typ Field Line Word     Key Typ Field Line Word
 1   a    1     1    1        2                           3
 4        ▲                   5                           6
 7                            8                           9
Select


Action                   Order                    Type
Sort                     Ascending                Merge sort

Type: a = Alphanumeric; n = Numeric;  Use arrows;  Press Exit when done
```

3 Type **2** for the field number, then press **Right Arrow** to move to the line number.

Using Negative Numbers

A field can have several lines, so WordPerfect needs to know in which line of the field the ZIP Code is located. The lines in a record are also counted from top to bottom. Robin Pierce's address has three lines, but do all the addresses have three lines?

1 Press **Exit** (F7) to leave the key for a moment.

2 Select **View** (2), press **Home,↓** then press **Down Arrow** (↓) to display Jayna Wilder-Smith's entire address on the screen.

While Robin's address is three lines long, Jayna's address is only two lines long.

A THREE LINES
B TWO LINES

```
    InterChange, Inc.
    544 Westminster Circle NW
A  Atlanta, GA 30327{END FIELD}
    Robin{END FIELD}
    (404) 359-2828{END FIELD}
    {END RECORD}
    ============================================================
    Jayna Wilder-Smith{END FIELD}
    8611 Market St.
B  San Francisco, CA 94102{END FIELD}
    View:  Press Exit when done                Doc 2 Pg 2 Ln 1.33" Pos 1"
    ▲   ▲   ▲   ▲   ▲   ▲   ▲   ▲   ▲   ▲   ▲  }  ▲   ▲   ▲
    -------------------- Sort Secondary Merge File --------------------

    Key Typ Field Line Word    Key Typ Field Line Word    Key Typ Field Line Word
     1   a    2    1    1        2                          3
     4                           5                          6
     7                           8                          9
    Select


    Action                     Order                      Type
    Sort                       Ascending                  Merge sort

      1 Perform Action; 2 View; 3 Keys; 4 Select; 5 Action; 6 Order; 7 Type: 2
```

If you use 3 for the line number in the key, then WordPerfect will not find the ZIP Code in line 2 of Jayna's record. However, if you use 2 for the line number, then WordPerfect will not find the ZIP Code in Robin's record.

Fortunately, Sort provides a way of solving the problem by letting you use *negative* numbers. If you count the lines from the top of the field to the bottom, then the line number for the ZIP Code will vary. However, if you count the lines from *bottom to top*, then the ZIP Code will always be in the first line of the field.

By using a negative sign, you can tell WordPerfect to count the lines in the opposite direction (bottom to top), and always make sure that WordPerfect is looking in the correct line for the ZIP Code.

3 Press **Exit** to return to the Sort menu.

4 Select **K**eys (3) to return to the first key.

5 Press **Right Arrow** (→) twice to move to the line number, then type **-1** to indicate the first line from the bottom of the field.

Now that you've identified the correct line, the final step is to identify which word in the line is the ZIP Code.

Robin's address (city, state and ZIP Code) is three words long, while Jayna's address is four words long. If you try using a 3 or 4 to identify the word in the line, then the ZIP Code will be sorted on some records and missed on others.

The problem can be solved by also using a negative number to identify the ZIP Code.

6 Press **Right Arrow**, then type **-1** to have WordPerfect sort on the first word from the *end* of the line (the ZIP Code).

By using a negative sign, you can have WordPerfect count the words from the end of the line instead of the beginning of the line.

7 Press **Exit** to save the key and display the Sort menu.

Performing the Sort

With the position of the ZIP Code identified for each record, WordPerfect can now sort the records by ZIP Code.

1 Select **P**erform Action (1) to begin the sort.

A counter at the bottom of the screen keeps you updated on the progress of the sort. When sorting is completed, WordPerfect replaces the original records on your screen with those that are sorted by ZIP Code.

```
Ted Mortinthal{END FIELD}
{END FIELD}
Ted{END FIELD}
(301) 522-8700{END FIELD}
{END RECORD}
=================================================================
Kathleen O'Hara{END FIELD}
678 Forestvale Road
Boston, MA 02136{END FIELD}
Kathy{END FIELD}
(617) 789-2027{END FIELD}
{END RECORD}
=================================================================
Joseph Corrales, Jr.{END FIELD}
Kensington House, #312
176 West 45th
Manhattan, NY 10036{END FIELD}
Joe{END FIELD}
(212) 687-1203{END FIELD}
{END RECORD}
=================================================================
Rosanne Jacobsen{END FIELD}
555 Lafayette Ave.
Brooklyn, NY 11205{END FIELD}
C:\CUSTOMER.WKB                              Doc 1 Pg 1 Ln 1" Pos 1"
```

Notice that WordPerfect placed Ted Mortinthal's record at the top of the secondary file. Any records that WordPerfect cannot sort because the field is empty are placed at the top of the file. In this case, Ted's record is missing an address.

Sorting on a field is a good way of finding out which records in a secondary file are missing information in that field.

Sorting to a File

Let's try sorting the records again, but this time save the sorted records to a file on disk.

1 Press **Merge/Sort** (Ctrl-F9), then select **S**ort (2).

⌨ *Select Sort from the Tools menu.*

2 Press **Enter** to sort the records on the screen, then enter **customer.zip** for the output filename.

When the Sort menu is displayed, notice that the settings have not changed for the type of sort or the key being used to sort the record. This feature makes it convenient to sort several files using the same key.

Changing the Sort Order

Another Sort feature lets you change the order in which the records are sorted.

1 Select **O**rder (6) from the menu at the bottom of the screen.

Notice that you can sort the records in ascending or descending order.

A ASCENDING ORDER

B DESCENDING ORDER

```
Ted Mortinthal{END FIELD}
{END FIELD}
Ted{END FIELD}
(301) 522-8700{END FIELD}
{END RECORD}
=====================================================================
Kathleen O'Hara{END FIELD}
678 Forestvale Road
Boston, MA 02136{END FIELD}
Kathy{END FIELD}
                                              Doc 2 Pg 1 Ln 1" Pos 1"
[    ▲    ▲    ▲    ▲    ▲    ▲    ▲    ▲    ▲    ▲    }  ▲    ▲    ]
----------------------- Sort Secondary Merge File -----------------------
Key Typ Field Line Word    Key Typ Field Line Word    Key Typ Field Line Word
 1   a    2    -1    -1      2                           3
 4                           5                           6
 7                           8                           9
Select


Action                     Order                      Type
Sort        ▲         ▲     Ascending                  Merge sort
            A         B
Order: 1 Ascending; 2 Descending: 0
```

Ascending means that words are sorted from A to Z, while numbers are sorted from lowest to highest. *Descending* means that words are sorted from Z to A, while numbers are sorted from highest to lowest.

The records in the customer list were sorted in an ascending order, which means that the record with the lowest ZIP Code number was placed at the top of the list (Kathleen O'Hara), while the record with the highest ZIP Code number was placed at the bottom of the list (Samuel A. Roberts).

Let's sort the records in descending order before saving them in the customer file on disk.

2 Select **D**escending (2), then select **P**erform Action (1) to begin sorting the records.

3 Press **Switch** (Shift-F3) to display the document 2 editing screen.

⌨ *Select Switch Document from the Edit menu.*

4 Press **Retrieve** (Shift-F10) and enter **customer.zip** to retrieve the sorted records.

⌨ *Select Retrieve from the File menu.*

As you can see, the first record is Samuel A. Roberts, while the rest of the list is in descending ZIP Code order.

Merging the Letters

Let's clear both editing screens and try merging a letter with the sorted secondary file.

1 Press **Exit** (F7), type **n**, then type **y** to exit the document 2 editing screen.

2 Press **Exit** and type **n** twice to clear the document 1 editing screen.

3 Press **Merge/Sort** (Ctrl-F9), then select **Merge** (1).

⌨ *Select Merge from the Tools menu.*

4 Enter **stores.wkb** for the primary file, then enter **customer.zip** for the secondary file.

5 When the merge is completed, press **Home,Home,↑** to move the cursor to the beginning of the first letter.

The first record in the secondary file (Samuel A. Roberts) should be the first letter in the merged document.

6 Press **Exit** and type **n** twice to clear the document screen.

Sorting by Name

Another common way of sorting records is by last name. However, in case there is more than one person with the same last name, you need to create two keys.

1 Press **Merge/Sort** (Ctrl-F9), then select **Sort** (2).

⌨ *Select Sort from the Tools menu.*

2 Enter **customer.zip** for the file you want sorted, then press **Enter** to have the records sorted to the screen.

3 Select **Keys** (3), then type the following for the first key (key 1):

a 1 1 -1

The first key tells WordPerfect to sort the records by the last name, which is the first word from the right (-1) in the first line (1) of the first field (1). Like the ZIP Code sort, you needed to use a negative number because some customers have a first and last name only, while others include a middle name or initial.

Because there may be more than one customer with the same last name, you also need to tell WordPerfect to sort by first name. You can do this by creating a second key.

4 Press **Right Arrow** (→) to move to the second key (key 2), then press **Right Arrow** again to fill in the key with "a 1 1 1".

After sorting the records by last name (key 1), WordPerfect makes a second pass through the records. Any records with identical last names will then be sorted by first name (key 2).

5 Press **Exit** (F7) to save the two keys.

6 Select **O**rder (6), then select **A**scending (1) to have the records sorted alphabetically from A to Z.

7 Select **P**erform Action (1) to begin sorting the records.

When the sorting is completed, the records are displayed on your screen.

Notice that the record for Joseph Corrales, Jr. has been sorted before the record for Rosanne Jacobsen. Normally, WordPerfect would have seen "Jr." as the last name, and sorted "Corrales, Jr." *after* "Jacobsen" in the list.

However, a special Hard Space (Home-Space Bar) has been placed between Corrales and Jr. to have WordPerfect treat both as one word. The Hard Space can be seen in Reveal Codes as a space between two brackets.

8 Press **Reveal Codes** (Alt-F3) to display the codes in the secondary file.

⌨ *Select **R**eveal Codes from the **E**dit menu.*

▲ HARD SPACE

```
Joseph Corrales, Jr.{END FIELD}
Kensington House, #312
176 West 45th
Manhattan, NY 10036{END FIELD}
Joe{END FIELD}
(212) 687-1203{END FIELD}
{END RECORD}
==================================================================
Rosanne Jacobsen{END FIELD}
555 Lafayette Ave.
Brooklyn, NY 11205{END FIELD}
                                          Doc 1 Pg 1 Ln 1" Pos 1"
[      ]
Joseph Corrales,[ ]Jr.[Mrg:END FIELD][HRt]
Kensington House, #312[HRt]
176 West 45th[HRt]
Manhattan, NY 10036[Mrg:END FIELD][HRt]
Joe[Mrg:END FIELD][HRt]
(212) 687[-]1203[Mrg:END FIELD][HRt]
[Mrg:END RECORD][HPg]
Rosanne Jacobsen[Mrg:END FIELD][HRt]
555 Lafayette Ave.[HRt]
Brooklyn, NY 11205[Mrg:END FIELD][HRt]

Press Reveal Codes to restore screen
```

By using a Hard Space, WordPerfect sorts "Corrales, Jr." instead of "Jr." and the record is placed in the correct order in the customer list.

9 Press **Reveal Codes** to display the normal editing screen.

⌨ *Select **R**eveal Codes from the **E**dit menu.*

Selecting and Sorting   Now let's introduce the other half of the sorting process—selecting records.

Unless you indicate otherwise, WordPerfect sorts *all* the records in the secondary file each time you use Sort. However, there may be times when you only want to select part of the records from the file and then sort them.

For example, letters need to be sent immediately to customers in Boston and New York City, informing them of a January grand opening. The rest of the letters can be sent later in the month.

The records for the two cities need to be selected, then sorted by ZIP Code to get the bulk mailing discount.

1 Press **Merge/Sort** (Ctrl-F9), then select **S**ort (2).

⊞ *Select Sort from the **T**ools menu.*

2 Press **Enter** twice to select and sort the records already on the screen.

You can select records by defining a key (or keys), and then identifying a word for each key in a select statement. When you start the sort, WordPerfect compares the word you identified to the defined key and selects only those records that match.

Because WordPerfect selects the records first *then* sorts them, the key for the ZIP Code needs to come first, followed by any keys for selecting records by city.

3 Select **K**eys (3), then type **a 2 -1 -1** for key 1 (to sort the selected records by ZIP Code).

Although "Boston" is one word, "New York" is two words. Let's create one key for Boston, then create a second key for York (just in case another city starts with "New").

4 Press **Right Arrow** (→), then type **a 2 -1 1** for key 2 (to find the word "Boston").

5 Press **Right Arrow** (→), then type **a 2 -1 2** for key 3 (to find the word "York").

6 When you finish, press **Exit** (F7) to return to the Sort menu.

The first key identifies the ZIP Code in the address field, while the second and third keys identify the first and second words (the city name) in the last line of the address field.

Now that you have set up the keys for selecting and sorting the records, you are ready to create the select statement.

7 Type **4** for Select, then type the following Select statement:

   key2=boston + key3=york

Important: Make sure that there is a space before and after the plus sign (+).

The select statement tells WordPerfect to select all records that have either Boston in key 2 (the first word in the line), or York in key 3 (the second word in the line). The plus sign (+) represents the "or" in the statement.

All the available select symbols are displayed at the bottom of your screen. For a detailed explanation of the symbols, turn to the Sort, Select Records *heading in the* WordPerfect Reference Manual.

8 Press **Exit** (F7) to display the Sort menu.

The settings below the keys should now read "Select and Sort" for the Action, "Ascending" for the Order, and "Merge Sort" for the Type of Sort.

9 Select **P**erform Action (1) to begin selecting and sorting the records.

When the selecting and sorting is completed, you should have the records for Kathleen O'Hara and Joseph Corrales, Jr. on the screen, with the records sorted by ZIP Code (Kathleen's record before Joseph's).

10 Press **Exit** and type **n** twice to clear the screen.

Sorting and selecting increases the efficiency of mass mailings. After using Sort a few times, you'll begin to see a variety of ways in which sorting can help you at the office or at home.

Lesson 33: Styles

A Style feature is included in WordPerfect that can help you automate the process of formatting a document. If you need to format the same text (headings, lesson steps, lists) several times in the same document, or need to use the same formats for several documents, then you may want to try creating styles to make formatting quicker and more dependable.

In this lesson, you are introduced to the Style feature by creating and editing three styles for a newsletter.

Creating a Paired Style

Whenever a document such as a newsletter or report is first created, the formatting is usually in a draft form, with plenty of space between lines for editing comments. After the editing is completed, the document is ready for its final formatting.

Let's retrieve three newsletter articles, then create three styles for the draft of the newsletter, one for the article headings, one for a masthead (the title of the newsletter), and one for the entire newsletter.

1 Press **Retrieve** (Shift-F10), then enter **newstext.wkb** to retrieve the newsletter.

⌨ *Select **Retrieve** from the **File** menu.*

Let's begin by creating a style that underlines the article headings.

2 Press **Style** (Alt-F8) to display a style list (currently empty).

⌨ *Select **Styles** from the **Layout** menu.*

If you have used Setup to indicate a Style Library Filename, then a list of styles will be retrieved and displayed in your screen. Use the Delete (5) and Definition Only (3) options to delete the styles before continuing the lesson.

3 Select **Create** (3) from the menu at the bottom of the screen to add a style to the list.

A Style Edit menu is displayed on the screen that includes options for entering a style name, type, description, and the actual formatting codes you want included in the style.

```
Styles: Edit
      1 - Name
      2 - Type              Paired
      3 - Description
      4 - Codes
      5 - Enter             HRt




Selection: 0
```

For details on the Enter option, turn to the Style, Create *heading in the* WordPerfect Reference Manual.

4   Select **N**ame (1), then enter **Headings** for the name of the style.

5   Select **D**escription (3), then enter **Underlined Heading** to describe the style.

The Type option lets you select from an open or paired style. The open type (like a Margin setting) inserts a single code into the document. The formats in the open style code affect all the text in the document from the style code forward through the document.

The paired type (like Bold and Underline) inserts an on and off code, and can be used to format part of the text without affecting the text before or after the on and off codes.

A third type, Outline, is introduced in lesson 18 of the workbook.

Because the default setting for Type is "Paired," all you need to do is insert the Underline codes into the style.

6   Select **C**odes (4) to insert the formatting codes for the style.

A Style Editor is displayed with Reveal Codes on (to let you see the formatting codes you insert), and a comment on the screen.

```
 ▷ ┌──────────────────────────────────────────────────────────────┐
   │ Place Style On Codes above, and Style Off Codes below.        │
   └──────────────────────────────────────────────────────────────┘




   Style:   Press Exit when done                    Doc 1 Pg 1 Ln 1" Pos 1"
   [    ▲     ▲     ▲     ▲     ▲     ▲     ▲     ▲     ▲     ▲    }    ▲     ▲
   [Comment]
```

The comment is only displayed for paired styles and represents the text in the document that you will be formatting with the style. Any formatting codes inserted to the left of the [Comment] code are placed in the Style On code, while any formatting codes to the right of the Comment code are placed in the Style Off code.

7 Press **Underline** (F8) to place an Underline On code [UND] to the left of the Comment code.

8 Press **Exit** (F7) twice to return to the list of styles.

Formatting the Article Headings

The Headings style is now included in the list. Because it is a paired type, it can be used with or without Block (like all paired codes in WordPerfect) to format text.

1 Press **Exit** (F7) to return to the normal editing screen.

2 Make sure the cursor is at the beginning of the newsletter.

3 Press **Block** (Alt-F4), then press **End** to highlight the Sales Up by Two Million heading.

⌨ *Block with the mouse by clicking and dragging or by selecting* **Block** *from the* **Edit** *menu and pressing* **End**.

4 Press **Style** (Alt-F8), make sure the cursor is on the Headings style, then select **On** (1).

⌨ *Select Style from the* **Layout** *menu.*

You are returned to the normal editing screen where the heading for the first article is now underlined.

LESSON 33: STYLES **409**

5 Press **Reveal Codes** (Alt-F3) to see the Style On and Off codes.

🖳 *Select **R**eveal Codes from the **E**dit menu.*

Both the style codes include the name of the style (Heading).

6 Press **Home,Home,Home,←** to place the cursor on the Style On code.

The Style On code expands to display any formatting codes that you placed to the left of the Comment code. In this case, an [UND] code is displayed.

7 Press **End**, then press **Left Arrow** (←) to place the cursor on the Style Off code.

The Style Off code expands to display the contents of the code. Notice that an Underline Off code [und] has been automatically inserted for you to turn off underlining at the end of the heading.

▲ UNDERLINE OFF CODE

```
Sales Up by Two Million

Record sales of the new line of music boxes has boosted first quarter revenues t
the tune of 2 million dollars.  It is expected that by the year 1995, one out of
3 people in the United States and Canada will own a music box.

On the drawing boards are music box watches, dash-board models for cars,
waterproof boxes for showers, ultra-light boxes for backpackers, and even an
amplified music box that plays a disco version of "Que Sera Sera."

Music boxes with figurines depicting the following occupational motifs will be
C:\WP51\LEARN\NEWSTEXT.WKB             Doc 1 Pg 1 Ln 1" Pos 2.85"
[Style On:Headings]Sales Up by Two Million[Style Off:Headings;[und]][HRt]
[HRt]
Record sales of the new line of music boxes has boosted first quarter revenues t
o[SRt]
the tune of 2 million dollars.  It is expected that by the year 1995, one out of
 every[SRt]
3 people in the United States and Canada will own a music box.[HRt]
[HRt]
On the drawing boards are music box watches, dash[-]board models for cars,[SRt]
waterproof boxes for showers, ultra[-]light boxes for backpackers, and even an[S

Press Reveal Codes to restore screen
```

To make sure that text following the Style Off code uses the current format settings for the document, WordPerfect inserts format codes for you in the Style Off code. For a paired code such as Bold or Underline, a [bold] or [und] code is inserted. If the current base font is Roman 10pt and you place [Font:Helvetica 12pt] in the Style On code, then WordPerfect will place [Font:Roman 10pt] in the Style Off code for you.

8 Press **Reveal Codes** to display the normal editing screen.

🖳 *Select **R**eveal Codes from the **E**dit menu.*

Now that you have formatted the first heading in the newsletter, use steps 3 and 4 as a guide to format the other two headings in the newsletter.

9 Format "Training Classes and Seminars" and "HALVA Goes Retail" with the Headings style.

Creating a Masthead Style

Although creating a style to simply underline text may seem unnecessary, styles are much more useful if they include more than one format.

Let's return to the list of styles and create a style that selects the Roman 18pt font for the masthead, bolds the masthead title, then centers the title between margins.

1 Press **Style** (Alt-F8), then select **Create** (3).

⊞ *Select Styles from the Layout menu.*

The Style Edit menu is displayed on the screen.

2 Select **Name** (1), then enter **Masthead** for the style name.

3 Select **Description** (3), then enter **Roman 18pt -- Bolded and Centered** to describe the style.

4 Select **Codes** (4) to insert the formatting codes for the style.

The Style Editor is displayed with Reveal Codes on.

5 Press **Font** (Ctrl-F8), then select **Base Font** (4).

⊞ *Select Base Font from the Font menu.*

6 Press **Home,Home,↓** then press **Up Arrow** (↑) three times to highlight the Roman 18pt font.

7 Press **Enter** to select the font.

A [Font:Roman 18pt] code is displayed in the Style Editor to the left of the [Comment] code.

8 Press **Bold** (F6), then press **Center** (Shift-F6) to place a [BOLD] and a [Center] code to the left of the [Comment] code.

9 Press **Exit** (F7) twice to return to the list of styles.

The Masthead style is now included in the list.

10 Press **Exit** (F7) to return to the normal editing screen.

Formatting the Masthead

You have already formatted existing text with a paired style by blocking the article headings, then selecting the Headings style. You can also select a paired style *first*, then type the text.

1 Press **Reveal Codes** (Alt-F3) to turn on the Reveal Codes screen.

⊞ *Select Reveal Codes from the Edit menu.*

2 Press **Home,Home,Home,↑** to place the cursor at the very beginning of the newsletter (on the Style On code for the first heading).

3 Press **Enter** twice, then press **Up Arrow** (↑) twice to place the cursor in the first empty line of the newsletter.

4 Press **Style** (Alt-F8), press **Down Arrow** (↓) to highlight the Masthead style, then select **On** (1).

⌨ *Select Styles from the Layout menu.*

A Style On and a Style Off code are inserted into the normal editing screen for the Masthead style. The Style Off code is highlighted in Reveal Codes, and includes a [Font:Helvetica 10pt] and [bold] code inserted by WordPerfect.

5 Type **HALVA Herald** for the title of the masthead.

As you type the title, the text is bolded and centered between the margins.

6 Press **Left Arrow** (←) until the cursor is on the Style On code for the masthead.

The code expands to display the formatting codes you inserted when creating the Masthead style.

7 Press **Print** (Shift-F7), select **V**iew Document (6), then select Full Page (3).

⌨ *Select Print from the File menu.*

The masthead title is centered, bolded and in a large font, with the article headings underlined.

🔺 MASTHEAD TITLE

🔺 ARTICLE HEADINGS

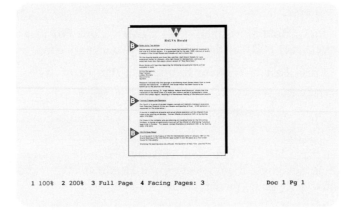

Creating an Open Style

Formats that affect an entire document (e.g., page numbering, headers) are normally placed in a group at the beginning of a document. By including these codes in a style, all you need to do is select the style to format the document.

For example, let's create a Format style that contains a header, page numbering, double spacing, and a Courier 10cpi font code, then select the style for the draft of newsletter.

1 Press **Exit** (F7) to return to the editing screen.

2 Press **Style** (Alt-F8), then select **C**reate (3) to display the Style Edit menu.

⊞ *Select Styles from the Layout menu.*

3 Select **N**ame (1), then enter **Format** for the style name.

Because the formats will affect the entire newsletter (instead of a heading, a masthead title, etc.), they should be placed in an Open style.

4 Select **T**ype (2), then select **O**pen (2).

The Enter option disappears from the menu because the option only affects formatting with paired styles.

5 Select **D**escription (3), then enter **Draft Format Style** to describe the style.

6 Select **C**odes (4) to display the Style Editor.

Let's create a header that includes the name of the author and the date the draft is printed.

7 Press **Format** (Shift-F8), select **P**age (2), then select **H**eaders (3).

⊞ *Select Page from the Layout menu.*

8 Select Header **A** (1), then select Every **P**age (2).

9 Type **NEWSLETTER DRAFT--Terry Brown** at the left margin.

10 Press **Flush Right** (Alt-F6), type **Printed on** then press the **Space Bar**.

11 Press **Date/Outline** (Shift-F5), then select Date **C**ode (2).

12 Press **Exit** (F7) once to return to the Page Format menu.

Now that the header has been added, let's finish creating the style by adding page numbering, double spacing, and a base font code.

13 Select Page Numbering (6), select Page Number **P**osition (4), then type **7** to print a page number in the bottom right corner of every page.

14 Press **Enter** twice to return to the main Format menu.

15 Select **L**ine (1), select Line **S**pacing (6), enter **2** for double spacing, then press **Exit** (F7) to return to the Style Editor.

16 Press **Font** (Ctrl-F8), then select Base **F**ont (4).

⊞ *Select Base **F**ont from the Font menu.*

17 Press **Home,↑** to place the cursor on the Courier 10cpi font, then press **Enter** to select the font.

The formatting codes in your Style Editor should look like those illustrated in the screen below.

△ FORMATTING CODES

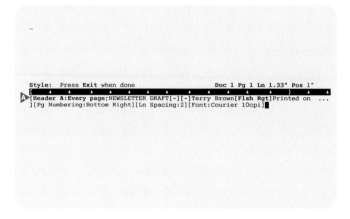

```
Style:  Press Exit when done                Doc 1 Pg 1 Ln 1.33" Pos 1"
▲[Header A:Every page;NEWSLETTER DRAFT[-][-]Terry Brown[Flsh Rgt]Printed on  ...
][Pg Numbering:Bottom Right][Ln Spacing:2][Font:Courier 10cpi]█
```

18 Press **Exit** (F7) three times to return to the normal editing screen.

Formatting the Entire Newsletter

Now that the Format style has been created, all you need to do is select the style to format the entire newsletter.

1 Press **Home,Home,Home,↑** to make sure that the cursor is at the very beginning of the newsletter.

2 Press **Style** (Alt-F8), make sure the cursor is on the Format style, then press **Enter** to select the style.

⌨ *Select Styles from the Layout menu.*

3 Press **Left Arrow** (←) to place the cursor on the [Open Style:Format] code.

The newsletter is formatted with all the formatting codes you inserted into the style.

4 Press **Print** (Shift-F7), then select **V**iew Document (6).

⌨ *Select Print from the File menu.*

The header and page number are in place, with the text of the newsletter double spaced. You can check the Courier 10cpi font by selecting 100% (1) or 200% (2).

5 When you finish, press **Exit** (F7) to return to the editing screen.

6 Press **Reveal Codes** (Alt-F3) to display the normal editing screen.

▢ *Select Reveal Codes from the Edit menu.*

Saving a List of Styles

Once you create a list of styles, you may want to use the same styles to format other documents. By saving the list as a file, you can retrieve the list into any WordPerfect document.

For example, the draft styles for the newsletter could be used to format other newsletters for editing.

1 Press **Style** (Alt-F8), then select **Save** (6).

▢ *Select Styles from the Layout menu.*

2 Enter **draft.sty** for the filename.

The .STY filename extension is not necessary, but it can help you quickly identify files that contain styles.

The styles are now saved in the DRAFT.STY file, and can be retrieved into any other WordPerfect document.

3 Press **Exit** (F7) to return to the editing screen.

Retrieving Styles

Let's save the draft version of the newsletter, then retrieve NEWSTEXT.WKB and try retrieving the styles into the original newsletter document.

1 Press **Exit** (F7), type **y**, then enter **newsltr.dft** for the name of the document.

▢ *Select Exit from the File menu.*

2 Type **n** to clear the screen.

The draft styles are saved with the formatted newsletter, and can be used or edited each time you retrieve the NEWSLTR.DFT file.

3 Press **Retrieve** (Shift-F10), then enter **newstext.wkb** to retrieve the original newsletter articles.

▢ *Select Retrieve from the File menu.*

4 Press **Style** (Alt-F8), then select **Retrieve** (7).

▢ *Select Styles from the Layout menu.*

5 Enter **draft.sty** to retrieve the list of draft styles.

The same styles you saved earlier are retrieved into the list of styles, and can be used for formatting the newsletter.

6 Press **Exit** (F7) to return to the editing screen.

You may want to try formatting part or all of the newsletter with the draft styles before continuing the lesson.

7 When you finish, press **Exit** (F7) from the normal editing screen, then type **n** twice to clear the screen.

⌨ *Select Exit from the File menu.*

If you want a list of styles automatically retrieved into a document each time you press the Style key, you can use the Setup key to indicate which file to retrieve. For details, turn to the Style *heading in the* WordPerfect Reference Manual.

Editing the Headings Style

After the newsletter is edited, the final formatting also needs to be done. Because styles were used to format the draft of the newsletter, all you need to do is edit the styles to reformat the newsletter for the final printing.

1 Press **Retrieve** (Shift-F10), then enter **newsltr.dft** to retrieve the draft version of the newsletter.

⌨ *Select Retrieve from the File menu.*

2 Press **Style** (Alt-F8) to display the list of styles.

⌨ *Select Styles from the Layout menu.*

Let's begin by reformatting the article headings for Helvetica 12pt bolded text with italics.

3 Press **Up Arrow** (↑) to highlight the Headings style, select **Edit** (4), then select **Codes** (4) to display the Style Editor.

4 Press **Delete** (Del) to delete the [UND] code.

5 Press **Font** (Ctrl-F8), then select Base Font (4).

⌨ *Select Base Font from the Font menu.*

6 Press **Down Arrow** (↓) until the Helvetica 12pt Italic font is highlighted, then press **Enter** to select the font.

7 Press **Bold** (F6) to insert a Bold On code.

8 Press **Exit** (F7) to return to the Style Edit menu, then select **Description** (3).

9 Press **Delete to End of Line** (Ctrl-End), then enter **Helvetica 12pt Italic -- Bolded** for the new description.

10 Press **Exit** twice to return to the normal editing screen.

The Sales Up by Two Million heading is now bolded instead of underlined. However, to see all the formatting changes to the heading, you need to display the newsletter in the View Document screen.

11 Press **Print** (Shift-F7), select **V**iew Document (6), then select 100% (1).

⊞ *Select Print from the File menu.*

12 Press **Page Down** (PgDn) to see the formatting for all three article headings in the newsletter.

If you find that you need to format and reformat text in a document, using the Styles feature can save you a lot of time and effort. By editing a style once, you can change the formatting for all text in a document that is formatted with that particular style.

13 Press **Exit** (F7) to return to the editing screen.

Editing the Masthead Style

The Masthead style also needs to be edited to reflect the final formatting of the newsletter.

1 Press **Style** (Alt-F8), then press **Home,↓** to highlight the Masthead style.

⊞ *Select Styles from the Layout menu.*

2 Select **E**dit (4), then select **C**odes (4) to display the Style Editor.

Let's begin by adding a graphics line above and below the masthead title.

3 Press **Right Arrow** (→) to place the cursor on the [BOLD] code.

4 Press **Graphics** (Alt-F9), select **L**ine (5), then select **H**orizontal (1).

⊞ *Select Line from the Graphics menu, then select Create Horizontal.*

5 Select **W**idth of Line (4), then enter **.04** to increase the width of the line.

6 Select **G**ray Shading (5), then enter **50** for 50% gray shading of the line.

7 Press **Exit** (F7) to return to the Style Editor.

Now that the first horizontal line has been created, let's use Backspace and Cancel to use the same line below the masthead title.

8 Press **Backspace** to delete the horizontal line.

9 Press **Cancel** (F1), then select **R**estore (1) to insert the horizontal line back into the Style Editor.

10 Press **Enter** to start the masthead title on a new line, then press **End** to place the cursor to the right of the [Comment] code.

11 Press **Enter** to start a new line, press **Cancel** (F1), then select **R**estore (1) to insert the same horizontal line below the masthead title.

12 Press **Up Arrow** (↑), then press **Left Arrow** (←) to place the cursor on the [BOLD] code.

To add some extra spacing between the horizontal lines and the masthead title, let's use the Advance feature.

13 Press **Format** (Shift-F8), select **O**ther (4), then select **A**dvance (1).

⊟ *Select **O**ther from the **L**ayout menu.*

14 Select **D**own (2), then enter **.15** to add extra spacing between the first horizontal line and the masthead title.

15 Press **Exit** (F7) to return to the Style Editor.

16 Press **Backspace** to delete the Advance Down code.

17 Press **Cancel** (F1), then select **R**estore (1) to insert the Advance Down code back into the document.

18 Press **Down Arrow** (↓), then press **Left Arrow** (←) to place the cursor on the second Horizontal Line code.

19 Press **Cancel**, then select **R**estore to insert a second Advance Down code to the left of the horizontal line.

When you finish, your Style Editor should contain the codes illustrated in the screen below.

▲ FORMATTING CODES

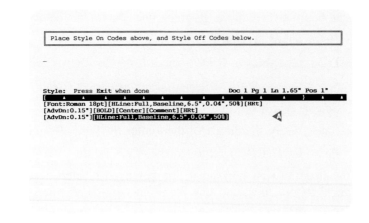

Graphics in a Style   Besides placing graphic lines in a style, you can also include graphics figures. However, because the actual figure cannot be placed in the style, WordPerfect provides a special method for including the graphics figure.

1 Place the cursor on the [BOLD] code.

2 Press **Graphics** (Alt-F9), select **U**ser Box (4), then select **C**reate (1).

⊟ *Select **U**ser Box from the **G**raphics menu, then select **C**reate.*

3 Select **F**ilename (1), then enter **buttrfly.wpg** for the name of the graphics file.

Notice that WordPerfect automatically selects "Graphic on Disk" and displays it next to the Contents option in the menu.

WordPerfect normally saves the graphics figure with the document when you retrieve the figure into a graphics box. However, when the "Graphic on Disk" setting is selected, only the filename of the graphics figure is saved with the document. WordPerfect uses the filename to retrieve the graphics figure when you display the document in the View Document screen or when you print the document.

The Graphic on Disk setting not only lets you place a graphics image in a style, but is also useful for decreasing the size of a document because the graphics figure is not stored in the document.

Let's finish formatting the User Box, place another butterfly to the right of the masthead title, then return to the list of styles.

4 Select Anchor **T**ype (4), then select **C**haracter (3).

5 Select **V**ertical Position (5), then select **C**enter (2).

6 Select **S**ize (7), select Set **W**idth/Auto Height (1), then enter **.4** to set the User Box for 4/10 of an inch in width.

7 Select **W**rap Text Around Box (8), then type **n** for No.

8 Press **Exit** (F7) to return to the Style Editor.

9 Press **Backspace** to delete the User Box code.

10 Press **Cancel** (F1), select **R**estore (1) to insert the User Box back into the style, then press **End** to move the cursor to the right of the [Comment] code.

11 Press **Cancel** again, then select **R**estore to insert another butterfly to the right of the masthead title.

12 Press **Left Arrow** (←), then press **Flush Right** (Alt-F6) to place the butterfly at the right margin.

By using Flush Right, the left border of the User Box lines up with the right margin and the butterfly will be printed in the margin (instead of in the masthead). To move the User Box back into the masthead, you need to insert an Advance Left code.

13 Press **Format** (Shift-F8), select **O**ther (4), then select **A**dvance (1).

⌨ *Select **O**ther from the **L**ayout menu.*

14 Select **L**eft (4), then enter **.4** for the 4/10 of an inch width of the User Box.

15 Press **Exit** (F7) to return to the Style Editor.

The formatting codes in your Masthead style should now look like those in the screen below.

```
┌────────────────────────────────────────────────────────────────┐
│ Place Style On Codes above, and Style Off Codes below.           │
└────────────────────────────────────────────────────────────────┘


                                                     ─

Style:   Press Exit when done                   Doc 1 Pg 1 Ln 1.22" Pos 7.1"
[       ▲      ▲      ▲      ▲      ▲      ▲      ▲      ]     ▲      ▲
[Font:Roman 18pt][HLine:Full,Baseline,6.5",0.04",50%][HRt]
[AdvDn:0.15"][Usr Box:1;BUTTRFLY.WPG;][BOLD][Center][Comment][Flsh Rt][AdvLft:0.
4"][Usr Box:2;BUTTRFLY.WPG;][HRt]
[AdvDn:0.15"][HLine:Full,Baseline,6.5",0.04",50%]
```

                                △

16 Press **Exit** (F7) to return to the Style Edit menu.

17 Select **D**escription (3), press **Delete to End of Line** (Ctrl-End), then enter **Horizontal Lines and Butterflies** for the new description.

18 Press **Exit** (F7) to return to the list of styles.

Deleting a Style

The last style that needs to be edited is the Format style. Because this style sets the general formatting requirements for the entire newsletter, all the formatting codes in the style need to be deleted and replaced with new formats.

Instead of editing the Format style and typing a new description, it would be just as easy to delete the style and create it again.

1 Press **Up Arrow** (↑) twice to place the cursor on the Format style.

2 Select **D**elete (5) to delete the Format style.

Three options are displayed on a menu at the bottom of the list. The first two options remove all the Style codes from the document, but let you have the choice of leaving the formatting codes behind or having the formatting codes deleted with the Style codes. The third option deletes the definition from the list, but leaves all the Style codes in the document.

Because there is only one Format style code in the document, let's delete the style from the list and the Style code (including formats) from the newsletter.

3 Select **I**ncluding Codes (2) from the Delete menu.

Creating a New Format Style

Now that the Format style is deleted, you are ready to re-create the style.

1 Select **C**reate (3) to display the Style Edit menu.

2 Select **N**ame (1), then enter **Format** for the name of the description.

3 Select **T**ype (2), then select **O**pen (2).

4 Select **D**escription (3), then enter **Final Format Style** for the description.

5 Select **C**odes (4) to display the Style Editor.

6 Press **Font** (Ctrl-F8), then select Base Font (4).

⌨ *Select Base Font from the Font menu.*

7 Press **Down Arrow** (↓) until the Roman 10pt font is highlighted, then press **Enter** to select the font.

8 Press **Format** (Shift-F8), select **L**ine (1), select **J**ustification (3), then select **F**ull (4).

⌨ *Select Line from the Layout menu.*

9 Press **Exit** (F7) to return to the Style Editor.

The last formatting code that needs to be placed in the style is a Text Column definition for newspaper columns.

10 Press **Columns/Table** (Alt-F7), select **C**olumns (1), then select **D**efine (3).

⌨ *Select Columns from the Layout menu, then select Define.*

11 Press **Exit** (F7) to use the default settings for two newspaper columns.

Although the Columns menu is displayed at this point for selecting Columns On (or Off), the Column On code would be at the beginning of the newsletter (above the masthead) instead of at the beginning of the first article if you were to place it in the Format style.

12 Press **Exit** (F7) to exit the Columns menu.

You should now have the following formatting codes for the Format style.

⚠ FORMATTING CODES

```
Style:  Press Exit when done                    Doc 1 Pg 1 Ln 1" Pos 1"
[                                                                       ]
[Font:Roman 10pt][Just:Full][Col Def:Newspaper;2;1",4";4.5",7.5"]
```

Both the newsletter formats and column definition are combined into one style for the purposes of this lesson. However, you could create a separate paired style for the Column Definition and Column On codes, then format only the articles with the style.

13 Press **Exit** (F7) three times to return to the normal editing screen.

14 Press **Reveal Codes** (Alt-F3) to display the codes in the newsletter.

▭ *Select Reveal Codes from the Edit menu.*

15 Press **Page Up** (Page Up) to place the cursor at the very beginning of the first page.

The cursor in the Reveal Codes screen highlights the Style On code for the Masthead style, displaying all the codes you inserted before the comment.

The Format style code needs to be inserted back into the document because it was deleted when you removed the Format style from the style list.

16 Press **Style** (Alt-F8), make sure the Format style is highlighted, then press **Enter** to select the style.

▭ *Select Styles from the Layout menu.*

Finishing the Formatting

A code for the Format style is inserted at the beginning of the document. Now all you need to do is turn on columns to finish formatting the newsletter.

1 Press **Down Arrow** (↓) four times, then press **Left Arrow** (←) to place the cursor on the Style On code for the Headings style.

2 Press **Columns/Table** (Alt-F7), select Columns (1), then select **On** (1).

⌨ *Select Columns from the Layout menu, then select On.*

3 Press **Page Up** (PgUp) to place the cursor at the top of the page.

4 Press **Reveal Codes** (Alt-F3) to display the normal editing screen.

⌨ *Select Reveal Codes from the Edit menu.*

5 Press **Print** (Shift-F7), then select View Document (6).

⌨ *Select Print from the File menu.*

The masthead is formatted with horizontal lines and butterflies, the article headings are bolded and italicized, and the articles are in newspaper columns.

```
1 100%  2 200%  3 Full Page  4 Facing Pages: 3                Doc 1 Pg 1
```

Let's return to the list of styles and save them in a FINAL.STY file.

6 Press **Exit** (F7) to return to the editing screen.

7 Press **Style** (Alt-F8), then select **S**ave (6).

⌨ *Select Styles from the Layout menu.*

8 Enter **final.sty** to save the list of styles on your screen.

Replacing a List of Styles

You have already retrieved styles into a document that had no styles (NEWSTEXT.WKB) earlier in the lesson. However, what happens if you retrieve styles into document that already has a list of styles?

For example, let's try retrieving the DRAFT.STY styles into the list displayed on your screen.

1 Select **R**etrieve (7), then enter **draft.sty** for the name of the file.

A "Style(s) already exist. Replace?" message is displayed on the screen. If you decide to retrieve the list of styles, then WordPerfect needs to know if you want any styles on the screen replaced by styles on disk that have the same style names. All other styles are simply added to the list on the screen.

The Draft styles and the Final styles both have exactly the same style names (Format, Headings, and Masthead). Let's type "y" to replace the Final styles with the Draft styles and see what happens.

2 Type **y** to replace the existing styles.

The descriptions for the Final styles are replaced with the Draft style descriptions, but what about the formatting codes?

3 Press **Exit** (F7) to return to the editing screen.

4 Press **Print** (Shift-F7), then select **V**iew Document (6).

⌨ *Select **P**rint from the **F**ile menu.*

All the final formatting for the newsletter has been replaced by the draft formatting that you created at the beginning of the lesson.

By keeping two sets of styles with exactly the same style names, you can quickly switch the formatting of a document as many times as you like by simply retrieving a new file.

5 Press **Exit** (F7) to return to the editing screen.

At this point you may want to retrieve FINAL.STY to format the newsletter with the final formatting codes, try editing a style, or create your own style.

6 When you finish, press **Exit** (F7), then type **n** twice to clear the screen.

For additional details on styles, turn to the *Style* and *Style, Create* headings in the *WordPerfect Reference Manual*.

Lesson 34: Tables—Part I

The Table feature can help you quickly organize information into columns and rows without using tabs or tab settings. Graphic lines divide the table into cells which can include text, numbers, or even formulas to help calculate numbers in the table.

In this lesson you are introduced to some basic techniques for building and editing tables. For details on all the Table features, turn to the *Table* headings in the *WordPerfect Reference Manual*.

Creating a Table

An article for the HALVA International newsletter needs a table that lists music box sales for several countries.

1 Press **Retrieve** (Shift-F10), then enter **newstabl.wkb** to retrieve the newsletter article.

*Select **Retrieve** from the **File** menu.*

A simple table has already been created using tabs. The table includes four rows (lines) of information and a row of column titles. Each line contains a column for the country, the gross sales, and the number (units) of music boxes sold.

A COLUMN TITLES
B COLUMN
C ROW

Tradition in the Marketplace
The scene is familiar around the world. Mary Smith enters a retail store looking for the perfect gift for an anniversary or family birthday. Attracted to the music boxes, she finds just the right one, only to turn over the price tag and decide that a box of expensive chocolates would be a much more sensible gift.

Customers like Mary Smith are often viewed by retailers as hopelessly frugal. However, recent studies indicate that tradition may play a key role in purchasing a music box.

Country	Gross Sales	Units Sold
Brazil	560,000.00	9,000
England	1,250,000.00	10,000
Holland	2,400,000.00	20,000
Norway	960,000.00	4,800

The above table lists the average price customers paid for a music box in several different countries. In those countries where the music box is seen as a good investment or a gift of quality and tradition, the average price is significantly higher.
C:\WP51\LEARN\NEWSTABL.WKB   Doc 1 Pg 1 Ln 1" Pos 1"

Let's try creating the same table *without* setting tabs by using the Table feature.

2 Move the cursor to the Country title (above Brazil, England, etc.).

3 Press **Home,Home,Home,←** to move the cursor to the very beginning of the line.

4 Press **Block** (Alt-F4), then type **800** to move the cursor to the end of the last line in the table.

You can type a character when Block is on to move the cursor to that character.

5 Press **Backspace**, then type **y** to delete the existing table.

To set up a table with the Table feature, all you need to do is let WordPerfect know how many rows and columns you want in the table (no tab settings are needed).

6 Press **Columns/Table** (Alt-F7), select **T**ables (2), then select **C**reate (1).

⌨ *Select **T**ables from the Layout menu, then select **C**reate.*

7 Enter **3** for the number of columns, then enter **5** for the number of rows (four countries plus the column titles).

A table is displayed on your screen that is surrounded by a double line border, with single line borders dividing the rows and columns into cells.

The borders are created using graphic lines (the same type used for graphic boxes). If your printer can print graphics, then the borders will be printed. If not, then the information in the table will be printed without the borders (even though the borders are displayed on the editing screen).

▲ ROW
▲ COLUMNS
▲ CELL

```
    retail store looking for the perfect gift for an anniversary or
    family birthday.  Attracted to the music boxes, she finds just
    the right one, only to turn over the price tag and decide that a
    box of expensive chocolates would be a much more sensible gift.

   Customers like Mary Smith are often viewed by retailers as
   hopelessly frugal.  However, recent studies indicate that
   tradition may play a key role in purchasing a music box.
```

```
Table Edit:  Press Exit when done     Cell A1 Doc 1 Pg 1 Ln 3.14" Pos 1.12"
Ctrl-Arrows Column Widths; Ins Insert; Del Delete; Move Move/Copy;
1 Size; 2 Format; 3 Lines; 4 Header; 5 Math; 6 Options; 7 Join; 8 Split: 0
```

Each cell is like a small editing window in which you can enter text, numbers, or a formula.

8 Press **Right Arrow** (→) three times to move the cursor to the beginning of the second row.

As you move the cursor through the table, the entire cell is highlighted. The status line includes a "Cell" message that updates as you move the cursor from cell to cell. The message lets you know the *address* of the current cell.

A CURSOR
B CELL MESSAGE
C CELL ADDRESS

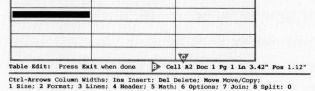

For example, the address for the first cell in the second row is A2 (column A, row 2). Columns are labeled with letters, while rows are labeled with numbers. Cell addresses help you reference cells, and are important when creating formulas in a table.

The menu at the bottom of the screen lets you change the structure and format of the table. Many of the menu options will be covered as you continue on through the lesson.

 TABLE EDIT MENU

retail store looking for the perfect gift for an anniversary or
family birthday. Attracted to the music boxes, she finds just
the right one, only to turn over the price tag and decide that a
box of expensive chocolates would be a much more sensible gift.

Customers like Mary Smith are often viewed by retailers as
hopelessly frugal. However, recent studies indicate that
tradition may play a key role in purchasing a music box.

Table Edit: Press Exit when done   Cell A2 Doc 1 Pg 1 Ln 3.42" Pos 1.12"

Ctrl-Arrows Column Widths; Ins Insert; Del Delete; Move Move/Copy;
1 Size; 2 Format; 3 Lines; 4 Header; 5 Math; 6 Options; 7 Join; 8 Split: 0

While you are in the Table Editor, you can select menu options with the mouse by placing the mouse pointer on the option and clicking the left button.

With the table created, let's start filling in the table information.

9 Try typing **Brazil** for the name of the first country.

WordPerfect did not let you type the country in the cell. However, by typing the "l" in "Brazil," you selected the Lines option from the Table Edit menu.

⚠ TABLE EDIT MESSAGE

⚠ LINES MENU

retail store looking for the perfect gift for an anniversary or
family birthday. Attracted to the music boxes, she finds just
the right one, only to turn over the price tag and decide that a
box of expensive chocolates would be a much more sensible gift.

Customers like Mary Smith are often.viewed by retailers as
hopelessly frugal. However, recent studies indicate that
tradition may play a key role in purchasing a music box.

Ⓐ Table Edit: Press Exit when done   Cell A2 Doc 1 Pg 1 Ln 3.42" Pos 1.12"

Ⓑ Lines: 1 Left; 2 Right; 3 Top; 4 Bottom; 5 Inside; 6 Outside; 7 All; 8 Shade: 0

WordPerfect lets you move the cursor from cell to cell in the Table Editor to format the cells. However, to fill in the table information, you need to return to the normal editing screen.

10 Press **Cancel** (F1) to back out of the Lines menu.

11 Press **Exit** (F7) to return to the normal editing screen.

Filling in the Table Information

After exiting the Table Editor, the cell is no longer highlighted with the cursor. However, WordPerfect still displays the "Cell" message on the status line as long as the cursor is in the table.

1 Press **Reveal Codes** (Alt-F3) to display the codes for the table.

⌨ *Select **R**eveal Codes from the **E**dit menu.*

```
box of expensive chocolates would be a much more sensible gift.

Customers like Mary Smith are often viewed by retailers as
hopelessly frugal.  However, recent studies indicate that
tradition may play a key role in purchasing a music box.




C:\WP51\LEARN\NEWSTABL.WKB                 Cell A2 Doc 1 Pg 1 Ln 3.42" Pos 1.12"
[                 ▲        ▲       ▲     ]▲[      ▲       ▲       ▲     ▲][   ▲       ▲       ▲     ]
[HRt]
[Tbl Def:I;3,2.17",2.17",2.17"]
[Row][Cell][Cell][Cell]
[Row][Cell][Cell][Cell]
[Row][Cell][Cell][Cell]
[Row][Cell][Cell][Cell]
[Row][Cell][Cell][Cell][Tbl Off][HRt]
[HRt]
[HRt]
The above table lists the average price customers paid for a[SRt]

Press Reveal Codes to restore screen
```

The Table Definition code and the Table Off code let WordPerfect know where the table begins and ends. The Row and Cell codes let WordPerfect know where the rows and cells begin and end.

2 Press **Backspace** to try to delete the Cell code to the left of the cursor.

WordPerfect did not let you delete the Cell code. As long as the Table Definition code exists, you cannot delete the Cell, Row, or Table Off codes.

If you delete the Table Definition code, then WordPerfect places tabs between the columns using the current tab settings. Although you can block the tabbed information again and create another table (Alt-F7,2,1), you may need to reformat the table. You cannot Undelete (F1) a Table Definition code unless you deleted both the table and the Table Definition code at the same time.

Because you cannot accidentally change the structure of a table in the normal editing screen (and because there are borders around each cell), you may never need to use Reveal Codes when creating a table.

3 Press **Reveal Codes** to display the normal editing screen.

⌨ *Select **R**eveal Codes from the **E**dit menu.*

As long as the "Cell" message is displayed on the status line, you know you are in the table.

4 Press **Left Arrow** (←) twice to place the cursor in cell A1 (check the status line).

⌨ *While in the normal editing screen, you can position the cursor in any cell of the table by placing the mouse pointer in the cell and clicking the left button.*

5 Type **Country** for the first column title, then press **Right Arrow** (→) to move the cursor to cell B1.

6 Type **Gross Sales** for the second column title, then press **Right Arrow** to move the cursor to cell C1.

7 Type **Units Sold** for the third column title, then press **Left Arrow** until the cursor returns to the beginning of the row (cell A1).

Whenever the cells in a table are empty, pressing the Left or Right Arrow key moves the cursor a cell at a time through the table. However, as soon as you enter text in a cell, pressing the Left or Right Arrow key in the normal editing screen moves the cursor a *character* at a time to let you edit the text in a cell.

To move forward a cell at a time through a table (text or no text in a cell), use the Tab key.

8 Press **Tab** until the cursor stops at cell A2.

If you need to move back to a cell, use the Shift-Tab key.

9 Press **Shift-Tab** until the cursor stops at cell A1.

Now that you know how to move through the table, and how to enter text in a cell, let's finish filling in the table for the newsletter article.

10 Type the following information in rows 2 through 5 of the table:

Brazil	**560,000.00**	**9,000**
England	**1,250,000.00**	**10,000**
Holland	**2,400,000.00**	**20,000**
Norway	**960,000.00**	**4,800**

If you press Enter accidentally, press Backspace to restore the row back to its original height.

Each country should be in a different row. When you finish, your table should look like the one illustrated below.

```
box of expensive chocolates would be a much more sensible gift.

Customers like Mary Smith are often viewed by retailers as
hopelessly frugal.  However, recent studies indicate that
tradition may play a key role in purchasing a music box.
```

Country	Gross Sales	Units Sold
Brazil	560,000.00	9,000
England	1,250,000.00	10,000
Holland	2,400,000.00	20,000
Norway	960,000.00	4,800_

```
The above table lists the average price customers paid for a
music box in several different countries.  In those countries
where the music box is seen as a good investment or a gift of
C:\WP51\LEARN\NEWSTABL.WKB          Cell C5 Doc 1 Pg 1 Ln 4.26" Pos 5.93"
```

Formatting a Cell

Let's return to the Table Editor and try using some of the formatting features to enhance the appearance of the table.

1 Make sure the cursor is in the table (check for the "Cell" message on the status line), then press **Columns/Table** (Alt-F7).

⌨ *Select* **Tables** *from the* **Layout** *menu, then select* **Edit**.

Because you are in a table, WordPerfect assumes that you want to edit that table and takes you directly to the Table Editor. However, you must still select the Edit option if you are using the pull-down menus.

2 Move the cursor to cell B2 (560,000.00).

The cursor highlights the entire cell for formatting.

3 Select **Format** (2), select **Cell** (1), then select **Justify** (3).

4 Select **Decimal Align** (5).

The number is aligned on the decimal point, just as if you had set a special Decimal tab for the cell.

A ALIGNED NUMBER

Country	Gross Sales ▼	Units Sold
Brazil	560,000.00	9,000
England	1,250,000.00	10,000
Holland	2,400,000.00	20,000
Norway	960,000.00	4,800

The above table lists the average price customers paid for a
music box in several different countries. In those countries
where the music box is seen as a good investment or a gift of
quality and tradition, the average price is significantly higher.

Table Edit: Press **Exit** when done **Align Cell B2 Doc 1 Pg 1 Ln 3.42" Pos 4.25"**

Ctrl-Arrows Column Widths; **Ins** Insert; **Del** Delete; **Move** Move/Copy;
1 Size; 2 Format; 3 Lines; 4 Header; 5 Math; 6 Options; 7 Join; 8 Split: 0

Formatting a Column

Instead of formatting a cell at a time, you can also format a column at a time.

1 Make sure the cursor is in column B (cell B2 is fine).

2 Select Format (2), then select Column (2) to format the column where the cursor is located (column B).

Whenever you select the Format option, information is displayed about the current cell and column.

A ALIGNMENT
B COLUMN WIDTH
C JUSTIFICATION
D ATTRIBUTES

Country	Gross Sales	Units Sold
Brazil	560,000.00	9,000
England	1,250,000.00	10,000
Holland	2,400,000.00	20,000
Norway	960,000.00	4,800

The above table lists the average price customers paid for a
music box in several different countries. In those countries
where the music box is seen as a good investment or a gift of
quality and tradition, the average price is significantly higher.

Table Edit: Press **Exit** when done **Align Cell B2 Doc 1 Pg 1 Ln 3.42" Pos 4.25"**

Cell: Top;Dec Algn;Normal   **Col:** 2.17";Left;Normal
Column: 1 Width; 2 Attributes; 3 Justify; 4 # Digits: 0

The justification for the cell is set to Decimal Align, but the justification for the column is set to Left.

3 Select **J**ustify (3), then select **D**ecimal Align (5).

The entire column is decimal aligned (including the Gross Sales title). Let's try changing the justification of the figures in column C.

4 Move the cursor to cell C2.

5 Select **F**ormat, select **C**olumn, then select **J**ustify.

6 Select **C**enter (2) to center the entire column of units sold.

The Format menus are designed to lead you through formatting a table. Even if you are unfamiliar with the Table feature, you should recognize most of the formatting options.

Formatting a Block of Cells

Although you can format a cell or column by using the Cell or Column options on the Format menu, you need to use the Block feature to indicate a row you want to format.

For example, let's bold and center the row of column titles using Block and Format.

1 Place the cursor in cell A1 (Country), then press **Block** (Alt-F4).

2 Press **Home,**→ to highlight the column titles.

3 Select **F**ormat (2), then select **C**ell (1) to format the cells in the block.

4 Select **J**ustify (3), then select **C**enter (2) to center the titles.

Because you are formatting individual cells, the column titles are all centered, even though the justification for the first and second columns is set to Left and Decimal Align. Cells can always be set to a different format than a column.

Now that the titles have been centered, let's try bolding them with Block and Format.

5 Make sure the cursor is at the end of the row (cell C1), press **Block**, then press **Home,**← to highlight the row.

6 Press **Bold** (F6) to bold the cells.

The column titles are bolded and centered above the columns in the table.

▲ COLUMN TITLES

Country	Gross Sales	Units Sold
Brazil	560,000.00	9,000
England	1,250,000.00	10,000
Holland	2,400,000.00	20,000
Norway	960,000.00	4,800

The above table lists the average price customers paid for a
music box in several different countries. In those countries
where the music box is seen as a good investment or a gift of
quality and tradition, the average price is significantly higher.

Table Edit: Press **Exit** when done   Cell C1 Doc 1 Pg 1 Ln 3.14" Pos 5.9"

Ctrl-Arrows Column Widths; **Ins** Insert; **Del** Delete; **Move** Move/Copy;
1 Size; 2 Format; 3 Lines; 4 Header; 5 Math; 6 Options; 7 Join; 8 Split: 0

Changing the Border Style

Not only can you format the justification and appearance of the text in a block of cells, but you can also change the style of the border around the cells.

1 Highlight the column title cells (A1 through C1) with **Block** (Alt-F4).

2 Select **L**ines (3), then select **B**ottom (4) to change the style of the bottom borders in all three cells.

3 Select **T**hick (6) for the border style.

WordPerfect displays a row of shaded characters that represent the thick line.

▲ SHADED CHARACTERS

Country	Gross Sales	Units Sold
Brazil	560,000.00	9,000
England	1,250,000.00	10,000
Holland	2,400,000.00	20,000
Norway	960,000.00	4,800

The above table lists the average price customers paid for a
music box in several different countries. In those countries
where the music box is seen as a good investment or a gift of
quality and tradition, the average price is significantly higher.

Table Edit: Press **Exit** when done   Cell A1 Doc 1 Pg 1 Ln 3.14" Pos 5.9"

Ctrl-Arrows Column Widths; **Ins** Insert; **Del** Delete; **Move** Move/Copy;
1 Size; 2 Format; 3 Lines; 4 Header; 5 Math; 6 Options; 7 Join; 8 Split: 0

The actual printed line is much thinner, but can only be seen in the View Document screen (with a graphics card).

4 Press **Exit** (F7) to return to the normal editing screen.

5 Press **Print** (Shift-F7), select **V**iew Document (6), then select 100% (1).

⌨ *Select **Print** from the **File** menu.*

The table is displayed as it will be printed, with the correct height for the thick line.

THICK LINE

```
Tradition in the Marketplace
The scene is familiar around the world.  Mary Smith enters a
retail store looking for the perfect gift for an anniversary or
family birthday.  Attracted to the music boxes, she finds just
the right one, only to turn over the price tag and decide that a
box of expensive chocolates would be a much more sensible gift.

Customers like Mary Smith are often viewed by retailers as
hopelessly frugal.  However, recent studies indicate that
tradition may play a key role in purchasing a music box.
```

Country	Gross Sales	Units Sold
Brazil	560,000.00	9,000
England	1,250,000.00	10,000
Holland	2,400,000.00	20,000
Norway	960,000.00	4,800

1 100%   2 200%   **3** Full Page   **4** Facing Pages: 1   Doc 1 Pg 1

6 Press **Exit** to return to the editing screen.

Now that you have created a table like the original one in the newsletter article, let's continue the lesson by introducing some additional Table features that can be useful when creating a table.

Inserting a Row

Whenever you need to add more information to a table, you can use the Insert key to insert another row or column.

1 Make sure the cursor is in the table, then press **Columns/Table** (Alt-F7) to display the Table Editor.

⌨ *Select **Tables** from the **Layout** menu, then select **Edit**.*

2 Place the cursor in cell A4 (Holland).

3 Press **Insert** (Ins), select **R**ows (1), then press **Enter** to insert a new row into the table.

LESSON 34: TABLES—PART I   **435**

An empty row with the same number of columns (3) is inserted at the cursor (between the England and Holland rows).

▲ NEW ROW

```
retail store looking for the perfect gift for an anniversary or
family birthday.  Attracted to the music boxes, she finds just
the right one, only to turn over the price tag and decide that a
box of expensive chocolates would be a much more sensible gift.

Customers like Mary Smith are often viewed by retailers as
hopelessly frugal.  However, recent studies indicate that
tradition may play a key role in purchasing a music box.
```

Country	Gross Sales	Units Sold
Brazil	560,000.00	9,000
England	1,250,000.00	10,000
▶		
Holland	2,400,000.00	20,000

```
Table Edit:   Press Exit when done          Cell A4 Doc 1 Pg 1 Ln 4.04" Pos 1.12"

Ctrl-Arrows Column Widths; Ins Insert; Del Delete; Move Move/Copy;
1 Size; 2 Format; 3 Lines; 4 Header; 5 Math; 6 Options; 7 Join; 8 Split: 0
```

4 Press **Exit** (F7) to return to the normal editing screen.

5 Fill in the empty row with the following information:

Japan   1,800,000.00   12,000

As you type the information in each cell, WordPerfect aligns the gross sales figure on the decimal point and centers the number of music boxes sold.

6 When you finish typing, press **Reveal Codes** (Alt-F3).

⊟ Select **Reveal Codes** from the **Edit** menu.

Notice that only the information is displayed with the Cell codes in the table.

▲ CELL CODE
▲ INFORMATION

```
tradition may play a key role in purchasing a music box.
```

Country	Gross Sales	Units Sold
Brazil	560,000.00	9,000
England	1,250,000.00	10,000
Japan	1,800,000.00	12,000

```
C:\WP51\LEARN\NEWSTABL.WKB                 Cell C4 Doc 1 Pg 1 Ln 4.04" Pos 6.7"

[Row][Cell]Country[Cell]Gross Sales[Cell]Units Sold
[Row][Cell]Brazil[Cell]560,000.00[Cell]9,000
[Row][Cell]England[Cell]1,250,000.00[Cell]10,000
[Row][Cell]Japan[Cell]1,800,000.00[Cell]12,000
[Row][Cell]Holland[Cell]2,400,000.00[Cell]20,000
[Row][Cell]Norway[Cell]960,000.00[Cell]4,800[Tbl Off][HRt]
[HRt]
[HRt]
The above table lists the average price customers paid for a[SRt]

Press Reveal Codes to restore screen
```

The formats for justification and bolding (column titles) are stored in the Table Definition code. As you use the Table Editor to change the formats, they are changed in the code.

You can insert a row while in the normal editing screen by pressing Ctrl-Insert.

7 Press **Reveal Codes** to display the normal editing screen.

⌨ Select **R**eveal Codes from the **E**dit menu.

8 Move the cursor to cell A4 (Japan), then press **Ctrl-Insert** to insert a new row.

9 Type the following sales information for Iceland:

Iceland   490,000.00   7,000

You should now have a row of column titles, followed by six rows of information about sales of music boxes in several countries.

tradition may play a key role in purchasing a music box.

Country	Gross Sales	Units Sold
Brazil	560,000.00	9,000
England	1,250,000.00	10,000
Iceland	490,000.00	7,000_
Japan	1,800,000.00	12,000
Holland	2,400,000.00	20,000
Norway	960,000.00	4,800

The above table lists the average price customers paid for a
music box in several different countries. In those countries
where the music box is seen as a good investment or a gift of
C:\WP51\LEARN\NEWSTABL.WKB   Cell C4 Doc 1 Pg 1 Ln 4.04" Pos 6.65"

Joining Cells

Sometimes you may want to change the structure of the table by joining cells.

1 Make sure the cursor is in the table, then press **Columns/Table** (Alt-F7) to display the Table Editor.

⌨ Select **T**ables from the **L**ayout menu, then select **E**dit.

Let's add a table heading by inserting another row at the top of the table.

2 Press **Home,Home,↑** to place the cursor in cell A1 of the table.

3 Press **Insert** (Ins), select **R**ows (1), then press **Enter** to insert a new row into the table.

Whenever you add a row or column to a table, WordPerfect duplicates the same number of columns and rows that already exist.

However, you only need one cell (not three) for the table title.

4   Highlight the new row (A1 through C1) with **Block** (Alt-F4).

5   Select **J**oin (7), then type a **y** to combine all three cells in the row into one large cell.

The Join option only works when Block is on, and lets you quickly change the basic structure of the table.

Row Height

The three cells in the row are now one cell (A1) that stretches from the left margin to the right margin.

1   Press **Exit** (F7) to return to the normal editing screen.

2   Make sure the cursor is in cell A1, then type **HALVA International** for the first line of the title.

The first line of the title is centered and bolded because WordPerfect copied the formats of the column titles when the row was inserted.

Whenever you insert a row, WordPerfect assigns the new row the same formats as the row on which the cursor is resting.

3   Press **Enter** to start a new line.

The height of the cell increases for the new line.

4   Type **Music Box Sales** for the subtitle.

As lines are added to a cell, the height of the entire row automatically expands to the correct size. This row height feature is called Automatic Multi-Line.

However, there may be times when you only want one line of text in a row, even when the Enter key is pressed (or text automatically wraps). For example, let's set the row height for the countries to Automatic Single Line.

5   Make sure the cursor is in the table, then press **Columns/Table** (Alt-F7) to display the Table Editor.

⌨ *Select Tables from the Layout menu, then select Edit.*

6   Place the cursor in cell A3 (Brazil), press **Block** (Alt-F4), then press **Home,**↓ to highlight all the country rows.

7   Select **F**ormat (2), then select **R**ow Height (3).

A menu of row height options is displayed.

▲ ROW HEIGHT OPTIONS

hopelessly frugal. However, recent studies indicate that
tradition may play a key role in purchasing a music box.

HALVA International Music Box Sales		
Country	Gross Sales	Units Sold
Brazil	560,000.00	9,000
England	1,250,000.00	10,000
Iceland	490,000.00	7,000
Japan	1,800,000.00	12,000
Holland	2,400,000.00	20,000
Norway	960,000.00	4,800

Block on   Cell A8 Doc 1 Pg 1 Ln 5.42" Pos 1.12"

Cell: Top;Left;Normal   Col: 2.17";Left;Normal
Row Height -- Single line: 1 Fixed; 2 Auto; Multi-line: 3 Fixed; 4 Auto: <u>4</u>

You can format rows for single line or multi-line, and fixed or automatic. Fixed lets you enter a line height for each line in the row. Automatic adjusts the line height to the tallest font in the row.

8 Select Single Line: Auto (2) to format all the highlighted rows.

9 Press **Exit** to return to the normal editing screen.

10 Press **Up Arrow** (↑) until the cursor is in cell A3, then press **Home,**→ to move to the end of the line in the cell.

11 Press **Enter** to start a new line.

Because you have only allowed one line in the row, WordPerfect moves the cursor to the next cell instead of adding a new line to the row.

12 Press **Enter** several times to test the Automatic Single Line feature.

If you have rows that only need one line of text, and want to use the Enter key for moving forward through the cells (instead of adding lines), you may want to format the rows for automatic single lines.

Attributes in a Cell

Whenever you format a cell, the format is stored in the Cell code and affects all the text in the cell.

1 Make sure the cursor is in the table, then press **Columns/Table** (Alt-F7) to display the Table Editor.

⌨ *Select **Tables** from the Layout menu, then select **Edit**.*

2 Press **Home,Home,**↑ to place the cursor in cell A1 (the table heading).

3 Select Format (2), select Cell (1), then select Attributes (2).

4 Select **Size** (1), then select **Large** (5) to format the entire cell for large text.

Whatever text you add to the table heading will now be formatted with the Large and Bold attributes.

If you want to format only part of the text in the cell, then you need to format the text from the normal editing screen.

5 Press **Exit** (F7) to return to the normal editing screen.

6 Place the cursor on the "M" of the Music Box Sales subtitle.

7 Press **Block** (Alt-F4), then press **Home→,** to highlight the subtitle.

8 Press **Font** (Ctrl-F8), select **Appearance** (2), then select **Italics** (4).

⌨ *Select* **Appearance** *from the* **Font** *menu, then select* **Italics**.

9 Press **Reveal Codes** (Alt-F3) to display the codes in the table.

⌨ *Select* **Reveal Codes** *from the* **Edit** *menu*.

A set of Italic codes is placed around the subtitle to format it for italicized text.

▲ ITALIC CODES

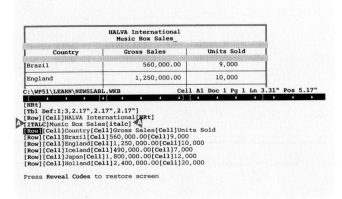

While you can format text in a table from the normal editing screen, the format codes (e.g., [ITALC][italc]) are not included as part of the format in the Cell code.

If you delete the Table Definition, the format codes remain with the text.

Once you format part or all of a cell or table with formatting codes that can be seen in Reveal Codes, then you need to make changes to the formats from the normal editing screen (instead of the Table Editor).

For example, you could only change the Music Box Sales subtitle from Italics to Underline by using Font attributes in the normal editing screen.

Cell Borders

Let's display the formatting for cell A1 in the View Document screen.

1 Press **Print** (Shift-F7), then select **View Document** (6) to see the results of the formatting.

⌨ *Select Print from the File menu.*

Notice that the top border of row 2 is still a double line, while the bottom border of cell A1 is a thick line.

A BOTTOM BORDER OF CELL A1

B TOP BORDER OF ROW 2

When you inserted a new row for the table heading, the same border style for all *four* borders of each cell (including top and bottom) were copied to the new row.

If you do not want one of the four borders printed, you can set a border style to None. For example, let's set the border style to None for the top border of row 2.

2 Press **Exit** (F7) to return to the editing screen.

3 Press **Reveal Codes** (Alt-F3) to display the normal editing screen.

⌨ *Select Reveal Codes from the Edit menu.*

4 Make sure the cursor is in the table, then press **Columns/Table** (Alt-F7) to display the Table Editor.

⌨ *Select Tables from the Layout menu, then select Edit.*

5 Highlight cells A2 through C2 with **Block** (Alt-F4).

6 Select **Lines** (3), select **Top** (3), then select **None** (1).

Let's check the results of selecting None as the border style in the View Document screen.

7 Press **Exit** to return to the normal editing screen.

8 Press **Print**, then select **View Document**.

⌨ *Select Print from the File menu.*

The top border is no longer displayed (or printed) for the cells in row 2.

9 Press **Exit** to return to the editing screen.

Adding a Row to the Table

While many tables you create may only need text and numbers, there may be times when you want to calculate the numbers in the table.

Before finishing the lesson, let's create a row at the bottom of the table that gives you a total for the gross sales and number of music boxes sold.

1 Make sure the cursor is in the table, then press **Columns/Table** (Alt-F7) to display the Table Editor.

⌨ *Select Tables from the Layout menu, then select Edit.*

From the Table Editor, you can use Go To to move the cursor to a specific cell in the table.

2 Press **Go To** (Ctrl-Home), then enter **a8** to move the cursor to cell A8 (Norway).

3 Press **Insert** (Ins), select **R**ows (1), then press **Enter** to insert a new row into the table.

4 Press **Home,↓** to display the bottom of the table.

The row is inserted at the cursor between Holland and Norway. However, the row needs to be added to the bottom of the table, not inserted in the middle.

5 Press **Up Arrow** (↑) to place the cursor in cell A8 (the new row).

6 Press **Delete** (Del), select **R**ows (1), then press **Enter** to delete the row in which the cursor is located.

Important: *You can undelete the last column or row you deleted by pressing Cancel (F1) and typing* **y**. *Only one deletion is saved at a time, and the feature only works in the Table Editor.*

Whenever you want to add rows to the bottom of a table, or columns to the right side of a table, use the Size option to increase the size of the table.

7 Select **Size** (1), then select **R**ows (1).

8 Enter **9** to increase the number of rows from eight to nine.

A new row is added to the bottom of the table for the totals.

▲ NEW ROW

	HALVA International Music Box Sales	
Country	Gross Sales	Units Sold
Brazil	560,000.00	9,000
England	1,250,000.00	10,000
Iceland	490,000.00	7,000
Japan	1,800,000.00	12,000
Holland	2,400,000.00	20,000
Norway	960,000.00	4,800

Table Edit: Press Exit when done   Cell A9 Doc 1 Pg 1 Ln 5.71" Pos 1.12"

Ctrl-Arrows Column Widths; Ins Insert; Del Delete; Move Move/Copy;
1 Size; 2 Format; 3 Lines; 4 Header; 5 Math; 6 Options; 7 Join; 8 Split: 0

Before continuing, let's format the cells in the new row for a double line top border and bolded text.

9 Make sure the cursor is in cell A9 (beginning of the new row), then highlight cells A9 through C9 with **Block** (Alt-F4).

10 Select **Lines** (3), **Top** (3), then **Double** (3) to separate the totals from the rest of the table with a double line border.

11 Press **Block**, then press **Home,←** to highlight the same row.

12 Select **Format** (2), select **Cell** (1), then select **Attributes** (2).

13 Select **Appearance** (2), then select **Bold** (1) to format the cells for bolded text.

Totaling Columns

Whenever you want to calculate the numbers in a table, you need to create a formula that does the calculating. The simplest type of formula you can create is one that adds the numbers in a column.

1 Place the cursor in cell B9 (bottom of the Gross Sales column).

2 Select **Math** (5) to display the options available for creating and calculating formulas.

The last three options in the menu let you insert a formula in a cell for adding a subtotal (+), total (=), and grand total (*). These single-character formulas are called *functions*.

All three functions add numbers above them in the column. However, the grand total function adds only calculated totals (=), and the total function only adds subtotals (+). The subtotal function is used most often and only adds numbers.

A function adds numbers above itself in the column up to the same type of function. For example, the subtotal function adds all numbers above it in the column to the next subtotal function.

3   Type **4** to insert the subtotal function into the cell.

A "* Please Wait *" message is briefly displayed, then the total appears in the cell. The calculated number for a formula is often called the *result*.

A RESULT
B FORMULA

HALVA International Music Box Sales		
Country	**Gross Sales**	**Units Sold**
Brazil	560,000.00	9,000
England	1,250,000.00	10,000
Iceland	490,000.00	7,000
Japan	1,800,000.00	12,000
Holland	2,400,000.00	20,000
Norway	960,000.00	4,800
7,460,000.00		

B =+

Cell B9 Doc 1 Pg 1 Ln 5.74" Pos 5.25"

Ctrl-Arrows Column Widths; **Ins** Insert; **Del** Delete; **Move** Move/Copy;
1 Size; 2 Format; 3 Lines; 4 Header; 5 Math; 6 Options; 7 Join; 8 Split: 0

The subtotal function is displayed on the status line, and an Align Char message lets you know that the total will be aligned on the decimal character.

4   Place the cursor in cell C9, select **Math**, then type **4** to insert a subtotal function in the cell.

Formula results are normally displayed with two digits to the right of the decimal point. You can adjust the number of digits by using the Format option.

5   Make sure the cursor is in cell C9, then select **Format** (2).

6   Select Column (2), select # **D**igits (4), then enter **0** (zero) for no decimal point.

Whenever you change the number of digits to the right of a decimal point for a formula cell, the formula needs to be calculated to see the results of the formatting.

7   Select **Math** (5), then select **Calculate** (1).

Each time you select the Calculate option, WordPerfect calculates all the formulas in the table.

The total number of music boxes sold (62,800) is displayed without a decimal point, just like the numbers you entered in the column.

Placing a Tab in a Cell	Now that you have totaled the two columns, let's add a title to the row.

1 Press **Exit** (F7) to return to the normal editing screen.

2 Press **Shift-Tab** twice to place the cursor in cell A9 (the empty cell at the beginning of the row).

3 Type **Totals** for the row title.

The word "Totals" lines up on the left side of the cell with the names of the countries.

4 Press **Home,←** to place the cursor on the "T" at the beginning of the cell.

5 Press **Home**, then press **Tab** to insert a Hard Left Tab in front of the title.

A [TAB] code is inserted in front of the title, and the title moves to the next tab stop.

By pressing Home *before* pressing Tab in the normal editing screen, WordPerfect inserts a tab into a cell instead of moving the cursor to the next cell.

Saving and Printing the Table	With the lesson completed, you need to save the table if you want to continue on with the Tables—Part II lesson.

1 Press **Save** (F10), then enter **newstabl** for the filename.

⬛ *Select Save from the File menu.*

If you want to print the table, you need to select your own printer before sending the newsletter article to the printer.

2 Press **Print** (Shift-F7).

⬛ *Select Print from the File menu.*

3 Choose **S**elect Printer, highlight the name of your printer, then press **Enter** to select the printer.

4 Select **F**ull Document (1) to send the newsletter article with the table to the printer.

⬛ *Select Print from the File menu.*

If your printer cannot print graphics, then the border lines around the cells will not be printed.

5 Press **Exit** (F7), then type **n** twice to clear the screen.

To learn more about the Table feature, you can continue on with the Tables—Part II lesson, or turn to the *Table* headings in the *WordPerfect Reference Manual*.

Lesson 35: Tables—Part II

In this lesson you continue editing the table created in the Tables—Part I lesson by adding a column of formulas, moving cells in the table, creating a table header, formatting the cell borders, and shading cells. Along the way you are introduced to several techniques that can help you when creating a table.

Splitting a Column

Besides using the totals functions, you can create your own formula to insert into a cell.

1 Press **Retrieve** (Shift-F10), then enter **newstabl** to retrieve the table created in the Tables—Part I lesson.

⌨ Select *Retrieve from the File menu.*

Let's add a column on the right side of the table for calculating the average price paid for a music box.

2 Place the cursor in cell A1 of the table, then press **Columns/Table** (Alt-F7).

⌨ Select *Tables from the Layout menu, then select Edit.*

You could use the Size option to add an extra column to the table. However, you can also divide the Units Sold column in half by using the Split option.

3 Press **Go To** (Ctrl-Home), then enter **c2** to place the cursor in cell C2 (Units Sold).

⌨ Select *Goto from the Search menu, then enter c2.*

4 Press **Block** (Alt-F4), then press **Home,↓** to highlight the cells that you want to split.

You can use Split without Block to split only the cell where the cursor is located.

5 Select S**p**lit (8), then select **Columns** (2).

6 Enter **2** to split the cells into two columns.

A fourth column is added to the right side of the table, with the width of the Units Sold column decreased to make room for the new column.

🅐 UNITS SOLD
🅐 NEW COLUMN

	HALVA International Music Box Sales 🔻🔻		🅑
Country	Gross Sales	Units Sold	
Brazil	560,000.00	9,000	
England	1,250,000.00	10,000	
Iceland	490,000.00	7,000	
Japan	1,800,000.00	12,000	
Holland	2,400,000.00	20,000	
Norway	960,000.00	4,800	
Totals	7,460,000.00	**62,800**	0

=+   Cell C9 Doc 1 Pg 1 Ln 5.85" Pos 5.58"

Ctrl-Arrows Column Widths; Ins Insert; Del Delete; Move Move/Copy;
1 Size; 2 Format; 3 Lines; 4 Header; 5 Math; 6 Options; 7 Join; 8 Split: 0

Adjusting the Column Width

Whenever you add columns, WordPerfect adjusts the width of the existing columns to keep the table width between the left and right margins.

You can adjust the width of a column to exactly the size you want by using the Format option on the Table Format menu.

1 Place the cursor in cell A3 (Brazil).

2 Select **F**ormat (2), select **C**olumn (2), then select **W**idth (1).

3 Enter **1.37** for the width of the current column (column A).

As you reduce the width of a column, WordPerfect keeps the rest of the columns at the same size. Changing the width of the columns yourself is a good way of reducing the overall width of the table.

If the position of the table is set to Full on the Table Options menu (Alt-F7,6), then WordPerfect adjusts the other columns as you reduce or increase a column width to make sure that the table fills the page from the left to the right margin.

If you do not have an exact width in mind for a column, an easier way of changing the column width is to use the Ctrl key with the Left and Right Arrows.

4 Place the cursor in cell B3 (560,000.00).

5 Hold down **Ctrl**, then press **Left Arrow** (←) four times to reduce the width of the Gross Sales column.

With the first two columns narrower, there is enough room to increase the width of the last two columns.

6 Place the cursor in cell C3 (9,000).

7 Hold down **Ctrl**, then press **Right Arrow** ($\rightarrow$) five times to increase the width of the Units Sold column.

8 Place the cursor in cell D3 (empty column), hold down **Ctrl**, then press **Right Arrow** six times to increase the width of the new column.

The table is now approximately 6.55" wide (the Position number on the status line may vary slightly with different monitors), and fills the width of the page from the left margin to the right margin.

▲ WIDTH OF TABLE

Now that you have adjusted the columns, let's add a double line border to the left side of the cells in the column and a column title.

9 Place the cursor in cell D2.

10 Press **Block** (Alt-F4), then press **Home,↓** to highlight the cells in column D.

11 Select **Lines** (3), select **Left** (1), then select **Double** (3).

12 Press **Exit** (F7) to return to the normal editing screen.

13 Place the cursor in cell D2, then type **Average Price** for the column title.

Your table should now look like the one illustrated below.

A DOUBLE LINE
B COLUMN TITLE

	HALVA International Music Box Sales	**B**	
Country	Gross Sales	Units Sold	Average Price
Brazil	560,000.00	9,000	
England	1,250,000.00	10,000	
Iceland	490,000.00	7,000	**A**
Japan	1,800,000.00	12,000	
Holland	2,400,000.00	20,000	
Norway	960,000.00	4,800	
Totals	7,460,000.00	62,800	0

C:\WP51\LEARN\NEWSTABL   Cell D2 Doc 1 Pg 1 Ln 3.64" Pos 7.21"

Creating a Formula

A formula is a statement that you create to let WordPerfect know how you want certain numbers calculated.

For example, to find the average price that a customer in Brazil spends on a music box, you need to divide the gross sales (560,000.00) by the units sold (9,000). The formula could be written using the division sign (/) and the two amounts:

> 560,000/9,000

However, if you ever changed the amounts in the table for Brazil, then you would also need to change the amounts in the formula.

A better way of creating the formula would be to use the cell addresses instead of the amounts:

> B3/C3

> *B3 = Gross Sales; C3 = Units Sold.*

If you enter cell addresses, then WordPerfect uses the amount currently in the cell to calculate the formula.

1 Make sure the cursor is in the table, then press **Columns/Table** (Alt-F7) to display the Table Editor.

▭ *Select* **Tables** *from the Layout menu, then select* **Edit**.

2 Place the cursor in cell D3 (in the new column).

3 Select **M**ath (5), then select **F**ormula (2).

4 Enter **b3/c3** for the formula (you can use uppercase or lowercase letters for the cell addresses).

When the calculation is completed, the result of the formula is displayed in the cell.

▲ RESULT
▲ FORMULA

box of expensive chocolates would be a much more sensible gift.

Customers like Mary Smith are often viewed by retailers as hopelessly frugal. However, recent studies indicate that tradition may play a key role in purchasing a music box.

HALVA International Music Box Sales			
Country	Gross Sales	Units Sold	Average Price
Brazil	560,000.00	9,000	62
England	1,250,000.00	10,000	
Iceland	490,000.00	7,000	
Japan	1,800,000.00	12,000	

=B3/C3   Cell D3 Doc 1 Pg 1 Ln 3.98" Pos 6.66"

Ctrl-Arrows Column Widths; Ins Insert; Del Delete; Move Move/Copy;
1 Size; 2 Format; 3 Lines; 4 Header; 5 Math; 6 Options; 7 Join; 8 Split: 0

Let's try changing the units sold for Brazil, then see what happens when you recalculate the Average Price formula.

5 Press **Exit** (F7) to return to the normal editing screen.

6 Press **Shift-Tab** to place the cursor in cell C3 (9,000).

Let's delete the 9,000 number and replace it with a new number for the units sold in Brazil.

7 Press **Delete to End of Line** (Ctrl-End) to erase the number in the cell.

Only the text in the cell is deleted (not to the end of the row). When you are in the normal editing screen, the delete keys only erase the text in the cell where the cursor is located.

8 Type **7,000** for the new Units Sold number.

9 Press **Columns/Table** to display the Table Editor.

⌨ Select **Tables** from the **Layout** menu, then select **Edit**.

10 Select **Math** (5), then select **Calculate** (1).

The Average Price formula is recalculated for Brazil (along with all the other formulas in the table), and a new result is displayed in the table.

```
Customers like Mary Smith are often viewed by retailers as
hopelessly frugal.  However, recent studies indicate that
tradition may play a key role in purchasing a music box.


                       HALVA International
                       Music Box Sales

     Country  |  Gross Sales  |  Units Sold  |  Average Price
   Brazil        560,000.0A      7,000             80  B
   England     1,250,000.00     10,000
   Iceland       490,000.00      7,000
   Japan       1,800,000.00     12,000
   Holland     2,400,000.00     20,000

   Table Edit:  Press Exit when done      Cell C3 Doc 1 Pg 1 Ln 3.98" Pos 4.69"

   Ctrl-Arrows Column Widths; Ins Insert; Del Delete; Move Move/Copy;
   1 Size; 2 Format; 3 Lines; 4 Header; 5 Math; 6 Options; 7 Join; 8 Split: 0
```

By using cell addresses in a formula instead of the actual amounts, WordPerfect can easily update the results of your formulas each time you change the information in a table.

Copying a Formula

Once you create a formula in a table, you may want to use the same formula for several rows or columns.

For example, the Average Price formula you just created is the same type of formula you need for the entire column. Only the cell addresses need to be updated for each row.

1 Press **Right Arrow** (→) to place the cursor in cell D3.

2 Select **M**ath (5), then select **C**opy Formula (3).

A menu is displayed that lets you copy the formula to another cell in the table, down the current column, or across the row to the right of the current cell.

3 Select **D**own (2), then enter **6** to copy the formula down the column six times.

The results of the copied formulas are displayed in column D.

4 Press **Down Arrow** (↓) to place the cursor in cell D4 (the first copied formula).

Notice that the cell addresses in the copied formula are for the gross sales (B4) and units sold (C4) in England.

Customers like Mary Smith are often viewed by retailers as
hopelessly frugal. However, recent studies indicate that
tradition may play a key role in purchasing a music box.

·HALVA International Music Box Sales			
Country	Gross Sales	Units Sold	Average Price
Brazil	560,000.00	7,000	80
England	1,250,000.00	10,000	125
Iceland	490,000.00	7,000	70
Japan	1,800,000.00	12,000	150
Holland	2,400,000.00	20,000	120

=B4/C4   Cell D4 Doc 1 Pg 1 Ln 4.26" Pos 6.41"

Ctrl-Arrows Column Widths; **Ins** Insert; **Del** Delete; **Move** Move/Copy;
1 Size; 2 Format; 3 Lines; 4 Header; 5 Math; 6 Options; 7 Join; 8 Split: 0

If you use cell addresses in a formula, then addresses are updated when you copy the formula.

5 Press **Down Arrow** to move down the column a row at a time.

Check the cell addresses in the copied formulas as you move down the column. WordPerfect updates the cell addresses in each formula you copy so that the formulas will work for each row.

Moving a Block

Whenever you change your mind about the arrangement of information in a table, you can use the Move feature to help you move the information.

For example, let's add Thailand to the table. Because the totals row needs to stay at the bottom of the table, you will need to use Insert instead of Size to add a new row.

1 Press **Go To** (Ctrl-Home), then enter **a8** to place the cursor in cell A8 (Norway).

⊞ Select *Goto* from the *Search menu*, then enter **a8**.

2 Press **Insert** (Ins), select **R**ows (1), then press **Enter** to insert a row for Thailand.

The new row is inserted above the row for Norway with a double question mark (??) in the Average Price column (cell D8). Cell D8 contains a copied formula, but a ?? appears because there is no Units Sold number to divide by in cell C8. The question marks will disappear as soon as you enter numbers in the empty cells (B8 & C8) and calculate the formula.

To keep the countries in alphabetical order, Norway needs to be moved to the new row.

3 Press **Down Arrow** (↓) to place the cursor in cell A9 (Norway), then highlight cells A9 through D9 with **Block** (Alt-F4).

4 Press **Move** (Ctrl-F4), select **B**lock (1), then select **M**ove (1).

The information in row 9 is cleared from the cells, but the cells are not deleted from the table.

5 Place the cursor in cell A8, then press **Enter** to retrieve the information for Norway.

The information is retrieved into row 8, starting at cell A8.

If there is text or formulas in the cells where you want to move information, then the text in the cells is replaced by the information being moved.

6 Press **Exit** (F7) to return to the normal editing screen.

7 Press **Down Arrow** (↓) to place the cursor in cell A9, then type the following information for Thailand:

Thailand   1,215,000.00   9,000

8 Place the cursor in cell D9, then press **Columns/Table** (Alt-F7) to display the Table Editor.

⌨ *Select Tables from the Layout menu, then select Edit.*

9 Select **M**ath (5), select **F**ormula (2), then enter **b9/c9** for the Average Price formula.

A "135" average price is displayed for Thailand in cell D9.

Moving a Column

When you move a block of cells, only the information in the cells is moved. However, if you move an entire row or column, both the cells and the cell information are moved to the new location.

For example, let's switch the position of the Gross Sales and Units Sold columns in the table.

1 Place the cursor in cell B2 (Gross Sales).

2 Press **Move** (Ctrl-F4), select **C**olumn (3), then select **M**ove (1).

The column is deleted from the table. All you need to do is move the cursor to the right of the column where you want the gross sales inserted, then press **Enter**.

3 Press **Right Arrow** (→) to place the cursor in cell C2 (Average Price), then press **Enter** to retrieve the Gross Sales column.

Although the column has been inserted in the correct place, a couple of adjustments need to be made to the table structure.

4 Press **Home,Home,↑** to place the cursor in cell A1.

5 Press **Block** (Alt-F4), then press **Home,→** to highlight the three cells in row 1.

6 Select **Join** (7), then type **y** to create one cell again.

7 Place the cursor in cell C2 (Gross Sales).

8 Press **Block**, then press **Home,↓** to highlight the cells in the column.

9 Select **Lines** (3), select **Left** (1), then select **Single** (2).

The first row is one cell again, with the left border of column C set for a single line style.

Editing a Formula

Now that the columns have been switched, the Average Price formulas need to be changed.

For example, the Average Price formula for Brazil needs to be changed from B3/C3 to C3/B3.

1 Place the cursor in cell D3 (80).

2 Select **Math** (5), then select **Formula** (2).

The formula in the current cell is displayed for editing next to the "Enter Formula:" message.

Country	Units Sold	Gross Sales	Average Price
Brazil	7,000	560,000.00	80
England	10,000	1,250,000.00	125
Iceland	7,000	490,000.00	70
Japan	12,000	1,800,000.00	150
Holland	20,000	2,400,000.00	120
Norway	4,800	960,000.00	200
Thailand	9,000	1,215,000.00	135
Totals	60,800	7,460,000.00	123

HALVA International
Music Box Sales

=B3/C3

Cell D3 Doc 1 Pg 1 Ln 3.99" Pos 6.46"

Enter formula: B3/C3

A   B

3 Press **Delete** (Del) to delete the "B," then type **c** for the new column.

4 Press **Right Arrow** (→) twice, press **Delete** to delete the "C," then type **b** for the new column.

The edited formula should look like the one displayed in the screen below.

HALVA International Music Box Sales			
Country	Units Sold	Gross Sales	Average Price
Brazil	7,000	560,000.00	80
England	10,000	1,250,000.00	125
Iceland	7,000	490,000.00	70
Japan	12,000	1,800,000.00	150
Holland	20,000	2,400,000.00	120
Norway	4,800	960,000.00	200
Thailand	9,000	1,215,000.00	135
Totals	60,800	7,460,000.00	123

=B3/C3
Cell D3 Doc 1 Pg 1 Ln 3.99" Pos 6.46"

Enter formula: c3/b3
▲

5 Press **Enter** to place the formula in the cell.

Another way of changing a formula is to clear the cell, then type a completely new formula.

6 Press **Down Arrow** (↓) to place the cursor in cell D4 (125).

7 Press **Backspace** to clear the cell.

Not only is the result (125) deleted from the cell, but also the formula (there is no formula displayed on the status line).

If you use Backspace (or any other delete key) in a formula cell in the normal editing screen, only the result is deleted from the cell. The formula remains in the cell, and can only be deleted from the Table Editor.

8 Select **M**ath, select **F**ormula, then enter **c4/b4** for the new formula.

The formula is entered into the cell and displayed on the status line. Let's finish changing the formulas by clearing the rest of the cells in the column, then copying the formula from cell D4 down the column.

9 Press **Down Arrow** to place the cursor in cell D5.

10 Press **Block** (Alt-F4), then press **Home,**↓ to highlight the rest of the cells in the column.

11 Press **Backspace**, then type **y** to delete (clear) the contents of the cells.

12 Press **Up Arrow** (↑) until the cursor is in cell D4.

13 Select **M**ath (5), select **C**opy Formula (3), select **D**own (2), then enter **6** for the number of times.

Because the formulas have been changed, the results should be exactly the same as the original average prices.

Inserting Multiple Rows

Whenever a table becomes long enough, WordPerfect splits the table with a page break. For example, let's add several rows to the table for additional countries.

1 Place the cursor in cell A4 (England).

2 Press **Insert** (Ins), select **R**ows (1), then enter **20** to insert twenty new rows into the table.

Now that the rows have been added, let's take a look at the table in the View Document screen.

3 Press **Exit** (F7) to return to the normal editing screen.

4 Press **Print** (Shift-F7), select **V**iew Document (6), then select Full Page (3).

⌨ *Select **P**rint from the **F**ile menu.*

The table is split cleanly at the bottom of the first page, with the rest of the table at the top of the second page.

5 Press **Page Down** (PgDn) to view the second page of the newsletter article.

⚠ BOTTOM OF TABLE

1 100%   2 200%   3 Full Page   4 Facing Pages: 3   Doc 1 Pg 2

WordPerfect always splits a table with a page break between two rows of cells. A row is never split in half by a page break.

Creating a Header

Whenever you have a table that is split between two or more pages, you may want to use the same heading at the top of each new page that appears at the beginning of the table.

1 Press **Exit** (F7) to return to the editing screen.

2 Press **Columns/Table** (Alt-F7) to display the Table Editor.

⊞ *Select* ***Tables*** *from the* ***Layout*** *menu, then select* ***Edit.***

3 Select **Header** (4), then enter **2**.

The heading and the column titles in the first two rows of the table will now be repeated at the top of every page where the table is continued.

4 Press **Exit** to return to the normal editing screen.

The table header is not displayed in the normal editing screen. However, you can see it in the View Document screen.

5 Press **Print** (Shift-F7), then select **V**iew Document (6).

⊞ *Select* ***Print*** *from the* ***File*** *menu.*

The two header rows from the beginning of the table are added to the second part of the table on page 2.

▲ HEADER ROWS

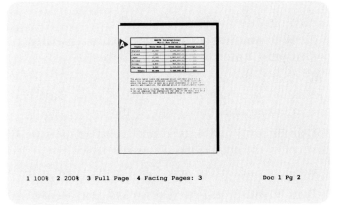

1 100%   2 200%   3 Full Page   4 Facing Pages: 3   Doc 1 Pg 2

An asterisk is included with the cell address (e.g., A2*) to identify the cells in a table that are selected for a header.

Deleting Multiple Rows

Now that you have inserted several rows and created a table header, let's return the table to its original size.

1 Press **Exit** (F7) to return to the editing screen.

2 Press **Columns/Table** (Alt-F7) to display the Table Editor.

⊞ *Select* ***Tables*** *from the* ***Layout*** *menu, then select* ***Edit.***

3 Press **Home,Home,↑** to move to the top of the table, then place the cursor in cell A4.

4 Press **Delete** (Del), select **R**ows (1), then enter **20** to delete the empty twenty rows.

The empty rows are deleted, and the finished table is displayed on the screen.

The header rows can be turned off by entering zero (0) for the number of rows.

5 Select **H**eader (4), then enter **0** for the number of header rows you want in the table.

Changing the Base Font

The text in the table uses the current base font for the document. By placing a Base Font code at the beginning of the table, you can change the font used for the table.

1 Press **Exit** (F7) to return to the normal editing screen.

2 Place the cursor in the empty line above the table.

3 Press **Font** (Ctrl-F8), then select Base Font (4).

⌨ *Select Base Font from the Font menu.*

4 Press **Down Arrow** (↓) until the cursor highlights the Helvetica 8pt font, then press **Enter** to select the font.

If the table is surrounded by text in a document (such as the Music Box Sales table), you may need to insert another Base Font code at the end of the table to change the font again for the rest of the document.

5 Using steps 3 and 4 as a guide, change the base font back to Courier 10cpi in the empty line below the table.

Let's take a look at the new font for the table in the View Document screen.

6 Press **Print** (Shift-F7), select **V**iew Document (6), then select 100% (1).

⌨ *Select Print from the File menu.*

Although the characters in the table are smaller, the width of the table is still the same.

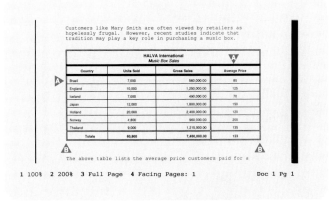

Even though you changed the base font, the columns in the table kept the same width. You need to use the Ctrl and arrow keys, or the Column Width format option if you want to adjust the column widths.

7 Press **Exit** to return to the editing screen.

8 Place the cursor in cell A1, then press **Columns\Table** (Alt-F7) to display the Table Editor.

⌨ *Select Tables from the Layout menu, then select Edit.*

9 Place the cursor in cell A2 (Country), then press **Ctrl-←** six times to decrease the width of column A.

10 Place the cursor in cells B2, C2, and D2, then repeat step 9 to decrease the width of columns B, C, and D by the same amount.

11 Press **Exit** to return to the normal editing screen.

12 Press **Print**, select **View** Document, then select 100% (1).

⌨ *Select Print from the File menu.*

Both the column widths and the width of the entire table are narrower. Notice that the Totals title has wrapped to a second line.

⚠ NARROWER TABLE WIDTH

⚠ WRAPPED TITLE

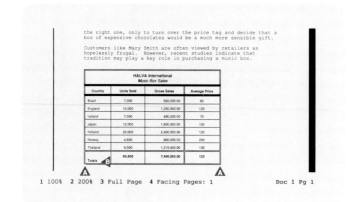

the right one, only to turn over the price tag and decide that a
box of expensive chocolates would be a much more sensible gift.

Customers like Mary Smith are often viewed by retailers as
hopelessly frugal. However, recent studies indicate that
tradition may play a key role in purchasing a music box.

HALVA International Music Box Sales		
Country	Units Sold	Gross Sales	Average Price
Brazil	7,000	560,000.00	80
England	10,000	1,250,000.00	125
Iceland	7,000	490,000.00	70
Japan	12,000	1,800,000.00	150
Holland	20,000	2,400,000.00	120
Norway	4,800	960,000.00	200
Thailand	9,000	1,215,000.00	135
Totals B	69,800	7,460,000.00	123

1 100%   2 200%   3 Full Page   4 Facing Pages: 1   Doc 1 Pg 1

13 Press **Exit** to return to the editing screen.

14 Place the cursor in cell A10, then delete the tab in the cell.

15 Press the **Space Bar** three times to indent the Totals title.

Positioning the Table Between Margins

Now that the table is narrower than the left and right margins, you may want to center it between the margins.

1 Make sure the cursor is in the table, then press **Columns/Table** (Alt-F7) to display the Table Editor.

⌨ *Select Tables from the Layout menu, then select Edit.*

2 Select **O**ptions (6), then select **P**osition of Table (3).

Left is the default setting for the position of tables between the left and right margins. However, you can also select Right, Center, Full, or Set Position.

The Full option forces the table to fill the margins, even when you decrease the width of a column. The Set Position option lets you set a horizontal position for the table from the left edge of the page.

3 Select **C**enter (3) to center the table between the left and right margins.

4 Press **Exit** (F7) to return to the normal editing screen.

5 Press **Print** (Shift-F7), select **V**iew Document (6), then select Full Page (3).

▣ Select **P**rint from the **F**ile menu.

▲ CENTERED TABLE

1 100% 2 200% 3 Full Page 4 Facing Pages: 3   Doc 1 Pg 1

The table will remain centered between the margins, even if you increase or decrease the width of the columns in the table.

6 Press **Exit** to return to the editing screen.

Changing the Inside and Outside Borders

You can change the borders inside or outside of a block of cells with the Inside and Outside options.

1 Make sure the cursor is in the table, then press **Columns/Table** (Alt-F7) to display the Table Editor.

▣ Select **T**ables from the **L**ayout menu, then select **E**dit.

Let's begin by changing the border style to None for the outside borders of the table.

2 Press **Home,Home,↑** to place the cursor in cell A1.

3 Press **Block** (Alt-F4), then press **Home,Home,↓** to place the cursor in cell D10 (the last cell in the table).

4 Select **L**ines (3), select **O**utside (6), then select **N**one (1).

The double line border around the table disappears because the entire table was highlighted.

Graphics characters are used to display the borders in the normal editing screen. Because the characters are all one standard width, arrows appear at the ends of lines whenever a shorter graphic character is not available. The arrows do not appear in the View Document screen because actual graphics lines (not graphics characters) are used to print the table borders.

If you want to change the inside or outside borders for *part* of a table, highlight only the cells that you want affected. For example, let's try setting the vertical borders to None for the second row by using the Inside option.

5 Place the cursor in cell A2 (Country), then highlight cells A2 through D2 with **Block**.

6 Select **Lines** (3), select **Inside** (5), then select **None** (1).

Only the vertical lines between the cells disappear because they were the only lines inside the block of cells. Let's finish the exercise by setting the border style to None for all the borders below the column titles.

7 Place the cursor in cell A3 (Brazil), press **Block**, then press **Home,Home,↓** to move the cursor to the last cell in the table.

8 Select **Lines**, select **Inside**, then select **None**.

Both the horizontal and vertical lines inside the highlighted cells have disappeared from the table.

```
                        HALVA International
                         Music Box Sales

              Country   Units Sold    Gross Sales   Average Price

              Brazil       7,000       560,000.00        80

              England     10,000     1,250,000.00       125

              Iceland      7,000       490,000.00        70

              Japan       12,000     1,800,000.00       150

              Holland     20,000     2,400,000.00       120

              Norway       4,800       960,000.00       200

              Thailand     9,000     1,215,000.00       135

              Totals      60,800     7,460,000.00       123

=C10/B10                        Cell D10 Doc 1 Pg 1 Ln 5.54" Pos 5.84"

Ctrl-Arrows Column Widths; Ins Insert; Del Delete; Move Move/Copy;
1 Size; 2 Format; 3 Lines; 4 Header; 5 Math; 6 Options; 7 Join; 8 Split: 0
```

9 Press **Block**, then press **Home,←** to highlight the Totals row.

10 Select **Lines** (3), select **Top** (3), then select **Double** (3) to restore the double line above the Totals row.

11 Press **Home,Home,↑** to move the cursor to the beginning of the table.

Now the table should only have three horizontal lines displayed.

```
                          HALVA International
                            Music Box Sales
     ▲
     ▲      Country     Units Sold      Gross Sales    Average Price

            Brazil        7,000         560,000.00         80

            England      10,000       1,250,000.00        125

            Iceland       7,000         490,000.00         70

            Japan        12,000       1,800,000.00        150

            Holland      20,000       2,400,000.00        120

            Norway        4,800         960,000.00        200

            Thailand      9,000       1,215,000.00        135
     ▲
            Totals       60,800       7,460,000.00        123

  Table Edit:  Press Exit when done       Cell A1 Doc 1 Pg 1 Ln 3.04" Pos 3.45"

  Ctrl-Arrows Column Widths; Ins Insert; Del Delete; Move Move/Copy;
  1 Size; 2 Format; 3 Lines; 4 Header; 5 Math; 6 Options; 7 Join; 8 Split: 0
```

Shading Cells in a Table

Whenever rows of single lines are listed in a table, every other row is often shaded to make information easier to find in the table.

A Shade option is available on the Lines menu that you can use to shade one or more cells in the table. For example, let's uses the Shade option to shade rows 3, 5, 7, and 9 in the table.

1 Place the cursor in cell A3 (Brazil), then highlight cells A3 through D3 by pressing **Block** (Alt-F4).

2 Select **Lines** (3), select **Shade** (8), then select **On** (1).

The cell address on the status line is shown in reverse video to indicate that the cells are shaded.

3 Using steps 1 and 2 as a guide, shade rows 5, 7, and 9.

4 Press **Exit** (F7) to return to the normal editing screen.

5 Press **Print** (Shift-F7), select **View** Document (6), then select 100% (1).

⌨ *Select **Print** from the **File** menu.*

Every other country in the table should be shaded at a 10% setting.

6 Press **Exit** to return to the editing screen.

*You can change the shading percentage from the Table Editor by selecting **O**ptions (6), **G**ray Shading (4), then entering a new percentage. The shading percentage affects all the cells in the table that are shaded.*

Saving and Printing the Table

Now that you have completed the table, you may want to save it, then try printing the table using your own printer.

1 Press **Save** (F10), press **Enter** to use the NEWSTABL filename, then type **y** to replace the original table.

🖬 Select **S**ave from the **F**ile menu.

2 Press **Print** (Shift-F7).

🖬 Select **P**rint from the **F**ile menu.

3 Choose **S**elect Printer, highlight the name of your printer, then press **Enter** to select the printer. Select **V**iew Document (6) to see the table as it will be printed.

You may need to adjust the column widths for your printer's current base font, or you may want to select another base font for the table.

4 Press **Exit** (F7) to return to the editing screen.

5 Make any necessary adjustments to the table (you may not need to do anything).

6 Press **Print**, then select **F**ull Document (1) to send the newsletter article with the table to the printer.

🖬 Select **P**rint from the **F**ile menu.

7 Press **Exit**, then type **n** twice to clear the screen.

At this point, you can turn to the *WordPerfect Reference Manual* to find out more about the Table feature, or try using what you have already learned to create your own table.

The Graphics *lesson in the* WordPerfect Workbook *includes information on placing a table in newspaper columns.*

Lesson 36: Thesaurus

Whenever you need to find just the right word, you can use the Thesaurus feature to display a list of synonyms (words with a similar meaning) for a word that already exists in a document or a word that you type from the keyboard.

A list of antonyms (words with an opposite meaning) may also be displayed for some words in the Thesaurus. For details on all the Thesaurus features, turn to the Thesaurus *heading in the* WordPerfect Reference Manual.

Replacing a Word

Let's retrieve the newsletter articles (from lesson 16), then use the Thesaurus to replace some of the words in the articles.

1 Press **Retrieve** (Shift-F10), then enter **newstext.wkb** to retrieve the newsletter articles.

⌨ *Select* Retrieve *from the* File *menu.*

If you are running WordPerfect from a two disk drive system, replace the Learn diskette with the Thesaurus diskette after the newsletter articles appear on the screen.

The word "revenues" in the first paragraph needs to be replaced with a word that is more accurate.

2 Press ♦**Search** (F2), type **revenues**, then press ♦**Search** again to place the cursor to the right of the word "revenues."

⌨ *Select* Forward *from the* Search *menu, type* revenues, *then click the right-hand mouse button.*

Whenever the cursor is on or to the right of a word in a document, you can quickly look up the word with a single keystroke.

3 Press **Thesaurus** (Alt-F1) to display a list of synonyms for the word.

⌨ *Select* Thesaurus *from the* Tools *menu.*

If an "ERROR: File not found -- WP[WP]US.THS" message is displayed, then the Thesaurus file was probably not copied to your hard disk (or Theaurss diskette) when installing WordPerfect. Try running the Install program and select the Custom Option to install the Thesaurus file.

A list of nouns (n) is displayed under "revenue" with a column of letters to the left of the words.

A HEADWORD

B REFERENCE MENU

C REFERENCE

D SUBGROUP

```
Sales Up by Two Million

Record sales of the new line of music boxes has boosted first quarter revenues t
the tune of 2 million dollars.  It is expected that by the year 1995, one out of
3 people in the United States and Canada will own a music box.
revenue=(n)=
  1 A ·gain
    B ·gross
    C ·income
    D  profits
    E  receipts

  2 F ·capital
    G ·money
    H ·wealth
```

```
1 Replace Word; 2 View Doc; 3 Look Up Word; 4 Clear Column: 0
```

The word "revenue" is called a *headword* because it can be looked up in the Thesaurus. The words in the list are called *references*. References are often divided into numbered *subgroups* of words that have the same basic meaning.

The bolded letters to the left of the words make up the *Reference menu* which can be used to select a listed reference.

4 Select Replace Word (1), then type **d** to select "profits" from the list.

WordPerfect exits the Thesaurus, then replaces the word "revenues" with the word "profits" in the newsletter article.

Moving the Reference Menu

Sometimes a word in your document may not be found in the Thesaurus.

1 Press ♦**Search** (F2), type **figurines**, then press ♦**Search** again to place the cursor to the right of the word "figurines."

⌨ *Select Forward from the Search menu, type figurines, then click the right-hand mouse button.*

2 Press **Thesaurus** (Alt-F1) to display a list of references for the word.

⌨ *Select Thesaurus from the Tools menu.*

A "Word not found" message is briefly displayed on the status line to let you know that "figurines" is not a headword in the Thesaurus. In fact, it may not be listed at all in the Thesaurus.

A second message (Word:) is displayed that lets you enter another word instead of "figurines."

3   Type **figure** and press **Enter** to see if "figure" is a headword in the Thesaurus.

A list of references fills all three columns of the Thesaurus menu. Whenever there are references in more than one column, you can move the Reference menu from column to column with the Left Arrow or Right Arrow keys.

4   Press **Right Arrow** (→) three times to move the Reference menu through the columns.

5   Press **Left Arrow** (←) twice to place the Reference menu in the second column.

6   Select Replace Word (1), then type **a** to select the word "character."

WordPerfect replaces the word "figurines" in the document with "character."

7   Type **s** to make the word "character" plural.

Looking Up a Word

Besides using the Thesaurus to replace a word in a document, you can also look up words in the Thesaurus.

1   Make sure the cursor is to the right of "characters," then press **Thesaurus** (Alt-F1).

⊞ *Select Thesaurus from the Tools menu.*

A list of references for "character" is displayed on the screen. Part of the list has spilled over into the second column so that all the references can be displayed on the screen at the same time.

Even though the Thesaurus is displaying references for the word "character," you can still look up another word.

2   Select Look Up Word (3), then enter **sale** to look up the word in the Thesaurus.

A list of references is displayed in the second column for the word "sale," but what happened to the references for "character" that were in the second column?

3   Press **Left Arrow** (←) to move the Reference menu back to the first column.

4   Press **Down Arrow** (↓) three times to display the missing references.

The references for "character" have been shifted to the bottom of the first column because there was no room for them in second column.

5   Press **Exit** (F7) to return to the normal editing screen.

Selecting Headwords

Let's continue the lesson by finding a replacement for the word "illustrious" in the last newsletter article.

1 Press ♦**Search** (F2), type **illustrious**, then press ♦**Search** again to place the cursor to the right of the word "illustrious."

⌨ *Select* **Forward** *from the Search menu, type* **illustrious***, then click the right-hand mouse button.*

2 Press **Thesaurus** (Alt-F1) to display a list of references for the word.

⌨ *Select* **Thesaurus** *from the Tools menu.*

A list of adjectives (a) and antonyms (ant) is displayed from which you can select an alternative. Notice that some of the adjectives in the list are marked with a bullet (•).

⚠ BULLETED REFERENCE

```
Attending the opening were city officials, the Governor of New York, and the Pri
Minister of Atlantis.  Our own illustrious President was there for the occasion,
warmly greeted all in attendance.

┌illustrious=(a)
  1 A   acclaimed
    B  ·celebrated
    C  ·famous
    D  ·prominent
    E  ·renowned

  2 F  ·brilliant
    G  ·distinguished
    H  ·glorious
    I  ·magnificent

│illustrious-(ant)
  3 J  ·ignominious
    K  ·mediocre
         ⚠

1 Replace Word; 2 View Doc; 3 Look Up Word; 4 Clear Column: 0
```

The bullets indicate those references that are headwords in the Thesaurus. By using the Reference menu, you can select a headword to display an additional list of references.

Those references that are not marked with a bullet can be selected to replace the word in the document, but cannot be displayed as a headword in the Thesaurus menu.

For example, of all the references listed for "illustrious," the adjective "famous" comes closest to describing the President of HALVA International. However, there may be a better alternative.

3 Type **c** to select "famous."

A list of references for "famous" is displayed in the second column of the Thesaurus menu.

4 Type **b** to select "renowned."

A list of references for "renowned" is displayed in the third column.

5 Type **f** to select "popular."

A list of references for "popular" is displayed in the third column, replacing the list of references for "renowned."

6 Press **Home,**↓ to display the end of the list in the third column.

7 Press **Home,**↑ to display the beginning of the list.

None of the references for "popular" seem to describe the president. You could continue displaying other headwords, but it would probably be a good idea to use a reference already displayed.

8 Press **Left Arrow** (←) to move the cursor to the second column under the "famous" headword.

9 Select Replace Word (1), then type **g** to select "distinguished" from the list of references.

Clearing a Column

Besides listing nouns (n), adjectives (a), and antonyms (ant), the Thesaurus can also list alternatives for verbs (v) in your document.

1 Press ♦**Search** (F2), type **impressed**, then press ♦**Search** again to move the cursor to the right of the word "impressed."

⌨ *Select Forward from the Search menu, type **impressed**, then click the right-hand mouse button.*

2 Press **Thesaurus** (Alt-F1), then type **h** to display a list of references for "excite."

⌨ *Select Thesaurus from the Tools menu.*

3 Type **a** to display a list of references for "delight."

Now there are three headwords listed across the Thesaurus menu—impress, excite, and delight. You could continue looking by selecting a headword under "delight," but what if you want to keep the "delight" list on the screen instead of having it replaced by the selected headword?

4 Press **Left Arrow** (←) twice to move the Reference menu to the first column (under "impress").

5 Select Clear Column (4) to clear the list of references from the column.

As soon as the column is cleared, the list of references for "excite" and "delight" are shifted one column to the left.

6 Press **Right Arrow** (→) to move the Reference menu to the second column (under "delight").

7 Type **c** to display a list of references for "enchant."

While several alternatives are now displayed on the screen, none of them seem to work as well as the word "impressed" which is already in the newsletter article.

| **Viewing the Document** | Before exiting the Thesaurus menu, let's scroll through the rest of the document to see if there are any other words that may need to be replaced. |

1 Select View Document (2).

The cursor moves up into the newsletter and the status line is displayed at the top of the Thesaurus menu. You can use the cursor keys to scroll through the document.

2 Press **Down Arrow** (↓) four times to move the cursor to the last line of text in the document.

3 Press **Home,Home,**→ to shift the screen to the end of the lines in the last paragraph.

If you see another word that you want to look up in the Thesaurus, you can use the Look Up Word option. However, to use the Replace option, you need to have the cursor on the word *before* selecting the Thesaurus feature.

4 Press **Exit** (F7) to return to the Thesaurus menu.

WordPerfect highlights the word "impressed" again to return you to the same place in the article.

5 Press **Exit** to return to the newsletter.

6 Press **Exit** again, then type **n** twice to clear the screen.

If you are running WordPerfect from a two disk drive system, replace the Thesaurus diskette with the Learn diskette before continuing to use the workbook.

The Thesaurus is a wonderful tool for looking up synonyms (and antonyms) when creating or editing a document. However, you may also find it just as useful for confirming that the word you are using is already the best alternative.

Appendix A—Feature List (Alphabetical)

This table is designed to help you find which lessons discuss each feature of WordPerfect.

Feature	Lesson(s)
Advance	14, 25, 30
Attributes, Font	3, 5, 17
Backup	11, 12
Block	4, 9, 10, 12, 20
Block Protect	21, 25
Cancel	5, 7, 8
Capitalization	1, 2
Center Page	3, 4, 5
Center Text	3
Columns, Newspaper	13, 16, 31
Columns, Parallel	25
Compose	26, 29
Cross-Reference	25
Cursor Movement	1, 2, 4, 5
Dates	3, 5, 6, 10, 12
Delete Codes	5, 10
Delete Files	11
Delete Text	4, 5, 8
Directories	11, 27
Document Comments	27, 30
Document Summary	27
Edit-Screen Options	25
Equations	29
Exit	1, 2, 7
Find	27
Flush Right	21
Font	12, 16, 17, 29, 31, 35
Footnotes and Endnotes	21, 22
Format	3, 4, 13, 16
Generate	22, 25
Go To	16
Graphics	16, 17, 21, 22, 31
Graphics Lines	14, 16, 21, 22, 31
Headers and Footers	10, 14, 21
Help	7
Hyphenation	25

Feature	Lesson(s)
Indent	13, 19
Indexing	22
Initial Codes	12, 28
Initial Settings	12
Justification	2, 12
Keyboards	26
Labels	28
Line Height	13
Line Spacing	13, 19
List Files	2, 4, 11, 12, 27
Look	4, 27
Macros	15, 26
Margins	3, 4, 5, 13, 14, 16, 17, 19
Merge	23, 24, 25, 28, 30
Move	4, 9, 12, 20, 21
Outline	18
Page Numbering	8, 10, 14, 17, 21, 22
Page, Soft and Hard	8
Paper Size/Type	28
Printing	1, 4, 12, 24, 28
Repeat Value	3, 5, 9
Replace	14
Retrieve	4, 6
Return, Soft and Hard	1, 5
Reveal Codes	3, 4
Rewrite	2
Save	1, 2, 4
Screen	23, 25
Search	10, 12, 14, 21, 25, 27
Setup	12, 28
Sort	10, 12, 32
Speller	6, 10, 14
Styles	33
Switch	9
Tabs	3, 4, 5, 13, 19, 20, 25
Tables	34, 35
Table of Contents	22
Text In/Out	27
Thesaurus	36
Typeover	2, 4
Undelete	7, 8, 12

Appendix B—Feature List (By Lesson)

This table is designed to help you identify which features of WordPerfect are discussed in each lesson.

Lesson 1: Notes
Capitalization
Cursor Movement
Exit
Printing
Return, Soft and Hard
Save
View Document

Lesson 2: Letter 1—First Draft
Capitalization
Cursor Movement
Exit
Justification
List Files
Rewrite
Save
Typeover

Lesson 3: Memo Form
Attributes
Center Page
Center Text
Dates
Format
Margins
Repeat Value
Reveal Codes
Tabs

Lesson 4: Letter 1—Second Draft
Block
Center Page
Cursor Movement
Delete Text
Format
List Files
Look
Margins
Move
Printing
Retrieve
Reveal Codes
Save
Tabs
Typeover
View Document

Lesson 5: Memo Fill-in
Attributes
Cancel
Center Page
Cursor Movement
Dates
Delete Codes
Delete Text
Margins
Repeat Value
Return, Soft and Hard
Tabs

Lesson 6: Letter 1—Final Draft
Dates
Retrieve
Speller

Lesson 7: Getting Help
Cancel
Exit
Help
Undelete

Lesson 8: Letter 2—First Draft
Cancel
Delete Text
Page, Soft and Hard
Page Numbering
Undelete

Lesson 9: Editing Screens
Block
Move
Repeat Value
Switch

Lesson 10: Letter 2—Final Draft
Block
Dates
Delete Codes
Headers and Footers
Page Numbering
Search
Sort

Lesson 11: File Management
Backup
Delete Files
Directories
List Files

Lesson 12: Special Techniques
Backup
Block
Dates
Font
Initial Codes
Initial Settings
Justification
List Files
Move
Printing
Search
Setup
Sort
Undelete
Window

Lesson 13: Formatting a Letter—Part I
Columns, Newspaper
Format
Indent
Line Height
Line Spacing
Margins
Tabs

Lesson 14: Formatting a Letter—Part II
Advance
Graphics Lines
Headers and Footers
Margins
Page Numbering
Replace
Search
Speller
Widow/Orphan

Lesson 15: Office Automation
Macros

Lesson 16: Formatting a Newsletter—Part I
Columns, Newspaper
Font
Format
Go To
Graphics
Graphics Lines
Margins

Lesson 17: Formatting a Newsletter—Part II
Attributes
Font
Graphics
Margins
Page Numbering

Lesson 18: Corporate Report—Outline
Outline

Lesson 19: Corporate Report—Indents and Line Spacing
Indent
Line Spacing
Margins
Tabs

Lesson 20: Corporate Report—Tabs
Block
Move
Tabs

Lesson 21: Corporate Report—Footers, Footnotes, and Endnotes
Block Protect
Footnotes and Endnotes
Graphics
Graphics Lines
Headers and Footers
Move
Page Numbering
Search

Lesson 22: Corporate Report—Table of Contents and Index
Footnotes and Endnotes
Generate
Graphics
Graphics Lines
Indexing
Page Numbering
Table of Contents

Lesson 23: Merge Fundamentals
Merge
Screen
Window

Lesson 24: Mass Mailings
Merge
Printing

Lesson 25: Special Techniques
Advance
Block Protect
Columns, Parallel
Cross-Reference
Edit-Screen Options
Generate
Hyphenation
Merge
Screen
Search
Tabs
Window

Lesson 26: Characters and Keyboards
Compose
Keyboards
Macros

Lesson 27: Document Management
Directories
Document Comments
Document Summary
Find
List Files
Look
Search
Text In/Out

Lesson 28: Envelopes and Labels
Initial Codes
Labels
Merge
Paper Size/Type
Printing
Setup

Lesson 29: Equations
Compose
Equations
Font

Lesson 30: Forms Fill-in
Advance
Document Comments
Merge

Lesson 31: Graphics
Columns, Newspaper
Font
Graphics
Graphics Lines

Lesson 32: Sorting Records
Sort

Lesson 33: Styles
Styles

Lesson 34: Tables—Part I
Tables

Lesson 35: Tables—Part II
Font
Tables

Lesson 36: Thesaurus
Thesaurus

Appendix C: Two Disk Drives

WordPerfect can run from a hard disk or two disk drives. If you are running WordPerfect from two disk drives, you need the following diskettes to do the lessons in the workbook:

- WordPerfect 1
- WordPerfect 2
- Learning
- Macros/Keyboards
- Speller
- Thesaurus

These diskettes were created when you installed WordPerfect on your computer. The use of each diskette is described below. When you finish reading the information, return to the introduction for additional details that you may need to know before using the workbook.

Important: *To run WordPerfect 5.1 on a two disk drive system, it is necessary that each of your drives be at least 720K or larger. If you are not sure whether your drives are at least 720K, please refer to your computer manual or contact your dealer.*

**WordPerfect 1,
WordPerfect 2,
and Learning**

The WordPerfect 1 and WordPerfect 2 diskettes are used to start the WordPerfect program. The Learning diskette includes the files you need for the workbook lessons.

Each time you use the workbook, you need to make sure that you have started WordPerfect, that the default drive is B, and that the Learning diskette is in drive B.

For example,

1 After starting DOS, insert the WordPerfect 1 diskette into drive A.

2 Insert the Learning diskette into drive B.

3 Enter **b:** to change the default drive to B.

4 Enter **a:wp** to start WordPerfect.

5 When prompted, replace the WordPerfect 1 diskette with the WordPerfect 2 diskette.

After you are in WordPerfect (check for the status line at the bottom of the screen), you should check to make sure that the default drive is B.

6 Press **List** (F5), then check the bottom left corner of the screen.

⊟ *Select List **F**iles from the **F**ile menu.*

If a "Dir B:*.*" message is displayed, you know that the default drive is B.

7 Press **Enter** to display all the files on the Learning diskette.

8 Press **Exit** (F7) to return to the normal editing screen.

If your default drive is not B: when you press the List key, turn to the Before You Start *heading in the introduction for instructions on changing the default directory.*

Macros/Keyboards

Lessons 26 and 28 in the workbook use some of the files found on the Macros/Keyboards diskette.

In lesson 26, you need to replace the Learning diskette with the Macros/Keyboards diskette before creating a keyboard. In lesson 28, you need to replace the Learning diskette in drive B with the Macros/Keyboards diskette before starting the Labels macro.

After finishing each lesson, place the Learning diskette back into drive B before continuing on to the next lesson.

Speller

Before using Spell (Ctrl-F2) in a lesson, you need to replace the Learning diskette with the Speller diskette so that WordPerfect can find the Speller dictionary.

When you finish spell-checking a document, replace the Speller diskette with the Learning diskette before continuing the lesson.

Thesaurus

Before using Thesaurus (Alt-F1) in lesson 36, you need to replace the Learning diskette with the Thesaurus diskette. When you finish the lesson, place the Learning diskette back into drive B.

Index